Politicians and Part

Politicians
and Party Politics

Edited by John G. Geer

The Johns Hopkins University Press

Baltimore and London

© 1998 The Johns Hopkins University Press
All rights reserved. Published 1998
Printed in the United States of America on acid-free recycled paper
9 8 7 6 5 4 3 2 1

The Johns Hopkins University Press
2715 North Charles Street
Baltimore, Maryland 21218-4363
The Johns Hopkins Press Ltd., London
www.press.jhu.edu

Library of Congress Cataloging-in-Publication Data
will be found at the end of this book.
A catalog record for this book is available from the British Library.

ISBN 0-8018-5845-3
ISBN 0-8018-5846-1 (pbk.)

To Stanley Kelley Jr.
True scholar, dedicated teacher,
and great friend

Contents

Acknowledgments

Acknowledgments are always fun to write. Not only does crafting these paragraphs mean that the project is nearly complete, but the author (in this case, editor) gets a chance to thank the many people who have helped along the way. It is certainly no different here.

I owe Fred Greenstein and Walter Murphy a special note of thanks. They were the ones who originally encouraged me to organize a conference during the fall of 1995 around the theme of party politics. This conference provided an opportunity not only to test new ideas for studying party politics but also to acknowledge our intellectual and personal debt to Stanley Kelley Jr., whose own research and teaching had long centered on this very subject.

Since that conference, Fred has been closely involved in this project, helping me in many ways. Larry Bartels and Doug Arnold also provided invaluable counsel and support. They both spent a great deal of time making sure that the conference was a success and then provided astute advice on how best to proceed with the publication of the volume. I leaned heavily on them, and they were always helpful.

Of course, the authors of the essays published here were absolutely critical to making the conference and this subsequent book a success. They were always willing to meet any deadline I set and produced work of the highest quality. I thank each of them. The discussants also played an important role in making the two-day event in Princeton a hit. Each of the commentators—Doug Arnold, Nancy Bermeo, Tony Broh, Fred Greenstein, Jennifer Hochschild, Michael Kagay, Tali Mendelberg, Ron Rogowski, Tom Romer, Dennis Thompson, and Michael Traugott—made a series of astute observations. The level of commentary was extraordinary, with some discussants actually presenting their own data in an effort to advance the discussion. The end result was a conference of the highest caliber, which in turn encouraged the authors to improve even further the chapters included in this volume.

It is fitting that I now make special reference to Don Stokes, who passed away in January 1997. Don not only served ably as a discussant at the conference, but he was, more importantly, a true student of party politics. He will be missed.

I also want to acknowledge the help of the Departments of Political Science at Arizona State University and Vanderbilt University. Both departments helped to subsidize the costs of organizing this conference. I particularly appreciate

Steve Walker's and Erwin Hargrove's willingness to support me in this endeavor. Diane Price, assistant to the chair at Princeton, was helpful in the early and final stages of this project. In addition, I want to acknowledge the special efforts of Reggie Cohen. Reggie did the important legwork at Princeton and helped to put the finishing touches on the conference that ensured its success. She handled those duties with much skill and good cheer. I would be remiss if I did not thank Henry Tom at the Johns Hopkins University Press. Henry was very helpful in steering this book through the editorial waters.

Finally, I want to say a few words about Stanley Kelley—to whom this book is dedicated. Over the years Stan has been my teacher, mentor, and friend, and I have accumulated uncounted debts to him. It is difficult for me to describe those debts in a way that does them justice. But as I reflect on the years since I first met Stan, it is clear that he gave me the benefit of an apprenticeship in the study of politics. Stan has taught me (and continues to teach me) a great deal about politics and how best to study this fascinating subject. Stan is always teaching, whether in the classroom, in everyday conversation, or through his own research.

An excellent example of Stan's research can be found in the second to last chapter of this volume. Usually, the person to whom the book is dedicated does not contribute a chapter. But Stan decided to honor all the contributors with a chapter of his own. I am particularly grateful that Stan did so, because his essay is a wonderful discussion about politicians and how to think about these actors who are so central to understanding politics. It is also worth noting that this chapter comes from Stan's concluding lecture in his undergraduate party politics course. After reading this essay, one gets a taste of the kinds of ideas and arguments his students at Princeton have been exposed to over the years. It also underscores in dramatic ways that teaching and research can indeed be reinforcing endeavors.

Let me conclude by noting that the contributors to this volume are also pleased and proud to dedicate this book to Stan. They too hold Stan in the highest regard. But rather than speaking for them, I urge the reader to turn to the chapters of this book. In these pages one will find provocative ideas, new evidence, and much good sense. In the end, it is the quality of the scholarship contained in these essays that best expresses our feelings for Stanley Kelley Jr.

Introduction

CHAPTER 1

A Call for New Perspectives

John G. Geer

In the United States, the study of political parties has become specialized along three dimensions: parties as organizations, parties in government, and parties in the electorate. V. O. Key developed this approach in *Politics, Parties, and Pressure Groups* (1964), and Frank Sorauf's highly influential textbook, *Party Politics in America* (now, Beck 1997), made it standard. Research following the framework laid out by these scholars has resulted in an impressive accumulation of knowledge about how parties operate.

The present book, however, breaks away from this approach to pursue new lines of thought about parties. The essays that make up this volume slice the subject of party politics in a number of novel ways. Part of the explanation for why these essays depart from "party politics as usual" lies in the substantive interests of the authors. Few of the contributors are traditional party scholars. Rather, their specialties include political theory, constitutional law, political movements, electoral behavior, Congress, public opinion, political campaigns, and political methodology. This wide range of interests, and the essays inspired by them, help to make evident not only how artificial the separation of the study of party politics into three dimensions is but also that what is important for the governing of modern states is also important for party politics, and vice versa.

In addition, these essays offer a new way to think about party politics. Scholars usually treat political parties and party politics as interchangeable terms. We do not. The difference between the terms is carefully spelled out by Stanley Kelley:

A *political party* is a group whose members act in concert to win the support for leaders who seek to govern. It has formal procedures for making at least some of its decisions.

Party politics comprises the activities of such groups. (Kelley n.d., 24)

Under the Kelley approach, "party politics" casts a much wider net than the typical study of "political parties"—a net wide enough to capture the multifaceted interplay between party politics and government. Party politics, for instance, does much more than just describe the workings of political parties. Standard treatments of the subject usually include discussion of party systems, when they began and ended, and whether or not we are currently witnessing such a transformation. At the same time, there is also likely to be an accounting of party organizations and assessments of how they have adapted to changing times. But we rarely ask how the ability to organize affects the kind and degree of change party leaders can forge in the political system. Nor do we consider carefully enough how best to interpret the often contradictory actions of politicians as they try to build majorities in both the electorate and the legislature. The scholarly examination of party politics, as defined here, encourages the asking of such crosscutting questions by treating the subject as a unity, rather than carving it into separate dimensions, and by expanding the scope of study. The end result is a book that not only examines new topics but also considers old ones in new light.

Consider Thomas Rochon and Ikuo Kabashima's essay on the mobilization of blacks during the civil rights movement. We might expect to find such work in a book on racial politics or social movements. But because of the importance of the entrance of African Americans into the electorate, their contribution shows why this development not only affected the behavior of the two major parties but has had implications for democratic theory, as well. Larry Bartels breathes new life into a long-standing concern—the coalitional makeup of the parties. Rather than treating party coalitions as made up of loyal supporters, he turns his attention to marginal voters. It is these individuals who draw the attention of victory-seeking candidates, since they not only hold the balance of power in elections but also are susceptible to influence during the campaign. Using this perspective, Bartels offers a new view of the American party system.

To develop a more theoretically coherent account of party politics, we have adopted a definition of parties that centers on the politician (see, also, Schlesinger 1991 and Aldrich 1995). Gerald Pomper's essay sets this tone by arguing that parties are best thought of as teams of politicians. This politician-centered approach works its way, either explicitly or implicitly, into all these essays. John Zaller, for example, employs the approach to greatly improve our understanding of incumbency advantage in congressional elections. And David Mayhew uses it to deflate the standard assumptions about the impact of partisan divisions within the national government.

To advance the politician-centered approach, this book examines three topics: mobilization, campaigning, and governing. These tasks are critical for party politicians to be successful at their trade, and this division allows the authors to cut across the normal three-part division within the field of political parties. For instance, "mobilization" encourages us to consider more than just who votes and why but also whom politicians might try to get to the polls and whether such mobilization is good or bad for the political process. "Campaigning" involves more than just seeking votes. Politicians in the midst of an election make numerous decisions that have consequences for the choices voters face and the kind of the government citizens will reap following the campaign.

These essays also offer lessons for party politics that extend beyond the three explicit topics. James DeNardo's contribution, for example, offers a new way to interpret aggregate turnout rates. After setting up his puzzle, DeNardo shows that to understand declining turnout one must look beyond the national trend, examining instead the skewed distribution of participation across the fifty states. In so doing, he makes it clear that the decline is much steeper and smoother than previous scholars have suggested. His findings offer insights for those who seek to interpret trends in participation, and his results have disturbing implications about the health of the party system.

To set the context for these chapters, I shall illustrate some of the problems with the traditional way of studying political parties and show why our approach offers at least a partial solution. With those tasks complete, I shall draw a road map highlighting the contributions, individually and collectively, of these thirteen essays.

A Need for New Perspectives

V. O. Key's approach to the study of political parties was fundamentally empirical. He (and others) saw that parties affected the operation of government, that they structured the electoral process, and that they had organizational features as well. Given these realities, it made good sense to adopt an approach that cast a wide conceptual net. As Morris Fiorina observes, "Party is a simple term that covers a multitude of complicated organizations and processes. It manifests itself most concretely as the set of party organizations that exist principally at the state and local levels. It manifests itself most elusively as a psychological presence in the mind of the citizen. Somewhere in between, and partly a function of the first two, is the manifestation of party as a force in government" (1980, 28). Because parties are complex entities, a reasonable response has been to focus on one part of the complexity and put the other pieces of this puzzle to the side. The outcome of this strategy, as mentioned earlier, has been a significant accumulation of information about parties and how they work within these three arenas. But there have been costs.

First, party scholars have often talked past each other. Part of the reason is that they have had their own working definitions of *party*, which has encouraged them to toil within the bounds of that concept. For instance, political scientists working on parties in the electorate have tended not to integrate their findings and theories with those of scholars examining parties as organizations. The upside of this approach was the development of sophisticated and careful work in particular subfields. The downside was that it tended to foster insulation from developments in the other arenas. An excellent illustration of this pattern involves the scholarly debate over the "decline of parties."

Since the 1960s, the central question in the field involved evaluating the strength of parties (Aldrich 1995). The initial conclusion of this research was that a significant decline in the influence and power of parties *at all levels* was under way (e.g., Ranney 1975; Kirkpatrick 1978; Fiorina 1980; Polsby 1983; Wattenberg 1984). Looking back over that debate, however, it is clear that the "decline" of parties was not across the board. Part of the reason was that scholars working in the arena of "parties in the electorate" dominated the debate and usually did not extend their interest much beyond that arena. Yet political scientists working in other parts of the triad found far less support for this thesis. Cornelius Cotter and some of his colleagues, for instance, reported a good deal of evidence that party organizations were still alive and well, especially at the state level (see also Herrnson 1988; Bibby 1994). Interestingly, Cotter and associates observe in a preface to the 1989 edition of their book that the decline of party within the electorate was accepted as a basis "for inferring the decline of party organizations" (Cotter et al. [1984] 1989, xi). But their data from the 1960s and 1970s show that such inferences were unwarranted.[1]

Despite evidence that parties are gaining strength in some quarters, it is still common to hear that parties are withering and that their functions have been replaced by the news media (e.g., Wattenberg 1991; Patterson 1993). Such claims are even harder to support in light of the pitched partisan battles of the 104th Congress. These kinds of miscommunications are unfortunate, because, besides making inefficient use of our scholarly time, we send mixed signals to academics in other fields and to the pundits who follow our debates.

A second, and related, problem with the approach is that changes in party strength have been unfolding differently within Key's three dimensions. Proponents of this approach usually assume that all three arenas move in tandem (e.g., Key 1964, 164). But that assumption, as has just been pointed out, is wrong. Given that these three levels work in different ways, we have even more reason to look beyond this traditional division of labor. The three-prong approach simply does not provide answers to why parties could be weakening at one level while strengthening at another. We need to consider approaches that examine the interconnections between and within these three levels.

A third problem with this framework is that the sticky issue of defining a party is cast in the background. Scholars have tended to adopt their own preferred definition and march forward. Perhaps because of this choice, little progress has been made in forging consensus on what constitutes a party (Pomper 1992; Janda 1993; Ware 1996). Paul Allen Beck and Frank Sorauf reflect the conventional view, observing that "because political parties can be different things to different people, they may be defined in [a number of] ways" (1992, 7).

Although Beck and Sorauf's position has appeal, we need to put our conceptual house in order. Without a clear and agreed-upon definition of parties, the problems noted above are likely to persist. Scholars will continue to talk past each other because they define *party* in ways that best fit their own research. Such outcomes make cumulative progress slow. In short, we need ways to take new cuts at party politics that rest on a firmer conceptual foundation.

Such a conceptual foundation can be found in rational choice theory.[2] The analytical power of rational choice is due, in part, to the use of a simple and abstract definition of *party*. For most rational choice scholars, a party is something akin to "a team seeking to control the governing apparatus by gaining office in a duly constituted election" (Downs 1957, 25). By viewing parties largely as teams of politicians, this approach eliminates an important source of confusion: voters do not constitute the parties. That point is adroitly developed by Gerald Pomper in the next chapter. Obviously, the preferences and choices of citizens are important to parties, but citizens are not, in Pomper's view, to be treated as parties. This focus allows us to turn our attention to politicians and how their actions and choices drive and shape party politics.

By casting politicians in a central role, we avoid reifying parties into political actors. It is not parties per se that seek to win elective office and to influence government. Rather, it is politicians, acting on the behalf of parties, who make decisions about how to secure additional votes in an election or how to build a coalition large enough to pass controversial legislation. And because party politicians usually make these decisions within a competitive environment and with limited resources, they must pursue those goals in a reasonable manner. If they do not, they may literally cease to be politicians (or at least successful ones). Hence, to understand political parties, we must understand the behavior of politicians and the contexts within which that behavior occurs.

Others have made exactly this point. Joseph Schlesinger (1991), for instance, has spent much of his career arguing that it is the "ambitious officeseeker" who creates and maintains the party. Or, as John Aldrich reminds us, political parties are "the creature of the politicians, the ambitious officeseeker, and the officeholder" (1995, 4). Thus, to understand parties we must understand politicians. Our attention to politicians, I should caution, is not always a direct one. Our multifaceted focus offers both direct and indirect evidence of the import of politicians and the many ramifications for party politics.

But in offering these new perspectives on party politics, we need to make sure that we bring along with us the empirical trappings of Key's approach. That is, we are not just in the business of offering theories about party politics. Rather, we want to gather and analyze data that will allow us not only to test our ideas but also to develop a better understanding of how party politics works.

A Road Map

Gerald Pomper begins this volume by providing a plethora of evidence that the many obituaries written for American political parties have been premature. This evidence leads him to argue that in many ways the strength of parties is increasing. Interestingly, Pomper makes this point within the existing framework set down by Key. Having shown that parties are alive and well, this book then moves into our substantive themes of mobilization, campaigning, and governing.

Larry Bartels introduces the theme of mobilization by advancing an innovative way to think about party systems from a politician's perspective. Rather than looking at core supporters that make up a party's electoral coalition, as Robert Axelrod (1972) and others have done, Bartels focuses on the marginal voter. He seeks to identify those individuals who are potential supporters of either team *and* are likely to vote. For the rational politician, these citizens are the real targets of campaigns, since they can be converted and are likely to show up on election day. The result of this tactic is a set of interesting and unexpected findings about the distribution of power in the American electorate.

James DeNardo examines the decline in participation in presidential elections, paying particular attention to the 1972 campaign. By disaggregating national turnout trends by state, DeNardo suggests that the electorate's partisan loyalties are weaker than ever before and that opportunities for strategic politicians to capitalize on low turnout are greater than just a few years ago. DeNardo's essay highlights the advantage of rethinking old problems from new perspectives and in so doing forges a better understanding of party politics.

Thomas Rochon and Ikuo Kabashima examine the mobilization of the African American electorate before, during, and after the civil rights movement. The entry of blacks into the voting public created both a threat and an opportunity for politicians of both parties. In the late 1950s, it was not clear which party would capture this group of voters. But with Lyndon Johnson's support of civil rights and Barry Goldwater's preference to let the states address the problem, African Americans began to embrace the Democratic Party. The result was a major shift in electoral politics in this country that has had enduring effects on the party system and on the politicians working within it.

John Zaller introduces the discussion of campaigning by arguing that the incumbency advantage in House elections has little to do with voters. The typical claim is that voters learn to love their members of Congress because of the "pork" they can supply to their districts. Zaller dismisses this argument, showing instead that incumbency advantage exists largely because sitting members of Congress, like heavyweight boxing champions, are simply better candidates than their opponents. The result is that they win, win often, and win by large margins.

The chapters by John Geer and Jonathan Krasno, in different ways, examine the link between politicians and voters. Geer evaluates the appeals candidates make to the electorate during presidential campaigns, showing, among other things, that the messages systematically differ from what the parties talk about in their platforms. This finding underscores the need to include the actions of campaigners in our models of party competition. All too often the behavior of politicians during the campaign is ignored in the typical account of party competition. But in an era of candidate-centered parties such an omission paints a misleading picture of how competition in elections works.

Krasno considers this link from the other end. What messages did voters send to Washington when casting their ballots during the 1994 midterm elections? We know from Robert Dahl's contribution in this book that politicians often make unwarranted claims of a mandate. Did Newt Gingrich and company interpret the elections as Dahl would expect? Krasno shows that the answer is yes—the Republicans did go too far in their interpretation of the elections as a mandate for the Contract with America. He finds, for instance, that only a handful of voters explicitly mentioned the Contract as a reason to support the Republican Party. Krasno also shows that New Deal issues remain at the center of congressional campaigns—even though it has been more than six decades since Franklin Roosevelt first took the oath of office.

Robert Dahl's argument about the theoretical basis for the electoral mandate serves as an important bridge between "campaigning" and "governing." Part of this bridge is crossed when Dahl himself laments the "pseudodemocratization" of the presidency. David Mayhew carries us even further into the arena of governing. He shows, for example, that members of Congress produce as much legislation under divided partisan control of government as under unified control. Party politicians are responsive to the national mood, and that is the critical variable in the legislative process. Carol Swain then takes us into new territory, examining the choices facing black members of Congress following the GOP victories in 1994. She considers the choice that members of the Congressional Black Caucus faced after the GOP took over. They had a good deal of influence when the Democrats were in power. But what should they do with the GOP in power? Should they try to maximize their limited influence or engage in what John Lewis called "protest politics"?

Walter Murphy concludes the section on governing by addressing whether elected officials have authority to "outlaw" political parties. Murphy offers the provocative argument that a constitutional democracy can justifiably ban certain kinds of parties. Using the Nazi Party in Germany as an example, Murphy explores the case in which a political party threatens the constitutional foundations of the regime. Under such circumstances, democratically elected politicians have good reason to restrict the rights of representatives of these parties to seek elective office. This idea will, of course, rub many "democrats" the wrong way. For that reason alone, it deserves careful consideration.

Stanley Kelley's contribution underscores the general theme (and title) of this book. Kelley argues that to understand politics, in general, and party politics, in particular, we must develop a better appreciation of what it takes to be a politician. Building on Max Weber's ideas of eighty years ago, Kelley provides an intriguing account of politicians, their motivations, and the talents needed for a successful career. This chapter illustrates the interplay of personal motivations and institutional dilemmas that politicians confront. Kelley highlights the special skills they must possess if they are to succeed, allowing a better appreciation of what it takes to be a politician. These ideas, as Kelley observes, take on even greater urgency in light of the frequent calls for citizen legislatures and the elimination of the professional politician.

The final word goes to Fred Greenstein. Greenstein, like many of the other authors, seeks to liberate the study of party politics from its normal boundaries. But rather than offering a theoretical or empirical argument, he weaves a commentary on the work of Stanley Kelley that highlights the many facets of party politics and the fascinating lessons they hold for democratic politics.

As these authors advance their arguments about party politics, some important underlying themes deserve special mention. First, racial politics is a topic that draws considerable attention in this volume. It is a central focus of the Rochon-Kabashima and Swain chapters and plays an important role in the chapters by DeNardo and Bartels. The fact that race enters into our discussion of party politics in American should come as no surprise. I would be hard pressed to imagine a good discussion of the topic without some reference to this issue that has so long tortured our nation. A second theme involves democratic theory—another topic of obvious relevance to party politics. Robert Dahl, Walter Murphy, and Stanley Kelley all speak directly to long-standing and important debates in democratic theory. Third, a number of chapters provide insight into the study of political change. DeNardo's analysis of turnout speaks to this topic, as does Bartels' analysis of party systems. Krasno's interpretation of the 1994 midterm elections, of course, addresses it. As with race and democratic theory, political change is central to any good understanding of party politics.

Finally, many of these essays make explicit statements about the normative implications of arguments for party politics. The contributions by Dahl, Geer, and Kelley are good examples. Such normative lessons provide an important link to the first generation of work on political parties. The debate over whether parties promote or hinder democracy was fundamentally normative (e.g., Bryce 1895; Ford 1898; Ostrogorski 1902; Michels [1915] 1949). But since that time, those kinds of debates have often simmered on the back burner. We hope our volume will move them to the front.

A normative approach takes on additional significance in light of our effort to put the party politician on center stage. Since we do not use the responsible party model as our normative standard, we must ask under what conditions competition between politicians promotes democratic ends. Walter Murphy tackles this question head on, arguing that democracies must sometimes restrict competition in order to survive. John Geer suggests that competition in campaigns has certain biases that may not yield the outcomes envisioned by E. E. Schattschneider and others. Larry Bartels shows that even in a competitive party system, many voting blocs will not have the same amount of electoral clout. Those kinds of arguments help to show whether our faith in the benefits of competition is warranted. It is these kinds of questions that need to be addressed if we are to understand fully the connection between party politics and democratic politics.

A Final Thought

In the preceding pages, I have tried to sketch why we need to develop new approaches to the study of party politics. Some will take issue with various arguments and ideas I have advanced. I suspect, however, that any doubts one might have will dwindle as one reads the enclosed essays. In the end, these chapters significantly improve our understanding of party politics.

In reading these essays, it may be useful to think of this book as making two distinct intellectual contributions to two different sets of readers: contributions that come from reading the volume as a whole and those that come from reading the essays individually. And each contribution has lessons for both the scholar and the beginning student of party politics. When reading the book as a whole, one gains an appreciation of the many ramifications of party politics and how new approaches can indeed illuminate new subjects and allow us to see old ones more clearly. From reading individual chapters, one gets new evidence, new ideas, and substantial elaborations of existing ideas that shed light on the behavior of politicians, parties, and interest groups.

Notes

I want to thank Fred Greenstein, Larry Bartels, Stan Kelley, and Bruce Oppenheimer for helpful comments on previous drafts of this introduction.

1. Good evidence also exists that parties remained important in government. David Rohde (1991), for instance, has shown that while party voting in Congress hit a low in the 1970s, it has been on the rise since then. It should be noted that even at their weakest point, parties remained highly consequential, whether influencing legislative votes or structuring the organization of committees. This latter point often gets overlooked when examining the temporary decline of parties within the halls of Congress.

2. The phrase "rational choice" holds different meanings for different people. For the purposes of this book, I am not advocating the adoption of the highly formal trappings often associated with this approach. My objective is simply to treat politicians as purposive actors. The work of Schumpeter (1950) and Schattschneider (1942) would fit this definition, since they, like rational choice scholars, view politicians as goal oriented.

References

Aldrich, John H. 1995. *Why Parties.* Chicago: University of Chicago Press.
Axelrod, Robert. 1972. "Where the Votes Come From." *American Political Science Review* 66:11–20.
Beck, Paul Allen. 1997. *Party Politics in America.* 8th ed. New York: Addison-Wesley.
Beck, Paul Allen, and Frank J. Sorauf. 1992. *Party Politics in America.* 7th ed. New York: Harper Collins.
Bibby, John F. 1994. "State Party Organizations: Coping and Adapting." In *The Parties Respond,* ed. Sandy Maisel. Boulder, Colo.: Westview Press.
Bryce, James. 1895. *The American Commonwealth.* New York: Macmillan.
Cotter, Cornelius P., James L. Gibson, John F. Bibby, and Robert Huckshorn. [1984] 1989. *Party Organizations in American Politics.* Pittsburgh: University of Pittsburgh Press.
Downs, Anthony. 1957. *An Economic Theory of Democracy.* New York: Harper and Row.
Fiorina, Morris P. 1980. "The Decline of Collective Responsibility in American Politics." *Daedalus* 109:25–45.
Ford, Henry Jones. 1898. *The Rise and Growth of American Politics.* New York: Macmillan.

Herrnson, Paul. 1988. *Party Campaigning in the 1980s*. Cambridge: Harvard University Press.

Janda, Kenneth. 1993. "Comparative Political Parties: Research and Theory." In *The State of the Discipline II*, ed. Ada W. Finifter. Washington, D.C.: American Political Science Association.

Kelley, Stanley, Jr. n.d. "Party Politics and Democratic Government." Unpublished manuscript, Department of Politics, Princeton University.

Key, V. O. 1964. *Politics, Parties, and Pressure Groups*. 5th ed. New York: Crowell.

Kirkpatrick, Jeane J. 1978. *Dismantling the Parties: Reflections on Party Reform and Party Decomposition*. Washington, D.C.: American Enterprise Institute.

Michels, Robert. [1915] 1949. *Political Parties*. New York: Free Press.

Ostrogorski, M. 1902. *Democracy and the Organization of Political Parties*. New York: Macmillan.

Patterson, Thomas. 1993. *Out of Order*. New York: Knopf.

Polsby, Nelson W. 1983. *Consequences of Party Reform*. New York: Oxford University Press.

Pomper, Gerald. 1992. "Concepts of Political Parties." *Journal of Theoretical Politics* 4:143–59.

Ranney, Austin. 1975. *Curing the Mischiefs of Faction*. Berkeley: University of California Press.

Rohde, David W. 1991. *Parties and Leaders in the Postreform House*. Chicago: University of Chicago Press.

Schattschneider, E. E. 1942. *Party Government*. New York: Rinehart.

Schlesinger, Joseph A. 1991. *Parties and the Winning of Office*. Ann Arbor: University of Michigan Press.

Schumpeter, Joseph. 1950. *Capitalism, Socialism, and Democracy*. New York: Harper Brothers.

Ware, Alan. 1996. *Political Parties and Party Systems*. New York: Oxford University Press.

Wattenberg, Martin P. 1984. *The Decline of American Political Parties*. Cambridge: Harvard University Press.

———. 1991. *The Decline of American Political Parties*. 3d ed. Cambridge: Harvard University Press.

CHAPTER 2

The Alleged Decline of American Parties

Gerald M. Pomper

Clichés are impressive, for their staying power if not their truth, and we have long held to clichéd but erroneous portrayals of American political parties. In this chapter, I contest the conventional characterization of the parties as weak and argue that we are now seeing the development of a semi-responsible party system in the United States.

What Parties?

A generation ago, a new and important textbook by Austin Ranney and Will-moore Kendall defended "our decentralized, office-oriented, and programmat-ically vague parties" (1956, 504). In our own time, a major comparative study, *How Parties Organize*, dismisses American "party organization as an empty vessel" (Katz and Kolodny 1994, 23). Over four decades, then, evaluations of the parties have changed from praise in the 1950s to scorn in the 1990s, but the characterizations remain the same.

Ranney and Kendall found the roots of American party politics in attitudes such as skepticism toward parties and in formal constitutional mechanisms such as federalism and the separation of powers. Currently, Richard Katz and Robin Kolodny similarly emphasize "three fundamental aspects of American politics. . . . These are the presidential system and the concomitant doctrine of separation of powers, a basic ambivalence about parties, and federalism" (1994, 24).

In terms of organization, according to the recent authors, "there is a prolif-eration of party bodies, most of which are not responsible to others, and the party national committees are only the 'national executives' of the presidential parties" (Katz and Kolodny 1994, 28). The authors echo the earlier statement that "the various committees, conventions, and officers do not—in theory, law, or fact—generally form a neat, pyramidal, hierarchical pattern, with lines of responsibility and authority clearly established. . . . The national committee is not, for either party, the formal supreme rule-making and policy-making body" (Ranney and Kendall 1956, 223, 230).

In their discussion of party government, Ranney and Kendall conclude that "most votes, in Senate and House alike, range Democrats and Republicans against Democrats and Republicans, not Democrats against Republicans. . . . Both party conferences in both houses meet infrequently, and they seldom attempt to 'bind' their members to vote a particular way" (392, 397). Little has changed in four decades, at least to judge by our current scholars, who write: "Congressional parties also differ from most parliamentary parties in that party discipline is virtually unknown. Relatively few votes divide a majority of one party from a majority of the other. . . . Caucus members do not want to be bound by party discipline, and thus do not try to impose it on others" (Katz and Kolodny 1994, 40, 42).

It is possible, of course, that the parties are unaltered after forty years. But during that time, the Cold War intensified and then ended; the national population exploded, diversified, and dispersed; Americans added five amendments to the Constitution; the federal budget increased almost thirtyfold; television saturated the nation; computers circled the globe; and men walked on the moon. Must we not expect party change in a period of such novelty?

In reality, there has been considerable change, even if we do not always recognize it. We must be wary of fixing too much on the past; instead, we must heed Tocqueville's warning: "Placed in the middle of a rapid stream, we obstinately fix our eyes on the ruins which may still be described upon the shore we have left, whilst the current hurries us away, and drags us backward toward the gulf" ([1835] 1956, 30).

Certainly, change has been dramatically evident in Washington. In 1995, a Republican majority took control of both houses of Congress for the first time in forty-two years (i.e., since before Ranney and Kendall's *Democracy and the American Party System* was published). The new House majority party pledged itself to an extensive program, the Contract with America. In organizing the House, that party centralized power in the hands of the Speaker, abolished institutionalized caucuses of constituency interests, distributed committee chairs on the basis of loyalty to the party program and in disregard of seniority, changed the ratios of party memberships on committees to foster passage of the party program, and rehearsed members to vote along party lines.

On the very first day in office, the majority unanimously supported the party program on fifteen roll calls. In subsequent weeks, even under more-open rules for debate, that party passed a series of major bills, including amendments to the Constitution that would seriously change the character of the national government and significant new public policies in regard to federal finance, law enforcement, taxes, and social welfare. After a brief recess, the House Republicans returned to legislate a fundamental change in environmental policy and the power of government in revision of the Clean Water Act. Perhaps most audaciously, they then passed a seven-year program to eliminate the federal budget deficit, reducing spending on behalf of the elderly, a few corporations, the arts, schoolchildren, and—of course—the poor. The Senate soon adopted a budget similar in its spending cuts, eventually also accepting the House Republicans' program of selective tax reductions. Some of these changes were thwarted by presidential vetoes and the subsequent shutdown of the government. Yet in the main the Republican program was accomplished, as President Bill Clinton accepted the principle of a balanced budget and the end of welfare entitlements. Impressive—not nice, but impressive.

Recent experience is significant beyond the immediate impact on public policy. The onset of the Republican majority, maintained in the 1996 elections, reveals two vital aspects of party change and the current state of U.S. parties. First, the Republicans' actions should clarify our understanding of party theory by focusing our attention on party as an alliance of politicians, not a collection of voters. Second, this activity is not a passing freak event but rather the culmination of long-term trends toward party strengthening.

In assessing contemporary parties, we encounter another cliché, the alleged decay of American political parties. Twenty-five years ago, David Broder (1972) told us in the title of his book that "the party's over." Martin Wattenberg (1984) underlines this conclusion in a number of related works emphasizing the theme that gave his first book its title, *The Decline of American Political Parties*. The evidence for decline is consistently found in voter attitudes rather than party characteristics. Voters are found to be increasingly neutral and occasionally negative toward political parties, to be less influenced by partisan identification in their vote choices, to be less consistent across tickets and across time, and, simply put, to see parties as of little relevance to contemporary American politics. As Wattenberg puts his argument, "Political parties are not perceived as particularly meaningful in today's political world. . . . The most potentially damaging attitude to the political parties' future, however, is the large percentage of the population which sees little need for parties altogether. . . . Most voters now view parties as a convenience rather than a necessity" (1991, 35, 45).

Wattenberg's belief that American parties are weak is widely shared. Indeed, it was so much the conventional wisdom that scholars were impressed, even relieved, when Cotter and his associates disputed the fashionable belief that parties were "verging on extinction . . . in an advanced state of decay" (Cotter et al. 1984, 1). These researchers used data on party organizational characteristics and activities to argue that parties had strengthened, not weakened. Their refutation is based, then, on contrary empirical evidence.

The thesis of party decline, however, is still more fundamentally flawed. It fails, regardless of the empirical evidence, because it rests on an erroneous theoretical foundation. The thesis depends on a view of parties as collectivities of voters. In this view, parties are weaker because fewer voters are strongly identified with the parties, and fewer are consistent supporters at the ballot box.

The problem with this argument is that parties are not properly considered as collections of voters. Indeed, they have never been considered theoretically in terms of voters. From Edmund Burke to the present, the appropriate conception of parties is quite different. Burke, the original party theorist, defined a party as "a body of men united, for promoting by their joint endeavors . . . some particular principle in which they are all agreed" ([1770] 1981, 317). Leaving principle aside, Anthony Downs, the most noted deductive party theorist, similarly characterizes a party as "a coalition of men seeking to control the governing apparatus by legal means" (1957, 24). After an extensive discussion of the nature of political parties, Leon Epstein comes to a similar basic definition of party as "any group, however loosely organized, seeking to elect governmental office-holders under a given label" (1980, 9). Or, as E. E. Schattschneider put it more bluntly, "A political party is first of all an organized attempt to get power" (1942, 35).

Voters are not members of the party organization but rather its clientele. This distinction has been obscured by the common textbook threefold division of party organization, party in government, party in the electorate. This "tripod" has become an iron cage, imprisoning party theory as well as distorting the meaning suggested by V. O. Key, its originator. Key clearly saw the electorate as the audience for parties. In introducing his text's section on the electorate, he writes: "The party apparatus, by posing alternative candidates and programs, arranges the situation to permit the electorate to play its role in the system of party government" (1964, 455). It is both confusing and inaccurate to think of voters as the party, even in the common usage of "party in the electorate." Anthony King dismisses this categorization: "It is rather as though one were to refer not to the buyers of Campbell's soup but to the Campbell-Soup-Company-in-the-Market" (quoted in Baer and Bositis 1993, 108).

The long tradition of party theory has consistently focused on the parties as organizations (Pomper 1992, chap. 1), while the newer and important research on voter partisanship properly constitutes a separate although related subject.

As argued by pathbreaking theorists such as Robert Michels and M. Ostrogorski, basic issues of democracy involve the relationship between parties and the electorate, but conflating the two elements confuses our understanding. Significantly, the major contemporary research on party organization (Katz and Mair 1992; 1995) does not even refer to any "party in the electorate."

We do better to think of the parties as seekers of voters, following Anthony Downs, Joseph Schumpeter, and Joseph Schlesinger. As Schlesinger elaborates, Downs' definition sparingly says only "that the political party is some kind of an organization. Yet the character of that organization—how it is arranged, what if any lines of authority it has, how disciplined it is, how much division of labor exists—is not part of this definition of party" (1984, 375).

We should think of parties as we think of commercial enterprises. As businesses seek customers in the economic market, parties seek voters in the political market (Frendreis 1996). In the automobile industry, we recognize the Ford and Toyota motor companies as the relevant organizations and car buyers as their market. In sports, we think of the Toronto Blue Jays (before the suicidal baseball strike) or the Green Bay Packers as the organization, competing for the loyalties of fans. We should think similarly of Republicans and Democrats as groups competing for voter loyalties.

If parties are competitive organizations like automakers and sports teams, we then should measure their strength in similar ways. In particular, we should determine their strength not by voter identification but by their ability to compete. This view of party, Schlesinger correctly emphasizes, "must exclude the voter. Voters are choosers among parties, not components of them." Certainly, "It is a great advantage to a party to have large numbers of voters inclined in its favor. Yet the ultimate test of a party's strength, at least within the electoral context, lies in its ability to win elections, not in its identification among the electorate." Indeed, parties may need to forge better organizations in response to declining voter identification (just as IBM improved its organization as it lost customers). "This seeming paradox, parties growing stronger while they are growing weaker, is a paradox only if we make the error of equating partisan strength with partisan identification" (1984, 377).

Building further on these rational choice premises, John Aldrich has made a major contribution to the understanding of political parties, developing what Schattschneider first termed "a politician's theory of parties" (1942, 11). Aldrich sees parties as institutions that meet three problems faced by officeholders and office seekers: ambition, collective action, and social choice. These politicians "have created and maintained, used or abused, reformed or ignored the political party when doing so has furthered their goals and ambitions" (Aldrich 1995, 4). They, not the electorates they court, are the empirical material for parties and the source of theoretical explanation.

The disjunction between the party as an organization and its electoral base is carried still further by Angelo Panebianco. Significantly, this creative contemporary theorist of political parties gives no focused attention to electorates, seeing the distribution of popular votes as simply one element in the parties' "contingent environment" (1988, chap. 11). To Panebianco, party strength is independent of votes (chaps. 5, 6, 13). Indeed, he argues, greater party institutionalization is more likely in parties that arise in opposition and lack governmental resources and in periods after electoral defeat. Perhaps the recent Republican strengthening can be seen as an American example of these comparative findings.

Stronger Parties?

From this proper theoretical perspective, we can see the growth of stronger, not weaker, political parties in recent American developments. Evidence can be found in four gauges of organizational strength: (1) recruitment of leadership; (2) group cohesion; (3) defined mission; and (4) institutional capacity, including command of resources and structural articulation (Barnard 1938; Blau and Scott 1962; March and Simon 1958). We consider the Green Bay Packers a strong organization, for example, because it is able to recruit its own leadership, works cohesively, has a clearly defined mission, and commands large amounts of money, while clearly articulating the players' roles. Politics is different, but party organizations can be assessed, using different data, by the same criteria.[1] The political analogues are presidential nominations, policy unity, party ideology, and party institutional capacity. In recent years, American parties have become stronger organizations on these standards.

Recruitment of Leadership: Presidential Nominations

If the ability to select its own leadership is one criterion of a strong organization, then American parties seem weak indeed, particularly in regard to their most important leaders, the presidential nominees. Since the "reforms" of the parties, beginning with the McGovern-Fraser Commission after 1968, in particular, presidential nominations have apparently become contests among self-starting aspirants who succeed by assembling a personal coalition that appeals directly to the voters in a series of uncoordinated state primaries.

Some observers, like Leon Epstein, accept the new "plebiscitary system" as no more than an extension of established state primaries that have made nominations "large-scale public rather than private organizational affairs" (1986, 108). Others, such as Austin Ranney, complain that "reform" got out of hand, confounding him and others who "preferred a reformed national convention to a national presidential primary or a major increase in the number of state presidential primaries" (1975, 206). But the consequences go beyond personal disappointment. According to Nelson Polsby, "what it takes to achieve the nomination differs nowadays so sharply from what it takes to govern effectively as to pose a [general] problem" (1983, 89).

Like the basic thesis of party decline, we have come to accept the disappearance of party influence in presidential nominations. We may find some solace in evidence of voter rationality in presidential primaries (Bartels 1988; Abramson et al. 1992, 55–69), but these explanations still see party as irrelevant. In the face of these analyses, the importance of the parties as sources of leadership recruitment may seem surprising. Since 1980, we have seen ten presidential nominations, all of them the choice of an established party leader, even in the face of significant insurgencies. These selections include three renominations of the sitting party leader with no or futile opposition (Ronald Reagan, 1984; George Bush, 1992; and Clinton, 1996); one renomination against a strong challenge (Jimmy Carter, 1980); three selections of the leader of the established dominant faction of the party (Reagan, 1980; Walter Mondale, 1984; and Bush, 1988); and three selections of the leader of a major-party faction (Michael Dukakis, 1988; Clinton, 1992; and Robert Dole, 1996).

Presidential nominations are certainly different today, but the differences are not clearly toward less, rather than different, party influence. Look back at the "traditional" convention system, as analyzed by Paul David, Ralph Goldman, and Richard Bain (1960). Historically, some presidents retired voluntarily or involuntarily after one term, but every chief executive since 1972 has been renominated, including Gerald Ford, who was never elected to national office. When nominations have been open, inheritance and factional victory have become the universal paths to success, as they were historically. In contrast, past patterns of inner group selection or compromise in stalemate have disappeared, but this change was already established over seventy years ago.[2]

The selection of presidential nominees still evidences influence by leaders of the organized parties or its factions, even if these choices have not been made primarily by the formal party leadership (such as Democratic "superdelegates" and similar Republican officials). These decisions are quite different from the selection of such insurgents as Barry Goldwater in 1964 and George McGovern in 1972, the typical illustrations of the asserted decline of party. While insurgents now have access to the contest for presidential nominations, the reality is that they fail in that contest, as shown by the examples of Democrats Edward Kennedy in 1980, Gary Hart in 1984, and Jesse Jackson in 1988 and the virtual absence of any Republican insurgents throughout the period until 1992.

The presidential nominations of 1992 and 1996 particularly evidence the party basis of recruitment. There were notable insurgent candidates: Republican Pat Buchanan twice attempted to reincarnate Goldwater, Jerry Brown imitated McGovern, and Paul Tsongas eschewed partisanship. In contrast with earlier years, however, all were soundly defeated by established party figures.

Among Republicans, Pat Buchanan illustrates the declining impact of insurgency, losing first to a weak incumbent, then losing by a wider margin to a flawed party leader. In 1992, George Bush not only was the incumbent leader but also typified the career of a party politician, served as national Republican chairman, and rose regularly in party ranks, securing his nomination as the heir of the retiring leader, Ronald Reagan. In 1996, Bob Dole—the congressional leader of the opposition and another former national chairman—was virtually the inevitable choice. As the established party leader, he easily withstood the well-heeled challenges of Phil Gramm, the senatorial spokesman of the party's conservative wing, and Steve Forbes, a classic if uniquely rich insurgent (Mayer 1997, chap. 1).

Bill Clinton came to party leadership from the position of governor, reflecting the variety of career opportunities available in a federal system, but Arkansas was hardly a robust power center. Clinton's real base was the Democratic Leadership Council (DLC), which provided much of his program, his source of contacts and finances, and his opportunity for national exposure. The DLC, composed of party officials and officeholders, is an organized party faction. Clinton's success is a testament to the influence of that faction far more than evidence of the decline of party and the substitution of unmediated access to the voters (Hale 1994, 249–63). By 1996, despite Clinton's manifold problems and inconstant approval ratings, nobody in the fractious Democratic Party dared challenge the incumbent party leader.

Contemporary presidential nominations have become comparable—although not identical—to the choice of leadership in a hypothetical U.S. parliamentary system. Is the selection of Reagan in 1980 that different from the British Tories' choice of Margaret Thatcher to lead the party's turn toward ideological free-market conservatism? In a parliamentary system, would not Bush and Dole, Reagan's successor and acolyte, respectively, be the ideal analogues to Britain's John Major? Is the selection of Mondale as the standard bearer of the liberal Democratic Party that different from the lineage of left-wing leaders in the British Labour Party? Within federal systems, with their diverse paths of recruitment, are the choices of Dukakis and Clinton much different from the selection of factional leaders with local bases of support in Canada and Australia? Is the Democratic turn toward the electoral center with Clinton not analogous to Labour's replacement of Michael Foot with Neil Kinnock, John Smith, and Tony Blair?

The analogy is not complete, to be sure. American political leadership is still quite open, the parties quite permeable. (Other strong organizations are also permeable, as corporations are subject to takeovers by "outsider" stockholders.) Presidential nominations do depend greatly on personal coalitions, and popular primaries are the decisive points of decision. Yet it is also true that leadership of the parties is still, and perhaps increasingly, related to prominence within the parties. On this first test, we find a significant degree of organizational strength.

Policy Cohesion

A second test of party strength is its cohesion on policy issues. In his classic text, Schattschneider, after reviewing congressional action and noting that "the testimony of competent scholars is unanimous," sadly concludes, "Yet, when all is said, it remains true that the roll calls demonstrate *the parties are unable to hold their lines in a controversial public issue when the pressure is on*" (1942, 131).

Contrast the action of the House Republican majority in the first months of 1995. On some three hundred roll calls, party loyalty was nearly total. In the process, a promise merely to vote on items in the Contract with America became a demand for actual passage of its far-reaching agenda. Eventually, that demand affected the Senate as well, although its members were not formally involved in the party pledges. The House held thirty-three roll calls on final passage of items in the Contract. Republicans were unanimous on sixteen of these votes, and the median number of Republican dissents was a mere *one*. Neither the British House of Commons nor the erstwhile Supreme Soviet could rival this record of party unity.

Altogether, there were but 156 dissenting votes on these roll calls, of which fully a quarter came on a single bill, the proposed constitutional limits on congressional terms (*Congressional Quarterly Weekly Report* 53 (1995): 1006). Even on this most divisive issue, 84 percent of the Republicans still voted for the party's position—and against their own personal interests. Significantly, Judiciary Committee chair Henry Hyde, who was personally and vehemently opposed to term limits, felt constrained by party commitments to bring the measure to the floor. In so doing, he exemplified the success of Majority Leader Dick Armey, who "exacted promises from most committee chairmen to hew closely to the contract when crafting their bills. When he could not win a guarantee from a chairman, he used the Rules Committee to keep members 'on contract' by instructing committee members to grant rules that did not leave the contract open to attack on the floor" (ibid., 987). Granting that these procedures, and indeed much of the Contract itself, are rather nasty, surely party had come to dominate the House of Representatives.

Republican cohesion continued past the euphoria of the first hundred days, even on measures that would be likely targets of parochial defection, most importantly the massive budget reductions. For all of 1995, the average Republican in the House supported the party on more than nine of ten roll calls (an average party unity score of 91 percent), and loyalty was virtually as high in the Senate (89 percent). Many expected this remarkable party unity would not last into the second session, as the centrifugal forces of local interests, decentralized elections, and factional presidential politics inevitably took hold. Despite these pressures, party unity fell only marginally in the House (to an average score of 87 percent) and not at all in the Senate (*Congressional Quarterly Weekly Report* 54 (1996): 3461).

The Republicans' unity in the 104th Congress is but an extreme illustration of a more general trend toward legislative party cohesion, depicted in figure 2.1. While the average party support score was less than 60 percent in both parties in 1970, by 1994 it had already risen to 83 percent for Republicans and 82 percent for Democrats.

Figure 2.1 Party Unity in Congress

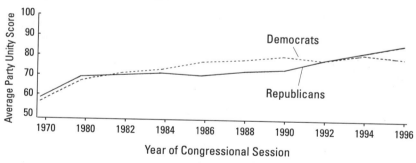

Source: Data from *Congressional Quarterly Weekly Report,* vols. 28–54 (1970–96).

Other measures provide further evidence of increased partisanship throughout the past generation. Not too long ago, in 1969, party conflict (a majority of Republicans opposing a majority of Democrats) was evident on only about a third of all roll calls. By 1993, as seen in figure 2.2, partisanship rose to two-thirds of both House and Senate votes. In 1995, nearly three-fourths of House votes

Figure 2.2 Partisan Roll Calls in Congress

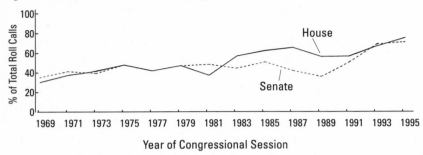

Source: Data from *Congressional Quarterly Weekly Report,* vols. 27–53 (1969–95).

and more than two-thirds of Senate roll calls showed these clear party differences. By contrast, appearances of the conservative coalition of Republicans and southern Democrats fell in the same period from 27 percent to 11 percent of all roll calls (*Congressional Quarterly Weekly Report* 52 (1994): 3658–64).

The effect of party in Congress increased with the arrival of President Clinton and unified party control of the legislative and executive branches and then with the advent of the Republican control of Congress. The increased impact of party, however, reflects more than current political lineups, for "by the mid- to late 1980s, a cohesive majority party led by an activist, policy-involved leadership had emerged in the House of Representatives" (Sinclair 1994, 299), as parties increasingly affected congressional behavior (Sinclair 1989; Rohde 1991). Once again, the evidence contradicts the wailing over the decline of party.

Party Ideology

Legislative cohesion is possible because contemporary parties also meet the third standard of strong organizations, a defined mission or, in political terms, a common ideology. Voters certainly see a difference between the parties. In 1992, a majority of the electorate chose either Democrats or Republicans as likely "to do a better job" on the nation's economy, foreign affairs, the problem of poverty, and "making health care more affordable." On only one issue, "keeping out of war," did the nation see no appreciable difference between the parties (Wattenberg 1993, 30). These attitudes reinforce the electorate's consistent attitude, unvarying even as party identification has fallen, that there are important differences in the parties' beliefs.

These mass attitudes accurately reflect the real differences that exist between the parties on the elite level. In research conducted forty years ago, Herbert Mc-

Closky and colleagues (1960, 406–27) described the large ideological differences among the two major parties' national convention delegates. Continuing party differences are also shown, sometimes inadvertently, in more recent studies of convention delegates. John Kessel and colleagues have drawn the ideological structures of these party representatives (Bruce, Clark, and Kessel 1991, 1089–1106). Though not monolithic, they are sharply distinct between the parties. These divisions persist within broader layers of party activists, such as contributors and campaign workers (Bruzios 1990, 581–601). Similarly, extensive surveys of state party convention delegates show consistent ideological differences, independent of state cultures. Republicans are always significantly more conservative than Democrats. Moreover, and more interestingly, Republicans in even the most liberal states, such as New York, are more to the right than Democrats in even the most conservatives states, such as Arizona (Abramowitz, McGlennon, and Rapoport 1986, chap. 3).

The most recent nominating conventions provide further support for the ideological cohesion of the national parties. A CBS/New York Times poll found massive differences between Republican and Democratic delegates on questions involving the scope of government, social issues, and international affairs. A majority of these partisans opposed each other on all of ten questions; they held remotely similar views on only one issue—international trade—and were in essentially different political worlds (fifty of more percentage points apart) on issues of governmental regulation, the environment, abortion, assault weapons, civil rights, affirmative action, and immigration (New York Times, Aug. 26, 1996, A12). There is, clearly, a difference.

Party leaders, at every level from campaign activists to members of Congress, differ on significant policies and act on their different ideological commitments. The presidential candidates of 1992 and 1996 are further testament to basic party differences. Bush and Dole were probably the most moderate Republicans, and Clinton the most moderate Democrat, who could conceivably be nominated. Nevertheless, there were major differences in policy and ideology between them —reflecting their basic party identities, even with President Clinton's professed turn toward moderation in the 1996 election.

The party platforms provide less subjective evidence. After examining major party manifestos over forty years (1948–88), Ian Budge concludes: "American Democrats and Republicans . . . consistently differentiate themselves from each other on such matters as support for welfare, government intervention, foreign aid and defence, individual initiative, and freedom. . . . Indeed, they remain as far apart as many European parties on these points, and more so than many" (1993, 696–97). A simple experiment can underline the point. Remove the labels from the Democratic and Republican platforms for 1996, and then read their positions on a series of issues, choosing from a long list including abortion, health insurance, education vouchers, regulation of the economy, endangered species legislation, and so on. Would any political scientist, or most voters, have great difficulty in matching the party to the position? The platform excerpts below, dealing with education policy, provide a quick test.

Party A

Americans should have the best education in the world. . . . Our formula is as simple as it is sweeping: the federal government has no constitutional authority to be involved in school curricula or to control jobs in the work place. That is why we will abolish the Department of Education . . . [and] call for prompt repeal of the Goals 2000 program and the School-to-Work Act. . . . We further urge that federal attempts to impose outcome- or performance-based education on local schools be ended.

We know what works in education . . . discipline, parental involvement, emphasis on basics including computer technology, phonics instead of look-say reading, and dedicated teaching. Abstinence education in the home will lead to less need for birth control services and fewer abortions. We support educational initiatives to promote chastity until marriage. . . . We encourage a reform agenda on the local level and urge State legislators to ensure quality education for all through programs of parental choice among public, private, and religious schools . . . [such as] school rebates, charter schools, and vouchers. . . . We will continue to work for the return of voluntary prayer to our schools. . . .

We support proposals to assist families to prepare for the financial strains of higher education, like the American Dream Savings Account, passed by [our party].

Party B

In the next four years, we must do even more to make sure America has the best public schools on earth. If we want to be the best, we should expect the best. . . . Students should be required to demonstrate competency and achievement for promotion or graduation. Teachers . . . should be required to meet high standards for professional performance. . . . Schools should be held accountable for results. We should redesign or overhaul schools that fail. We should expand public school choice, but we should not take American tax dollars from public schools and give them to private schools. We should promote public charter schools that are held to the highest standards of accountability and access. . . .

We must bring the twenty-first century into every classroom in America. . . . [We] have launched a partnership with high-tech companies, schools, state, and local governments to wire every classroom and library to the Information Superhighway by the year 2000.

We must make sure that every American has the opportunity to go to college. . . . We should expand work-study so one million students a year can work their way through college. . . . We should give a $1,000 honor scholarship for the top 5 percent of graduates in every high school. And we must make fourteen years of education the standard for every American [by offering] a $10,000 tax deduction for families to help pay for education after high school [and] a $1,500 tax credit.

Underlying these specific issues is a basic philosophical and historical disagreement between the major parties.[3] Republicans are individualists, Democrats communitarians. America tries to balance a commitment to individual liberty with a commitment to social equality, to balance the pursuit of our private interests with our search for a public community. We engage in a perpetual personal and national debate asking, to paraphrase John Kennedy, both what we can do for ourselves and what we can do for others. In that debate, Republicans are more likely to raise the banner of individualism: pursuit of individual goals will add up to the common good. Democrats are more likely to raise the banner of community: pursuing the social good will be better for each of us individually (Patterson 1992).

This philosophical difference leads to significant differences in the parties' attitudes toward power and politics. Republicans distrust government, even when they control it. They rely on the private sector, and particularly the accumulation of private capital, to meet social needs. The 104th Congress provides additional evidence of the point. As Republicans returned to power on Capitol Hill, they overwhelmingly supported constitutional amendments to limit their ability to spend money through the balanced budget amendment, to shift power to a Democratic president though the line-item veto, and to reduce their institutional wisdom through term limits. Only a congenital aversion to government can explain these actions.

By contrast, the Democratic Party, at least since the New Deal, has looked on government as a potentially benign force, able to take action, at the very least, to stimulate the private sector and, more ambitiously, to redistribute the national wealth. Only a Republican could give Reagan's 1981 inaugural address, proclaiming that "government is not the solution to our problem—government is the problem." Only a Democrat could give Clinton's 1993 speech, reiterating the party's call for "bold, persistent experimentation, a government for our tomorrows," or still claim, as Clinton did in 1997, that "where it can give Americans the power to make a real difference in their everyday lives, government should do more, not less."

These basic ideological distinctions were evident in the Clinton administration and in the 1996 election campaign, in such issues as family leave, capital gains taxation, minimum wages, social spending, and education. Health care is exemplary. While the president and Hillary Rodham Clinton developed a complex program involving government regulation, subsidies, and mandates, the Republicans looked to individualistic solutions such as private health insurance and tax credits. The futile congressional debate on health care reflected these continuing philosophical differences—and the parties' continuing character as organizations with distinct missions.

The American parties' policy differences may seem startling when we match them against the traditional description of nonideological power-seeking organizations. On a more theoretical level, however, we might expect these findings. Once we see parties as organizations, we immediately must look for incentives provided for members of these organizations. Downs posits purely utilitarian, self-interested motivations: party members "act solely in order to attain the income, prestige, and power which come from being in office" (1957, 28). While this postulate is highly productive in developing his theory, Downs— or any other observer—knows it is empirically untrue and theoretically incomplete. The rewards of office can explain neither the activity of party activists who never seek or hold office nor the persistence of activity among perennial losers. We also need to explain such recent anomalies as the superior political activity of Republicans, although they have been shown to be less interested in professional political careers (Fiorina 1988, 304–16).

Party programs clarify these problems. They provide a means to overcome the problems of effective social choice, as Aldrich demonstrates (1995, chaps. 2, 3). Even a Downsian party requires some policy program; after all, every business has a product. Furthermore, the dynamics of electoral politics will maintain some distinctiveness of policies. Parties in government become identified with particular policies, which they cannot abandon without losing credibility (Downs 1957, 107–11; Chappell and Keech 1986, 881–900). Parties also must maintain the loyalty of their core supporters, even as they attempt to cope with electoral uncertainty. All of these factors make the parties partially ideological in character. Committed to programs, they are hesitant to change their positions on public issues, a pattern demonstrated in comparative research on party platforms. In seeking to win elections, parties change not their views but their emphases, seeking not the more popular view on given and similar issues but the more popular issues (Budge 1994, 443–67).

These behavioral rules apply to all parties, but it is particularly notable that ideological incentives have become important to American parties, the presumed exemplars of unprincipled politics. As the availability and attractiveness of material incentives have declined, the parties must resort to "purpose, principle, and ideology as a major source of incentives" (Wilson 1973, 96). One reason for this necessity is recruitment. If patronage is insufficient, parties can attract active support through purposive incentives, which draw new and different people into politics, such as Republican conservatives. A second reason is financial. The parties today need more money, because of the higher cost of high-technology, high-capital politics. At the same time, money is harder to raise, because of legal limitations on the amount of individual contributions. Purposive incentives bridge the gap. They provide a motive for financial involvement by more people and by ideological interest groups.

Institutional Capacity

The parties also evidence greater strength on the last of our four criteria, institutional capacity. Money is one major measure of organizational strength. In 1996, vastly extending a trend of the 1980s, the political parties were major sources of campaign spending, particularly in the presidential race (Hernnson 1988). Reinforced by a supportive ruling of the Supreme Court, *Colorado Republican Federal Campaign Committee v. Federal Election Commission* (1996 U.S. Lexis 4258), they overcame the party-weakening provisions of election finance laws. "The Court's decision essentially freed the parties to spend unlimited amounts of money in the general election" and raised the distinct possibility that all limits on party spending would be removed in a future case (Corrado 1997, 149).

There were three large sources of party money in 1996: direct subsidies provided by the federal election law, individual "hard money" campaign contributions, and "soft money" contributions provided for "issue advocacy," state parties, and organizational work. Together, party funds totaled $880 million for the major candidates and their parties. Each major party received direct public grants of $12 million for its national conventions and another $62 million for the presidential campaign. Beyond these public funds, Republican national committees directly spent $400 million, and the Democrats $200 million. Piling their funds still higher, the Republicans spent $150 million, and the Democrats $120 million, in "soft money," in each case about two-and-a-half times the amount spent in 1992. Soft money was used to strengthen the organizational ladder of party federalism, with close to half of these funds transferred from the federal to the state level (Corrado 1997, 150–55).

These figures show a major change in the financial impact of the parties. The party role became evident in 1994, with the victory of a Republican majority originally recruited and financed by Newt Gingrich's GOPAC, a party body disguised as a political action committee. Beyond direct contributions and expenditures, the parties have developed a variety of ingenious devices, such as bundling, coordinated spending, and agency agreements, to again become significant players in the election finance game. Significantly, in 1996 national party funds ($880 million) far exceeded the record monies raised for all congressional campaigns ($661 million) (Corrado 1997, 150–64). The parties also now predominate over political action committees, which probably contributed less than $200 million to candidates in 1996.[4]

Underlining the impact of this party spending, the Republican and Democratic presidential campaigns in 1992 each spent twice as much money as did billionaire Ross Perot, whose candidacy is often seen as demonstrating the decline of the parties. By 1996, even he was overwhelmed, having spent a comparatively trifling amount of $29 million in federal funds while withholding his own fortune. Frank Sorauf shrewdly predicted, "the financial rebirth of the national parties offers hope of new influence for parties and a reversal of the much heralded 'decline' and 'decomposition' of the American parties" (1988, 132). The major American parties, holding a privileged position in government campaign funding, hardly seem to be extinct; rather, they have begun to resemble a European model of a state-sponsored "cartel party" (Katz and Mair 1995).

The evident structural viability of the parties is another mark of organizational strength. The national parties are now continuing institutions, with elaborate permanent headquarters—a marked response to earlier calls for party renewal programs (Ranney 1975, 45; Bailey 1959). They have large professional staffs, conducting party programs of candidate recruitment and training, opinion polling, research, campaign management, broadcasting, advertising, and finance. Campaign consultants and political action committees, which are often seen as competitors or potential replacements for the parties, are actually increasingly allied with them. The national parties, to be sure, do not dominate election campaigns, but the truth is that they never did. More accurately, the national parties have changed from the locus of "politics without power" to become active participants in coalitional politics (Cotter and Bibby 1980, 1–27).

State parties, it is now understood, rather than declining, have become stronger organizations. Even while electoral loyalty to the parties has dropped (and perhaps because it has dropped), the party organizations have been transformed and have actually "gained in organizational strength over a period when they were generally thought to be in decline" (Cotter et al. 1984, 102). That organizational strength was evident in the 1988, 1992, and 1996 presidential elections, when Democrats Dukakis and Clinton ran much of their campaigns through the state party organizations.

In summary, American parties now recruit their presidential candidates from among the most prominent national politicians, cohere strongly on policy issues, promote distinct ideological programs, and evidence growing financial resources and institutional capacity. Rather than organizations in decline, they are increasingly vibrant, active, and important. We may confidently look forward to their continued existence and, therefore, to continued fruitful research. We may even dare to speculate about the future.

Responsible Parties?

These developments may best be described as the partial advent of a "responsible party system." In the classic formulation of this normative goal, only two conditions were seen as necessary: "First, that the parties are able to bring forth programs to which they commit themselves and, second, that the parties possess sufficient internal cohesion to carry out these programs" (American Political Science Association 1950, 1) Although its ideological direction is certainly different from that expected by liberal advocates of responsible parties, the congressional Republicans, within the constraints of separated institutions, have fulfilled these conditions.

In this regard, we should remember that the "responsible party" model does not require that voters be ideologically motivated, only that parties be coherently programmatic. It is therefore irrelevant to the model, and to contemporary politics, that the voters in 1994 were not directly committed to the Contract with America (Wilcox 1995, 20–21). The Republican candidates were so committed and have followed through on their commitments.

If this trend exists, it might more accurately be called the development of a "semi-responsible" party system. American institutions, including federalism, the separation of national powers, and the local electoral system, remain as permanent barriers to realization of the Schattschneider model. And candidate-centered campaigning and the mass media are more recent, but equally important, barriers.

Nevertheless, we have reviewed evidence of greater party impact and cohesion. Perhaps the Contract with America is no more a harbinger of the future than was the freedom of contract that once prevented child labor laws. Two significant underlying factors, however, suggest that the movement toward strengthened political parties will endure. The first is change in the institutional balance within the federal government. The second is the realignment of the parties' electoral market.

We have become accustomed to thinking of American government as presidential government, a constitutional structure created through the informal transformation of institutions that began in the New Deal. As Charles Jones reminds us, however, the formal Constitution remains one of separated institutions in which the presidency is only one part of a complex arrangement. We have also tended to equate the presidency not only with American national government but also with the national political parties, leading to the "classic party responsibility model in which a winning political party, led by its president, is expected to carry out a governing mandate" (Jones 1995, 248). The connection between strong parties and a strong president is particularly clear in the APSA report of 1950 and in the advocacy of Schattschneider's intellectual heir, James MacGregor Burns. Strong congressional parties, Burns (1963) argues, led to the deadlock of a multiparty system, while effective two-party politics meant presidential politics.

We should remember that, historically, parties arose, and have exercised their most effective discipline, in legislatures. In the United States, parties first arose to meet legislative and political needs evident in the first Congresses, before they became oriented toward the election and the programs of the president. Recent scholarship actually suggests that there is both a temporal and a logical connection between the strengthening of the presidency since the New Deal and the weakening of the parties. Sidney Milkis (1993), for example, shows how Franklin Roosevelt's creation of the administrative state weakened the Democratic Party.

Since then, the chief responsibility of the president has been the conduct of foreign policy, from the onset of the Second World War through the Cold War. To fulfill this responsibility, all presidents have necessarily de-emphasized partisanship, even as their office grew in size and power. Significantly, virtually every president since Franklin Roosevelt has been criticized for neglecting his role as party leader, indicating the likely conflict between the roles of party leader and leader of foreign policy and national defense.

With the end of the Cold War, the presidency no longer embodies a clear national mission, and the inherent weaknesses of the office—elaborated by Richard Neustadt (1960) even at the height of international conflict—are again evident. The presidency cannot revert to its earlier partisan character, however, because it has been distanced from party governance by the growth of the administrative state and from state and local party politics by the transformation of the nominating process. The Clinton administration exemplifies these changes. President Clinton is often characterized as a weak president. Yet he is reasonably skilled, is experienced in executive-legislative relations, and actually achieved considerable success in his first two years. The difficulty he has faced is not simply personal or tactical incompetence—although some is surely evident—but the inherent limitations of an office unsupported by a party base. In strengthening his position before the 1996 election, Clinton moved further away from his party.

As the presidency weakens relative to Congress, the natural divisions of politics become centered more on Congress. There, party institutions have been strengthened over the past two decades, along with institutional capacity, in contrast with restrictions both on the presidency and on the autonomy of committee chairs and individual representatives. Party leaders—Democrats as well as the reborn Republicans—now have extensive powers over committee assignments, legislative scheduling, policy development, and individual perquisites (Jones 1995, 16–19). All of these trends are consistent, reflected in the increased unity of the legislative parties.

American politics now begins to resemble parliamentary competition, with alternative visions of public policy expressed by reasonably coherent parties, paralleling the classic conflicts of government and opposition. As even a skeptical observer conceded in advance of the 1996 elections, "If the Republicans remain in control, officeholders may attribute this success to the power of their agenda to focus choices for voters, and it may serve as a model for both parties for the future" (Kolodny 1996, 326).[5] In contrast to the opaque processes of the executive branch, these party visions are openly debated in Congress. Compare, for example, the secretive development of the Clinton health care program with the vivid debates on welfare policy in the House or on the balanced budget amendment in the Senate. Surely, the latter decisions—leaving substantive content aside—are better examples of vigorous party government—and of vigorous democratic deliberation.[6]

The trend toward "parliamentary government" will be strongly furthered by the Republican congressional victories of 1994 and 1996, even aside from its immediate policy consequences. Until November 1994, another tenet of conventional wisdom was the permanent overlay of party conflict with institutional conflict, a virtually constitutional division between a Democratic Congress (at least in the House) and a normally Republican president. With each party holding a secure base, write Benjamin Ginsberg and Martin Shefter,

> intense institutional struggles have increasingly come to supplant electoral competition as the central focus of politics in the United States. . . . The shift from an electorally to an institutionally centered politics in the United States means that efforts by opposing forces to attack and undermine governmental institutions have become major features of political combat. . . . As the Democrats seek to weaken the presidency and to strengthen the administrative and coercive capabilities of Congress while the Republicans attempt to undermine Congress and increase the autonomy of the White House, a system approaching dual sovereignty has emerged in the United States. (1990, 131, 162–63)

Since the Democratic capture of the White House in 1992, the Republican congressional triumph in 1994, and the continuation of the new partisan balance of power in 1996, the electoral-institutional overlay no longer exists. With party competition no longer equivalent to institutional competition, the parties can—and surely will—seek victory throughout the government. That pursuit of victory requires some increased cooperation between presidential and legislative candidates, some agreement on national policy issues, and still clearer delineation of the parties' ideologies.

These institutional changes are complemented by a change in the makeup of the parties' voting coalitions. Although I have emphasized the distinction between parties and their electoral markets, they are certainly affected by the character of their mass base. Parties with diverse electoral markets are like conglomerate corporations, offering different products to unrelated clienteles. In contrast, parties with a more restricted market are more likely to specialize in particular "brands," thereby presenting a more coherent program.

In the past two decades, the parties' markets have become more defined both socially and ideologically, reciprocally fostering greater coherence in the appeal parties make to the voters. The Democratic Party has lost its most conservative element, white southerners, as well as some conservative Catholics, while the influence of more liberal groups, such as blacks and feminists, has increased. Republican support among white Protestant fundamentalists has become almost as distinctive as the party's traditional base among the wealthy. "Considering these changes, it is time to declare the New Deal coalition dead" (Stanley and Niemi 1995, 237).

Change in the parties' electoral markets is seen in figures 2.3 and 2.4, which graph the ideological self-identifications of the electorate within partisan groups in 1974, 1984, and 1994. As the nation has moved toward the right, the Democrats have become the distinctive location of the left within the electorate. The relative proportion of liberals and conservatives has remained tilted to the left within the Democratic Party, with liberals outnumbering conservatives by nearly two to one. Conversely, liberals have virtually disappeared from the Republican market, and self-identified conservatives dominate the party base. Among independents, there is no clear pattern; liberal decline has not been matched by conservative growth.

The patterns in the four figures in this chapter thus illustrate parallel trends among party entrepreneurs and party clienteles. In the public mind as well, there is now a close relationship between liberals and the Democratic Party and between conservatives and the Republican Party. In a reprise of the conflicts of the 1960s, "the linkage of parties to the main ideological blocs has returned" (Weisberg et al. 1995, 255).

If American parties are not in decline, there may also be hope for American democracy. These parties have not always fulfilled the promise of their theoretical functions in promoting public understanding and control of govern-

Figure 2.3 Conservative Self-Identification

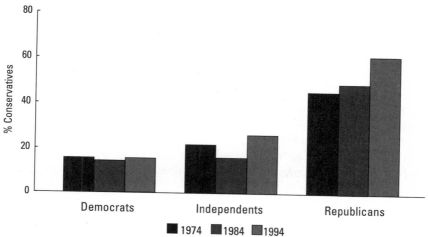

Source: National Election Studies website: www.umich.edu/~nes/nesguide/tab3_1.

Figure 2.4 Liberal Self-Identification

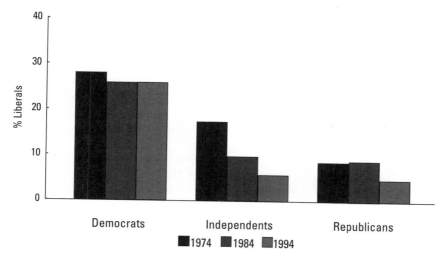

Source: National Election Studies website: www.umich.edu/~nes/nesguide/tab3_1.

ment. Describing their character in an earlier time, one observer writes, "Decentralization tends to encourage differences in the policy appeals of candidates of the same party and discourages, therefore, the development of any but the vaguest of party ideologies. It also encourages a lack of discipline in legislative parties, which, in turn, means that public discussion of legislative activities will fail to shape political issues in a way that is directly relevant to choices at the polls" (Kelley 1960, 148–49).

Parties now are different—more centralized, more ideological, more disciplined, more capable. They are currently conducting a great national dialogue on the purpose of American government and the goals of the American community. However it is resolved, that dialogue is a societal emblem of the personal and serious conversation that makes political parties essential to meaningful democracy in America.

Notes

1. Some, but not all, of these criteria are employed in Paul Beck's leading textbook, *Party Politics in America* (1997, 60).

2. Since 1924, the only exception to the trend away from inner party selection or compromise is Alf Landon's designation as the Republican candidate in 1936. The last president to "voluntarily" decline a second term was Lyndon Johnson in 1968. Another trend is the disappearance of second efforts by nominees defeated in a previous general election. Richard Nixon in 1968 represents the last exception.

3. Should there be any doubt, the Republicans are Party A (Republican National Committee 1996, 50–52), the Democrats, Party B (Democratic National Committee 1996, 13–14).

4. In the first eighteen months of the 1995–96 election cycle, political action committees (PACs) reported $127 million in campaign contributions (Federal Election Commission, Sept. 27, 1996, www.fec.gov\finance\finmenu.htm).

5. Writing before the conclusion of the 104th Congress, Kolodny seriously underestimates the fulfillment of the Contract.

6. To promote this development of "parliamentary" government, Theodore Lowi (1996) argues—incorrectly, I believe—for a third party.

References

Abramowitz, Alan, John McGlennon, and Ronald Rapoport. 1986. "An Analysis of State Party Activists." In *The Life of the Parties*, ed. Ronald Rapaport, Alan Abramowitz, and John McGlennon. Lexington: University Press of Kentucky.
Abramson, Paul, John Aldrich, Phil Paolino, and David Rohde. 1992. "'Sophisticated' Voting in the 1988 Presidential Primaries." *American Political Science Review* 86 (Mar.): 55–69.

Aldrich, John H. 1995. *Why Parties?: The Origin and Transformation of Party Politics in America*. Chicago: University of Chicago Press.

American Political Science Association, Committee on Political Parties. 1950. *Toward a More Responsible Two-Party System*. New York: Rinehart.

Baer, Denise, and David Bositis. 1993. *Politics and Linkage in a Democratic Society*. Englewood Cliffs, N.J.: Prentice-Hall.

Bailey, Stephen. 1959. *The Condition of Our National Political Parties*. New York: Fund for the Republic.

Barnard, Chester. 1938. *The Functions of the Executive*. Cambridge: Harvard University Press.

Bartels, Larry. 1988. *Presidential Primaries and the Dynamics of Public Choice*. Princeton: Princeton University Press.

Beck, Paul. 1997. *Party Politics in America*. 8th ed. New York: Addison-Wesley.

Blau, Peter, and W. Richard Scott. 1962. *Formal Organizations*. Scranton, Pa.: Chandler.

Broder, David. 1972. *The Party's Over*. New York: Harper and Row.

Bruce, John M., John A. Clark, and John H. Kessel. 1991. "Advocacy Politics in Presidential Parties." *American Political Science Review* 85 (Dec.): 1089–1106.

Bruzios, Christopher. 1990. "Democratic and Republican Party Activists and Followers." *Polity* 22 (summer): 581–601.

Budge, Ian. 1993. "Parties, Programs, and Policies: A Comparative and Theoretical Perspective." *American Review of Politics* 14 (winter): 695–716.

———. 1994. "A New Spatial Theory of Party Competition." *British Journal of Political Science* 24:443–67.

Burke, Edmund. [1770] 1981. *Thoughts on the Causes of the Present Discontents*. In *The Writings and Speeches of Edmund Burke*, ed. Paul Langford. Oxford: Clarendon Press.

Burns, James MacGregor. 1963. *The Deadlock of Democracy: Four-Party Politics in America*. Englewood Cliffs, N.J.: Prentice-Hall.

Chappell, Henry, and William Keech. 1986. "Policy Motivation and Party Differences." *American Political Science Review* (Sept.): 881–900.

Corrado, Anthony. 1997. "Financing the 1996 Elections." In *The Election of 1996*, ed. Gerald Pomper. Chatham, N.J.: Chatham House.

Cotter, Cornelius, and John Bibby. 1980. "Institutional Development of Parties and the Thesis of Party Decline." *Political Science Quarterly* 95 (spring): 1–27.

Cotter, Cornelius, James Gibson, John Bibby, and Robert Huckshorn. 1984. *Party Organizations in American Politics*. New York: Praeger.

David, Paul T., Ralph M. Goodman, and Richard C. Bain. 1960. *The Politics of National Party Conventions*. Washington, D.C.: Brookings Institution.

Democratic National Committee. 1996. *1996 Democratic National Platform*. Washington, D.C.: Democratic National Committee.

Downs, Anthony. 1957. *An Economic Theory of Democracy*. New York: Harper.

Epstein, Leon. 1980. *Political Parties in Western Democracies*. New Brunswick, N.J.: Transaction Publishers.

———. 1986. *Political Parties in the American Mold*. Madison: University of Wisconsin Press.

Fiorina, Morris. 1988. "Divided Government in the American States." *American Political Science Review* 88 (June): 304–16.

Frendreis, John. 1996. "Voters, Government Officials, and Party Organizations." In *The State of the Parties*, ed. John Green and Daniel Shea. 2d ed. Lanham, Md.: Rowman and Littlefield.

Ginsberg, Benjamin, and Martin Shefter. 1990. *Politics by Other Means*. New York: Basic Books.

Hale, Jon F. 1994. "The Democratic Leadership Council: Institutionalizing Party Faction." In *The State of the Parties*, ed. John Green and Daniel Shea. 2d ed. Lanham, Md.: Rowman and Littlefield.

Hernnson, Paul. 1988. *Party Campaigning in the 1980s*. Cambridge: Harvard University Press.

Jones, Charles. 1995. *Separate but Equal Branches*. Chatham, N.J.: Chatham House.

Katz, Richard S., and Robin Kolodny. 1994. "Party Organization as an Empty Vessel: Parties in American Politics." In *How Parties Organize,* ed. Richard S. Katz and Peter Mair. London: Sage Publications.

Katz, Richard S., and Peter Mair. 1992. *Party Organizations*. London: Sage Publications.

———. 1995. "Changing Models of Party Organization and Party Democracy: The Emergence of the Cartel Party." *Party Politics* 1 (Jan.): 5–28.

Kelley, Stanley, Jr. 1960. *Political Campaigning*. Washington, D.C.: Brookings Institution.

Key, V. O. 1964. *Politics, Parties, and Pressure Groups*. 5th ed. New York: Thomas Y. Crowell.

Kolodny, Robin. 1996. "The Contract with America in the 104th Congress." In *The State of the Parties,* ed. John Green and Daniel Shea. 2d ed. Lanham, Md.: Rowman and Littlefield.

Lowi, Theodore. 1996. "Toward a Responsible Three-Party System." In *The State of the Parties,* ed. John Green and Daniel Shea. 2d ed. Lanham, Md.: Rowman and Littlefield.

March, James, and Herbert Simon. 1958. *Organizations*. New York: Wiley.

Mayer, William. 1997. "The Presidential Nominations." In *The Election of 1996*, ed. Gerald Pomper. Chatham, N.J.: Chatham House.

McClosky, Herbert, Paul J. Hoffmann, and Rosemary O'Hara. 1960. "Issue Conflict and Consensus among Party Leaders and Followers." *American Political Science Review* 54 (June): 406–27.

Milkis, Sidney. 1993. *The President and the Parties*. New York: Oxford University Press.

Neustadt, Richard. 1960. *Presidential Power*. New York: Wiley.

Panebianco, Angelo. 1988. *Political Parties: Organization and Power*. Cambridge: Cambridge University Press.

Patterson, Orlando. 1992. "Our History versus Clinton's Covenant." *New York Times,* Nov. 13.

Polsby, Nelson. 1983. *Consequences of Party Reform*. New York: Oxford University Press.

Pomper, Gerald. 1992. *Passions and Interests: Political Party Concepts of American Democracy*. Lawrence: University Press of Kansas.

Ranney, Austin. 1975. *Curing the Mischiefs of Faction*. Berkeley: University of California Press.

Ranney, Austin, and Willmoore Kendall. 1956. *Democracy and the American Party System*. New York: Harcourt Brace.

Republican National Committee. 1996. *Restoring the American Dream*. Washington, D.C.: Republican National Committee.

Rohde, David. 1991. *Parties and Leaders in the Postreform House*. Chicago: University of Chicago Press.

Schattschneider, E. E. 1942. *Party Government*. New York: Holt, Rinehart and Winston.

Schlesinger, Joseph. 1984. "On the Theory of Party Organization." *Journal of Politics* 46 (May): 369–400.

Sinclair, Barbara. 1989. *The Transformation of the U.S. Senate*. Baltimore: Johns Hopkins University Press.

———. 1994. "The Congressional Party." In *The Parties Respond*, ed. Sandy Maisel. 2d ed. Boulder, Colo.: Westview.

Sorauf, Frank. 1988. *Money in American Elections*. Glenview, Ill.: Scott, Foresman.

Stanley, Harold, and Richard Niemi. 1995. "The Demise of the New Deal Coalition: Partisanship and Group Support, 1952–1992." In *Democracy's Feast*, ed. Herbert Weisberg. Chatham, N.J.: Chatham House.

Tocqueville, Alexis de. [1835] 1956. *Democracy in America*. Edited by Richard Heffner. New York: Mentor.

Wattenberg, Martin. 1984. *The Decline of American Political Parties*. Cambridge: Harvard University Press.

———. 1991. *The Rise of Candidate-Centered Politics*. Cambridge: Harvard University Press.

———. 1993. "The 1992 Election." Paper presented at meeting of the American Political Science Association, Washington, D.C., Sept.

Weisberg, Herbert F., Audrey A. Haines, and Jon A. Krosnick. 1995. "Social Group Polarization in 1992." In *Democracy's Feast*, ed. Herbert F. Weisberg. Chatham, N.J.: Chatham House.

Wilcox, Clyde. 1995. *The Latest American Revolution?* New York: St. Martin's Press.

Wilson, James Q. 1973. *Political Organizations*. New York: Basic Books.

Part I

Mobilizing

CHAPTER 3

Where the Ducks Are
Voting Power in a Party System

Larry M. Bartels

> We're not going to get the Negro vote as a bloc in 1964 and 1968,
> so we ought to go hunting where the ducks are.
> Barry Goldwater, Atlanta, 1961

Rational candidates seeking to maximize their electoral prospects must "go hunting where the ducks are," tailoring their appeals to those prospective voters who are both likely to turn out and susceptible to conversion. This chapter examines the political implications of that strategic imperative. In particular, it describes a new measure of voting power that makes it possible to quantify inequalities in the electoral influence of individuals or groups arising from variations in the extent to which they are politically mobilized and in the extent to which they are predisposed to support one party or the other.

Equality of electoral influence is a powerful ideal in the American political system, as it must be in any representative democracy. "Each and every citizen," the United States Supreme Court ruled in *Reynolds v. Sims* (377 U.S. 533 [1964]), "has an inalienable right to full and effective participation . . . an equally effective voice" (565). But exactly what that means has never been clear. For the last thirty years, the attention of the courts, legislatures, and the public has focused on two kinds of especially egregious violations of the ideal of equal influence: the open, often violent, disenfranchisement of most African Americans in most of the South throughout most of the last century and the widespread malapportionment of legislative districts at the federal, state, and local levels. The first of these violations has been mitigated by a constellation of private, judicial, legislative, and executive actions, including the passage and implementation of the

1965 Voting Rights Act and its successors, while the latter violation has been drastically circumscribed by a series of court rulings enshrining the principle of "One person, one vote" as a binding rule for legislative apportionment.[1]

Despite these advances, "the courts, Congress, attorneys, and scholars are still fumbling to define the vote at 'full value without dilution or discount'" (Thernstrom 1987, 232, quoting Supreme Court Justice William O. Douglas). Inequalities in voting power that are subtler and less institutionalized than those typically addressed by courts and legislatures are especially problematic. The principle of "One person, one vote" has clearly been extended, at least for certain protected groups, to entail a right to cast an *effective* vote, somehow defined. But if a legislative districting plan that can be said to "dilute" the electoral influence of recognized minorities is objectionable, is not a functioning system of electoral competition, with an associated constellation of standing partisan loyalties that can be just as cogently said to "dilute" the electoral influence of the same minorities, equally objectionable? Perhaps; but it is much harder to legislate and litigate party strategies and campaign appeals than the boundaries of legislative districts.

Here, I aim to provide a richer, more realistic framework for thinking about inequalities of electoral influence in functioning party systems. Section 1 introduces the two key concepts in my analysis of voting power: *participation* and *centrality*. In section 2, I propose a formal measure of voting power based on these concepts and explicitly derived from a familiar model of prospective voters as utility maximizers and candidates as vote (plurality) maximizers. In section 3, I modify the measure of voting power to take account of the impact of additional inequalities in electoral influence introduced by the operation of the unit rule within the electoral college in U.S. presidential elections.[2]

In sections 4, 5, and 6, I use the measure of voting power proposed in section 2 and modified in section 3 to analyze patterns of electoral influence in eleven recent U.S. presidential elections. Section 4 examines the distribution of voting power among individuals, as well as changes in that distribution from the 1950s to the present; the analysis suggests that although the distribution of voting power is somewhat more egalitarian in the contemporary party system than it was in the 1950s, the most influential third of the electorate still has about as much voting power as the least influential two-thirds. Section 5 examines the distribution of voting power among social groups, presenting estimates of both the per capita influence and the share of total voting power wielded by each of thirty-eight different groups in the American party system.

Section 6 focuses on the electoral fortunes of two especially interesting groups in the American party system, African Americans and southern whites. For African Americans, the analysis suggests that the impact of rapid electoral mobilization in the 1950s and 1960s was significantly diluted by the impact of increasing Democratic partisan loyalty, leaving the average black American with only about 70 percent as much voting power as the average white American in the contemporary party system. On the other hand, the analysis suggests that the increasing Republican partisan loyalty of southern whites produced by the "southern strategy" of Barry Goldwater and Richard Nixon in the 1960s actually produced significant declines in both the relative and absolute voting power of southern whites, despite notable increases in their numbers and turnout rate.

1: Elements of Voting Power

The abstract ideal of equal electoral influence is clearly violated in a variety of ways in real electoral systems. From the perspective of parties and candidates, two sorts of inequalities seem especially consequential: those stemming from unequal rates of electoral *participation* and those having to do with unequal *centrality* in a functioning party system.[3] On one hand, vote-maximizing politicians must care more, other things being equal, about the views of regular voters than about the views of people who seldom or never get to the polls. At the same time, candidates have little incentive to appeal to prospective voters whose minds are already made up, except insofar as such appeals may impel likely supporters to turn out or likely opponents to stay home. Thus, other things again being equal, the preferences and concerns of prospective voters without strong preexisting loyalties to either party are likely to receive more weight at the margin than the preferences and concerns of prospective voters already strongly predisposed to support one party or the other.[4]

Significant differences in rates of electoral participation among individuals and groups are, of course, well documented in the literature on American electoral politics (e.g., Wolfinger and Rosenstone 1980). However, these variations are seldom explicitly related to any observed or potential impact they may have upon the strategic decisions of candidates or the policy outcomes produced by the electoral process.[5] By examining electoral mobilization from the candidates' point of view, in the context of a broader framework for measuring voting power, I hope to offer a clearer picture of the potential political consequences of observed patterns of voting and nonvoting.

My emphasis on the partisan centrality of pivotal individuals or groups in a party system as a second important element of voting power contrasts markedly with the traditional focus, in both the scholarly and popular literatures on party systems, upon the most loyal groups in each party's ranks during a given era of partisan competition. Thus, for example, the New Deal party system is invariably characterized by the list of loyal constituent groups in the Democratic coalition constructed by Franklin D. Roosevelt (Axelrod 1972; Petrocik 1981; Stanley, Bianco, and Niemi 1986; Erikson, Lancaster, and Romero 1989). Here,

I propose to focus not upon the most loyal elements of each party's electoral coalition but upon the individuals and groups occupying the strategically important center of a more or less stable distribution of partisan predispositions. In this respect I follow a lead suggested by Kelley's description in *Interpreting Elections* of the characteristics and concerns of "marginal voters" in the landslide elections of 1964 and 1972 (1983, 147–66).

My focus on centrality is motivated in part by the theoretical importance of the median or mean voter in spatial theories of party competition (e.g., Downs 1957; Enelow and Hinich 1989). An interesting implication of such theories—but one that has only recently been recognized explicitly in the literature on party competition (Erikson and Romero 1990)—is that vote-maximizing candidates should be especially responsive to the views of potential voters located near the center of the distribution of partisan predispositions. Although the analysis presented here does not attempt to test that proposition directly, it does provide much of the framework necessary to construct such a test.[6]

Obviously, partisan loyalties—and, hence, the relative electoral centrality of a given individual or group—are not immutable. If either party appeals more successfully than the other to some previously uncommitted voters, those voters may develop new loyalties and become correspondingly less central to the ongoing party competition. By the same token, strong predispositions to support one party or the other may be eroded by changes in the parties' images, policies, and performance. These changes may be relatively sudden (Key 1955) or more gradual (Key 1959); in either case, when they are of sufficient political import, analysts declare a transition from one party system to another. The political loyalties characteristic of the new party system will, in turn, be malleable in the long run. But in the short run politicians will tend to take them as given and construct their appeals accordingly.

The notion of electoral centrality proposed here bears some similarities to formal measures of voting power such as the Shapley and Banzhaf values (Shapley and Shubik 1954; Banzhaf 1965), which are based on the probability that a given voter or bloc will be pivotal in determining the outcome of an election. However, I dispense with the highly unrealistic assumption upon which those formal measures are invariably based, that any pattern of preferences is as likely to arise as any other. Instead, I use observed voting behavior to estimate how likely it is that any given voter might be induced to cross party lines and thus, by extension, the centrality of that voter's concerns in the existing party system.

An important feature of the notion of voting power proposed here is that its two central elements, participation and centrality, *interact* to produce electoral *influence*. Centrality alone is insufficient to guarantee influence if a potential voter is very unlikely to actually turn out to vote. By the same token, participation alone is insufficient to guarantee influence if a voter is situated at the periphery of the party system, almost certain to vote in a predictable way whatever the competing candidates may do or say. Thus, analyses focusing upon either turnout propensities or partisan predispositions in isolation may be misleading, since advantages or disadvantages with respect to either factor may be reinforced, mitigated, or reversed by advantages or disadvantages with respect to the other.

2: Measuring Voting Power

The measure of *voting power* proposed here is derived from an explicit model of the behavior of candidates and prospective voters in a functioning two-party system. I assume that the behavior of prospective voters is consistent with a random utility model of the form

$$\omega_i = x_i' \beta + \epsilon_i$$

$$\tau_i = x_i' \alpha + (x_i' \beta)^2 \gamma + \delta_i,$$

where i indexes prospective voters; x_i' is a row vector of characteristics of prospective voter i; α, β, and γ are constant parameters to be estimated; δ_i and ϵ_i are random variables with uncorrelated standard normal distributions for all i; and the latent variables τ_i and ω_i represent prospective voter i's random utilities for turning out and for voting Republican conditional upon turning out, respectively. Prospective voter i is assumed to turn out if and only if τ_i is greater than or equal to zero, to vote Republican (conditional upon turning out) if and only if ω_i is greater than or equal to zero, and to vote Democratic (conditional upon turning out) if and only if ω_i is less than zero. Thus,

$$\text{prob}_i (\text{Republican vote} \mid \text{turnout}) = \Phi(x_i' \beta),$$

$$\text{prob}_i (\text{Democratic vote} \mid \text{turnout}) = 1 - \Phi(x_i' \beta),$$

and

$$\text{prob}_i (\text{turnout}) = \Phi(x_i' \alpha + (x_i' \beta)^2 \gamma),$$

where $\Phi(\cdot)$ represents the cumulative normal distribution function.

It follows that the ith prospective voter's expected contribution to the Republican vote plurality is

$$\text{prob}_i (\text{Republican vote}) - \text{prob}_i (\text{Democratic vote}) =$$

$$\Phi(x_i' \beta) \Phi(x_i' \alpha + (x_i' \beta)^2 \gamma) - [1 - \Phi(x_i' \beta)] \Phi(x_i' \alpha + (x_i' \beta)^2 \gamma) =$$

$$2[\Phi(x_i' \beta) - .5] \Phi(x_i' \alpha + (x_i' \beta)^2 \gamma). \tag{1}$$

We may think of candidates as vote plurality maximizers attempting to improve their electoral fortunes by effecting marginal alterations in prospective voters' partisan propensities—for example, by committing themselves to policies offering some group-specific benefits. Of course, not all such commitments are simultaneously feasible; candidates must choose, at least to a significant degree, to placate some prospective voters while ignoring (or even offending) others. Equation (1) implies that, at the margin, some prospective voters are more likely than others to be placated by rational, plurality-maximizing candidates. The value to either candidate of a marginal change in the ith prospective voter's partisan propensity, $x_i' \beta$, depends precisely upon the effect of that change on the ith prospective voter's expected contribution to the Republican plurality:

$$\frac{\partial \{2[\Phi(x_i' \beta) - .5] \, \Phi(x_i' \alpha + (x_i' \beta)^2 \gamma)\}}{\partial x_i' \beta}$$

$$= 2\Phi(x_i' \beta) \, \Phi(x_i' \alpha + (x_i' \beta)^2 \gamma) + 2[\Phi(x_i' \beta) - .5] \, \Phi(x_i' \alpha + (x_i' \beta)^2 \gamma) \, 2x_i' \beta \gamma \quad (2)$$

where $\Phi(\cdot)$ represents the normal density function.

Since equation (2) represents the marginal change in an election outcome with changes in voter i's partisan preference $x_i' \beta$, it conforms to Jack Nagel's definition of *power* as "an actual or potential causal relation between the preferences of an actor regarding an outcome and the outcome itself" (1975, 29). Voter i's power over the election outcome derives not simply from his or her right to vote but additionally, and more subtly, from the candidates' strategic imperative to compete for his or her vote; disparities in the force of that strategic imperative can produce disparities in electoral influence, even in a system in which every person is legally entitled to cast one vote.

In particular, in deciding whether to commit to any proposed policy, a rational, plurality-maximizing candidate must be guided not by the net changes in partisan propensities summed across the electorate that are expected to result from that commitment but by the net changes in partisan propensities, *each weighted by the corresponding marginal impact in equation (2)*. Facing a choice between two equally costly appeals, one that will change prospective voter i's partisan propensity $x_i' \beta$ by some small amount (and leave every other prospective voter's partisan propensity unchanged) and another that will change prospective voter j's partisan propensity $x_j' \beta$ by the same amount (and leave every other prospective voter's partisan propensity unchanged), the margin-maximizing candidate must choose to placate the prospective voter for whom the magnitude of the reaction in equation (2) is larger. In this sense, equation (2) provides an index of prospective voter i's relative electoral influence.

It is convenient to normalize equation (2) by expressing it as a fraction of its maximum value (for plausible values of γ), $2\phi(0)$. Applying this normalization (and rearranging) produces our proposed measure of prospective voter i's voting power:

$$\pi_i = \Phi(x_i'\alpha + (x_i'\beta)^2\gamma)\ \phi(x_i'\beta)\ /\phi(0)$$
$$+ 2x_i'\beta\gamma\ [\Phi(x_i'\beta) - .5]\ \phi(x_i'\alpha + (x_i'\beta)^2\gamma)\ /\ \phi(0). \tag{3}$$

The index of *voting power* π_i consists of two distinct terms, corresponding to two distinct ways in which candidates can gain support by changing prospective voters' partisan predispositions. One possible effect of a marginal change in a prospective voter's partisan propensity is that it may convert the voter from voting for one candidate to voting for the opposing candidate. The other possible effect is that, if γ is greater than zero, a marginal change in partisan propensity may motivate the prospective voter to actually turn out (if he or she is a likely supporter) or to stay home (if he or she is a likely opponent). I refer to these two potential effects as *conversion* and *mobilization*, respectively.

The *conversion value* of prospective voter i,

$$\Phi(x_i'\alpha + (x_i'\beta)^2\gamma)\ \phi(x_i'\beta)\ /\phi(0),$$

is itself the product of two distinct factors: the voter's probability of actually voting, $\Phi(x_i'\alpha + (x_i'\beta)^2\gamma)$, and the voter's relative "availability" for partisan conversion, measured by the rate at which the voter's choice probabilities change with changes in his or her partisan propensity (relative to the corresponding rate for a totally uncommitted voter), $\phi(x_i'\beta)/\phi(0)$. Both factors are necessary components of prospective voter i's conversion value. Candidates have nothing to gain either by attempting to convince the already committed or by "converting" prospective voters who will not vote in any case.

The *mobilization value* of altering prospective voter i's partisan predisposition,[7]

$$2x_i'\beta\gamma\ [\Phi(x_i'\beta) - .5]\ \phi(x_i'\alpha + (x_i'\beta)^2\gamma)\ /\phi(0),$$

is the product of three distinct factors: the rate, $2x_i'\beta\gamma$, at which partisan predispositions affect turnout; voter i's partisan reliability, measured by the extent to which the voter's probability of voting Republican, $\Phi(x_i'\beta)$, departs from .5; and prospective voter i's "availability" for mobilization (or demobilization), measured by the relative sensitivity of his or her turnout probability to changes in his or her turnout propensity, $\phi(x_i'\alpha + (x_i'\beta)^2\gamma)/\phi(0)$. Again, all three factors are necessary components of prospective voter i's mobilization value. If γ

is zero, the strength of a prospective voter's preference for one candidate over the other does not affect his or her probability of turning out; in that case, the only reason for candidates to appeal to prospective voters is to produce conversion among those already likely to turn out.[8] If $\Phi(\mathbf{x}_i' \boldsymbol{\beta}) - .5$ is zero, a marginal change in partisan propensity may indeed make the prospective voter more likely to turn out, but neither candidate has anything to gain from mobilizing such a prospective voter, since the voter is just as likely to vote for the opponent as for the candidate doing the mobilizing. Finally, if $\phi(\mathbf{x}_i' \boldsymbol{\alpha} + (\mathbf{x}_i' \boldsymbol{\beta})^2 \gamma) / \phi(0)$ is zero, there is no marginal benefit to be had from attempting to mobilize even the most reliable partisan supporter, because he or she is already essentially certain to turn out (or to stay home).

It should be evident that the two distinct forms of voting power, *conversion value* and *mobilization value*, produce incentives for competing candidates to target their appeals to two distinct groups of prospective voters: likely voters without strong preexisting loyalties, who are most susceptible to conversion, and potential voters with strong preexisting loyalties, who can be mobilized to turn out (or *de*mobilized to stay home). The fact that rational candidates must attempt to identify and appeal to both groups in order to maximize their expected vote pluralities explains why real campaigns combine persuasive efforts at the margin with efforts to protect the candidate's own partisan base (and challenge the opponent's). Indeed, quantitative variations among party systems in prospective voters' conversion value and mobilization value may help to account for variations in the relative prevalence of these two forms of campaigning.

3: Two-Stage Voting and the Impact of the Electoral College

My analysis so far has treated rational party politicians as vote (plurality) maximizers.[9] But real electoral systems often create more complicated electoral incentives. Political parties competing in simultaneous legislative elections in many districts may—to the extent that they are unified teams rather than independent actors—attempt to maximize their share of seats in the legislature (or their probability of attaining a majority of seats) rather than their share of votes. By the same token, the peculiar institution of the electoral college—together with the customary unit rule in casting each state's electoral votes—requires candidates in U.S. presidential elections to attempt to achieve statewide vote pluralities in a set of states amounting to a majority of the electoral college rather than a simple plurality of popular votes nationwide.

The number of electoral votes allocated to each state is equal to the number of representatives it sends to Congress: two senators plus from one to fifty-two members of the House of Representatives, depending upon the state's population. By giving each state a minimum of three electoral votes, the electoral college system clearly advantages very small states. In 1992, for example, California cast only eighteen times as many electoral votes as Wyoming (fifty-four versus three), despite having fifty-five times as many voters (11.1 million versus 0.2 million). Paradoxically, however, the main effect of the electoral college system in practice seems to be to make large states even more important than their sheer size would warrant, due to the unit rule. Given the improbability of winning enough small states to build an electoral college majority, candidates regularly choose to concentrate their time and money in larger states, especially the nine largest "battleground" states (California, New York, Texas, Florida, Pennsylvania, Illinois, Ohio, Michigan, and New Jersey), which together cast 90 percent of the electoral votes needed to assemble a majority in the contemporary electoral college (Brams and Davis 1974; Colantoni, Levesque, and Ordeshook 1975; Bartels 1985).

Game theorists have used a variety of mathematical models to formalize the extent to which large states are advantaged by the unit rule in the electoral college (Mann and Shapley 1964; Banzhaf 1968; Owen 1975; Lake 1979). Perhaps the simplest formula is Steven Brams and Morton Davis's "3/2's rule," in which each state's influence is proportional to its electoral vote allocation raised to the power of 3/2 (Brams and Davis 1974). The "3/2's rule" agrees with other mathematical analyses based on slightly different assumptions and arguments in suggesting that the strategic advantage of large states due to the unit rule far outweighs the electoral vote bonus received by small states. For example, California has seventy-six times as much power as Wyoming in the electoral college of the 1990s by this measure, despite having only eighteen times as many electoral votes (and only fifty-five times as many voters).

If each state's strategic value is proportional to the number of its electoral votes to the power of 3/2, the strategic value of changing the expected plurality in a given state by one vote (whether by mobilization or conversion) should be proportional to the number of its electoral votes to the power of 3/2 divided by the number of voters (since the probability that a given voter will be pivotal within a state is assumed to be proportional to the number of voters in the state, other things being equal). This logic suggests that the index of voting power for individual voters defined in equation (3) should be modified to reflect the differential value of winning votes in different states. The *modified index of voting power* is

$$\omega_i = \pi_i \, (E_j^{3/2}/V_j) \, /(E^{3/2}/V), \qquad (4)$$

where π_i is the voting power of prospective voter i defined in equation (3), E_j is the number of electoral votes cast by voter i's state j in a given election, V_j is the number of popular votes for president cast in state j in that election, and

($E^{3/2}/V$) is the average value of ($E_j^{3/2}/V_j$) in that election, included in the denominator to normalize the modified index of voting power ω_i to the same scale as the original index π_i.

It is important to notice that the modified index of voting power ω_i depends upon the number of voters and electoral votes in each state but not upon the state's population. While electoral votes are distributed to states on the basis of their population, the state's total electoral influence is shared among those who actually turn out at the polls rather than among the population as a whole. This feature of the electoral college, which is often overlooked by commentators and analysts,[10] constitutes an additional source of potential bias in the electoral college system.

Turnout is, of course, roughly proportional to population in most places at most times. But it needn't always be so. The most glaring examples of "rotten boroughs" in recent U.S. history occurred in the unreformed South through the 1950s, when not only African Americans but also many whites were effectively disenfranchised by poll taxes, literacy tests, and other devices (Key 1949). As a result, Louisiana in the 1950s had as many electoral votes as Iowa but only half as many voters; Georgia and Virginia had as many electoral votes as Wisconsin but fewer than half as many voters; Mississippi had as many electoral votes as Kansas but fewer than one-third as many voters. It seems obvious that, other things being equal, the marginal value to candidates of a single vote must have been less in Kansas than in Mississippi, where one-third as many voters controlled the same number of electoral votes.

The regional implications of the electoral college biases stemming from the unit rule and differential turnout are displayed in table 3.1, which reports the positive or negative percentage deviation of the average value of the modified voting power index ω_i from the average value of the unmodified voting power index π_i in each region and election year. There are three major patterns evident in the table. First, as I have already suggested, the extraordinarily low turnout in the South in the late New Deal era made those southerners who did turn out disproportionately influential; in 1952 the electoral college inflated the value of the average southerner's vote by about 46 percent, although that advantage dissipated steadily and rapidly through the 1950s and 1960s with increasing southern turnout. Second, midwesterners have been disadvantaged by the electoral college system throughout this forty-year period, with the average midwestern vote in recent elections worth about 10 percent less than it would have been in a national popular vote system. Third, the electoral college system has made westerners disproportionately influential in recent elections, due primarily to the growing power of California, which by itself holds 18 percent of the total voting power in the contemporary electoral college according to the "3/2's rule," giving westerners a 24 percent electoral college bonus in 1992.

Table 3.1 Estimated Impact of the Electoral College on Average Voting Power, by Region and Election Year (percentage)

Year	South[a]	East[b]	Midwest[c]	West[d]
1952	+45.9	−8.2	−24.1	−17.8
1956	+37.8	−7.9	−22.1	−17.8
1960	+29.9	−0.1	−21.2	−23.0
1964	+10.4	+1.6	−12.4	−2.2
1968	+2.3	+8.9	−9.4	−3.2
1972	+4.6	−0.0	−7.4	+1.8
1976	−3.9	+7.5	−4.2	+5.5
1980	−8.7	+20.5	−6.3	+1.2
1984	−4.1	+5.7	−13.4	+17.5
1988	−4.2	+10.1	−11.7	+13.8
1992	+1.0	+0.4	−9.8	+24.0

Source: Data from American National Election Studies 1995.

Note: Percentage deviation of the average value of the modified index of voting power ω_i from the average value of the unmodified index of voting power π_i.

[a] Alabama, Arkansas, Delaware, District of Columbia, Florida, Georgia, Kentucky, Louisiana, Maryland, Mississippi, North Carolina, Oklahoma, South Carolina, Tennessee, Texas, Virginia, West Virginia.

[b] Connecticut, Maine, Massachusetts, New Hampshire, New Jersey, New York, Pennsylvania, Rhode Island, Vermont.

[c] Illinois, Indiana, Iowa, Kansas, Michigan, Minnesota, Missouri, Nebraska, North Dakota, Ohio, South Dakota, Wisconsin.

[d] Alaska, Arizona, California, Colorado, Hawaii, Idaho, Montana, Nevada, New Mexico, Oregon, Utah, Washington, Wyoming.

What are the broader political consequences of these regional disparities? They turn out to be surprisingly modest. In particular, the "urban minorities" often supposed to be the main beneficiaries of the electoral college's large state bias (Polsby and Wildavsky 1996, 292) have, on the whole, been virtually unaffected. African Americans benefited slightly from the electoral college—by 3–9 percent—between 1952 and 1980, but more through their concentration in the South than in the large industrial swing states. In any case, the average impact of the electoral college on their voting power in the three most recent presidential elections was, by my calculations, a minuscule (and negative) −0.4 percent. The corresponding figures for city dwellers, members of union house-

holds, Catholics, and Democrats—all groups that might be expected to benefit from a large-state bias—were +0.7 percent, +0.1 percent, +0.9 percent, and
−1.1 percent, respectively. It seems evident from these calculations that the regional biases engendered by the electoral college system do not significantly alter
the balance of power among other social groups in the contemporary American party system.

4: The Distribution of Voting Power in the American Party System

The empirical analysis presented in the remainder of this chapter applies the
definition of voting power proposed in section 2, and modified in section 3 to
reflect the impact of the electoral college system, to observed patterns of voting
and nonvoting in eleven recent U.S. presidential elections. The data for the
analysis are from the corresponding American National Election Studies (NES)
surveys.[11] A more detailed description of the analysis and results is presented in
the appendix to this chapter.

   Although all of my data analysis is conducted separately for each election, it
seems desirable both on theoretical grounds and for descriptive purposes to
minimize the effect of idiosyncratic, election-specific factors by summarizing
patterns of voting power in a series of elections fought out within a more or less
stable party system. Analysts can and do argue vigorously on both theoretical
and historical grounds about how to distinguish one more or less stable party
system from another.[12] But for my purposes it is sufficient—and simple—to
group the eleven elections examined here into three distinct periods: a "late New
Deal" period from 1952 through 1960, a "transitional" period from 1964 through
1976, and a "post–New Deal" period from 1980 through 1992. This rough classification recognizes the significance of the partisan changes that occurred in
the 1960s, especially among blacks and white southerners (Carmines and Stimson 1989), as well as the potential impact of the "Reagan revolution" on the
structure of party coalitions in the elections of the 1980s.

   Since the approach proposed here provides a straightforward way to estimate
the voting power of individual prospective voters, I begin with a consideration
of the overall distribution of voting power in the U.S. electorate. Figure 3.1 displays two estimated distributions of voting power, one for the "late New Deal"
elections of 1952, 1956, and 1960 (indicated by closed circles) and the other for
the "post–New Deal" elections of 1980, 1984, 1988, and 1992 (indicated by open
circles). In each case, the height of the distribution at any point indicates the
percentage of the electorate (averaged over the relevant election years) having
the indicated level of voting power.[13]

   It is clear from figure 3.1 that there were significant disparities in voting power
among prospective voters in both eras, but the distribution of voting power has

Figure 3.1 Distributions of Voting Power, 1952–1960 and 1980–1992

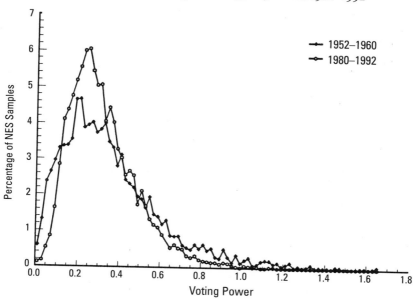

Source: Data from American National Election Studies 1995.

been somewhat more egalitarian in recent presidential elections than it was in the late New Deal period, with notable reductions in both the proportion of prospective voters with very little voting power ($\omega_i < 0.1$) and the fraction with very high levels of voting power ($\omega_i > 0.5$). From 1952 to 1960, the most influential tenth of the electorate and the least influential half each exercised about a quarter of the total voting power. By contrast, in the post–New Deal period, the most influential tenth of the electorate exercised only about 20 percent of the total voting power and the least influential half exercised about 30 percent, while the most influential third exercised about half of the total voting power.

Of course, even the more egalitarian distribution of voting power in recent presidential elections is a far cry from embodying the ideal of democratic equality. Some perspective on the magnitude of the political inequalities documented in figure 3.1 may be provided by comparisons with prevailing inequalities in other areas of social life. For example, figure 3.2 provides a graphical comparison of the relative inequality of the cumulative distributions of voting power and income in the U.S. from 1980 to 1992. The distribution of voting power (represented by the heavier line marked with diamonds) is only slightly more egalitarian than the distribution of income, even in the unusually inegalitarian

Figure 3.2 Cumulative Distributions of Voting Power and Income, 1980–1992

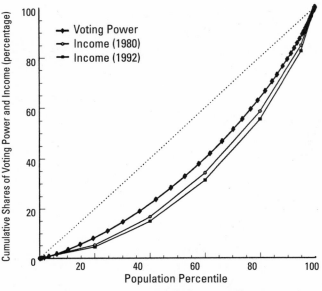

Source: Data from *American National Election Studies* 1995. and U.S. Bureau of the Census 1981, 1993.

economy of the 1990s. Indeed, the similarity is striking enough to suggest that the attention devoted by political scientists and political philosophers to the latter inequality might usefully be extended to the former, which is presumably at least as consequential for the workings of the political process.

5: The Voting Power of Social Groups

Although voting power is measured here at the level of individual prospective voters, it is also possible to pursue questions concerning the relative voting power of distinguishable social groups. Analyses of the group bases of voting behavior and party coalitions have a long history within political science, despite a wealth of evidence demonstrating that few groups in the American electorate are anything like monolithic in their partisan preferences (Lubell 1952; Axelrod 1972; Stanley, Bianco, and Niemi 1986; Erikson, Levesque, and Romero 1989). What is more, working politicians seem to think about electoral mobilization and conversion primarily in terms of identifiable social groups, despite the obvious complications produced by multiple group memberships and crosscutting cleavages.[14]

Table 3.2 presents estimates of the relative per capita voting power of 38 distinct groups in the U.S. electorate. Each group is defined by a shared race, region, residence, level of education or income, age, gender, religion, or strength of party identification. The figures presented in table 3.2 are averages of the estimated voting power of all the survey respondents in each group, averaged over the three or four elections within each of the three partisan eras ("late New Deal," "transitional," and "post–New Deal").

Table 3.2 Estimated Relative Per Capita Voting Power of Selected Social Groups (percentage)

Category	1952–1960	1964–1976	1980–1992
Race			
Black	−51.9	−56.6	−27.6
White	+4.7	+5.2	+3.7
Region/Race			
Southern black	−63.0	−57.5	−37.2
Nonsouthern black	−34.9	−55.5	−13.5
Southern white	+41.7	−2.4	−4.7
Nonsouthern white	−8.9	+8.2	+7.3
Region			
South	+23.5	−10.9	−11.3
East	+1.1	+12.1	+11.3
Midwest	−16.5	−0.5	−8.5
West	−17.1	+5.5	+20.8
Residence			
City	−5.0	−1.1	+1.5
Suburb	−7.1	+3.3	+5.0
Town/Rural	+6.3	−1.7	−7.5
Unionization			
Union household	−4.3	+8.3	+10.8
Nonunion household	+1.4	−2.7	−2.8
Income			
Low income	−13.3	−19.2	−17.2
Middle income	+2.2	+0.9	+0.2
High income	+11.2	+18.5	+16.6

Table 3.2 (*continued*)

Category	1952–1960	1964–1976	1980–1992
Education			
Grade school	–21.5	–29.0	–31.2
Some high school	+7.8	–3.0	–13.4
High school grad	+1.4	+9.2	–6.5
Some college	+15.6	+9.6	+6.3
College grad	+28.4	+14.7	+19.6
Age			
<30	–13.2	–14.1	–20.8
30–39	+3.1	+3.4	+0.5
40–49	+8.3	+13.7	+12.0
50–64	+4.2	+7.8	+11.8
65+	–13.3	–11.8	+2.1
Gender			
Male	+9.2	+5.2	+0.4
Female	–7.9	–3.9	–0.3
Religion			
Catholic	+2.8	+17.3	+13.1
Protestant	–0.7	–5.4	–4.6
Jewish	–1.6	+20.2	+23.4
Other/None	–10.4	–12.4	–8.2
Party Identification			
"Strong" identifier	–24.0	–12.5	–12.2
"Weak" identifier	+12.5	+8.1	+8.8
Independent "leaner"	+21.5	+13.2	+9.5
"Pure" independent	+3.7	–13.8	–14.6

Source: Data from *American National Election Studies* 1995.

Note: Percentage deviations from equal voting power, calculated from parameter estimates in tables 3.A1 and 3.A2.

Since the overall average level of voting power fluctuates from one election to the next for a variety of reasons (including changes in aggregate turnout rates, the average strength of partisan loyalties, and the presence of more or less popular independent candidates),[15] the estimated voting power of each individual in each election year is expressed as a percentage of the average voting power in that election year, and the relative voting power of social groups is expressed in terms of percentage deviations from these average levels. Thus, the average level of voting power for blacks from 1952 to 1960 (−51.9 percent) was only 48 percent of the overall average level in that period, while the average level for whites (+4.7 percent) was 105 percent of the overall average level.

Even given the fairly rough level of categorization in table 3.2, there are clearly quite significant variations among social groups in per capita voting power. In the contemporary post–New Deal period (1980–92), the most advantaged groups (as I have delineated them here) were Jews, westerners, and college graduates, each of which had an average level of voting power about 20 percent higher than for the population as a whole. The wealthiest third of the electorate, Catholics, and prospective voters in their forties and fifties also had significantly greater than average shares of electoral influence in the contemporary party system, with excesses in per capita voting power ranging from 12 to 17 percent. At the other extreme, people with grade school educations and African Americans had average levels of voting power less than 75 percent of the national average, with people under the age of thirty, the poorest third of the electorate, "strong" party identifiers, "pure" independents, and southerners also significantly disadvantaged (by twelve to twenty-one percentage points).

The separate estimates in table 3.2 of relative voting power for the various social groups in three different electoral eras not only facilitate comparisons among groups but also make it possible to chart the changing political circumstances of specific groups in the evolving U.S. party system. In particular, several social groups that were at least marginally disadvantaged in the party system of the 1950s had gained significantly in voting power by the 1980s. For example, the relative per capita voting power of westerners increased by thirty-eight percentage points, from 83 percent of the national average in the late New Deal period to 121 percent of the national average in the post–New Deal period; the relative per capita voting power of Jews increased by twenty-five percentage points, from 98 percent of the national average in the late New Deal period to 123 percent of the national average in the post–New Deal period; the relative per capita voting power of people over the age of sixty-five increased by fifteen percentage points, leaving voters under the age of thirty the only significantly disadvantaged age cohort in the American electorate; and the relative per capita voting power of women increased by almost eight percentage points, nearly eliminating the seventeen-point gap in voting power between men and women that existed in the 1950s.

One other, less familiar, disadvantaged group made gains in voting power that are worth noting: "strong" party identifiers. Much has been made of the fact that there are fewer committed partisans and more political independents in the U.S. electorate now than there were in the 1950s. Strong party identifiers made up 35 percent of the potential electorate in the late New Deal period but only 29 percent in the post–New Deal era; independents of all stripes increased from 28 percent of the potential electorate to 37 percent over the same period. However, an important countervailing trend has gone virtually unnoticed: since the 1950s, electoral participation has become increasingly sensitive to variations in the strength of prospective voters' partisan preferences, producing a sharp decline in turnout among independents and a significantly smaller decline among partisan loyalists.

The preferences of those independents who do turn out to vote are still disproportionately influential because of their greater availability for conversion, and the preferences of strong party identifiers are still heavily discounted because their votes are so unlikely to be won, or lost, in the short run. However, the relative per capita voting power of strong partisans has increased by twelve percentage points since the 1950s (from 76 percent of the national average in the late New Deal period to 88 percent of the national average in the transitional and post–New Deal periods), while the average voting power of pure independents has actually declined by eighteen percentage points (from 104 percent of the national average in the late New Deal period to about 85 percent of the national average in the transitional and post–New Deal periods). These changes in relative per capita voting power have completely offset the much-noted decrease in the proportion of "strong" party identifiers in the electorate during this period, leaving the relative total shares of electoral influence of the two groups essentially unchanged since the 1950s.

Finally, it is worth recognizing that the electoral influence of some social groups has changed significantly since the 1950s, even though their per capita voting power has remained relatively constant, simply due to demographic changes in the proportions of the electorate belonging to those groups. Changes of this sort are documented in table 3.3, which reports the share of total voting power, rather than per capita voting power, of each of the social groups listed in table 3.2 in the late New Deal, transitional, and post–New Deal party systems.

It is evident from table 3.3 that suburbanites, the college educated, and westerners are significantly more influential groups in the contemporary party system than they were in the 1950s. Although suburbanites and, especially, west-

Table 3.3 Estimated Share of Total Voting Power of Selected Social Groups (percentage)

Category	1952–1960	1964–1976	1980–1992
Race			
Black	4.1	4.9	8.6
White	95.9	95.1	91.4
Region/Race			
Southern black	1.9	2.8	4.5
Nonsouthern black	2.2	2.2	4.2
Southern white	34.7	25.9	26.5
Nonsouthern white	61.2	69.2	64.9
Region			
South	36.7	28.6	30.9
East	25.9	24.9	20.9
Midwest	26.7	29.6	25.2
West	10.8	16.9	23.0
Residence			
City	25.0	26.1	24.6
Suburb	25.6	33.2	43.6
Town/Rural	49.3	40.8	31.7
Unionization			
Union household	25.1	26.4	22.7
Nonunion household	74.9	73.6	77.3
Income			
Low income	30.6	28.1	27.1
Middle income	28.2	31.6	34.4
High income	41.2	40.4	38.5
Education			
Grade school	26.7	14.6	6.8
Some high school	21.9	17.3	10.9
High school grad	18.5	22.7	24.2
Some college	22.8	29.8	34.1
College grad	10.2	15.5	24.0

Table 3.3 (*continued*)

Category	1952–1960	1964–1976	1980–1992
Age			
<30	12.7	19.5	18.3
30–39	25.6	19.0	24.2
40–49	24.2	21.3	17.7
50–64	25.4	25.5	21.6
65+	12.1	14.6	18.2
Gender			
Male	50.7	45.2	44.4
Female	49.3	54.8	55.6
Religion			
Catholic	21.3	26.9	26.8
Protestant	71.0	65.6	59.7
Jewish	3.2	2.8	2.7
Other/None	4.6	4.7	10.7
Party Identification			
"Strong" identifier	27.0	25.5	25.6
"Weak" identifier	41.6	42.3	36.6
Independent "leaner"	17.6	21.4	26.7
"Pure" independent	13.9	10.7	11.1

Source: Data from *American National Election Studies* 1995.

Note: Percentage shares of total voting power, calculated from parameter estimates in tables 3.A1 AND 3.A2.

erners have also made gains in per capita voting power, the growing influence of these groups stems primarily from their increasing numbers. College graduates have made even more dramatic numerical gains, allowing them to more than double their share of total voting power despite suffering a decline in per capita electoral influence. At the same time, those without high school diplomas have gone from being more than half of the electorate in the 1950s to less than a quarter of the electorate in recent years, accentuating a marked decline in their per capita electoral influence over the same period.

Many of these patterns of group voting power—for example, that people with grade school educations are less influential than college graduates or that suburbanites' share of total voting power has increased significantly since the 1950s—will come as no surprise to anyone familiar with American electoral politics. However, even in those cases, it seems useful to have a framework facilitating systematic measurement of the relevant disparities in voting power. That the average voting power of citizens with grade school educations is about 58 percent of the average for college graduates, rather than 28 percent or 88 percent, seems to me to be an important fact, and not an obvious one, about the contemporary American party system. What is more, some of the patterns of voting power suggested by my analysis are more surprising, even in their basic outlines. In the next section I examine a particularly significant example, focusing on the changing electoral fortunes of blacks and southern whites in the American party system over the last forty years.

6: The Ironies of African American Enfranchisement

The electoral mobilization of African Americans beginning in the 1950s and continuing through the 1960s represents one of the great triumphs of the American civil rights movement. By my calculations, blacks turned out at only about 40 percent of the rate of whites in the 1950s, but that fraction increased to 48 percent in 1960, 77 percent in 1964, and 97 percent in 1968. Thus, an observer might expect to find that African Americans have moved into the mainstream of political competition in the contemporary American party system. However, that expectation is contradicted by the estimates of per capita voting power in table 3.2, which suggest that blacks actually had less voting power in the transitional period from 1964 to 1976 than they had had before 1964 and continued to have substantially less than a proportionate share of voting power even in the post–New Deal period, two decades and more after the passage of the landmark Voting Rights Act of 1965. The calculus of voting power outlined above makes it possible not only to quantify but also to explain the striking failure of massive African American electoral mobilization to produce anything close to equality of electoral influence for African Americans in the contemporary American party system.

In the 1950s, blacks outside the South were already sufficiently attached to the party of Franklin Delano Roosevelt to be relegated to the fringes of the competitive party system. This fringe status was by no means unique. For example, Democratic Jews and the Republican rich were at least as marginal as non-southern blacks in the party system of the 1950s; but unlike both Jews and the rich, who compensated for their marginality by turning out at rates significantly in excess of the national average, black turnout lagged behind white turnout even outside the South. Nevertheless, the voting power of blacks outside the

South exceeded 60 percent of the national average in 1952 and had reached 74 percent of the national average by 1960.

The situation of southern blacks in the 1950s was quite different from that of blacks outside the South. For southern blacks, the memory of FDR could not erase the memory of Abraham Lincoln and Jim Crow. As a result, the political loyalties of southern blacks were very much up for grabs, making them tempting targets for partisan conversion. Moreover, although the vast majority of southern blacks were still systematically excluded from the electoral process by an elaborate complex of discriminatory state laws and local customs dating back to the turn of the century (Kousser 1974; Key 1949, pt. 5), by 1960 that system of exclusion was beginning to erode. Southern black turnout doubled from about 12 percent in 1956 to about 24 percent in 1960 and would double again by 1964. The result was that the average southern black already had about half as much voting power as the average American in 1960 and seemed poised to make much greater gains.

What happened to frustrate the drive toward electoral equality of African Americans? The answer is evident in figure 3.3, which graphs the trends over time in black turnout probabilities and partisan preferences. One trend line (in-

Figure 3.3 African American Turnout and Republican Vote Probabilities, 1952–199?

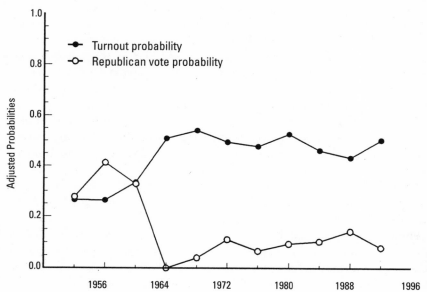

Source: Data from *American National Election Studies* 1995.

dicated by closed circles) documents the massive electoral mobilization of African Americans between 1956 and 1964. (Black turnout remained relatively constant after 1964 despite the passage of the Voting Rights Act, fluctuating between 43 percent and 54 percent, while white turnout declined significantly.) The other trend line (indicated by open circles) documents the massive consolidation of Democratic loyalties among African Americans over the same period of time. The average African American's Republican vote propensity—the estimated probability of voting Republican in a close election—was more than 40 percent in 1956 and 33 percent even in 1960 but fell to almost zero in 1964. What is more, it averaged less than 10 percent for the next three decades, making African Americans by far the least pivotal group in the American electorate.

One need not look far for the underpinnings of this massive electoral change. In his eleven months as president before standing for election in his own right, Lyndon Johnson built upon his martyred predecessor's symbolic support for black equality by pushing through Congress the most celebrated civil rights legislation in modern history, the Civil Rights Act of 1964. What is more, the Republican presidential nominee, Barry Goldwater, was one of only eight senators from outside the South to vote against the Civil Rights Act. Those two facts had profound consequences for the future of the American party system and especially for the role of African Americans within that party system (Carmines and Stimson 1989). Given their overwhelming loyalty to the Democratic Party in 1964 and after, blacks became practically unavailable for partisan conversion and, therefore, marginalized in the party system, despite their higher rates of electoral participation.

The political impact of these crosscutting trends in electoral mobilization and electoral centrality is evident in figure 3.4, which displays the relative voting power of southern and nonsouthern blacks in each presidential election from 1952 through 1992. In the 1950s southern blacks had only about 22 percent of the voting power of southern whites, while nonsouthern blacks had about 65 percent of the voting power of nonsouthern whites. These figures increased markedly in 1960 but plunged in 1964 as southern and nonsouthern blacks alike moved virtually unanimously into the Democratic column. The relative voting power of African Americans in the South has been roughly constant since 1968 (at about two-thirds of the southern white level), while the relative voting power of African Americans outside the South has, if anything, declined since the mid-1970s (to about four-fifths of the nonsouthern white level in the last four presidential elections). Southern blacks now resemble blacks outside the South in turnout and vote propensities, while blacks outside the South have themselves become even more extreme partisans (and to that degree, captives) of the national Democratic Party.

Figure 3.4 Relative Voting Power of African Americans, 1952–1992

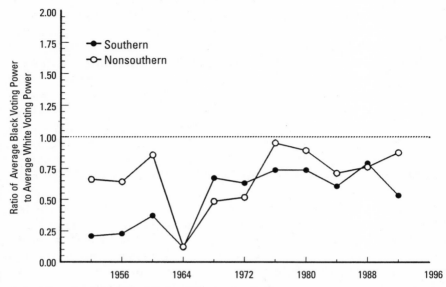

Source: Data from *American National Election Studies* 1995.

The result is that the average black American's presidential voting power continues to lag far behind that of the average white American. After increasing from about 40 percent in the 1950s to about 60 percent in 1960, the average black's voting power as a fraction of the average white's peaked at about 80 percent in 1976 and 1980 before falling to between 63 and 71 percent in the three most recent presidential elections examined here. Thus, despite the many legal and social advances of the 1960s and 1970s, African Americans remain among the most disadvantaged groups in the contemporary party system.

Blacks not only have significantly less voting power than whites in the contemporary party system; the voting power they do have tends to be of a different sort. Given their position on the Democratic fringe of the contemporary party system, African Americans cannot credibly promise or threaten to convert to the Republicans in substantial numbers. Instead, their primary leverage over both parties resides in the prospect of greater or lesser turnout. Thus, mobilization value accounted for 55 percent of blacks' total voting power in the four presidential elections of the post–New Deal period; the corresponding fraction for whites was about 18 percent. It does not seem far-fetched to suppose that much of what is distinctive about the role of African Americans in the contemporary American party system can be explained by the disproportional importance of mobilization as a component of their voting power.

In a final irony, the relative stagnation in voting power experienced by the African Americans whom Senator Goldwater wrote off in the early 1960s was actually less bad than the absolute decline in voting power experienced by the white southerners he embraced. White southerners in the 1950s were already so loosened from their traditional Democratic loyalties (at the presidential level) that they were disproportionately pivotal in the party system. Their turnout was relatively low but increasing, while their absolute numbers were also increasing. (As table 3.1 indicates, they also benefited from a significant electoral college bias.) The existence of an unusually pivotal group comprising one-fourth of the potential electorate, growing steadily, and mobilizing at a rapid rate seems to have invited precisely the sort of "southern strategy" pursued by Goldwater (and later by Richard Nixon) in the transitional period after 1960.

But the very success of the Republicans' "southern strategy" significantly diluted the voting power of white southerners by pushing them away from the center and toward the loyal Republican periphery of the (presidential) party system. At the same time, the electoral mobilization of large numbers of south-

Figure 3.5 Relative Voting Power of Southern Whites, 1952–1992

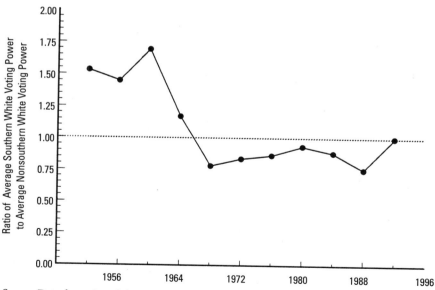

Source: Data from *American National Election Studies* 1995.

ern whites and blacks alike eroded the substantial electoral college bias enjoyed by southern voters in the 1950s. The combined result, shown in figure 3.5, is that the relative per capita voting power of southern whites was reduced by almost half over an eight-year period, from 156 percent of the nonsouthern white level before 1964 to 86 percent of the nonsouthern white level after 1964.

Southern whites' share of total voting power in the American party system was bolstered by major population gains throughout the four decades covered by my analysis. Nevertheless, as the estimates in table 3.3 indicate, the changes in the party system produced by the watershed events of the 1960s significantly reduced even the total voting power of southern whites, from about 37 percent before 1964 to about 30 percent after 1964. Thus, while blacks gained surprisingly little from the realignment of the party system, white southerners actually experienced significant declines in both relative and absolute voting power. Clearly, if Senator Goldwater proposed today to "go hunting where the ducks are," he would have no particular reason to target southern whites.[16]

7: Conclusion

Rational candidates are impelled by the goal of vote maximization to discriminate among prospective voters, appealing primarily to those who either are likely to vote and susceptible to partisan conversion or are reliable supporters susceptible to mobilization (or likely opponents susceptible to demobilization). The resulting strategic imperatives produce significant inequalities in the voting power of individuals and groups in functioning party systems. In the late New Deal party system of the 1950s, for example, the most influential tenth of the electorate had about a quarter of the voting power in American presidential elections. Even in the more egalitarian post–New Deal party system of the 1980s and early 1990s, the most influential tenth of the electorate had about twice as much voting power as their numbers warranted, while the most influential third of the electorate had as much total voting power as the remaining two-thirds.

Inequalities in voting power can be remedied in part—but only in part—by electoral mobilization of the disadvantaged. This fact is clearest in the case of African Americans, who have consistently participated at about 90 percent of the white rate in presidential elections over the last three decades but, because of their position on the loyal Democratic periphery of the party system, have consistently had only about two-thirds as much per capita voting power as white Americans.

Inequalities of this sort cannot simply be wished away, as Jesse Jackson and other African American political leaders have discovered to their frustration.

But neither are the issues and cleavages defining a given party system immutable or entirely predictable. Rather, they are the byproducts of strategic choices made by working politicians—choices constrained, but by no means entirely determined, by existing and developing political circumstances.[17] Party systems are constructed, not discovered; and their specific blueprints have significant political consequences for the individuals and groups competing within them.

Appendix: Estimation

The parameters α, β, and γ in equation (3) above were estimated separately for each of the eleven U.S. presidential elections from 1952 through 1992 using survey data from the American National Election Studies. The probit parameter estimates for the vote equation conditional upon turnout (estimates of β) are presented in table 3.A1, and the probit parameter estimates for the turnout equation (estimates of α and γ) are presented in table 3.A2.

The calculations of voting power reported in the body of this chapter are based upon these parameter estimates with three adjustments. First, in order to incorporate the impact of the unit rule in the electoral college, all of my analysis is based on the modified index of voting power ω_i introduced in section 3 rather than on the unmodified index of voting power π_i.

Second, in order to allow for overreporting of turnout in the surveys, the estimated probabilities of turnout for each election were adjusted to produce aggregate turnout in the sample consistent with published aggregate turnout statistics. These adjustments are based on the assumption that each respondent's probability of misreporting when he or she fails to vote is proportional to his or her probability of turning out in the first place.[18] The required coefficients of proportionality for each election year are reported in table 3.A3.

Third, to simulate the distribution of partisan propensities in a close election, the intercept in the vote equation for each election was adjusted to produce an average Republican vote propensity in the sample (with each respondent weighted by his or her adjusted probability of turning out) of zero. The coefficients used to make these adjustments are also reported in table 3.A3.

The calculations of voting power reported here ignore one additional relevant complication: the presidential candidate's need to appeal sequentially to primary and general election constituencies (Aranson and Ordeshook 1972). Adequate incorporation of the nominating process in an analysis of voting power will require additional theoretical work as well as more and better data.

Table 3.A1 Republican Vote Propensities, 1952–1992

Category	1952	1956	1960	1964	1968
Intercept	−.089 (.508)	.026 (.614)	−.105 (.851)	−1.597 (.589)	−.773 (.667)
Partisanship	1.555 (.086)	1.744 (.090)	1.468 (.095)	1.326 (.081)	1.575 (.101)
Black	−1.100 (.349)	−.674 (.281)	−1.361 (.364)	−4.727 (20.222)	−1.626 (.475)
Southern black	.664 (.551)	.467 (.510)	.750 (.544)	−.067 (30.229)	.100 (.634)
South	.116 (.127)	.409 (.136)	.336 (.154)	.673 (.141)	.204 (.164)
East	−.029 (.124)	.252 (.133)	.374 (.169)	−.299 (.143)	−.123 (.157)
West	.101 (.152)	.288 (.146)	−.162 (.197)	.223 (.154)	.161 (.171)
City	−.098 (.126)	.362 (.132)	.125 (.168)	.089 (.139)	−.086 (.154)
Suburb	−.012 (.116)	.022 (.122)	.008 (.147)	.020 (.125)	−.045 (.142)
Homeowner	.053 (.099)	.018 (.113)	−.194 (.138)	−.019 (.123)	.041 (.145)
Children	.074 (.105)	−.049 (.114)	.007 (.141)	.223 (.154)	−.302 (.138)
Age (in years)	−.0060 (.0184)	.0088 (.0211)	−.0324 (.0285)	.0042 (.0202)	.0451 (.023
Age squared	.000105 (.000187)	−.000173 (.000220)	.000378 (.000278)	.000078 (.000206)	−.000523 (.000
Female	−.002 (.096)	.121 (.095)	.135 (.115)	−.119 (.102)	−.026 (.117)
Education (in years)	.0217 (.0156)	.0012 (.0170)	.0214 (.0207)	.0441 (.0192)	.0207 (.022
Income	.113 (.192)	.039 (.207)	.278 (.273)	.356 (.223)	−.564 (.270
Union household	−.375 (.112)	−.317 (.108)	−.090 (.134)	−.267 (.131)	−.104 (.134
Protestant	.572 (.168)	.439 (.291)	.866 (.405)	.149 (.261)	.823 (.299
Catholic	.544 (.191)	.453 (.299)	−.390 (.422)	−.084 (.276)	.485 (.307
Jewish	.138 (.282)	−.962 (.382)	−1.270 (.554)	−.278 (.402)	−.541 (.484
log likelihood	−509.6	−469.9	−324.2	−406.3	−318.8
N of obs	1,235	1,266	898	1,111	882
% classified	79.6	83.3	82.5	83.5	84.7
sample % Republican	58.1	59.6	50.3	32.5	53.4

Source: Data from *American National Election Studies* 1995.

Note: Probit parameter estimates with standard errors in parentheses.

1972	1976	1980	1984	1988	1992
−.829 (.386)	−.557 (.435)	−.281 (.543)	−.085 (.469)	−.936 (.514)	−1.107 (.489)
1.176 (.069)	1.353 (.073)	1.459 (.096)	1.599 (.078)	1.624 (.083)	1.786 (.084)
−1.272 (.291)	−.754 (.320)	−.928 (.356)	−.841 (.278)	−1.172 (.474)	−.626 (.294)
−.295 (.352)	−.412 (.472)	−.330 (.458)	−.388 (.366)	.417 (.520)	−1.012 (.430)
.578 (.110)	.254 (.115)	.074 (.149)	.224 (.128)	.407 (.138)	.234 (.129)
−.054 (.108)	−.094 (.119)	−.203 (.172)	.060 (.139)	.181 (.150)	−.083 (.145)
.150 (.120)	.015 (.130)	.043 (.170)	−.172 (.134)	−.163 (.141)	−.142 (.146)
−.149 (.103)	.025 (.115)	−.192 (.156)	−.071 (.134)	−.012 (.144)	.026 (.140)
.120 (.097)	−.024 (.104)	.014 (.134)	.112 (.110)	.187 (.116)	−.070 (.114)
.160 (.095)	.044 (.110)	.209 (.141)	.179 (.119)	−.071 (.122)	.286 (.119)
.042 (.088)	.075 (.101)	.285 (.130)	.150 (.107)	.277 (.117)	.102 (.111)
.0447 (.0135)	−.0287 (.0158)	.0291 (.0198)	.0067 (.0162)	.0236 (.0177)	.0174 (.0179)
−.000394 (.000144)	.000340 (.000165)	−.000302 (.000204)	−.000077 (.000167)	−.000188 (.000175)	−.000169 (.000179)
−.208 (.079)	−.028 (.086)	−.295 (.114)	−.199 (.095)	−.072 (.102)	.082 (.098)
−.0322 (.0155)	.0386 (.0174)	.0334 (.0227)	.0042 (.0204)	−.0057 (.0211)	.0113 (.0225)
.105 (.176)	.547 (.197)	−.321 (.259)	.524 (.207)	.284 (.229)	−.313 (.210)
−.135 (.090)	−.139 (.102)	−.308 (.131)	−.472 (.111)	−.202 (.125)	−.039 (.131)
.690 (.176)	.407 (.185)	−.024 (.215)	.249 (.160)	.401 (.185)	.503 (.151)
.722 (.182)	.439 (.196)	.094 (.234)	.037 (.170)	.144 (.197)	.514 (.169)
−.122 (.301)	−.012 (.332)	.356 (.353)	−.627 (.318)	−.369 (.377)	−.469 (.490)
−694.7	−585.0	−345.4	−484.7	−435.1	−439.2
1,587	1,322	877	1,376	1,195	1,357
78.6	80.0	81.6	84.3	84.9	88.3
64.3	49.3	56.3	58.2	52.9	41.6

Table 3.A2 Turnout Propensities, 1952–1992

Category	1952	1956	1960	1964	1968
Intercept	−2.386 (.384)	−2.032 (.426)	−3.447 (.656)	−3.345 (.456)	−3.765 (.447)
Partisan strength	.604 (.133)	.594 (.116)	.685 (.167)	.934 (.145)	.717 (.141)
Black	−.085 (.225)	−.331 (.183)	−.624 (.253)	.642 (.664)	−.394 (.208)
Southern black	−1.060 (.282)	−.511 (.258)	−.129 (.328)	−.433 (.296)	.997 (.259)
South	−.591 (.101)	−.572 (.095)	−.514 (.137)	−.437 (.108)	−.684 (.105)
East	.012 (.107)	.017 (.104)	.320 (.163)	.113 (.122)	.039 (.115)
West	−.309 (.122)	−.099 (.113)	−.410 (.160)	−.101 (.127)	−.023 (.125)
City	.064 (.101)	−.204 (.100)	−.124 (.152)	−.212 (.107)	.118 (.105)
Suburb	.085 (.095)	−.093 (.090)	−.173 (.128)	−.157 (.105)	.043 (.099)
Homeowner	.314 (.082)	−.035 (.084)	.021 (.125)	.347 (.091)	.295 (.093)
Children	−.049 (.086)	−.137 (.086)	−.060 (.125)	.092 (.098)	−.196 (.094)
Age (in years)	−.0612 (.0138)	.0525 (.0141)	.0935 (.0215)	.0677 (.0150)	.0432 (.0148)
Age squared	−.000533 (.000138)	−.000375 (.000147)	−.000833 (.000206)	−.000581 (000151)	−.000359 (.00014
Female	−.401 (.079)	−.323 (.073)	−.317 (.103)	−.094 (.082)	.117 (.079)
Education (in years)	.0977 (.0132)	.1067 (.0129)	.1012 (.0184)	.0912 (.0147)	.1174 (.0148)
Income	.386 (.153)	.426 (.161)	.448 (.237)	.286 (.171)	.574 (.180)
Union household	−.181 (.093)	.116 (.084)	−.128 (.118)	.165 (.102)	−.213 (.092)
Protestant	.474 (.133)	.047 (.213)	.518 (.279)	.343 (.186)	.395 (.187)
Catholic	.644 (.160)	.304 (.223)	.601 (.303)	.587 (.200)	.500 (.200)
Jewish	.939 (.288)	.781 (.352)	.478 (.446)	1.132 (.401)	.513 (.348)
Residence	−.051 (.032)	−.017 (.030)	.038 (.042)	.052 (.036)	.121 (.032)
Preference strength	.0805 (.0277)	.0073 (.0187)	.0887 (.0368)	−.0110 (.0168)	.0540 (.0267)
log likelihood	−763.4	−843.8	−417.0	−658.4	−703.8
N of obs	1,714	1,762	1,109	1,450	1,346
% classified	79.9	77.8	83.7	79.9	74.7
% reported voting	72.0	71.8	81.0	76.6	65.5

Source: Data from American National Election Studies 1995.

Note: Probit parameter estimates with standard errors in parentheses.

1972	1976	1980	1984	1988	1992
−2.510 (.289)	−3.696 (.328)	−3.544 (.357)	−3.426 (.320)	−3.771 (.352)	−3.022 (.291)
.911 (.099)	.564 (.143)	.609 (.130)	.554 (.117)	.605 (.145)	.844 (.133)
−.403 (.171)	−.293 (.209)	−.299 (.188)	−.128 (.164)	−.513 (.210)	.256 (.160)
.522 (.209)	−.101 (.236)	.255 (.238)	.205 (.205)	.524 (.237)	−.431 (.196)
−.387 (.080)	−.309 (.090)	.014 (.101)	−.154 (.087)	−.469 (.096)	−.043 (.078)
.011 (.089)	−.082 (.098)	−.187 (.111)	−.023 (.100)	−.273 (.111)	−.073 (.088)
−.107 (.097)	−.243 (.104)	.043 (.115)	.035 (.098)	.009 (.111)	−.148 (.088)
.021 (.081)	−.088 (.089)	−.056 (.106)	.067 (.092)	.158 (.103)	.290 (.081)
−.018 (.076)	−.091 (.081)	−.112 (.090)	−.001 (.075)	.180 (.083)	.162 (.068)
.070 (.072)	.168 (.079)	.176 (.090)	.307 (.078)	.216 (.086)	.225 (.069)
−.067 (.068)	.059 (.078)	−.004 (.085)	−.048 (.075)	−.094 (.080)	−.094 (.066)
.0287 (.0096)	.0539 (.0106)	.0247 (.0124)	.0482 (.0105)	.0471 (.0117)	.0231 (.0101)
−.000272 (.000100)	−.000445 (.000110)	−.000133 (.000129)	−.000405 (.000109)	−.000335 (.000117)	−.000119 (.000101)
−.159 (.061)	−.249 (.068)	−.075 (.077)	.110 (.066)	−.030 (.073)	.180 (.059)
.1092 (.0112)	.1176 (.0133)	.1052 (.0153)	.1182 (.0138)	.1228 (.0146)	.1085 (.0130)
.540 (.135)	.497 (.152)	.285 (.167)	.414 (.145)	.704 (.160)	.209 (.125)
−.023 (.073)	.152 (.083)	.102 (.090)	.056 (.081)	−.122 (.094)	.118 (.081)
−.024 (.134)	.521 (.121)	.423 (.120)	.019 (.109)	.260 (.122)	.110 (.085)
.095 (.143)	.474 (.134)	.431 (.136)	.281 (.120)	.438 (.136)	.166 (.096)
.208 (.285)	.189 (.249)	.322 (.243)	.109 (.255)	.171 (.306)	.337 (.266)
.107 (.025)	.098 (.029)	.157 (.030)	.064 (.027)	.060 (.029)	.011 (.023)
.0609 (.0218)	.1570 (.0489)	.1284 (.0304)	.0739 (.0228)	.1335 (.0343)	.0497 (.0258)
−1199.6	−984.0	−786.7	−1038.9	−876.6	−1308.0
2,283	1,909	1,407	1,989	1,773	2,254
73.7	74.1	72.1	74.2	77.4	68.3
69.5	69.2	62.3	69.2	67.4	60.2

Table 3.A3 Election-Specific Averages and Adjustments

Year	Coefficient of Turnout Overreporting ρ_t[a]	Adjustment to Republican Vote Propensity[b]	Average Electoral College Power $(E^{3/2}/V)$[c]	Average Modified Voting Power ω_i[d]
1952	.4535	−.2872	.00003794	.3807
1956	.5330	−.3308	.00003680	.3073
1960	.7948	−.0545	.00003337	.3814
1964	.6341	+.6560	.00003058	.3618
1968	.5253	−.1070	.00002902	.3098
1972	.6159	−.3021	.00002713	.3926
1976	.6713	−.0013	.00002540	.4224
1980	.5647	−.1462	.00002517	.3540
1984	.6592	−.2441	.00002350	.3252
1988	.7112	−.0747	.00002358	.3540
1992	.6384	+.1876	.00002078	.2476

Source: Data from *American National Election Studies* 1995.

[a] The coefficient of turnout overreporting is $\rho_t = (R_t - V_t)/V_t (1 - V_t)$, where R_t is the proportion of the NES sample that reported voting for a major party candidate for president and V_t is the proportion of the voting-age population that voted for a major party candidate according to published turnout figures (U.S. Bureau of the Census 1994, tables 423 and 449).

[b] To measure the availability of prospective voters for partisan conversion in a close election, each prospective voter's Republican vote propensity $x_i'\beta$ calculated from the parameter estimates in table 3.A1 is adjusted by the indicated amount to produce an average adjusted partisan propensity (weighting each prospective voter by his or her estimated probability of turning out) of zero.

[c] The electoral college power of voter i in state j in election t is $E_{jt}^{3/2}/V_{jt}$, where E_{jt} is the number of electoral votes cast by state j in election t and V_{jt} is the number of popular votes for president cast in state j in election t.

[d] The indicated average value of the modified voting power index ω_i is used as a baseline for calculating the percentage deviations in per capita voting power reported in table 3.2.

Notes

The analysis presented here was originally conceived at the Center for Advanced Study in the Behavioral Sciences. Earlier versions were presented at the 1990 meeting of the American Political Science Association and in the Political Economy Workshop at Princeton University. Robert Erikson, Stanley Kelley Jr., John Londregan, Tali Mendelberg, James Pope, and Harold Stanley provided especially helpful comments on various drafts.

1. Of course, the U.S. Senate remains a notable constitutionally mandated exception to the principle of equal apportionment, and thus so too does the electoral college. The implications of the electoral college system for voting power in U.S. presidential elections is examined in section 3, below.

2. Either by state law or by custom, each state's electoral votes are cast as a bloc for the candidate receiving a plurality of popular votes in that state. Thus, a pivotal voter in a populous state may be much more influential than a pivotal voter in a state with fewer electoral votes.

3. Phillips Shively's (1992) analysis of changing patterns of abstention and conversion provides a related perspective on partisan competition over a longer historical period.

4. Both my model and my empirical analysis deal with the simplest case of a two-party system. The measure proposed here could in principle be extended to deal with multiparty systems, perhaps along the lines suggested by Richard Katz's notion of an "optimal enemy" (1980, chap. 2). However, the resulting theoretical and empirical complications are beyond the scope of the present analysis. In any case, the fluidity of support for independent (as distinct from third-party) candidates in the American setting renders historical analysis of the sort proposed here tenuous, at best. Thus, I focus solely on major-party voters, treating Ross Perot, George Wallace, and John Anderson voters as nonvoters throughout my analysis.

5. Important, though more or less partial, exceptions to this generalization include Wolfinger and Rosenstone 1980, Cavanagh 1981, Stanley 1987, and Piven and Cloward 1988. Sidney Verba, Kay Schlozman, and Henry Brady (1995) analyzed forms of political participation other than voting with an eye toward the likely impact (but offered no evidence about the actual impact) of the inequalities they observed.

6. The closest approaches to a direct test of which I am aware appear in the literature on constituency representation in legislatures. For example, Douglas Rivers found that congressional representatives responded most strongly to the preferences of independents, "presumably the pivotal group in most constituencies" (n.d., 2).

7. I ignore here direct efforts to mobilize supporters by altering features of their turnout propensity other than those captured by the "strength of preference" term $(\mathbf{x}_i{}' \boldsymbol{\beta})^2 \gamma$. Direct efforts to mobilize supporters (for example, by offering rides to the polls) are certainly an important feature of election campaigns; but since by definition they leave prospective voters' partisan propensities unchanged, they are unlikely to have the same political significance as the indirect efforts considered here.

8. In that case, *voting power* reduces to a simplified version of *conversion value* reflecting the *product* of turnout probability and availability for partisan conversion:

$$\pi_i = \Phi(\mathbf{x}_i{}'\boldsymbol{\alpha}) \, \phi(\mathbf{x}_i{}'\boldsymbol{\beta}) / \phi(0),$$

However, in the empirical analyses below, preference strength is clearly, and fairly strongly, related to turnout (the average estimate of the γ parameter is .075 with an average *t*-ratio of 2.4 over all eleven elections, and .108 with an average *t*-ratio of 3.3 over the five most recent elections), making the complications embodied in the notion of *mobilization value* worth pursuing here.

9. It would probably make more sense to assume that politicians attempt to maximize their probability of winning a vote plurality rather than simply maximizing their expected vote. I ignore this potential complication, since the strategic implications of the distinction are unlikely to be significant in relatively close elections.

10. For example, all of Brams and Davis's calculations of electoral college bias use state population rather than presidential turnout as the relevant denominator (1974, table 5).

11. The data analyzed here are from the 1952–92 Cumulative Data File disseminated on *American National Election Studies, 1948–1994*, a CD-ROM issued in May 1995 and available through the Inter-University Consortium for Political and Social Research, University of Michigan. The data were originally gathered by Warren E. Miller and the American National Election Studies project, Center for Political Studies, University of Michigan.

12. The seminal works are by V. O. Key Jr. (1955, 1959). The single most thorough theoretical and historical treatment is James Sundquist's (1983).

13. Although the measure of voting power proposed in equation (3) has a theoretical maximum value of 1.0, the modified index of voting power proposed in equation (4) can produce scores greater than 1.0 for prospective voters in states favored by the electoral college system. Since all of my analysis incorporates the electoral college adjustment, a few such voters appear in the distributions shown in figure 3.1.

14. For example, "The New Jersey Catholic Conference is sponsoring statewide voter-registration drives at more than five hundred parishes this weekend. A conference coordinator . . . said the purpose was to deliver votes to candidates 'who will respond to the concerns that Catholics have' about legalized abortion, private school vouchers, and other issues. A spokesman for the Diocese of Trenton . . . said that although the drives could strengthen the voice of Roman Catholic voters, 'there's no monolithic Catholic voting bloc; there's conscientiousness and concern'" ("Catholic Voter-Registration Push" 1995).

15. The overall average level of voting power in each election (modified to take account of the impact of the electoral college) is shown in the last column of table 3.A3 in the appendix. The average level of voting power ranges from a low of .25 in 1992 (when Ross Perot drew about 10 percent of the potential electorate out of the major-party ranks) to a high of .42 in 1976. However, there is no clear trend over time, despite the fact that turnout in presidential elections declined by more than ten percentage points during this period. How did the electorate as a whole participate less but remain about as powerful? The key factor was the increasing sensitivity of turnout to the strength of prospective voters' partisan preferences. The average estimated value of the γ parameter intro-

duced in section 2 increased by almost two-thirds between the late New Deal and post–New Deal periods. As a result, the average prospective voter's mobilization value increased substantially, roughly compensating for the loss of conversion value entailed by the aggregate decline in turnout.

16. Of course, strategic perceptions often lag behind strategic realities, as both parties have demonstrated by continuing to cater to white southerners despite their relatively marginal status in the current party system.

17. The importance of this point has been emphasized in a theoretical context by William Riker (1982, chaps. 7–9) and in a historical context by Amy Bridges (n.d.).

18. This assumption is a stylized representation of the pattern of misreporting observed by Brian Silver, Barbara Anderson, and Paul Abramson: "Respondents most inclined to overreport their voting are those who are highly educated, those most supportive of the regime norm of voting, and those to whom the norm of voting is most salient—the same characteristics that are related to the probability that a person actually votes" (1986, 613). The coefficient of overreporting is

$$\rho_t = (R_t - V_t)/V_t(1 - V_t),$$

where R_t is the proportion of the sample reported voting in election t and V_t is the proportion of the population actually voting in election t. The adjusted turnout probability V_i for respondent i can be expressed as a function of the apparent turnout probability R_i estimated from the probit analyses reported in table 3.A2 and the coefficient of overreporting ρ_t:

$$V_i = \left\{ 1 + \rho_t - \left[(1 + \rho_t)^2 - 4\rho_t R_i \right]^{1/2} \right\}/2\rho_t.$$

My adjustment does not rely on the National Election Studies' "validated vote" measure, as many other analyses of turnout do, because that measure is consistently available only since 1976 and, in any case, suffers from measurement errors nearly as daunting as those affecting self-reported turnout (Traugott, Traugott, and Presser 1992).

References

American National Election Studies, 1948–1994. 1995. CD-ROM issued in May. Available through the Inter-University Consortium for Political and Social Research, University of Michigan, Ann Arbor.

Aranson, Peter H., and Peter C. Ordeshook. 1972. "Spatial Strategies for Sequential Elections." In *Probability Models of Collective Decision Making*, ed. Richard G. Niemi and Herbert F. Weisberg. Columbus, Ohio: Charles E. Merrill.

Axelrod, Robert. 1972. "Where the Votes Come From: An Analysis of Electoral Coalitions." *American Political Science Review* 66:11–20.

Banzhaf, John F., III. 1965. "Weighted Voting Doesn't Work: A Mathematical Analysis." *Rutgers Law Review* 19:317–45.

———. 1968. "One Man, 3.312 Votes: A Mathematical Analysis of the Electoral College." *Villanova Law Review* 13:304–22.

Bartels, Larry M. 1985. "Resource Allocation in a Presidential Campaign." *Journal of Politics* 47:928–36.

Brams, Steven J., and Morton D. Davis. 1974. "The 3/2's Rule in Presidential Campaigning." *American Political Science Review* 68:113–34.

Bridges, Amy. n.d. "Republicans Come to Power, 1860 and 1980." Unpublished paper, Department of Political Science, University of California, San Diego.

Carmines, Edward G., and James A. Stimson. 1989. *Issue Evolution: Race and the Transformation of American Politics.* Princeton: Princeton University Press.

"Catholic Voter-Registration Push." 1995. *New York Times,* Sept. 22.

Cavanagh, Thomas E. 1981. "Changes in American Voter Turnout, 1964–1976." *Political Science Quarterly* 96:53–65.

Colantoni, C. S., T. J. Levesque, and Peter C. Ordeshook. 1975. "Campaign Resource Allocation under the Electoral College." *American Political Science Review* 69:141–61.

Downs, Anthony. 1957. *An Economic Theory of Democracy.* New York: Harper and Row.

Enelow, James M., and Melvin J. Hinich. 1989. "A General Probabilistic Spatial Theory of Elections." *Public Choice* 61:101–13.

Erikson, Robert S., Thomas D. Lancaster, and David W. Romero. 1989. "Group Components of the Presidential Vote, 1952–1984." *Journal of Politics* 51:337–46.

Erikson, Robert S., and David W. Romero. 1990. "Candidate Equilibrium and the Behavioral Model of the Vote." *American Political Science Review* 84:1103–26.

Katz, Richard S. 1980. *A Theory of Parties and Electoral Systems.* Baltimore: Johns Hopkins University Press.

Kelley, Stanley, Jr. 1983. *Interpreting Elections.* Princeton: Princeton University Press.

Key, V. O. [1949] 1984. *Southern Politics in State and Nation.* Knoxville: University of Tennessee Press.

———. 1955. "A Theory of Critical Elections." *Journal of Politics* 17:3–18.

———. 1959. "Secular Realignment and the Party System." *Journal of Politics* 21:198–210.

Kousser, J. Morgan. 1974. *The Shaping of Southern Politics: Suffrage Restriction and the Establishment of the One-Party South, 1880–1910.* New Haven: Yale University Press.

Lake, Mark. 1979. "A New Campaign Resource Allocation Model." In *Applied Game Theory,* ed. S. J. Brams, A. Schotter, and G. Schwödiaver. Wurzburg, West Germany: Physica-Verlag.

Lubell, Samuel. 1952. *The Future of American Politics.* New York: Harper and Brothers.

Mann, I., and L. S. Shapley. 1964. "The A Priori Voting Strength of the Electoral College." In *Game Theory and Related Approaches to Social Behavior,* ed. Martin Shubik. New York: Wiley.

Nagel, Jack H. 1975. *The Descriptive Analysis of Power.* New Haven: Yale University Press.

Owen, Guillermo. 1975. "Evaluation of a Presidential Election Game." *American Political Science Review* 69:947–53.

Petrocik, John R. 1981. *Party Coalitions: Realignment and the Decline of the New Deal Party System.* Chicago: University of Chicago Press.

Piven, Frances Fox, and Richard A. Cloward. 1988. *Why Americans Don't Vote.* New York: Pantheon.

Polsby, Nelson W., and Aaron Wildavsky. 1996. *Presidential Elections: Strategies and Structures of American Politics.* 9th ed. Chatham, N.J.: Chatham House.

Riker, William H. 1982. *Liberalism against Populism: A Confrontation between the Theory of Democracy and the Theory of Social Choice.* San Francisco: W. H. Freeman.

Rivers, Douglas. n.d. "Partisan Representation in Congress." Unpublished paper, Department of Political Science, University of California, Los Angeles.

Shapley, L. S., and Martin Shubik. 1954. "A Method of Evaluating the Distribution of Power in a Committee System." *American Political Science Review* 48:787–92.

Shively, W. Phillips. 1992. "From Differential Abstention to Conversion: A Change in Electoral Change, 1864–1988." *American Journal of Political Science* 36:309–30.

Silver, Brian D., Barbara A. Anderson, and Paul R. Abramson. 1986. "Who Overreports Voting?" *American Political Science Review* 80:613–24.

Stanley, Harold W. 1987. *Voter Mobilization and the Politics of Race: The South and Universal Suffrage, 1952–1984.* New York: Praeger.

Stanley, Harold W., William T. Bianco, and Richard G. Niemi. 1986. "Partisanship and Group Support over Time: A Multivariate Analysis." *American Political Science Review* 80:969–76.

Sundquist, James L. 1983. *Dynamics of the Party System: Alignment and Realignment of Political Parties in the United States.* Rev. ed. Washington, D.C.: Brookings Institution Press.

Thernstrom, Abigail M. 1987. *Whose Votes Count? Affirmative Action and Minority Voting Rights.* Cambridge: Harvard University Press.

Traugott, Michael W., Santa Traugott, and Stanley Presser. 1992. "Revalidation of Self-Reported Vote." Paper prepared for presentation at the annual meeting of the American Association for Public Opinion Research, St. Petersburg Beach, Fla.

U.S. Bureau of the Census. 1981, 1993, 1994. *Statistical Abstract of the United States, 1981, 1993, 1994.* Washington, D.C.

Verba, Sidney, Kay Lehman Schlozman, and Henry E. Brady. 1995. *Voice and Equality: Civic Voluntarism in American Politics.* Cambridge: Harvard University Press.

Wolfinger, Raymond E., and Steven J. Rosenstone. 1980. *Who Votes?* New Haven: Yale University Press.

CHAPTER 4

The Turnout Crash of 1972
Hard-Won Lessons in Electoral Interpretation

James DeNardo

A central problem in party politics—for leaders in government, members of the press, political scientists, and citizens at large—is how to extract meaning from electoral outcomes. What does the division of the vote tell us about the "will of the people?" What does declining turnout reveal about the voters' loyalties to the parties? When should landslides be understood as electoral mandates? Answering such questions requires that concrete political messages somehow be distilled from large aggregations of ballots, each cast for reasons that remain hidden from view.

The privacy of the electorate's motivations creates fascinating analytical puzzles that sustain a long and distinguished literature.[1] In this chapter, I consider one particular strand of electoral interpretation that enjoys wide currency among scholars, journalists, and politicians. When voter turnout declines, as it has very dramatically in the United States since 1960, analysts of all persuasions seem drawn to a single troubling conclusion: the voters' withdrawal from the electoral process conveys their alienation from party competition and democratic life. Without doing justice to many variations on the theme, the following examples illustrate the kind of argument I have in mind:

> The rhetoric of political advertising is often vicious, strident, and shallow. . . . The toll on the electorate has been considerable. . . . Political advertising—at least as it is currently practiced—is slowly eroding the participatory ethos in America. In election after election, citizens have registered their disgust with the negativity of contemporary political campaigns by tuning out and staying home.[2]
>
> The continued growth of the "party of nonvoters" in the United States in current elections can only be evaluated as a critical and major limit on democracy itself. It marks the degeneration of an electoral market deriving from the

forces that have led to the degeneration of its primary institutions, the parties.[3]
     Consider the well-known decline in turnout in national elections over the last three decades. From a relative high point in the early 1960s, voter turnout had by 1990 declined by nearly a quarter; tens of millions of Americans had forsaken their parents' habitual readiness to engage in the simplest act of citizenship. . . . Not coincidentally, Americans have also disengaged psychologically from politics and government over this era. The proportion of Americans who reply that they "trust the government in Washington" only "some of the time" or "almost never" has risen steadily from 30 percent in 1966 to 75 percent in 1992.[4]

     In this chapter, I consider an interesting and amusing case study that illustrates both the perils and the potential of this fallible electoral barometer. Though we shall see how easy it is to misconstrue observed trends in voter turnout, especially at the national level, my point is not to dismiss the possibility of extracting from them interesting information about our system of party government. Rather, I show that the measure of turnout one selects can have dramatic effects on the received political message. In developing my case, I explain why turnout in the United States has declined much more dramatically than the literature on voting recognizes and, paradoxically, why the national turnouts themselves conceal the real pattern of decline. My results should give pause about the uncritical use of turnout statistics as diagnostic indicators of our democratic well-being. At the same time, my alternative measures suggest that the contraction of the American electorate is even more disturbing than previously thought.

The Crash of 1972

Among American citizens of voting age (the so-called voting-age population, or VAP), 60.9 percent cast ballots for president in 1968. In 1972, only 55.2 percent did so. What did this ominous downturn, one of the largest on record, signal about the condition of the American party system? What did it bode for the election of 1976? The dominant interpretation at the time attributed the crash to the electorate's sharply escalating disdain for politics. After years of military and moral disaster in Vietnam and tumultuous civil disorders at home, the voters became so disillusioned that they withdrew in droves from the democratic process. Here is how the columnist Tom Wicker described the situation in October 1976, shortly before the approaching presidential election:

     The decline of voter participation in America is causing much weeping, wailing, and gnashing of teeth, and well it might. Authoritative estimates are that for the first time since 1920—when women first had the vote in Presidential elections—less than 50 percent of those eligible may cast a vote this year. The record is depressing. In 1972, the year of the Nixon landslide, 55 percent of those eligible voted. . . . The general apathy evident in the 1976 campaign and the drastic reduction in campaign spending this year [along with lower registration] argue for a reduced turnout on November 2. . . . Numerous potential voters have been alienated from the political system—turned off by war, Watergate, corruption, bureaucracy, indifference, unresponsiveness, and 'the mess in Washington.'[5]

Wicker's analysis clearly belongs to the interpretative tradition described above. In fact, it rests on two inferential rules that typify the whole genre:

1. the amount that turnout declines measures the severity of alienation in the electorate, while
2. the timing of the decline and its proximity to surrounding events defines the causes.

I want to reconsider Wicker's forecast that turnout would fall below 50 percent in 1976 and his supporting inferences about disillusionment in the electorate. The turnout crash of 1972 is an instructive example of the analytical dilemmas that surround such inferences and a delightful electoral puzzle. To appreciate these dilemmas better, let us suspend the wisdom that comes from hindsight and transport ourselves back to the aftermath of the crash. Did the evidence at hand support Wicker's troubling analysis or not?

Historical Perspectives on the Turnout Crash

One way to gain perspective on declining turnout is by studying time series data from earlier elections. Figure 4.1 shows what the presidential turnouts looked like between the New Deal period and 1972. The turnouts are expressed as a fraction of the voting-age population, as reported by the Census Bureau. You can see that turnout really did drop abruptly in 1972, and with very little warning. Nevertheless, several considerations weigh against a knee-jerk reaction to the dire-looking decline. First, turnout was even lower in 1932 (a pretty bad year during the height of the depression) and in 1948 (a better year, following victory in World War II). In neither case had democracy collapsed in the United States. Turnout in 1972 was only slightly lower than the average level during the 1930s and 1940s. Also striking is the rebound turnout made in 1952, erasing the 4.9 percent crash of 1948. And finally, 1948 and 1972 seem to be anomalous deviations from an otherwise rising, long-term trend.

Figure 4.2 shows two attempts to separate the long-term trend in the turnout series from the short-term fluctuations that arise in particular years. A simple linear fit, computed by ordinary least squares (OLS), is probably the most common approach to such problems. As a general proposition, however, the OLS

Figure 4.1 Turnout in Presidential Elections, 1932–1972

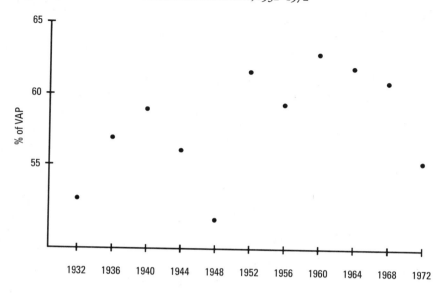

Figure 4.2 Two Summaries of Trends in Turnout, 1932–1972

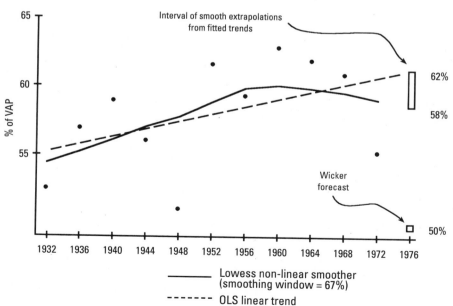

method has some questionable aspects. First, it assumes that the trend must be linear and thereby imposes the most drastic imaginable smoothing on the data. All bumps are flattened and troughs filled in, resulting in severe erosion if the actual trend has ups and downs. At the same time, the OLS technique is highly sensitive to outliers in the data.

Modern nonlinear smoothers like lowess do not impose linearity on the smooth and are much more resistant to outliers.[6] Despite these virtues, however, the smooths in figure 4.2 are very similar. The key point to notice is that virtually any smoother that embodies a reasonably long time horizon gives projections for 1976 that lie well above the observed turnout in 1972.

Extending our historical perspective throws doubt on Wicker's gloomy forecast while raising difficult questions about how to understand the evidence from 1972. Is the turnout crash simply an abnormal deviation from the long-term trend, or does it mark a real change in electoral fundamentals? Is 1972 an "outlier" in the statistical sense, or is it a turning point in American electoral history? Would the far more optimistic extrapolations in figure 4.2 provide a better forecast than Wicker's 50 percent?

Without answers to some difficult substantive questions, it would be hard to know. How relevant is the experience of the 1930s and 1940s to that of 1976? Did the same mechanisms generate turnouts in the two periods? Did the factors that influence turnout remain at stable levels? How much weight should be given to the unusual experience of 1972, relative to the evidence from previous elections? How far back must one go before earlier elections no longer provide information about future outcomes? A basic analytical dilemma arises here, because answering such questions requires more detailed theoretical understanding of voter turnout than now exists. Political scientists still have not satisfactorily explained why people vote at all, much less whether the laws of turnout remain stable across historical periods. With no powerful theory in hand, an open-minded, exploratory approach seems inescapable.

In this spirit, let's narrow our focus to the elections after 1948, which form a homogeneous-looking subset of the longer time series considered above. Figure 4.3 shows these more recent elections in closer detail.

Readers should select their own smooth for the data and then extrapolate to make a forecast for 1976. Putting oneself on the line with a firm prediction makes the cardinal question come to life—just how much influence should the observation from 1972 exert over the projection from past experience? Clearly, the more weight we give to this election, the lower will be our forecast for 1976.

Figure 4.4 displays several choices for the new, shorter-horizon smooth. The two linear trends compare what happens when the observation from 1972 is included or excluded from the fitting sample. One can see that 1972 observation

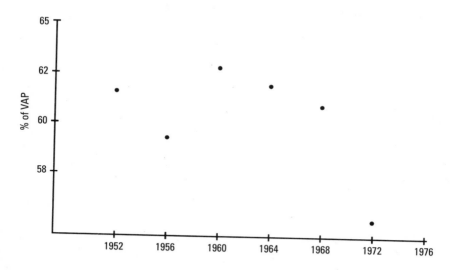

Figure 4.3 Presidential Turnout, 1952–1972

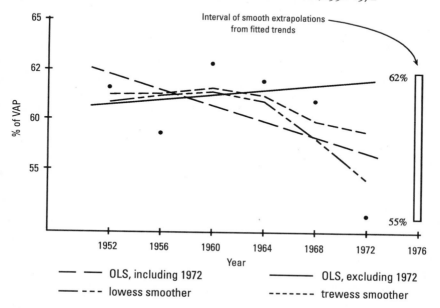

Figure 4.4 Alternative Smooths for Presidential Turnout, 1952–1972

exerts a lot of influence on the fitted trend. (Modern robust regression techniques fit lines between these two extremes.) The other two smooths are of the nonlinear, resistant kind. Of course, with only six observations we are straining these techniques to their limit, and maybe beyond. Still, all produce reasonable-looking smooths, differing mainly in the weight given to 1972. The main point to notice is that despite our shortened time horizon, and allowing different weights for 1972, the range of smooth extrapolations still lies above the rate of turnout observed in 1972. The turnout crash of 1972 still appears to be a negative deviation from the underlying trend.

Our trend-fitting exercises give a strong indication that 1972 should be considered a political anomaly, like the election of 1948. Such evidence clearly invites closer reflection about the political environment in 1972 and a comparison with conditions in 1976. Here, three factors stand out, all of which support the idea that 1972 was an aberration. First, the presidential election that year, pitting Richard Nixon against George McGovern, was one of the biggest landslides of all time—a twenty-three-point blowout that never got close after the nominating conventions. In 1976, Jimmy Carter and Gerald Ford were running neck and neck (Carter won by one of the narrowest margins in presidential history). If close elections induce higher turnout, as many analysts believe, then the too-close-to-call horse race of 1976 should have stimulated greater interest and participation than the cakewalk of 1972.

The election of 1972 was special in another way, too. It was the first time that eighteen-year-olds became eligible to vote. In an ordinary year, four new birth-year cohorts become old enough to vote for president. These cohorts traditionally turn out at the lowest rates in the eligible electorate. In 1972, however, the set of first-time presidential voters included an additional three cohorts between the ages of eighteen and twenty, making a total of seven cohorts. This distortion of the electorate's normal composition was unique to the transition year. In 1976 (and thereafter), the usual four new cohorts would enter the presidential electorate.

Finally, the presumed cause of the voters' alienation, the war in Vietnam, was over. True, the alienating Watergate scandal had unfolded after the 1972 election (quite probably without affecting turnout during that year), but the bad guys had been caught red-handed and justice prevailed with gratifying completeness. In all of these ways, 1972 looks like an especially bad year for turnout, while 1976 does not.

At least, so our group at Princeton University concluded in late October 1976, after becoming intrigued by Wicker's forecast.[7] One of our members, Mike Kagay, wrote up our analysis for the *Daily Princetonian* (if memory serves), and shortly thereafter Wicker picked up our corrective to the conventional wisdom.

Far from crashing through the psychologically devastating barrier of 50 percent, or even declining at all, turnout in 1976 would rebound to 58 percent or more:

> Looked at another way, 1972 turnout dipped six points below the average of the 1950s and 1960s (61 percent). Assuming that half the drop was due to alienation and the other half to the "peculiar features" of 1972 (no horse race, the new voters), Mr. Kagay believes that half the drop might be regained in 1976 by the absence of "peculiar features," even if alienation is as bad this year as it was then. ... He expects a turnout "several points" above the 55 percent recorded in 1972 and points out that if participation reached 58 percent this time, that would just equal the overall average of the forty years from 1932 to 1968.[8]

Our analysis echoed the conclusions reached by Philip E. Converse in an earlier debate about falling turnout at the turn of the century: "[Turnout levels] are susceptible to a wide range of influences, many of which have little or nothing to do with variations in voter apathy, involvement, or system alienation that naive observers take for granted they reflect."[9]

Summary

Our forecasting problem raises two of the central analytical dilemmas that occupy the recent statistical literature on smoothers (a literature that exploded in the late 1970s). Choosing an appropriate interval of observations on which to compute the fit (the so-called window width) is tantamount to deciding how smooth the fitted trend will be. The general goal is to capture the basic pattern of the data with the smoothest curve possible or, equivalently, to make the residuals from the fitted trend fluctuate as little as possible in level. If the fitting window becomes too wide, the fit becomes too smooth, and medium-scale patterns are relegated to the residuals (also called "the rough"). When the window becomes too narrow, on the other hand, the fitted trend starts tracking every "blip" in the data series. Taken to extremes, the fitted curve "connects the dots." Smooths based on very narrow time horizons tend toward all fit and no residual, as if stochastic or chance factors played no role in the phenomenon under study. Though tracking the observed cases with impressive precision, such fits "capitalize on chance" and do very poorly in forecasting future observations (where the configuration of chance factors is unlikely to be repeated.)[10] A critical problem, then, is figuring out when one has gone beyond fitting the trend and started fitting the noise. The question is closely related to deciding what observations to include when forming a prediction. We experimented with several time horizons and kept getting the same answer—the crash of 1972 did not appear to fit the underlying trend at all.

A related issue raised by our problem is sensitivity to "spikes," or outliers. A good smoother is resistant to spikes, allowing them little influence on the final fit. One way to reduce influence of single observations, of course, is to widen the window width, but the question of resistance goes to how the fitting should be done inside the fitting window. The huge literature on robust inference takes as its first canon that rogue observations are commonplace in real data (as they are not in the classical normal distribution). The second canon is that such observations should receive less weight than classical techniques allow (nonresistant techniques like least squares have optimal properties when distributions are normal). In our case, the question was how much weight to give to the data point from 1972. Because it appeared to be an outlier on both statistical and substantive grounds, we resisted the appearance it gave that turnout was in free fall.

To justify a forecast lower than 50 percent in 1976, one would have to ignore all of the special political features of the 1972 election, ignore the recent historical record on turnout, and compute what amounts to a naive linear extrapolation from the two adjacent elections. Figure 4.5 illustrates the kind of sky-is-falling prediction that Wicker described as "the most conventional wisdom."[11] But these forecasts seem statistically and politically highly dubious. The window of experience on which they rest is only two periods wide, and the most anomalous observation of the postwar period dominates the whole story. When we extend our historical perspective even slightly, de-emphasizing the 1972 case, we reach conclusions very unlike the prevailing scenarios of doom and gloom.[12]

Figure 4.5 Forecasting Turnout in 1976 with a Two-Period Linear Trend

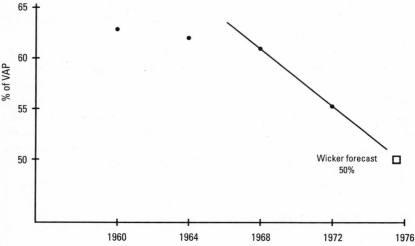

What Happened in 1976?

One can imagine the surprise and chagrin of our Princeton group when turnout fell in 1976 to 53.5 percent—considerably lower than in 1972. What had gone wrong with our carefully considered, statistically robust forecast? Was 1972 really a watershed year in modern electoral history, marking the sudden disengagement of the electorate and the onset of a dangerous new period of instability? Having convinced ourselves that the crash of 1972 could not be understood by using the interpretive rules of the alienation genre, it now seemed more mysterious than ever.

In fact, the entire drift of our analysis—that 1972 was an anomalous deviation from the ongoing trend, that the crash originated in singular features of the 1972 election (especially the lack of a horse race and the eighteen-year-old vote), the whole idea that 1972 was "peculiar"—missed the boat. Had we understood better what the national turnouts measured, we would have concluded that none of those peculiar features of 1972 was critical. Indeed, the startling one-period crash that year was largely a mirage, originating in the sultry backwaters of southern politics. The mirage fooled others too, of course. Because the conventional alienation hypothesis was driven by the conspicuous drop in turnout that happened in 1972, it misconstrued what was happening as well: turnout had been falling faster and longer than even the gloomiest pessimists believed.

What I want to explain next is why everyone was so badly deceived and why the severity of declining turnout still hasn't been properly understood. The heart of the mystery lies in the turnout figures themselves. Although the data considered so far seem to provide a direct barometer of electoral engagement, they actually conceal basic patterns in voter participation. To appreciate the source of the problem, let us investigate next the presidential turnouts enumerated by state.[13]

Figure 4.6 shows the distribution of the statewide turnouts in the presidential election of 1960, the high tide before turnout went downhill.

The most striking feature of the distribution is its extreme skewness. A long tail originates just below the modal turnout near 70 percent and trails off to shockingly low levels (25 percent turnout for a whole state in a presidential election?). In such a distribution, the median provides a better description of the typical state than does the mean. Because it is not a resistant statistic, the mean is more heavily influenced by the least typical observations in the skewed tail. Put another way, the mean conceals a surprising fact that the median makes obvious—most states turn out at much higher rates than the national-level turnouts we've been studying. The summary statistics in figure 4.6 also reveal another, more subtle, surprise. The mean rate of turnout in the states is virtu-

Figure 4.6 Distribution of Presidential Turnouts by State, 1960

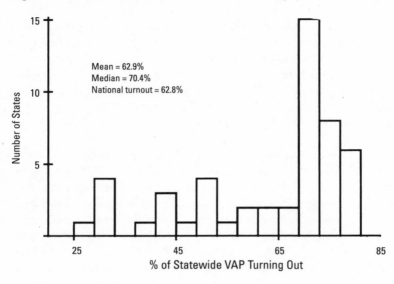

ally identical to the national rate of turnout. Certainly, one can derive the national turnout from the statewide rates by using a straightforward formula, but the simple average is not it. Figuring out why the simple average gives essentially the right answer, when by all rights it should not, provides a critical clue for unraveling the puzzling crash of 1972.

Why Is the Mean Turnout among States like the National Turnout?

The following quantities define the relationship between state and national turnouts in a given election year:

v_i	the number of votes cast in the ith state
vap_i	the size of the eligible electorate in state i
$t_i \equiv \dfrac{v_i}{vap_i}$	the rate of turnout in state i
$V \equiv \sum_i v_i$	the total number of votes cast in all states
$VAP \equiv \sum_i vap_i$	the total size of the national electorate
$T \equiv \dfrac{V}{VAP}$	the national rate of turnout

It should be evident that one can not simply average the statewide rates, the t_i, to recover the national turnout, T. In general,

$$\bar{t} \equiv \sum_{i=1}^{n} \frac{t_i}{n} = \sum_i t_i \left(\frac{1}{n}\right) \neq T.$$

The simple average gives every observation the same weight $(1/n)$. But turnout in California has to count more heavily than turnout in Delaware in determining T. The national turnout is properly calculated by a weighted average of the statewide rates:

$$T = \sum_i t_i \frac{vap_i}{VAP,} = \sum_i \frac{v_i}{vap_i} \frac{vap_i}{VAP} = \sum_i \frac{v_i}{VAP} = \frac{V}{VAP}.$$

The variable weights (vap_i/VAP), control for the relative size of each state's electorate. Since the states differ greatly in size, you can see now why it is surprising that a simple (unweighted) average nevertheless gives essentially the right answer for T.

Although the states do vary in size, there are still some special situations when the simple average of the statewide turnouts equals the national turnout. If turnout were the same fixed constant in every state, (call it t), then it is trivially true that

$$\bar{t} = t = T.$$

Figure 4.6 shows, however, that turnout rates are anything but fixed across the states. Another far-fetched possibility arises when the covariance (or correlation) between the turnouts and populations of the states happens to be zero. Using the simple average does no harm in this case, because all the weighting errors exactly cancel out:

$$Cov\left(t_i, vap_i\right) = 0 \Rightarrow T = \bar{t}$$

Proof:

$$Cov\left(t_i, vap_i\right) = 0 \Rightarrow \sum_i \left(t_i - \bar{t}\right)\left(vap_i - \overline{vap}\right) = 0$$

So,

$$0 = \sum_i \left(t_i\, vap_i - \bar{t}\, vap_i - t_i\, \overline{vap} + \bar{t}\, \overline{vap}\right)$$

$$= \sum_i \frac{v_i}{vap_i}\, vap_i - \bar{t} \sum_i vap_i - \overline{vap} \sum_i t_i + \sum_i \bar{t}\, \overline{vap}$$

$$= \sum_i v_i - \bar{t} \sum_i vap_i - \overline{vap}\, n\, \bar{t} + n\, \bar{t}\, \overline{vap}$$

$$= V - \bar{t}\, VAP$$

Thus,

$$Cov\left(t_i, vap_i\right)= 0 \Rightarrow V - \bar{t}\, VAP = 0 \Rightarrow \frac{V}{VAP} = \bar{t}.$$

And here, remarkably, is the answer to our question. Because turnout rates are virtually uncorrelated with the size of the states, the mean turnout in the states is very close to the national turnout—not just in 1960, but year after year, as a structural feature of the electoral system. Table 4.1 shows just how little turnout rates covaried with population between 1948 and 1972.

We can now appreciate a critical fact that escaped us in 1976 and still remains unnoticed in the literature: because of a highly improbable statistical coincidence, $Corr(t_i, vap_i) = 0$, the national turnouts are essentially the average of the statewide turnouts in disguise. When I said earlier that we did not understand what the national turnouts "measured," this is what I meant. But if national turnouts are the average of state turnouts, then the national turnouts inherit all the undesirable, nonresistant characteristics of the simple average when describing typical behavior in skewed distributions. In particular, the national turnouts will be extremely sensitive to the least typical, high-leverage cases in the skewed tail of the distribution. To show who those cases might be, figure 4.7 reconstructs the 1960 distribution in greater detail.[14]

As you might have guessed, all the observations down in the tail are southern states (save for the new state, Alaska). In 1960, electoral turnout in the Deep South was dismally lower than everywhere else. Not only were African Americans widely disenfranchised, but southern politics followed a unique pattern of single-party domination, making most elections foregone conclusions.[15]

Figure 4.7 also contains a Tukey box-plot that neatly summarizes the pattern

Table 4.1 Relationship between State-Level and National Measures of Turnout, 1948–1972

Year	Corr (t_i, vap_i)	Total (T)	Mean (t_i)	Median (t_i)
1948	.005	51.1	51.7	58.8
1952	−.031	61.6	63.5	71.0
1956	−.009	59.3	60.6	67.0
1960	.016	62.8	62.9	70.4
1964	.022	61.9	61.7	66.6
1968	−.040	60.9	61.3	64.3
1972	−.041	55.2	55.9	59.0

of distribution in 1960. The box contains the middle 50 percent of states, after they have been ranked in order of turnout (the so-called interquartile range, or IQR). The line inside the box locates the median (the 50th percentile), while the cross shows the average (the national turnout). The whiskers extend to the extremes of the distribution (excluding outliers, which are shown separately, as circles or asterisks, when they arise). Like the intervals between the median and the ends of the box, each whisker contains about a quarter of the cases. Notice how the asymmetry of the box-plot captures the skewness of the distribution. The picture also conveys the range, the typical value (median), and a robust measure of spread in the data (the IQR).

Explaining the Turnout Crash of 1972

We are now in a position to understand why turnout crashed in 1972. Figure 4.8 shows how the shape, the spread, and the location of the turnout distribution all changed dramatically in the twelve years after 1960.

Figure 4.7 Presidential Turnout by State, 1960

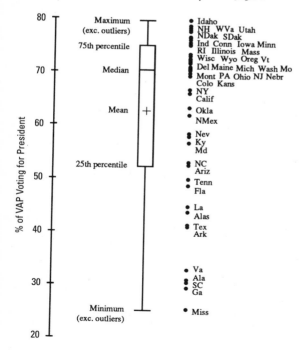

Figure 4.8 Declining Turnout in the States, 1960–1972

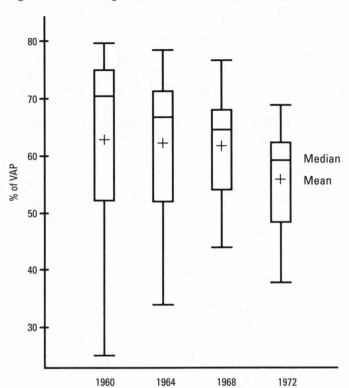

Let us first examine how the location (or center) of the distribution shifted. The median turnout, the more robust of the two measures shown in each box, fell a remarkable 11.4 points from 70.4 percent to 59 percent (more than twice as much as the "crash" that originally captured everyone's attention). The average turnout, by contrast, fell only 7 points, from 62.9 percent to 55.9 percent. Notice, too, how the median descended in a smoother, more continuous fashion. By 1968, the median had already dropped more than 6 percent, while the mean turnout remained virtually flat. The mean fell off the table only in 1972, when it (like the national-level turnout) crashed 5.4 percent in one period.

The competing measures of location tell such different stories because the distribution of turnouts undergoes two separate transformations at once. These confounding trends appear in figures 4.9 to 4.11, which distinguish the nonsouthern states from the Deep South.

Figure 4.9 Voter Turnout in the Nonsouthern States, 1960–1972

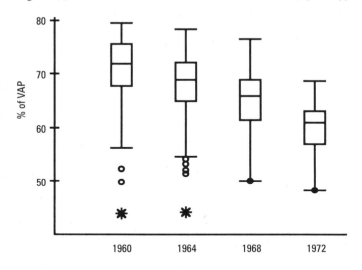

Figure 4.10 Turnout Paths in Individual Nonsouthern States, 1960–72

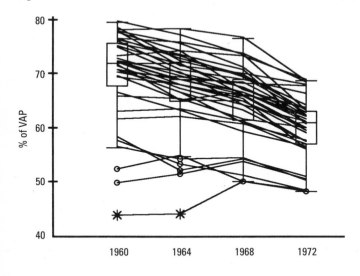

In the forty nonsouthern states, turnout declined sharply throughout the period, in a remarkably smooth, virtually linear fashion. There is no hint of discontinuity in 1972, nor any deviation from the *already established* pattern. Figure 4.10 shows that this dominant trend operates on a truly national scale, with nearly every state showing a similar pattern of decline (each line records the path of a single state). The whole distribution shifts in an amazingly uniform way (with rare exceptions like Alaska, Hawaii, and Arizona, all on the low end of the scale).

Figure 4.11 shows how voting followed a very different pattern in the Deep South. It appears that the civil rights movement propelled a sharp increase in turnout until 1968, mobilizing newly registered black voters and probably a backlash turnout among whites. This countervailing regional trend peaked in 1968 and then reversed course in 1972—a critical feature to notice. The reversal followed the decapitation of the civil rights movement in 1968, when Dr. Martin Luther King Jr. was assassinated, and the severe polarization of the movement thereafter.

Returning to the combined distribution of all the states' turnouts (fig. 4.8), we see that the median turnout, which is quite insensitive to goings-on in the skewed tail, marches smoothly downward, reflecting a pervasive decline in the vast majority of states. The nonresistant mean, however, is highly sensitive to the atypical southern states, which experience a rising trend through 1968. This

Figure 4.11 Voter Turnout in the Southern States, 1960–1972

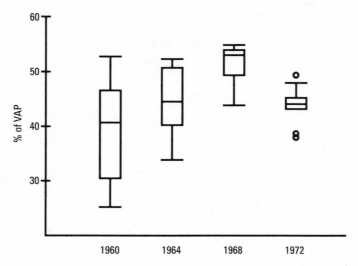

countervailing regional trend attenuates the downward movement of the mean, disguising almost completely the rapid erosion of turnout outside the South. When the southern trend reverses course in 1972, the countervailing pressure on the mean is relieved, and it crashes in one fell swoop.

Naturally, the shape of the turnout distribution changes, too, as it gets pulled in two different directions. With the southern states elevating toward the national norm and the nonsouthern states descending en masse, the pattern of distribution becomes more symmetric and compact. The mean and median converge as a result (making the mean and the national turnout better, though still understated, descriptions of typical behavior in the states).

Because of its nonresistant properties and the anomalous behavior of the southern states, the average turnout in the states badly misrepresents the contraction of the electorate between 1960 and 1972. The mean understates the steepness of the decline (by nearly a factor of two), it misrepresents the timing of the decline (by concealing all of the movement between 1960 and 1968), and it misrepresents the continuity of the process (by crashing in 1972, for reasons incidental to the bigger picture). Had we realized that the national-level turnouts were just these averages in disguise, our story in the fall of 1976 would have changed dramatically. No one would have understood declining turnout to be a one-period crash. Our Princeton group would not have perceived the 1972 election as an outlier from the underlying trend nor mined for peculiar features of the 1972 election to explain what happened. In the same way, explanations that identified causes for the decline in the early 1970s (like Wicker's war weariness, Watergate, and "the mess in Washington") would have appeared doubtful. A good explanation would recognize that turnout began falling sharply in the early 1960s. Everyone would have been less sanguine about the health of the electoral system and more persuaded that basic electoral changes were afoot (and Wicker would not have changed his tune so easily). Our group would not have been surprised when turnout in 1976 followed the well-established pattern. Indeed, we could have predicted the course of declining turnout over the next several elections by extrapolating smoothly from the box-plots in figure 4.8.[16]

Figures 4.12 to 4.14 show what happened after 1976, extending the story through 1992. I believe this picture vindicates the turnout rates as worthy objects of electoral interpretation, notwithstanding their subtle and delicate properties. The national turnouts, like any aggregated electoral totals, can be highly misleading when they embody confounding effects. By replacing them with the state-level distributions, a wealth of political ore comes to the surface. These statewide turnouts reveal beautifully some of the basic large-scale patterns of contemporary American politics. We can see the steady, long-term withdrawal

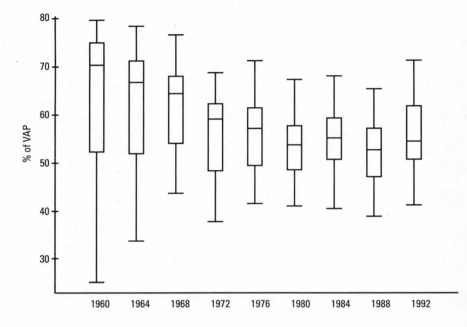

Figure 4.12 Declining Turnout in the States, 1960–1992

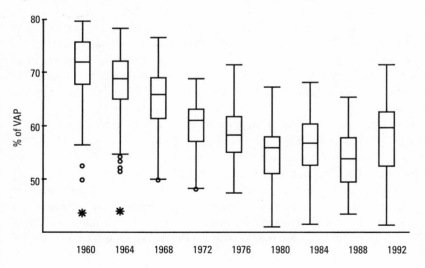

Figure 4.13 Turnout in the Nonsouthern States, 1960–1992

Figure 4.14 Turnout in the Southern States, 1960–1992

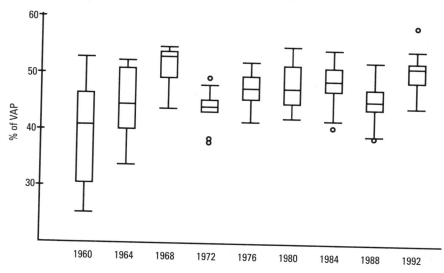

of the electorate from the democratic process, the early success of the civil rights movement and its subsequent exhaustion, and the ongoing, though uncompleted, integration of the South into the national mainstream. It also becomes apparent how severely the electorate contracted after 1960. Measured by the median rate among the states, turnout fell much more drastically than most people realize.

Notes

First and foremost, thanks go to Stanley Kelley Jr. for sharing so much friendship and wisdom. For helpful comments and ideas, I am grateful to Larry Bartels, Susanne Lohmann, Mohan Penubarti, Thomas Romer, Thomas Schwartz, and John Zaller. The essay would not have been written without the tireless efforts of John Geer.

1. Stanley Kelley's contributions to this intellectual lineage are exceptionally thoughtful and interesting. Of particular relevance here are his book, *Interpreting Elections* (Princeton: Princeton University Press, 1983), and the classic article on voter turnout, Stanley Kelley Jr., Richard E. Ayres, and William G. Bowen, "Registration and Voting: Putting First Things First," *American Political Science Review* 61 (June 1967): 359–79.

2. Steven Ansolabehere and Shanto Iyengar, *Going Negative: How Political Advertisements Shrink and Polarize the Electorate* (New York: Free Press, 1995), 99.

3. Walter Dean Burnham, *The Current Crisis in American Politics* (New York: Oxford University Press, 1982), 12.

4. Robert Putnam, "Bowling Alone," *Journal of Democracy* 6 (Jan. 1995): 65–78.

5. Tom Wicker, "It Sells Toothpaste, Doesn't It?" *New York Times*, Oct. 17, 1976.

6. The basic idea of lowess is simple, though it should be noted that the technique was not yet available in 1976: at each value of x (here, x is year), fit a regression line to nearby observations (x, y) and take as the smooth the y-*hat* value of the fitted line at x. Then move to the next x value, shifting over the window of observations on which the regression is computed, and repeat the procedure. An adjustable smoothing parameter in lowess describes the fraction of the observations contained in the fitting window. The wider the window, the heavier the smooth. For resistance, lowess computes an iteratively reweighted regression that de-emphasizes the influence of cases with large residuals from the fitted lines. It also applies declining weights to observations that grow more distant from x. For a clear discussion of lowess by its inventor, see W. S. Cleveland, "Robust Locally Weighted Regression and Smoothing Scatterplots," *Journal of the American Statistical Association* 74 (1979): 829–36. For a careful survey that compares lowess with other modern smoothers, see Colin Goodall, "A Survey of Smoothing Techniques," in *Modern Methods of Data Analysis*, ed. John Fox and J. Scott Long (Newbury Park, Calif.: Sage Publications, 1990).

7. The group in question included Stanley Kelley Jr., Michael Kagay, now pollster for the *New York Times*, and me. Kagay and I were preceptors in Kelley's course on party politics. To avoid assigning credit or blame, I have portrayed our ill-fated, lunch-hour deliberations as a collective effort.

8. Tom Wicker, "In a Real Horse Race, Maybe Turnout Will Go Up," *New York Times*, Oct. 29, 1976.

9. Philip E. Converse, "Change in the American Electorate," in *The Human Meaning of Social Change*, ed. Angus Campbell and Philip E. Converse (New York: Russell Sage Foundation, 1972), 288.

10. The statistical literature on chance capitalization and cross-validation develops these themes with many striking examples.

11. Wicker, "It Sells Toothpaste."

12. Estimating an autoregressive model like $\gamma_t = \alpha + \beta\gamma_{t-1} + \mu_t$ is another approach that tends to attach a lot of weight to the observations immediately preceding the forecast period. Evidence from earlier periods nevertheless affects the estimated coefficients in such models. For presidential turnouts, a one-period autoregression estimated on data from 1932–1972 yields an estimated turnout of 57.9 percent in 1976.

13. Although the state-level data contain a gold mine of information, they rarely appear in the literature on voter turnout. For some reason, the very interesting distributions considered below are not a natural object of study.

14. Figure 4.7 recalls the interesting semi-graphical display in Donald S. Collat, Stanley Kelley Jr., and Ronald Rogowski, "The End Game in Presidential Nominations," *American Political Science Review* 75 (June 1981): 421–35.

15. The general lesson here is too little appreciated: When interpreting national electoral statistics, one must be deeply wary about quantities that are sensitive to anomalous behavior in the southern states. As my colleague Douglas Rivers once put it, the first question to ask when considering American electoral data is, "What about the South?"

16. After learning these lessons in the late 1970s, I wrote a paper suggesting how turnout might fall in the 1990s before hitting a floor near 50 percent. In fact, presidential turnout hit bottom in 1988, at 50.1 percent. For the reasoning that identified the floor, while supporting further inferences about the underlying condition of the parties' core followings, see James DeNardo, "Declining Turnout in an Era of Waning Partisanship," *British Journal of Political Science* 17 (Oct. 1987): 435–56. A corrective to Wicker's "next most conventional wisdom . . . that a big turnout would inevitably help the majority party" appears in James DeNardo, "Turnout and the Vote: The Joke's on the Democrats," *American Political Science Review* 74 (June 1980): 406–20. This paper was another direct outgrowth of Stanley Kelley's course on party politics at Princeton, where its figure 1 was a handout presented to students. Further discussion and debate appear in James DeNardo, "Does Heavy Turnout Help Democrats in Presidential Elections?" *American Political Science Review* 80 (Dec. 1986): 1298–1304; Benjamin Radcliff, "Turnout and the Democratic Vote," *American Politics Quarterly* 22 (July 1994): 259–76; Alexander Pacek and Benjamin Radcliff, "Turnout and the Vote for Left-of-Center Parties: A Cross-National Analysis," *British Journal of Political Science* 25 (Jan. 1995): 137–43; Robert Erikson, "State Turnout and Presidential Voting: A Closer Look," *American Politics Quarterly* 23 (Oct. 1995): 387–96; and Jack Nagel and John McNulty, "Partisan Effects of Voter Turnout in Senatorial and Gubernatorial Elections," *American Political Science Review* 90 (Dec. 1996): 780–94.

CHAPTER 5

Movement and Aftermath
Mobilization of the African American Electorate, 1952–1992

Thomas R. Rochon
Ikuo Kabashima

> Democracy is not the multiplication of ignorant opinions.
> Beatrice Webb

Extensive political mobilization is the stuff of dreams for some; for others it is a nightmare. The differing values attached to political mobilization depend largely on what one assumes to be the relationship between expanded participation and the skills of the electorate. There are two schools of thought on this question; one claims that increased participation dilutes the skills of the electorate, while the other asserts that participation enhances political skills.

The first view, which has come to be known as the "elite theory" of citizenship, finds its classical expression in Joseph Schumpeter's (1942) definition of democracy as a set of procedures for electing leaders on the basis of free competition between rival political parties. The purpose of mass participation in the process is confined to selecting leaders in the controlled forum of electoral contests. A more active public role in politics is not necessary to a democracy. Nor is extensive participation useful, since, as Schumpeter puts it, "when we move still farther away from the private concerns of the family and the business office into those regions of national and international affairs that lack a direct and unmistakable link with those private concerns, individual volition, command of facts, and methods of inference soon cease to fulfill the requirements of the classical doctrine [of citizenship]" (1942, 261). Indeed, for Schumpeter, "the electoral mass is incapable of action other than a stampede" (283). Schumpeter's theory of citizenship, then, places heavy reliance on elites to bring rationality to the political process.

Subsequent investigations of the contours of public opinion provided a great deal of support for the elite theory of citizenship. The mass public has proved to hold inconsistent attitudes about political issues, to change opinions in response to stimuli as slight as variations in the wording of questions, and to hold opinions based on little or no information about the object of their attitudes (for reviews, see Converse 1975; Luskin 1987). Recent work on the theory of the survey response suggests that people generate issue positions on demand by linking issues to one of the relatively few general beliefs they hold (Zaller 1992). As the chain of inference from general belief to specific issue lengthens, the consistency of issue belief declines.

Not all investigators of public opinion reach the same conclusions about democratic theory, but Bernard Berelson, Paul Lazarsfeld, and William McPhee (1954) summed up the lessons drawn by many others when they expressed the view that people do not generally meet the criteria of citizenship laid down by democratic theory. Berelson concluded that it was therefore probably a good thing that the least informed segment of the population is also the least likely to take any active political role.

As Carole Pateman (1970), Dennis Thompson (1970), and others have pointed out, this reasoning stands classical democratic theory on its head. The school of thought that we label the "participation theory" of citizenship values participation precisely because it provides an opportunity for the public to become more educated and responsible about politics.[1] The participation school of citizenship asserts that political skills are developed only when individuals have an opportunity to be active citizens. If the present political skills of the public are weak, then the answer is to offer more opportunities for participation rather than to enshrine limitations on public influence as necessary to a functioning democracy.

Tensions arise between the elite and participation theories of citizenship whenever mass political participation expands, whether due to an extension of citizenship rights or to the mobilization of a mass movement. According to the elite theory of citizenship, expanded political participation brings what Samuel Huntington calls "creedal passions" into politics (1981). The competence of the electorate is diluted by the expansion of participation to previously apathetic and ill-informed individuals. Elite theorists conclude that democracy is vulnerable to rapid mobilizations that outrun the capacity of institutions to channel participation.

The participation theory of citizenship holds that any such dilution of competence is at most temporary, since expanded participation leads to growth in political skills and engagement. Participation theorists anticipate that new mobilizations may challenge existing political agendas and policies, but they do not anticipate a challenge to the political process arising from unfamiliarity or inability to engage with existing institutions. Donald Matthews and James Prothro drew upon the participation theory of citizenship as an argument to speed the enfranchisement of African Americans in the 1960s.

> The "cycle" of poverty exists not just in economics but in the cognitive and political life of southern Negroes as well. Negroes will have little chance to rise permanently above their present status as "second class citizens" until this cycle of ignorance and inactivity has been broken. But once it has been broken, participation, interest, and knowledge will further the development of one another. The vicious circle will become benign. (1966, 275)

This confrontation between elite and participation theories can be broken out into a number of specific disagreements, as illustrated in figure 5.1. Scholars within the tradition of the elite theory of citizenship claim that increased political participation leads to increased policy demands, which in turn lead to declining governmental performance, lowered participation, and reduced political skills on the part of citizens. In Huntington's influential formulation of the problem, a surfeit of participation will create a cycle of mobilization, increased demands, and decreased performance that could ultimately destroy democratic governments (1975, 84ff.).

Participation theorists predict a positive cycle between precisely the same variables. The expansion of participation leads to an enhancement of political skills among the public and to increased effectiveness of the political machinery. This increases further the desire and ability to participate. As Carole Pateman puts it, "The existence of a participatory society would mean that [the cit-

Figure 5.1 Elite and Participation Theories of Citizenship

Elite Theory	Participation Theory
Inclusive political rules	Inclusive political rules
↓	↓
Expanded participation	Expanded participation
↓	↓
Increased political demands	Increased efficacy and trust
↓	↓
Lowered governmental efficiency	Increased governmental efficiency,
↓	due to wider basis of consent
Lowered efficacy and trust	

izen] was better able to assess the performance of representatives at the national level, better equipped to take decisions of national scope when the opportunity arose to do so, and better able to weigh up the impact of decisions taken by national representatives on his own life and immediate surroundings" (1970, 110).

Despite the importance of the dispute between participation and elite theorists, there is remarkably little evidence supporting either set of claims about the consequences of an expansion of citizenship. One reason for this may be the dynamic nature of the theories, which makes testing difficult. In order to generate evidence capable of discriminating between the participation and elite theories of citizenship, it is necessary to focus on a group that is newly admitted to the polity. This group must be tracked across the period of its inclusion in order to see the effect of inclusion on its political skills and attitudes. This means that comparable survey data on participation, knowledge, and efficacy must be available for the group reaching back to the period before it began to take part in the political process.[2]

These data requirements are sufficiently stringent to drastically limit the number of instances that can be used to test elite and participation theories of citizenship. One case that does meet these requirements, however, is that of African Americans. African American mobilization in the civil rights movement of the 1950s and 1960s, leading to elimination of the legal barriers to black political participation, offers an ideal opportunity to study the effects of expanded participation on political skills. Blacks entered the electoral system in large numbers in a short period of time, between 1956 and 1965. As late as 1960, black registration in eleven southern states averaged only 29 percent, compared with 61 percent for whites (U.S. Bureau of the Census 1981, table 822). In the next decade, black registration in the South gained rapidly (Carmines and Stimson 1989, 49; Thernstrom 1987). The most dramatic case is that of Mississippi, which had a 6 percent black registration rate in 1960 and a 60 percent black registration rate in 1970. Clearly, African Americans meet the test criterion of rapid admission to citizenship rights.

Had admission to the polls been the only change in the political life of African Americans, their mobilization would not be a fair test of the participation theory of citizenship. John Stuart Mill claimed that a vote cast only "once in a few years, and for which nothing in the daily habits of the citizen has prepared him, leaves his intellect and his moral dispositions very much as it found them" (as cited in Thompson 1976, 41). Steven Finkel posits that voting has virtually no impact on the self-perceived efficacy of Americans or West Germans (1985, 1987). Finkel concludes that "voting is not a means of personal empowerment, as [has] been hypothesized by Thompson and other citizenship theorists, and thus cannot be justified on these kinds of developmental grounds" (1987, 461).

But Finkel does find that more demanding forms of participation, such as campaign activities or protesting, do affect individual attitudes. Kent Jennings (1987) also finds that the experience of participating in antiwar protests while in college left substantial marks on individual political attitudes over a decade later.[3]

These considerations add a second element to the examination of elite and participation theories of citizenship in the context of African American mobilization. For black Americans, admission to the polls followed a decade of political struggle. The civil rights movement was simultaneously a national movement and a movement with a great number of local targets and campaigns. It was a movement that required exceptional dedication and courage on the part of a great number of individuals (see, e.g., McAdam 1982; Morris 1984; Chong 1991). Its effects on the rate of black political participation were dramatic, particularly among those with low levels of education (Verba and Nie 1972; Nie et al. 1988).

There is, however, a second and less storied phase of the mobilization of the African American citizenry, the movement aftermath. In this phase, which might be dated from the presidential election of 1964 and which continues to the present, party politics has replaced movement politics as the vehicle of mobilization. Political involvement through the party system differs from involvement through movements in a number of ways. As African Americans aligned themselves with the Democratic Party, their political fortunes rose and fell with those of the party. Over the ensuing three decades, Democratic Party leaders were also inconsistent in the extent of their efforts to mobilize black voters. Finally, movement mobilization was a more or less continuous phenomenon, while party mobilization is concentrated around election campaigns.

Each of these considerations suggests that the participation theory of citizenship will find more support during movement mobilizations than in the context of party mobilization. The electoral mobilization of African Americans from 1952 to 1992 thus permits us to examine the elite and participation theories of citizenship under conditions of movement campaigns as well as in the context of party mobilization for electoral campaigns. Levels of African American engagement in politics may be expected to have increased substantially during the civil rights movement and subsequently to have fluctuated from election to election.

Mobilization and Its Consequences

Did African Americans become more knowledgeable and efficacious about government after gaining access to the rights of citizenship, or did their enfranchisement simply introduce into the electorate a large group of people whose

lack of political skills could destabilize the political system? If black mobilization was followed by increasing interest in and knowledge about politics, then
the contention of participation theorists that participation breeds political responsibility is confirmed for that group. If electoral mobilization of the black
population did not affect its political interest or knowledge, then elite theorists
are correct in their assumption that extension of the franchise to less educated
classes permanently dilutes the political competence of the electorate.[4]

To see which of these two theories of the consequences of political mobilization is correct, we must first examine the process of mobilization itself. This
process can be thought of as the progressive diminution of the difference in the
extent to which the probability of voting depends on the contingency of race.
At any one point in time, this model can be described as

$$P_t = [1 + \exp(a_0 + a_1 R_t)]^{-1}, \tag{1}$$

where

P_t is the probability of voting,
a_0 is a constant,
a_1 describes the effect of race on the probability of voting, and
R_t represents race.

The term a_1 in equation (1) expresses the total effect of race on the probability
of voting, an effect that is augmented by a variety of confounding variables. It
requires only a slight complication of the model to add to the equation a control for other factors that would affect the size of a_1.

$$P_t = [1 + \exp(b_0 + b_1 R_t + b_2 S_t)]^{-1}, \tag{2}$$

where

b_0 is a constant,
b_1 represents the effect of race on the probability of voting, controlling for
    the variables summarized as S_t,
b_2 represents the cumulative change in the probability of voting due to the
    variables S_t, and
S_t represents the socioeconomic variables that are associated with both race
    and the probability of voting.

Thus, a_1 gives us the total effect of race on voting, and b_1 is the partial effect,
controlling for the socioeconomic variables S_t.[5]

We have repeated the analysis presented in equations (1) and (2) for presidential elections between 1952 and 1992 to see how the effect of race on electoral
turnout has changed over time.[6] The total and partial effects in this model por-

tray African American political behavior and beliefs compared with the behavior and beliefs of whites. While the "white standard" is arbitrary, and other standards for measuring attitudinal change among African Americans are certainly possible, using white Americans as a comparison group has the useful trait of controlling for general trends in society, which over this period saw substantial declines in both turnout and efficacy. Whites serve in effect as a control group in order to measure changes in black political behavior and attitudes, net of wider trends in American culture.

Figure 5.2 presents the results of that analysis in two forms (white turnout, both adjusted and unadjusted, is represented by the horizontal line running across the figure). First, we looked at the mobilization of African Americans into the electoral system controlling for socioeconomic status and demographics. This "partial effect" tracks the value of $\exp(b_1)$ (from equation [2]) for each election. It shows the distinctively racial elements of mobilization, setting aside the effects of education, income, urbanicity, and other demographic variables that are associated with both race and the likelihood of turning out to vote. We also looked at the uncorrected difference between the races in electoral participation. This is the a_1 of equation (1) and is labeled "total effect" in figure 5.2.

Figure 5.2 shows that turnout among blacks relative to turnout among whites began to increase in 1956 and accelerated sharply in 1964. Already in 1964, African American turnout reached levels comparable to that of whites, controlling for differences in social status.

Figure 5.2 Effect of Race on Voter Turnout, All States, 1952–1992

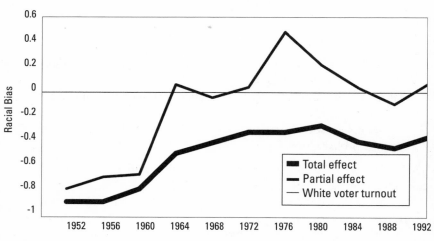

In figure 5.3 we have given separate consideration to the electoral mobilization of African Americans in the South. Exclusion from the electoral process was concentrated in the South, as were the remedies of the 1965 Voting Rights Act. Figure 5.3 shows that federal intervention into the electoral system after 1964 did indeed have a large impact on the southern vote. Controlling for socioeconomic factors, southern blacks were more likely than southern whites to vote in presidential elections beginning in 1968. Even without correction for differences in education and other demographic factors, differences in voting turnout between southern blacks and southern whites vanished in 1972.

The effects of federal legislation on turnout among southern blacks were not a gift from above but occurred rather as the culmination of a process of political mobilization that had begun a decade earlier. Beginning in 1956, the turnout rates of African Americans across the country moved closer to that of whites in each election. This gain was particularly striking in the 1964 election, the last presidential election before the effects of federal legislation on voting rights became apparent. This is, of course, the election in which voters were offered "a choice, not an echo" on race (among other topics), the election shown by

Figure 5.3 Effect of Race on Voter Turnout, South Only, 1952–1992

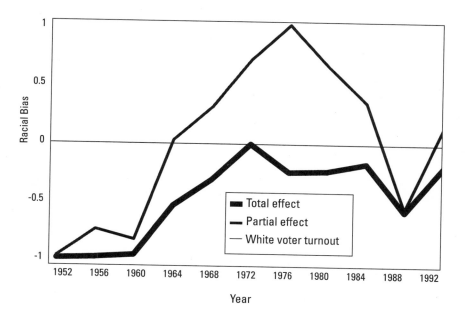

Carmines and Stimson (1989) to have marked a turning point in the partisan clarity of racial issues.

The lesson of figures 5.2 and 5.3 is that although federal legislation helped southern blacks enter the electoral process, the greater share of the mobilization of the black vote predated federal involvement. As important as the 1964 Civil Rights Act and the 1965 Voting Rights Act were, two-thirds of the national increase in turnout among African Americans (and nearly half of the increase in the South) occurred between 1952 and 1964, during the campaigns of the civil rights movement. That movement, whose voter registration activities were also focused largely on the South, had already by 1964 brought voting rates among southern African Americans up nearly to the level of African Americans in the North.

There was little in the actions of the federal or state governments prior to 1964 that could account for the large observed changes in turnout among African Americans. To the limited extent that it became easier for blacks to register to vote in the years prior to 1964, these changes were due to the efforts of the civil rights movement rather than to legislative change. This is the phase of movement mobilization. At issue, then, is the question of whether this mobilization was also accompanied by an increase in the political engagement and skills of African Americans.

Historical evidence on the development of political attitudes among African Americans during this period is ambiguous. On the one hand, blacks clearly showed a tendency to reward the political institutions that had helped them gain their civil rights. African Americans voted in massive numbers for the Democratic Party in 1964 and 1968, and trust in the Supreme Court among blacks reached remarkably high levels in the mid-1960s (Murphy and Tannenhaus 1968). On the other hand, a four-year cycle of urban riots began with an outburst in Harlem in July 1964, only weeks after the passage of the 1964 Civil Rights Act. The "Black Power" slogan first used by Stokely Carmichael in 1966 seemed also to express alienation and withdrawal from established political institutions rather than engagement with them.

Of course, such events were the well-publicized activities of a minority of blacks. We can examine evidence that is both more systematic and more germane to the dispute between participation and elite theorists by adapting the model we used to examine the incorporation of African Americans into the electoral system. We simply substitute the appropriate political behaviors and attitudes for turnout in equations (1) and (2). Thus, for example, figure 5.4 shows the total and partial effects of race on the use of the mass media as a source of information about the presidential campaigns.[7]

Figures 5.4 through 5.6 show that enfranchisement of African Americans did have the wider effects on political engagement and information forecast by the participation theory of citizenship. At the same time, those effects are concentrated in the period of movement mobilization. The phase of party mobilization, which begins with the 1964 presidential election, presents a more mixed picture in which the extent of African American engagement with the political system varies from election to election.

Figure 5.4, for example, shows that African Americans gained rapidly from the 1950s to the 1960s in their use of the mass media for information about presidential candidates and campaigns. Already in 1964 the adjusted rate of media use placed blacks substantially above whites in attention to the media. In 1972 the black rate of media use was slightly above the white rate, even without controls for social status and demographics applied. Succeeding elections display a variable pattern of media use. The overall pattern is one of rapid growth in media use among blacks (compared with whites) until 1964, followed by variability from election to election.

Exposure to political information tells us part of what we want to know about the effects of gaining citizenship rights, but it may not be the most important indicator of the development of citizen skills. If the participation theory of citizenship is correct, we must expect the electoral mobilization of African Americans to be accompanied by increased levels of political information.

Figure 5.5 shows that African Americans in 1960 were much less likely to retain certain information they heard and read in the media, such as knowledge of which party held a majority of seats in the House of Representatives before

Figure 5.4 Effect of Race on Media Use, 1952–1992

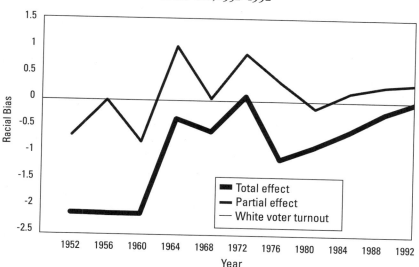

and after the most recent election.[8] Blacks in 1960 (the first year these questions were asked) were substantially less informed than whites, even controlling for education and other aspects of socioeconomic status. Four years later, the difference between black and white was almost completely effaced, when the controls are applied. Between 1972 and 1980 there was very little difference, on average, between the two races in levels of information, again with controls taken into account. Since 1972, however, there has been a decline in the level of information among African Americans, compared with whites. As with media use, we see the positive effects of movement mobilization on political engagement, while party mobilization provides only the conditions for the maintenance of approximate parity.

Political knowledge is, of course, only one of a number of elements required for effective participation in the electoral process. The dispute between elite and participation theorists of citizenship reaches beyond the retention of political facts to the development of feelings of political competence, or internal efficacy. Figure 5.6 displays racial differences in internal efficacy between 1952 and 1992.[9] These trends follow a pattern that is by now becoming familiar. In the 1950s African Americans had relatively weak feelings of political competence, but by 1960 the partial differences (i.e., controlling for socioeconomic status) show the self-perception of efficacy to be higher for blacks than for whites. In 1968 blacks surpassed whites in perceived political efficacy—by a slight margin—even without the controls for different levels of education and social status applied. Since

Figure 5.5 Effect of Race on Political Information, 1960–1992

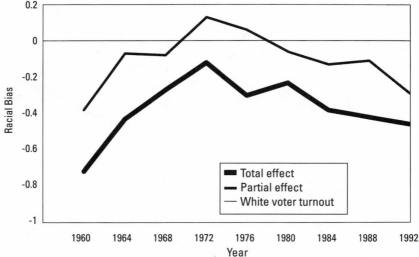

that date, relative levels of perceived efficacy among African Americans have fluctuated from campaign to campaign, being noticeably higher in years when a Democrat gains election to the White House. As with rates of political information, though, the overall trend is one of gradual decay from the remarkable peak of internal efficacy reached toward the end of the civil rights movement. Party mobilization has not been as effective as movement mobilization in cultivating feelings of political efficacy among African Americans.

The sea change in the relative levels of media use, political information, and perceived efficacy among African Americans between 1952 and 1964 fully bears out the expectations of participation theorists of citizenship. But the clarity of the trend line prior to 1964 is subsequently replaced by a trendless sawtooth pattern, one that (if anything) tends to decay over time. These short-term fluctuations suggest some dynamic other than the mobilization-learning pattern projected by participation theorists of citizenship.

The Postmobilization Steady State

Based on his 1955 survey of both races using an open-ended exercise called the "Picture Arrangement Test," psychologist Bertram Karon concluded that "the American caste system" created among African Americans feelings of low self-esteem, "over-conformity to white ideals," apathy, resignation, anxiety, and elevated rates of depression (1958, 169–75). Karon found particularly among

Figure 5.6 Effect of Race on Internal Efficacy, 1952–1992

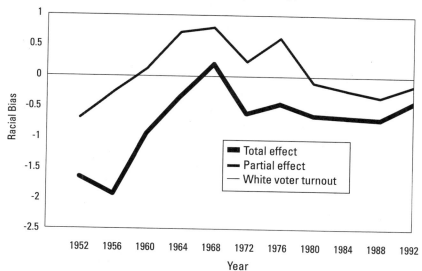

southern blacks a feeling of hopelessness about discrimination, a readiness to deny situations involving anger, and more generally a pattern of deadened emotions.

Although Karon's methodology has never been repeated, the survey evidence presented here suggests that low self-esteem has been replaced by remarkably high levels of perceived efficacy, apathy by an increased degree of political awareness, and feelings of resignation by elevated rates of electoral participation. A number of studies of race and participation undertaken in the 1970s suggest that the source of this change was the development among African Americans of racial pride and the increased use of race as a referent in political issues (Olson 1970; Verba and Nie 1972). The specific contribution of the civil rights movement to this change appears to have been to foster increased levels of internal efficacy, which, combined with the relatively low levels of political trust among blacks, generated participation oriented to achieving political change. Richard Shingles has demonstrated that "the combination of political mistrust and a sense of internal political efficacy optimizes high-initiative, conventional policy[-oriented] behavior for otherwise unmotivated citizens" (1981, 81).

The systemic consequences of this resurgence of African American participation have been massive. There were two black members of the House of Representatives in 1952; by 1996 this number had risen to thirty-nine (Swain, chap. 11, below). There were only five hundred black elected officials at all levels of government nationwide in the early 1970s; by the early 1990s there were nearly seventy-five hundred (Barnes and Proctor 1994, 84; see also Lawson 1985). This surge in black office holding is a consequence of the civil rights movement not only because the movement mobilized voters but also because it created a cadre of political activists who would later run for office. A 1972 study by Lester Salamon found that 66 percent of black elected officials in Mississippi had been active in the civil rights movement between 1960 and 1966; 59 percent of them had taken part in an activity defined as "risky" (cited in Coleman 1994, 78).

The surge in political participation and office holding among African Americans has also led to a reconfiguration of legislative and regulatory policies ranging from federal rules on affirmative action policies and the design of electoral districts to the distribution of city services and access to municipal jobs. James Button and Minion Morrison show that local black office holding, particularly control of the mayor's office, generates increased minority employment in fire and police departments, greater police protection, and better streets and parks in minority neighborhoods (Button 1989; Morrison 1987).

Over the two-decade period spanning the late 1950s to the late 1970s, African American mobilization was translated first into access to the ballot box, then to an increase in black office holding, and finally to a reorientation of public policy to take greater account of the needs of black communities. This sequence is close to the process depicted in figure 5.1 as the participation theory of citizenship. Expanded participation has led to new political learning and a reorientation of policy achieved by working through existing institutions.

But the experience of black mobilization deviates from the expectations of the participation theory in one important respect. Political participation by African Americans has become normalized through the party system and is no longer dependent on the extraordinary stimulus of movement mobilization. The end of the civil rights movement has lowered the salience of mobilization as an expression of group solidarity. Turnout differences between blacks and whites in the entire nation remained approximately stable after 1972, but relative levels of information and efficacy among blacks have tended to fluctuate from election to election based on the same kinds of short-term forces that affect the white electorate.

Other investigations have also shown the importance of the immediate context in determining rates of black participation. Lawrence Bobo and Franklin Gilliam's (1990) investigation using the General Social Survey shows that African Americans are more likely to be politically involved in cities where there are blacks already in political office. Katherine Tate's (1994) analysis of the National Black Election Studies found patterns of surge and decline in black participation in the 1980s dependent on the Jesse Jackson presidential candidacies specifically and more generally on the issue appeals and candidate alternatives offered in each campaign. Priscilla Southwell (1988) found that the large increase in black turnout in the 1982 congressional elections was a response to conditions of high unemployment. The black working class increased its turnout over 1978, just as the white working class did; given the association of race with class, this translated into an increase of black turnout relative to white voting rates. These studies demonstrate the importance of specific issues and candidates in accounting for African American political participation, factors that affect blacks and whites alike. For blacks, though, this responsiveness to short-term forces is something new. It marks the end of the era in which the struggles of the civil rights movement created a generalized impulse toward high rates of political engagement and electoral participation among African Americans.

This is not to say that party mobilization has not succeeded in institutionalizing the changed levels of African American political skills and engagement originally developed in the context of movement mobilization. A return to the low rates of voter turnout and internal political efficacy characteristic of the early 1950s is all but unimaginable. But the spur to participation created by the heightened sense of group consciousness in the era of the civil rights movement has proved to be temporary. And although other investigations of this subject have focused solely on rates of registration and voting, the evidence presented here shows that the point can be extended to media use, political information, and perceived efficacy, as well.

The participation model of citizenship correctly predicted that extension of political rights to African Americans would result in significant increases in their political skills and degree of engagement with established institutions. The increases in voting, information, and perceived efficacy depicted in figures 5.2 through 5.6 tell us that the legacy of generations of exclusion from the political process was overcome in little more than a decade. And yet, the effect predicted by participation theorists has also proven to be temporally bounded. Having achieved a "normal" level of political participation and engagement (as defined by the rather lax standards of white America), African Americans no longer enjoy a "bonus" based upon group consciousness as fostered through movement mobilization.

Discussion

The earliest studies of the American electorate made it clear that the public possessed far less political information than one might think necessary for the proper exercise of the duties of citizenship. Although unwilling to tolerate "apathy without limit," Berelson, Lazarsfeld, and McPhee noted that "the apathetic segment of America probably has helped to hold the system together and cushioned the shock of disagreement, adjustment, and change" (1954, 322). Gabriel Almond and Sidney Verba's classic cross-national study of political cultures (1963) raised this finding to a general precept, concluding that the political culture best suited to democracy consists of a mixture of participant and deferential citizens. Too many deferential people and democracy has no defense against authoritarian leadership. Too many participants and democracy has no defense against the demands of the people.

Although formulated most clearly in the literature on democratic stability, the assumption of a trade-off between expanded participation and government authority is also found in debates on expansion of the suffrage that took place in Europe throughout the nineteenth century and in the spread of concern about the governability of democracies in the 1970s. The issues of universal manhood suffrage, later the vote for women, and then still later the propensity of citizen organizations to exert direct pressure on government were described time and again as innovations reducing the ability of public officials to govern effectively.

These are old battles for the liberal democracies, battles that are always eventually resolved in favor of inclusiveness. But these controversies have nonetheless affected social science research on participation. As Peter Natchez (1985) has shown, our images of voting are products of our visions of democracy. Political scientists generally view voting solely in instrumental terms, as a way of conveying public preferences to elites and of giving elites an incentive to be responsive to the public. Our studies of participation typically explore the effect of internal efficacy on turnout; only rarely do they examine the effect of turnout on internal efficacy.

And yet, our concern to understand the reasons for low levels of issue awareness among the electorate need not blind us to the fact that things can be otherwise. If it is normally rational for the electorate to be ill informed, it is easy enough to imagine conditions under which high levels of information are rational. The experience of African Americans in the 1950s and 1960s suggests that rates of information, internal efficacy, and participation increase when people anticipate an opportunity for increased political influence. Once the struggle for admission to the rights of citizenship had been joined through the civil rights movement, political knowledge and efficacy among African Americans increased dramatically.

If the experience of African Americans since the 1950s is representative, then movement mobilization and party mobilization work hand in hand. Movement mobilization raised blacks' levels of attentiveness, information, efficacy, and participation to unprecedented heights. The iron laws binding participation to socioeconomic status were temporarily abrogated. As party mobilization in periodic election campaigns has taken the place of civil rights movement campaigns, political engagement among African Americans has fallen back to expected levels based on socioeconomic status, levels that vary depending on the electoral context. This shows the ability of party politics to sustain advances in mobilization made through movements, even if they cannot maintain the atmosphere Aristide Zolberg has labeled a "moment of madness" (1972).

Ultimately, then, the optimism of the participation theorists of citizenship is affirmed. It would appear that in politics, as in other realms of life, we learn by doing. As Beverly Nash, a former slave elected to the Reconstruction era South Carolina Constitutional Convention, put it, "I believe, my friends and fellow-citizens, we are not prepared for this suffrage. But we can learn. Give a man tools and let him commence to use them, and in time he will learn the trade. So it is with voting. We may not understand it at the start, but in time we shall learn to do our duty" (cited in Morris 1975, 81).

The evidence presented here suggests that African Americans developed the attitudes and skills necessary to "learn the trade" of politics in a remarkably short period of time and to an extent one would not anticipate based on the elite theory of democracy. African Americans have responded to the experience of joining the electorate through movement mobilization as participation theorists predicted they would.

Notes

For helpful comments and other assistance on earlier versions of this chapter, we would like to thank John Geer, Jennifer Hochschild, Robert Luskin, Douglas Mills, Dennis Thompson, George Tsebelis, and Sidney Verba. If they have not discovered all our errors, the blame attaches solely to us.

1. What we have labeled the "elite" and "participation" theories of citizenship bear a close relationship to what others have called the "instrumental" and "developmental" perspectives on participation. For excellent reviews of these perspectives, see Bennett and Resnick 1988 and Dalton 1996, 277–83.

2. The American National Election Studies (NES) series provides questions in identical format for nearly all the data examined in this chapter. There are two exceptions. The media-use index in figure 5.4 required a recombination of categories to obtain approximate comparability for some years, and the political-information index in figure 5.5 is based on different questions in 1992 from those used for all prior years. These data are disseminated on *American National Election Studies, 1948–1994*, a CD-ROM issued in May 1995, available through the Inter-University Consortium for Political and Social Research, the University of Michigan, Ann Arbor.

3. For a review of evidence on the empowering effects of movement participation, see Rochon 1998, chaps. 4 and 5.

4. An elite theorist would not necessarily conclude that such groups as African Americans should not be enfranchised. However, the extension of citizenship rights does introduce painful trade-offs to an elite theorist and in practice may lead to proposals to moderate the pace or impact of change.

5. The demographic variables S_t, whose effects we wish to partial out, are education, income, occupational status, age, sex, and urbanization. Education is measured in years spent in school; along with income and age it is logarithmically transformed. Occupational status is the log of the occupational prestige score, urbanization is the log of a five-point scale, and sex is, of course, dichotomous. Figures 5.4 through 5.6 are based on ordinary least squares regression, since the dependent variables are continuous. Figures 5.2 and 5.3 are based on logistic regression, since their dependent variables are dichotomous. For other applications of a similar model, see Feldstein 1975, Verba, Nie, and Kim 1978, and Kabashima 1984.

6. This analysis uses self-reports of whether or not one voted and is therefore susceptible to errors stemming from misreporting. There is general agreement that blacks are more likely than whites to report falsely that they voted in the most recent election (Sigelman 1982; Silver, Anderson, and Abramson 1986; Abramson and Claggett 1984, 1986, 1989, and 1991). The reason for this appears to be the strong voting norm found in the black population; overreporting the vote is also more prevalent among educated whites who are most supportive of the idea that citizenship includes the duty to vote (Silver, Anderson, and Abramson 1986). Since we are more interested in trends than in the absolute difference between the races at any one point in time, the existence of overreporting is less important than its distribution over time. Paul Abramson and John Aldrich found

that there were no changes in the extent of overreported turnout in the NES data series since 1964, the first year in which a validated vote measure is available (Abramson and Aldrich 1982). As long as African Americans did not increase their overreporting of the vote between 1956 and 1964 (and as long as whites did not decrease their overreporting in that same period), the inferences from figures 5.2 and 5.3 concerning the timing and extent of electoral mobilization among African Americans are valid.

7. Respondents were asked how often they read newspapers and newsmagazines and how often they listen to the radio and watch television for political information. Responses to these four questions were combined into a single index of use of the mass media for political information. We were concerned that limited African American access to television in the 1950s might create artifactual increases in media use as television ownership spread. However, when we ran the analysis with a three-media index, leaving television out, we got the same results.

8. Knowing which party controls the House before and after the elections is the only objective question that has been put to respondents consistently since 1960. An objective question such as this is a better indicator of political knowledge than self-reported political interest, which was our prime alternative. In 1992 this measure was replaced by a lengthier battery of political information questions. Responses to those questions have been recoded to approximate the tripartite categorization of information levels generated by the "control of the House" questions.

9. Our measure of internal efficacy combines the questions on whether people like *R* have much say in politics and whether politics is too complicated for people like *R*.

References

Abramson, Paul, and John Aldrich. 1982. "The Decline of Electoral Participation in America." *American Political Science Review* 76 (Sept.): 502–21.

Abramson, Paul, and William Claggett. 1984. "Race-Related Differences in Self-Reported and Validated Turnout." *Journal of Politics* 46 (Aug.): 719–38.

———. 1986. "Race-Related Differences in Self-Reported and Validated Turnout in 1984." *Journal of Politics* 48 (May): 412–22.

———. 1989. "Race-Related Differences in Self-Reported and Validated Turnout in 1986." *Journal of Politics* 51 (May): 397–408.

———. 1991. "Racial Differences in Self-Reported and Validated Turnout in the 1988 Presidential Election." *Journal of Politics* 53 (Feb.): 186–97.

Almond, Gabriel, and Sidney Verba. 1963. *The Civic Culture.* Boston: Little, Brown.

Barnes, Elsie, and Ronald Proctor. 1994. "Black Politics in Tidewater, Virginia." In *Black Politics and Black Political Behavior,* ed. Hanes Walton Jr. Westport, Conn.: Praeger.

Bennett, Stephen Earl, and David Resnick. 1988. "Political Participation Reconsidered: Old Ideas and New Data." Paper presented at the annual meeting of the Midwest Political Science Association, Chicago, Apr.

Berelson, Bernard, Paul Lazarsfeld, and William McPhee. 1954. *Voting.* Chicago: University of Chicago Press.

Bobo, Lawrence, and Franklin Gilliam. 1990. "Race, Sociopolitical Participation, and Black Empowerment." *American Political Science Review* 84 (June): 377–93.

Button, James. 1989. *Blacks and Social Change: Impact of the Civil Rights Movement in Southern Communities.* Princeton: Princeton University Press.

Carmines, Edward, and James Stimson. 1989. *Issue Evolution: Race and the Transformation of American Politics.* Princeton: Princeton University Press.

Chong, Dennis. 1991. *Collective Action and the Civil Rights Movement.* Chicago: University of Chicago Press.

Coleman, Mary. 1994. "The Black Elected Elites in Mississippi: The Post–Civil Rights Apportionment Era." In *Black Politics and Black Political Behavior,* ed. Hanes Walton Jr. Westport, Conn.: Praeger.

Converse, Philip E. 1975. "Public Opinion and Voting Behavior." In *Handbook of Political Science,* vol. 4, ed. Fred Greenstein and Nelson Polsby. Reading, Mass.: Addison-Wesley.

Dalton, Russell. 1996. *Citizen Politics in Western Democracies.* 2d ed. Chatham, N.J.: Chatham House.

Feldstein, Martin. 1975. "Wealth, Neutrality, and Local Choice in Public Education." *American Economic Review* 65 (Mar.): 75–89.

Finkel, Steven. 1985. "Reciprocal Effects of Participation and Political Efficacy." *American Journal of Political Science* 29 (Nov.): 891–913.

———. 1987. "The Effect of Participation on Political Efficacy and Political Support: Evidence from a West German Panel." *Journal of Politics* 49 (May): 441–64.

Huntington, Samuel. 1975. "The United States." In *The Crisis of Democracy,* ed. Michel Crozier, Samuel Huntington, and Joji Watanuki. New York: New York University Press.

———. 1981. *American Politics: The Promise of Disharmony.* Cambridge: Harvard University Press.

Jennings, M. Kent. 1987. "Residues of a Movement." *American Political Science Review* 81 (June): 367–82.

Kabashima, Ikuo. 1984. "Supportive Participation with Economic Growth: The Case of Japan." *World Politics* 36 (Apr.): 309–38.

Karon, Bertram. 1958. *The Negro Personality.* New York: Springer.

Lawson, Steven. 1985. *In Pursuit of Power: Southern Blacks and Electoral Politics, 1965–1982.* New York: Columbia University Press.

Luskin, Robert. 1987. "Measuring Political Sophistication." *American Journal of Political Science* 31 (Nov.): 856–99.

Matthews, Donald, and James Prothro. 1966. *Negroes and the New Southern Politics.* New York: Harcourt, Brace and World.

McAdam, Doug. 1982. *Political Process and the Development of Black Insurgency, 1930–1970.* Chicago: University of Chicago Press.

Morris, Aldon. 1984. *The Origins of the Civil Rights Movement.* New York: Free Press.

Morris, Milton. 1975. *The Politics of Black America.* New York: Harper and Row.

Morrison, Minion K. C. 1987. *Black Political Mobilization: Leadership, Power, and Mass Behavior.* Albany: State University of New York Press.

Murphy, Walter, and Joseph Tannenhaus. 1968. "Public Opinion and Supreme Court: The Goldwater Campaign." *Public Opinion Quarterly* 32 (spring): 31–50.

Natchez, Peter. 1985. *Images of Voting/Visions of Democracy.* New York: Basic Books.

Nie, Norman, Sidney Verba, Henry Brady, Kay Schlozman, and Jane Junn. 1988. "Participation in America: Continuity and Change." Paper presented at the annual meeting of the Midwest Political Science Association, Chicago, Apr.

Olson, Marvin. 1970. "Social and Political Participation of Blacks." *American Sociological Review* 35 (Aug.): 682–97.

Pateman, Carole. 1970. *Participation and Democratic Theory.* Cambridge: Cambridge University Press.

Rochon, Thomas. 1998. *Culture Moves: Ideas, Activism, and Changing Values.* Princeton: Princeton University Press.

Schumpeter, Joseph. 1942. *Capitalism, Socialism, and Democracy.* New York: Harper and Row.

Shingles, Richard. 1981. "Black Consciousness and Political Participation: The Missing Link." *American Political Science Review* 75 (Mar.): 76–91.

Sigelman, Lee. 1982. "The Nonvoting Voter in Voting Research." *American Journal of Political Science* 26 (Feb.): 47–56.

Silver, Brian, Barbara Anderson, and Paul Abramson. 1986. "Who Overreports Voting?" *American Political Science Review* 80 (June): 613–24.

Southwell, Priscilla. 1988. "The Mobilization Hypothesis and Voter Turnout in Congressional Elections, 1974–1982." *Western Political Quarterly* 41 (June): 273–87.

Tate, Katherine. 1994. *From Protest to Politics: The New Black Voters in American Elections.* New York: Russell Sage Foundation.

Thernstrom, Abigail. 1987. *Whose Votes Count?* Cambridge: Harvard University Press.

Thompson, Dennis. 1970. *The Democratic Citizen: Social Science and Democratic Theory in the Twentieth Century.* New York: Cambridge University Press.

———. 1976. *John Stuart Mill and Representative Government.* Princeton: Princeton University Press.

U.S. Bureau of the Census. 1981. *Statistical Abstract of the United States: 1981.* Washington, D.C.: Government Printing Office.

Verba, Sidney, and Norman Nie. 1972. *Participation in America: Social Equality and Political Democracy.* New York: Harper and Row.

Verba, Sidney, Norman Nie, and Jae-on Kim. 1978. *Participation and Political Equality.* Cambridge: Cambridge University Press.

Zaller, John. 1992. *The Nature and Origins of Mass Opinion.* New York: Cambridge University Press.

Zolberg, Aristide. 1972. "Moments of Madness." *Politics and Society* 2 (winter): 183–207.

Part II

Campaigning

CHAPTER 6

Politicians as Prize Fighters
Electoral Selection and Incumbency Advantage

John Zaller

Leading accounts of congressional politics stress the capacity of House incumbents to develop strong ties with their constituents. By dint of strenuous effort—constant trips back to the district, chasing lost Social Security checks, helping win federal grants for the district—members of Congress (MCs) are said to cultivate electorates that trust them and are loyal to them personally, thereby creating an incumbency advantage over would-be challengers.

This essay challenges the notion that the loyalty of ordinary voters makes an important contribution to incumbency advantage. Voters develop attachments to politicians of their own party, but not, to judge from available data, to MCs independent of party. The reason that incumbent MCs win reelection at very high rates is the same reason that world heavyweight boxing champions win most of their title defenses: owing to their manner of selection, incumbent champions in both professions are simply better competitors than most of the opponents they face.

This chapter has three sections, two of which challenge the notion of voter loyalty and the last of which demonstrates that what Robert Erikson and Gerald Wright (1993) call electoral selection is a sufficient explanation for incumbency advantage. The first section argues that the best survey-based evidence for the existence of voter loyalty is undermined by an apparent artifact: the tendency of many survey respondents to concoct reports of personal contact with politicians they like or admire. If this admiration could withstand the attacks of strong challengers, it might be a basis for incumbency advantage, but this does not appear to be the case. The second section argues that the growth paths for incumbent vote margins and constituent attitudes toward incumbents are too dissimilar for the second to be a cause of the first. While the "personal vote" develops quickly in a "Sophomore Surge" at the time of first reelection, constituents develop attitudes toward their MCs much more slowly. Moreover, constituents' attitudes toward their MCs never become much more positive than at their first election. This and other evidence of a mismatch between vote margins and constituent attitudes belies the notion that voter loyalty underlies incumbency advantage. In light of these findings, the third part of the chapter considers sources of incumbency advantage that are not mediated by constituency attitudes, focusing in particular on electoral selection. The argument is that incumbents, who, in order to become incumbents, must either beat other incumbents or win open-seat contests, are a more selected group than challengers and hence likely to be more-skilled competitors—enough more skilled (as I seek to demonstrate by means of a Monte Carlo simulation) to explain the size and other specific features of incumbency advantage. The argument is buttressed by a comparison of career data from MCs and world heavyweight boxing champions, who are also a highly selected group.

Problems with Existing Evidence of Voter Loyalty

One would suppose that incumbency advantage would be one of the easier problems in political science to explain, but since its discovery some twenty-five years ago by Erikson (1971) and Mayhew (1974), concise understanding has been hard to come by. Gary Jacobson, in his authoritative synthesis of scholarship on congressional elections, offers the following explanation for how incumbents maintain themselves in office:

> A member's personal relationship with constituents can keep the district safely in the member's hands, but only through a continuing high level of personal attention, and only if potent new issues detrimental to the incumbent do not intrude. . . . A wide reelection margin is maintained only through unrelenting entrepreneurial effort; let there be a letup or a slip-up that attracts and is exploited by a formidable opponent and it can evaporate quickly. (1997b, 45)

Throughout his book, Jacobson places great importance on a "member's personal relationship with constituents," yet, as in this passage, he also acknowledges many complicating factors. In a later passage, he describes the benefits of ceaseless efforts to build trust among constituents:

> The payoffs are clear. A member who is trusted, accessible, and thought to be 'one of us' will have much less trouble defending against personal attacks. Explanations for controversial votes will be heard more sympathetically, institutional or partisan failures, even notorious ethical lapses, may go unpunished.
> This kind of relationship cannot be developed overnight, nor can it be maintained without continual reinforcement. (74)

Efforts to contact constituents, help them with problems they may have, and propagandize them through the mass media are part of the process by which MCs develop relationships with their constituents, and, as Jacobson finds, "the net effect of successful attempts to reach voters is clearly helpful to candidates" (104).

That the personal relationship MCs develop with their constituencies is a major component of incumbency advantage is the prevailing view in the congressional elections literature, most notably in the agenda-setting work of Richard Fenno (1978), Morris Fiorina (1989), Bruce Cain, John Ferejohn, and Morris Fiorina (1987), Thomas Mann (1978), Thomas Mann and Raymond Wolfinger (1980), and Gary Jacobson (1997b). It is easy, moreover, to gain the impression from this research that this personal relationship, built up by unrelenting effort on the part of the MC, is the most important component of incumbency advantage.

Significantly, much of the strongest evidence for the importance of the personal relationship comes from public opinion surveys, especially the National Elections Studies, in which citizens report both the contact they have had with their MC and their attitudes toward the MC. Studies that have measured actual MC activity (rather than measures derived from the reports of survey respondents) have generally found weaker, null, or even negative relations with constituent attitudes. One of the stronger pieces of positive evidence is reported by Albert Cover and Bruce Brumberg (1982), who find that the effects of sending baby care information with the MC's name on it to new parents improves the MC's image with the parents, but the general significance of this study is unclear.[1] Perhaps the most highly regarded study using direct measures of casework, that undertaken by Cain, Ferejohn, and Fiorina (1987), presents evidence that is decidedly mixed, at least for the American case. Jacobson's (1997b) recent review of the relevant evidence continues to describe it as equivocal.[2]

As Fiorina (1981) was the first to argue, this generally weak or even negative evidence cannot be taken at face value. The incumbents who work the hardest to cultivate support in their districts—those running for reelection in districts that, for one reason or another, are disinclined to worship at the feet of their local congressional representative—may well be the ones who face the toughest tasks. If so, higher levels of MC effort could be associated with somewhat low levels of political support—even if the efforts themselves were effective in increasing support from its initially low level.

Steven Levitt and James Snyder (1997) provide strong evidence for Fiorina's argument, concerning both the actual effect of MC activity and the confounds that make the effect difficult to observe. Their main finding is that higher levels of federal spending—for which the incumbent MC presumably claims credit—are associated with higher vote margins, but the effects of the spending do not show up clearly until the electoral weakness that motivates them is taken into account. The results of the Levitt and Snyder study say nothing, however, about attitudes of individual voters or the degree to which their loyalty may be won by particularistic benefits. It is, for example, consistent with their evidence that local politicians refrain from supporting challenges to MCs who are adept at bringing home "pork" (whether or not most voters know anything about it).

In order to show that the efforts of MCs to maintain themselves in office operate through their efforts on voter attitudes, as much literature asserts, it is necessary to examine those attitudes directly. This has the potential advantage, as Fiorina (1981) has pointed out, of identifying the particular individuals who have benefited from contacts with their MC, thereby avoiding the endogeneity problem that arises when vulnerable MCs make greater efforts at constituency service than do secure MCs. Survey data, however, have another sort of endogeneity problem: individuals may exaggerate or even concoct their degree of contact with their MC, perhaps to rationalize an intended vote. This problem was first raised by John McAdams and John Johannes (1981) and continues to reverberate in the literature. David Romero (1996) claims to have solved this problem, but the instrumental variable he uses in his analysis is a prime suspect for the same kind of endogeneity bias he is attempting to correct for (as I discuss below). More generally, this section provides what I believe is the first concrete evidence that standard indicators of MC contact are likely to be biased and hence unusable. In so doing, it undermines what I take to be the strongest existing evidence that MC efforts to woo constituents have any direct, widespread effect on constituents' attitudes.

This discussion begins with data on constituents who claim to have personally met their MC, a claim that appears on its face to be among the most concrete and hence least susceptible to biased reporting. This indicator of contact has an added advantage: it is, presumably, a reasonably simple task to figure out what plausible rates of MC contact ought to be and to check them. As it happens, personal contact is also one of the stronger determinants of MCs' evaluations (Cain, Ferejohn, and Fiorina 1987, 161, table 6.17).

Even a casual examination of survey reports of personal contact immediately raises the suspicion that they are flawed. Consider, by way of setting expectations for what reasonable rates of contact might be, the following passage from Jacobson:

> Most politicians have faith in the personal touch; if they can just talk to people and get them to listen, they can win their support. Some evidence supports this notion. Larry Pressler, now a senator from South Dakota, won his first House election in 1974 with a campaign that consisted largely of meeting people one-on-one. "I tried to shake 500 hard hands a day," Pressler has said.

"That is where you really take their hand and look at them and talk to them a bit. I succeeded in doing that seven days a week. I put in a lot of twelve-hour days, starting at a quarter to six in the morning at some plant in Sioux Falls or Madison." Pressler estimates that he shook 300 to 500 hands per day for 80 days. "You would not believe the physical and mental effort this requires." (1997b, 69)

The difficulty with this approach to winning office, Jacobson continues, is that "it is simply impossible to meet more than a small fraction of the electorate during a single campaign." This contention is surely correct. Let us take Pressler, who gained fame for having met what must be close to the maximum number of people it is possible to meet in a campaign. Meeting 400 people per day for eighty days comes out to 32,000 people. If we assume that a contemporary congressional district has about 575,000 people and that 70 percent of them are of voting age, then the number of people Pressler met would constitute about eight percent of the voting-age population of the district.

In light of this calculation of what is possible with maximum effort, what are we to make of the fact that, on average, nine percent of voters from districts with winning challengers in 1980—that is, candidates winning congressional office for the first time—claimed to have met the winner, and that this average figure was 23 percent in 1982?[3] In the 1990s, the reported rate of personal contact with candidates for open seats is around 8 percent (Jacobson 1997b, 100, table 5.7).

One can, of course, note that many contacts (even in Pressler's campaign) must involve something less than "really tak[ing] their hand and look[ing] them in the eye and talk[ing] to them a bit." One can also make some allowance for the possibility that candidates meet a higher proportion of voters than of all constituents[4] and that a few voters may have met candidates in connection with campaigns for other offices.[5] But even granting these allowances, it is hard to avoid concern that reported rates of contact are suspiciously high.

There are other reasons to be suspicious of reports of personal contact. Cain, Ferejohn, and Fiorina (1987) find that rates of personal contact are especially high for MCs who have large Washington staffs. Why large Washington staffs should foster high rates of personal contact with constituents is hard to explain, and it becomes still harder once it is revealed that MCs with larger staffs make fewer trips home to their districts. Could it be that MCs with large Washington staffs are more important and more heavily covered in the media, and that for this reason constituents feel they know them?

Another oddity is that reports of personal contact are as high for U.S. senators as for House members, despite the fact that most states are much larger than a typical House district.[6] Again, the suspicion that comes to mind is that citizens are overreporting contact with famous politicians they like or admire.

Without doubt, there is exaggeration in reports of contact with MCs. The only question is whether the overreporting is random or rather is systematically related to the respondent's attitude toward the MC. The argument for expecting random overreporting would be that overreporting is simply another form of social desirability bias akin to overreporting of voter turnout—and, as such, implies nothing about attitudes toward the particular MC with whom contact is claimed. Figure 6.1, however, suggests that the overreporting is systematic. This figure shows the 1992 and 1994 percentages of respondents who claimed to have met their Democratic MC in relation to the MCs' electoral fortunes. Survey respondents whose Democratic MC ran about as well in 1994 as in 1992 (fig. 6.1, "no change" on the x-axis) were about equally likely to report contact in each year; however, survey respondents whose MC suffered large electoral declines in 1994 (fig. 6.1, 10–15 and 15+ points) were significantly less likely to report contact in the latter year. The difference in contact rates between respondents whose MCs lost 10 or more points achieves statistical significance at the conventional level ($t = 2.41$). This reduction in reported contact is all the more notable in that it goes against the grain of a considerable element of brute reality, namely, that tougher campaigns inevitably involve more electioneering than easy ones, giving people more opportunities to actually meet their MC. Note that these results are based not on panel data but on simple sampling of respondents from the same districts at two points in time. Note also that the survey question asks whether the person has "ever" met the MC and that the measure of electoral success is actual election results rather than a possibly endogenous survey measure.[7]

The electoral duress necessary to produce the effects shown in figure 6.1 is relatively uncommon in congressional elections. Even in 1994, an electoral cataclysm for the Democrats, the average Democratic MC within the American National Election Studies (NES) sampling frame lost an average of only 3.7 points in support, compared with the previous election. Moreover, the 1994 NES sample includes only about a hundred respondents from districts whose MCs lost 10 points or more—barely enough to detect even large effects. The only other recent election producing such a large decline in vote share among MCs in the NES sampling frame was the 1980 election, for which the decline in support among Democratic MCs is also about 4 points.

Because of the difficulty in finding enough cases in any individual NES study, I have aggregated data from the 1978 to 1994 NES studies into a single test of the effect of electoral duress—that is, the effect of going from a very easy race to a very hard race—on reports of having personally met one's MC. The results are shown in table 6.1. The criterion for an easy race in the initial period is winning at least 60 percent of the vote in a contested election, while the criterion for a

Figure 6.1 Effect of Electoral Success on Claims to Having Personally Met Democratic MCs, 1992 and 1994

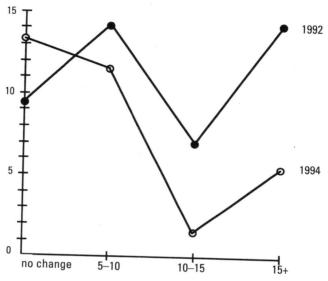

Percentage of voters who claim to have personally met their incumbent Democratic MC

Decline in Share of Two-Party Vote, 1992–1994 (percentage)

	no change	5–10%	10–15%	15%+
1992 *N*	426	181	57	77
1994 *N*	419	189	61	55

Districts in the NES sampling frame in each category having contested elections both years: Democratic vote loss less than five percentage points: 103, 509, 513, 526, 529, 535, 542, 703, 1005, 1304, 1309, 1312, 2003, 2004, 2005, 2101, 2102, 2205, 2101, 2102, 2205, 2209, 2212, 2215, 2304, 2308, 2504, 2506, 2509, 3001, 3009, 3010, 3206, 3207, 3217, 3218, 3229, 3503, 3704, 3801, 4315, 4604, 4608, 4609, 4707. Vote loss of five points to ten points: 3201, 4709, 508, 3307, 2305, 3301, 602, 512, 1301, 4311, 2216, 4402, 3814, 4309, 601, 1007, 3308, 3210, 519. Vote loss of ten points to fifteen points: 306, 902, 1303, 1305, 1319, 4205, 4904. Vote loss of fifteen points or more: 4313, 105, 1404, 1504, 4313. First one or two digits of the numbers refer to the alphabetical order of the states; last two digits refer to the congressional district number.

Source: American National Election Studies.

hard race is losing at least 10 percent of previous support and falling below 60 percent of the vote.

As table 6.1 shows, the tendency of respondents to report less contact with MCs who come under electoral duress holds for the period 1978 to 1994.[8] Though the tendency is not so strong overall as it seems to be in 1994, the effect is substantively important—a decline of about one-quarter in reported personal meetings—and achieves statistical significance at the level of $p = .10$.[9]

Since the question about meeting one's MC was first asked in 1978 and discontinued after 1994, table 6.1 includes the universe of NES data for which this test can be made. However, I investigated three additional hypotheses that I hoped would shed additional light on its significance:

• I expected that congressional voters would be more apt than nonvoters to report reduced contact with their MC. My reasoning was that voters would be more psychologically involved in and cognitively aware of congressional pol-

Table 6.1 Changes in Reported Claims of Having Met MC, 1978 to 1994

	All Respondents	Citizens Who Hardly or Never Follow Public Affairs	Citizens Who Usually or Always Follow Public Affairs	Mean Thermometer Score
Easy races	14.1%	7.1%	18.5%	64.4%
N	297	113	184	289
Hard races	10.6%	9.2%	11.7%	55.8%
N	263	98	163	278
Difference	−3.5	+2.1	−6.8	−8.5
One-tailed probability value of difference	.105	—	.037	.000

Source: American National Election Studies.

Note: Cell entries are percentage of respondents who report having ever personally met their member of Congress. Results are for MCs who went from very easy races in one election to very difficult races in the next election, according to criteria defined in the text. Reapportionment years are excluded. The following list gives the districts included in the data for each election: 1978–80: 542, 2509, 3004, 3509, 3824; 1982–84: 3307, 4203; 1984–86: 2202, 3231; 1986–88: 2212; 1988–1990: 509, 517, 2105, 2209, 2502, 2509, 3818, 4708; 1992–94: 105, 1319, 1303, 1404, 1504, 4313, 4904. The first digit or digits refer to the alphabetical order of the states; the second two digits refer to the congressional district number.

itics—both more motivated and more able to exaggerate contact with MCs who were doing well. The data supported this expectation, but very weakly.

• Continuing to pursue this idea, I reasoned that respondents who follow public affairs ought to be more likely to show the effect of electoral duress on reported contact, since they would be more likely to know which MCs were in electoral duress and which were not. This expectation was strongly supported by the data, as shown in table 6.1.[10]

• I expected that the respondents most likely to exaggerate contact with MCs and then abandon them in time of duress would be independents and out-party members. This expectation was entirely unsupported by the data; in fact, there was a modest tendency in the other direction.

I further investigated the effect of electoral duress on the tendency of respondents to report having contacted their MC's office and been "very satisfied" with the results of the contact. I expected that reported satisfaction would diminish as electoral duress increased. This expectation was supported, but very weakly; all three of the interactive expectations described in the previous paragraphs also held, but also weakly.[11] I also investigated more complicated hypotheses, but the results, most of which were somewhat encouraging to my general position, are not worth describing in detail.

Before drawing conclusions from all this, I would like to discuss the problem of statistical inference in small data sets of the sort I am using here. As is well known, tests of statistical significance depend on the assumption that one has clear a priori expectations about what to test for. Yet in this case, as in much research, I began my analysis with only hunches and proceeded to refine them through data analysis. How, then, can I say anything meaningful about the statistical properties of results I have turned up? I know of no models on how to proceed, but I think a thumbnail history of my investigation may help readers to judge what I have turned up.

Working initially with the 1978–80 pair of elections, I thoroughly explored the data. Everyone who has done data analysis knows what this means. For several ways of slicing the data, I could, from the beginning, find clear differences along the lines reported in table 6.1, but for other ways, little or nothing. Data from the 1992–94 pair of elections later became available. From my first look at these data, I found strong effects of the kind shown in figure 6.1 for the "ever personally met" item, and just about anything I tried left these effects more or less intact. I also investigated other items, especially the items asking whether respondents had ever contacted their MC's office. The results of some of these tests were encouraging and were circulated in earlier drafts of this chapter, but they were complicated, and in the end I decided not to rely on them.[12] Following the advice of a colleague, however, I decided to run a straight-up hypothesis test of the effect of electoral duress on the "ever personally met" item for all available data. The result is described in the first column of table 6.1. A key question about this test is how I chose the cutpoints for "easy" and "hard" elections, since the results would mean little if I had ransacked a small data set in search of the most favorable cutpoints. The answer is that I chose what I thought would be the best cutpoints—those that would maximize the difference between "easy" and "hard" elections while yet preserving as many cases as possible for analysis—and I ran the test only once.[13]

From these several pieces of evidence I draw two conclusions. One safe conclusion is that it is difficult to study incumbency advantage with standard survey designs. Sample sizes of fifteen hundred to two thousand cases may be adequate for making point estimates of public opinion on particular issues, but for the purposes of this section they are too small. Even aggregated over a sixteen-year period, NES surveys are still too small: the large majority of incumbent elections in recent decades have been essentially nonelections and, as such, are uninformative about the dynamics of the few real elections that do occur. Even in years of intense electoral turbulence, the percentage of voters facing a real electoral choice is small. Thus in 1994, the American National Election Studies interviewed only 182 people from districts in which Democratic incumbents got 55 percent of the vote or less, and of these, only 107 reported voting. This scarcity of data must be counted among the important reasons that incumbency advantage has been difficult to understand. *Inter alia*, it forces scholars into fine analyses of the sort undertaken in table 6.1—analyses that are as important to report as they are difficult to conduct in a credible manner.[14]

Not only is there a paucity of pertinent data, but much of what data exists is probably biased. This, I believe, is also a safe conclusion, for two reasons. First, the rate of reported contact with MCs is much too high, and it is even more exaggerated for better-known but less-accessible U.S. senators. This obvious overreport should occasion more caution than it often does. Second, and compounding the overreport, there is evidence, particularly in table 6.1, that overreporting is correlated with the incumbent's political standing.

Biased overreporting of contact with MCs can defeat almost any attempt to use data like that from the NES surveys to discern the true effect of such contact, including the most sophisticated of these attempts, that of Rivers and Fiorina (1989). They find that, after making a correction for endogeneity bias of the type Fiorina (1981) has identified, there are strong, positive links between member activity and an individual-level indicator of political support in the district. Any such analysis, however, depends on the assumption that respondents are reporting their contact more-or-less honestly rather that concocting it to fit the incumbent's level of popular support. Although my analysis reports no fault with the particular items they use, it raises doubt about any items that ask respondents to report their contact with political figures.[15] And it raises still more doubt about other analyses, such as Romero's (1996), that use the "personally met" item as an exogenous cause of constituent attitudes. Finally, if even these sophisticated analyses are suspect on grounds of endogeneity bias, then the large majority of more straightforward analyses—notably, those that simply use respondent reports of contact or satisfaction with the MC's response to contact as exogenous predictors of voting for the incumbent—are even more so.

In making this argument, I am challenging the strongest available evidence that MC efforts at constituency service have any widespread, direct effect on the attitudes of constituents. This questioning of existing evidence is an essentially negative task. In the next two sections, I begin to adduce positive evidence about what is happening.

Positive Evidence of Absence of Voter Loyalty

Many members of Congress win their first elections by something less than a landslide and then go immediately to work to consolidate their position. In a furious round of activity, they contact as many voters, activists, and group members as possible in an effort to increase their margin of electoral safety (Fenno 1978). Their payoff is the so-called Sophomore Surge, which is the amount by which incumbents' winning margin increases at the time of their first reelection (Alford and Brady 1993). On average, the Sophomore Surge is about seven to nine percentage points in share of the two-party vote.

Members of Congress do not, of course, cease working their districts after their first reelections. They continue intensive activities for several more elections in the "expansionist" phase of their careers. Later, in the "protectionist" phase of their careers, many members become more interested in lawmaking in Washington and consequently scale back their district-oriented activities.

To capture these three phases of a congressional career—that is, the Sophomore Surge, the more general expansionist phase, and the protectionist phase—I have estimated the following model:

$$\text{margin}_t = b_0 + b_1(\text{incumbent}_t) + b_2(\text{terms}_t) + b_3(\text{terms squared}_t), \qquad (1)$$

where

margin_t = margin of victory, as defined immediately below,

incumbent_t = a variable that takes the value of zero in the member's initial election and one in all elections thereafter,

terms_t = the number of prior terms served by MC of district t, and

terms squared_t = terms squared.

The expectation in specifying the model in this way is that the incumbency variable will capture the Sophomore Surge that occurs at the time of the first reelection; that the variable for number of terms will capture additional gains accruing to the incumbent in later terms of the expansionist phase; and that the variable for "terms squared" will capture whatever falloff may occur in the late years of the congressional career.

In estimating this model, I define margin of victory as

margin = percent of two-party vote − 50 percent.

Before applying this model, it is necessary to decide what to do with uncontested races. To set them aside, as is sometimes done, would be to set aside those cases in which incumbents have been most successful in generating electoral security, thereby understating the amount of electoral security that develops. On the other hand, to regard victory in an uncontested race as evidence that the MC has captured 100 percent of the vote would probably exaggerate MCs' actual level of support.

To resolve this problem, I calculated the average 1978 share of the vote for incumbents who were uncontested in 1980 but did have opponents in 1978. This figure, 85 percent, might plausibly be assigned as the average vote share in uncontested races. Yet 85 percent seems an underestimate of actual political support, for two reasons: first, some MCs were also uncontested in 1978, and second, lack of opposition, especially if it recurs, should be given some weight as an indicator of electoral security. In light of these data and considerations, I set the vote share of uncontested MCs at 90 percent rather than 85 percent.

The results of applying equation (1) to data on victory margins in 1980 and 1990 are shown in the first column of table 6.2. These two elections are near the extremes of electoral volatility, with 1980 a turbulent year and 1990 an unusually quiet one, so lumping them together, as I do in this analysis, may give a rough idea of general patterns.[16] As can be seen, the only significant coefficient is for the 0–1 variable intended to capture the Sophomore Surge effect. (The same is true for either set of data analyzed separately.) The other two coefficients, which do not approach statistical significance, suggest a gentle nonmonotonicity, such that victory margins rise slightly through the early terms of a member's career, the expansionist phase, and decline very slightly thereafter. A graph of this nonmonotonic effect is shown in figure 6.2. The figure shows results through seventeen terms because only 1 percent of MCs seeking reelection in those years had service longer than that, making it hard to tell what actual electoral trends might be above that point. The main finding is nonetheless clear: MCs gain essentially all the electoral security they are likely to get at the time of their first reelection to office. Subsequent efforts to cultivate support in the district, which continue well after the first reelection bid, generate scarcely any additional support.

Figure 6.2 Effect of Terms of Service on Average Margin of Victory and
Spending Patterns in 1980 and 1990 House Elections

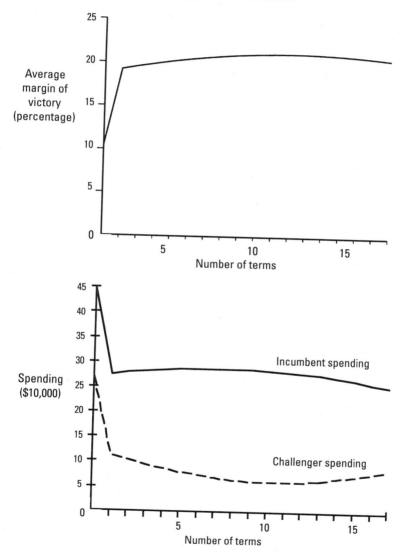

Source: Data from American National Election Studies.
Note: Victory margin in the top figure is defined as share of the vote minus 50 percent.
In open-seat contests in the lower figure, winners are defined as incumbents and losers
as challengers.

Table 6.2 Coefficients for Effect of Time in Office on Selected Indicators of MC Support among Voters

	Margin of Victory	Recall Name	Recognize Name	Rate at 51+	Rate at 61+	Thermometer Score	Net of Likes and Dislikes	Sum of Likes	Sum of Dislikes
Intercept	10.48	-0.08	1.85	0.36	-0.34	63.7	0.44	0.89	0.45
Incumbent "Sophomore Surge" (0 if open seat, 1 otherwise)	8.32 (1.72)	-0.26 (.15)	0.36 (.22)	0.59 (.15)	0.58 (.15)	8.57 (1.74)	0.58 (.13)	0.33 (.11)	-0.25 (.06)
Prior terms of service	0.41 (.33)	0.030 (.030)	0.11 (.06)	0.041 (.033)	0.033 (.030)	-0.25 (.34)	-0.030 (.029)	-0.010 (.025)	0.019 (.013)
Prior terms squared	-0.018 (.020)	-0.0022 (.0019)	-0.0047 (.0039)	-0.0013 (.0021)	-0.0008 (.0019)	0.031 (.021)	.0028 (.0018)	0.0017 (.0015)	-.0011 (.0008)
N	854	4213	4198	4194	4194	3863	1984	1984	1984
Adjusted r-square	.05	.001	.005	.013	.014	.014	.015	.009	.009
Range of dependent variable:	0-45	0-1	0-1	0-1	0-1	0-100	-4 to +4	0-4	0-4

Source: American National Election Studies, 1995.

Note: Model is equation (1) in text. Estimation is by OLS or logit, as appropriate, with standard errors of coefficients shown in parentheses. Margin of victory data are from 1980 and 1990; likes/dislikes data are from 1978 and 1986 NES studies; remaining analyses are based on pooled data from the 1978, 1980, 1986, 1988, and 1990 NES surveys. For the five-sample data set, dummies for year were added to model, though estimates of the dummy coefficients are not shown; the omitted category was 1978. All analyses exclude, on grounds of conceptual ambiguity, cases in which MC's most recent election was first election to office in a special election.

Admittedly, this conclusion rests on a highly simplified analysis, in that it uses cross-sectional evidence as a basis for making inferences about a dynamic process. The analysis is, in this respect, below the standard in the field, which has developed extremely sophisticated measures of incumbency advantage. But notwithstanding its simplicity, my approach yields results that are close to what others have found,[17] and at the same time—and this is the justification for it— the regression model at the core of my approach makes an excellent vehicle for summarizing a wide variety of evidence in a comparable format, as will be apparent shortly.

Let me, then, return to my substantive argument with this claim: The pattern of results in figure 6.2 is strong positive evidence against the view that MCs build up their "personal vote" by dint of the efforts they make to woo individual voters, for this reason: given the huge size of congressional districts, the first-year surge in support is too large in relation to the gains in the next few electoral cycles. If the personal vote really depended on the cultivation of individual voter support, it would develop more gradually over the first several years of an incumbent's service rather than all at once.

A more likely explanation for the observed pattern of surge and stasis is this: In their initial election to office, MCs face either a sitting incumbent or an open-seat race. In either case, their opponent is likely to be skilled and well funded. But strong challengers appear only intermittently. Hence, it is likely that the Sophomore Surge is the effect of a sudden decline in the average quality of electoral opposition.

To test this argument, I estimated the model in equation (1) for data on campaign spending by both incumbents and their opponents. The data are from 1980 and 1990, with no adjustment for inflation.[18] "Incumbent spending" refers to either sitting MCs or winners of open-seat contests. "Challenger spending" refers to either opponents of sitting MCs or losers in open-seat contests. As shown graphically in the bottom half of figure 6.2, there is a large fall in average level of spending at the time of an MC's first reelection—a sophomore slump in which spending by both candidates falls dramatically—and no strong temporal trend after that.[19] Since incumbents can usually spend as much as they need in order to be competitive, the tandem declines in spending should be interpreted to mean the absence of a strong opponent at the time of first reelection. It thus appears that the Sophomore Surge in the MC margin of victory may be due, in significant part, to a sharp decline in the level of effort or quality of the political opposition.

The spending data in this analysis refer to averages, which, in the case of opposition spending, is especially misleading. If we examine median spending, we find the following: In open-seat elections in 1990, the median level of spending by the loser was about $365,000; in races involving incumbents seeking their first reelection in that year, the median level of challenger spending was about

$36,000, which is a tenfold difference. For MCs in 1990, these figures were $640,000 in first elections and $470,000 in first reelections. It thus appears that, in the typical "sophomore" reelection bid, the typical incumbent is both adequately financed and without a strong opponent—a combination that could easily explain the one-time surge in margin of victory that occurs at that time.[20]

Before accepting this argument, however, let us examine some additional evidence. The notion that MCs build up the "personal vote" by building up credit with individual voters implies, in light of figure 6.2, that MCs should be substantially better known and better liked at the time of their first reelection than when they first won office. To test this implication, let us examine the relation between "terms of service" and each of several indicators of voter attitudes toward their MC:

- Name recall and name recognition
- Degree of warmth of ratings on the feeling thermometer
- Likes and dislikes of MC

I begin with the two indicators of cognitive awareness: whether voters can recall the name of their MC and whether they recognize the MC, in the sense of being willing to rate him or her on a hundred-point feeling thermometer. The model used to analyze these indicators is equation (1), including, as before, variables for Sophomore Surge, number of prior terms served, and prior terms squared. The data are from the set of recent NES surveys unaffected by reapportionment, namely, those of 1978, 1980, 1986, 1988, and 1990. Year dummy variables are included to capture any aggregate temporal or survey-related effects.[21]

The results on the effect of length of service on voter awareness are shown in the second and third columns of table 6.2. The main point is that the Sophomore Surge, so prominent in the analysis of margins of victory, fails to emerge consistently in these data. For name recall, the Sophomore Surge appears to run in reverse, and for name recognition, the effect is small. These effects are shown graphically in figure 6.3. The main story in figure 6.3 is that constituents are almost as familiar with their MCs at the time of first election as they are at any subsequent time. This is perhaps unavoidable in the case of name recognition, a low-threshold indicator already showing high levels of awareness at the first reading. But there is plenty of room for gain in name recall, and none occurs. Indeed, name recall declines slightly at first reelection.

I turn now to indicators of affect toward the MC, beginning with three open-ended measures: the sum of likes on the traditional NES question, the sum of dislikes, and a net score. The results of applying the model in equation (1) are shown in table 6.2 and figure 6.4. This analysis includes data only from the 1978 and 1986 surveys.

Figure 6.3 How Terms of Service Affect Voter Awareness of MC

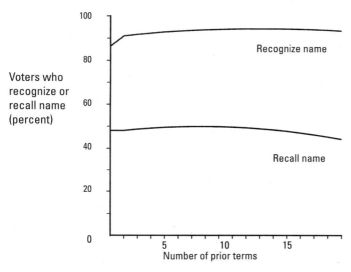

Source: Data from *American National Election Studies* 1995.
Note: Estimates are based on coefficients in table 6.2.

Figure 6.4 How Terms of Service Affect Voter Likes and Dislikes of MC

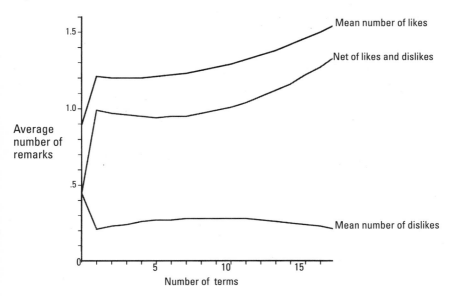

Note: Estimates based on coefficients in Table 6.2.

In contrast with the data on political awareness, these indicators exhibit un-equivocal evidence of a Sophomore Surge. The Surge variable picks up a decline in dislikes and a spike in likes, leading to a marked change in the indicator of net affect. In subsequent elections, likes continue to grow and dislikes to di-minish, thus generating a trend toward greater net liking of the incumbent.

These data articulate nicely with both the Sophomore Surge effect shown in figure 6.2 and the observational evidence on the continued district-oriented ac-tivity of MCs following their first reelections. In short, they appear to constitute confirming evidence for the standard view of the importance of the reelection-oriented activities of MCs.

There are, however, reasons to regard this evidence with reserve. First, the mean number of likes, though constantly rising, never gets very high. After thirty-five years in office, the average is still hovering around 1.5 comments, many of which have little substantive content. There may be, in addition, an im-portant element of social desirability in the expression of even this amount of regard for the MC, since it could be embarrassing to be unable to say anything at all about an official one has just rated on a feeling thermometer. (In both 1978 and 1986, the likes and dislikes questions immediately followed the set of ther-mometer ratings.)

A final piece of evidence comes from the standard NES feeling thermom-eters, which elicit constituents' feelings of warmth or coolness toward their MC. The thermometer scores have been recoded to create three alternative versions of the same variable: whether a person recognizes and rates the MC at 51 de-grees or higher; whether a person recognizes and rates the MC at 61 degrees or higher; and the average thermometer rating of those who make a rating. Plots of these indicators are shown in figure 6.5.

The pattern for these measures falls between that of the cognitive indicators, on one side, and the likes/dislikes measures, on the other—though, as I eyeball the data, they are more similar to the awareness measures. There is a statistically significant Sophomore Surge on all three affect measures, but it is not large. Thereafter, ratings commence a very slow rise. At its peak, the expected ther-mometer score for an MC has risen just 4.4 degrees above what it was at the time of the first reelection. The main story here is that, as in the case of candidate awareness, evaluations of MCs do not change much over the course of a con-gressional career.

The significance of these effects, small as they are, is by no means obvious. For one thing, some fraction of the increase may be due to selection effects, such that better-liked incumbents survive to become senior incumbents while less well-liked MCs get weeded out—without anyone actually becoming better liked. Another problem is that the gains on the thermometer scores appear to be, as

Daniel Lowenstein (1992) earlier maintained, quite ephemeral. This point can be seen by returning to table 6.1, which shows mean thermometer scores for sets of incumbents who had "easy" races in one election and "hard" ones in the next. Just before entering a "hard" race, these incumbents had scores on the feeling thermometers that were slightly above the mean of all MCs in the period 1978 to 1994,[22] but, as can be seen, their scores fell once they came under pressure in the following election. The average drop was 8.5 points, from 65.4 in one election to 55.8 in the next. What this quite dramatically shows is that the good feeling incumbents painstakingly build up over the years, small as it is, is only fair-weather support that vanishes under stress.

If, in addition to all this, we now take account of the fact that, as shown in figure 6.3, MCs are hardly better known after twenty or thirty years in office than they were when first elected, we must be skeptical of a conclusion that these increases in positive affect toward MCs, however exactly they are generated, have any political importance.

Figure 6.5 How Terms of Service Affect Voter Evaluations of MC

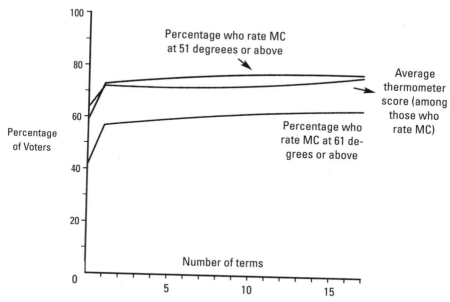

Source: Data from *American National Election Studies.*
Note: Estimates are based on coefficients in table 6.2. The *y*-axis, "percentage of constituents," also represents "degrees on feeling thermometer."

In the end, then, the largest and most portentous of the Sophomore Surge effects remains the huge downward surge in challenger spending. It is easy to imagine that this drop, in combination with continued, relatively heavy spending by the MC, could drive all the other indicators of Sophomore Surge. Of course, it can well be argued that the reason incumbents are able to enjoy a slump in the spending of their opponents is that potential opponents and their backers recognize that the incumbents would be difficult or impossible to beat in a full-out fight. I readily acknowledge this point. But I contend that the reason incumbents seem hard to beat is not that their constituents know and hold them in extremely high esteem. It is more likely for reasons of electoral selection (as I argue later).

One difficulty with all of the data examined so far is that they come from the fall election season and are therefore susceptible to campaign effects. My conclusions would be more certain if there were corroborating evidence from a nonelectoral period. Happily, such evidence exists. The 1993 NES Pilot Study (*American National Election Studies* 1993), carried out midway in the first term of a set of newly elected MCs, presented versions of all the attitudinal indicators examined in figures 6.4 and 6.5.[23] Hence, we are able to get "midcourse" readings on name recall, name recognition, feeling thermometer scores, and likes and dislikes. The results are shown in table 6.3.

The first point to notice is that citizens do not seem to become more familiar with their MCs during the interelection period; rather, the trend on the two cognitive variables—name recall and name recognition—is in the other direction. This is as true for newly elected MCs, who are presumably "working their districts" especially hard, as for established MCs.

At the same time, there is evidence that MCs are at work in their districts and that their work is having some effect. The decay rate for name recall of challengers—who in most cases do nothing to keep themselves alive in the minds of citizens after the election is over—is far greater than for name recall of winning candidates. This strongly suggests that winning candidates would fade more rapidly from the memory of constituents if they did nothing to counteract the natural tendency of memory to decay.[24]

The data on the three affective measures—thermometer scores, likes, and dislikes—must be summarized separately for newly elected and previously elected MCs. For previously elected MCs, the three affect measures show no clear pattern of gains or losses. For them, therefore, the story seems to be stasis, which is exactly what figures 6.4 and 6.5 would lead us to expect for this group. For newly elected members, all three affect indicators, each of which is measured independently, improved. This pattern would be expected to occur by chance only once in 2^3 (or one in eight) trials. The data thus give a reasonably strong indication that some real change has occurred.

The magnitudes of the overtime changes for newly elected MCs are, in absolute terms, unimpressive: a mean increase of .06 likes on a scale that potentially runs from 0 to 5.0 and has an SD of .91, a mean decrease of .01 dislikes on the same scale, and a rise of four degrees on the hundred-point feeling thermometer. Nonetheless, using the Sophomore Surge changes in figures 6.4 and 6.5 as the baseline, one can calculate that the comparable changes for members newly elected in 1992 are, on average, 37 percent as large—and all in just one year since election. If the new MCs continue to make gains in constituent liking at this rate, they will realize more than 75 percent of what each entering class typically gains over its first term in office, and do so before spending a penny in the fall campaign.[25]

From another analysis (data not shown), it appears that even during the short sixty-to-seventy-day period that NES postelection surveys are in the field, citi-

Table 6.3 Interelection Attitudes toward MCs

	Newly Elected MCs		Previously Elected MCs	
	Post election	Pilot Study	Post election	Pilot Study
Percent who recall name	18	17	33	23
Percent who recognize name	74	68	83	82
Mean number of likes	.44	.51	.81	.78
Mean number of dislikes	.24	.23	.31	.24
Mean thermometer score	54	58	57	57
Percent who rate at 51 or above	36	37	48	45
Percent who recall challenger's name	18	7	13	3

Source: American National Election Studies 1993.

Note: Sample totals for "Percent who recall name": newly elected MCs, $N = 154$; previously elected MCs, $N = 565$. Sample totals for all other categories: newly elected MCs, $N = 154$; previously elected MCs, $N = 592$.

zens begin to forget the name of their MC. Table 6.3 now shows that forgetting continues over the first year of the interelection period. Taken together, these findings suggest that an important part of whatever citizens know about their MCs is learned in the relatively partisan context of an election campaign and then gradually forgotten in the period between elections. But at the same time that citizens are forgetting the names of their MCs, constituents are also acquiring some new reasons to like their representatives, much of which comes from the MCs themselves and is therefore nonpartisan and favorable (Cook 1989; Vermeer 1987). The effect of this dual forgetting-and-learning process—forgetting campaign information and acquiring MC-supplied information—should be to make citizens gradually less partisan in their overall assessment of their MCs. And this seems to be what happens: for newly elected members, the correlation between constituents' party identification and their rating of the MC on the feeling thermometer at the time of the election is .42; but this same correlation, measured in the Pilot Study data during the interelection period, is .30. The comparable correlations for more-senior MCs are .24 and .12, respectively. Thus, for all MCs, constituent evaluations become less strongly associated with party identification over the interelection period.

This overall pattern of results—the relatively greater decay of constituent awareness of challengers, the small gains in affect for the MC, and the decoupling of MC evaluations from party attachment—cannot be explained without assuming that MCs' efforts to spread good news about themselves have at least some success. Yet, the magnitude of this success does not imply either large or durable effects.

Relations between MCs and voters are so superficial, in fact, that surveys that seek to study them risk creating the attitudes they are merely trying to measure. One case in point is a change in the NES vote report question in 1978, which, for the first time, began to mention the names of the candidates in the course of asking who the respondent had voted for. Previous questions had asked only which party the respondent had voted for. The result was a sudden increase in reports of voting for the incumbent, who was in most cases the better-known candidate. Further, as Robert Eubank and David John Gow (1983), Gerald Wright (1993), and Gary Jacobson and Douglas Rivers (1993) have shown, this increase in reported vote for incumbents was actually a substantial overreport.[26] Although the natural tendency is to regard this overreport as a methodological artifact, it is also an important substantive finding: many survey respondents simply do not know for whom they have voted.

Another artifact of voter disengagement from congressional politics turned up in the 1996 NES study. In an effort to study the effects of congressional campaigns on voter awareness, this study carried the standard NES battery of questions about congressional candidates on the September-October wave of the survey as well as on the postelection wave. Previously, these questions had only been asked on postelection surveys. The effect of this innovation was, as Jacobson (1997a) shows, to greatly increase the percent of congressional voters who could recall the name of their MC on the postelection wave, from a mean of 47 percent in seven previous surveys to 64 percent in 1996.[27] The effect was proportionally larger on name recall of challengers, from an average of 18 percent in seven previous surveys to 39 percent in 1996. The notable implication of these findings is that voters know so little about congressional candidates that even answering a few questions about them produces a major uptick in their overall information.[28]

The NES design innovation in 1996 disclosed one other notable finding. At the beginning of the campaign period in September, voter name recall of incumbents was about 30 percent, while at the end it had risen to 45 percent. This is not an artifact but rather a genuine effect of the campaign on voter awareness. But note how low the initial starting point is for a group of mostly seasoned incumbents and how much difference is made by a few weeks of mostly low-key campaigning.

To judge from the data examined in this section, the cliché that Americans hate Congress but love their congressman can be at best only half true. Americans hardly know their congressional representatives, let alone really like them. To cite one last statistic, in the 1993 Pilot Study, the proportion of all respondents who could recall their MC's name and rated him or her at 51 degrees or above on the feeling thermometer was 13 percent. Among those who had voted in the 1992 House elections, this figure was only slightly higher, 17 percent.

Findings like these help explain incumbency advantage primarily by making a clear positive demonstration of the direction in which an explanation does *not* lie. They show, that is, that whatever the actual explanation for incumbency advantage might be, it does not involve the development of any deep bonds of loyalty, trust, or affection between voters and their MC. As far as most voters are concerned, superficial is the best characterization of the relationship with their MC.

Alternative Models of Incumbency Advantage

The first two parts of this chapter have argued that there is little credible evidence that the arduous efforts of MCs to cultivate support among individual constituents have sizable, durable effects on their attitudes and, further, that there is positive reason to believe that they do not. Citizens are clearly hard to reach, and when they are reached most seem to form superficial attitudes that are of little use to incumbents in time of duress. This is not to deny that citizens have strong views about congressional politics; it is merely to say that these views are only infrequently linked with particular MCs.

It does not follow from these empirical findings that those MCs who work hard to cultivate support in their districts are wasting their time. Presumably, they are accomplishing something of importance. But what they are accomplishing and how it affects their ability to survive in office is, in light of these findings, something of a puzzle.[29]

The trick to resolving this puzzle is to find mechanisms that credit MC efforts with real effects but do not require these effects to be mediated by the attitudes of individual citizens. This, it turns out, is quite possible to do. I suggest two such models: elite co-optation and electoral selection.

Elite Co-optation

In one section of *The Politics of Congressional Elections*, Jacobson writes:

> Casework, trips back to the district, issuing newsletters, and all the other things members do to promote reelection are not aimed merely at winning votes in the next election. . . . If an incumbent can convince potentially formidable opponents and people who control campaign resources that he or she is invincible, he or she is very likely to avoid a serious challenge and so will be invincible—as long as the impression holds. (1997b, 34)

In a digression from their main analysis, Rivers and Fiorina describe the potential importance of an MC's reputation:

> In [some game-theoretic literature], reputation refers to seemingly irrational actions taken to deter an opponent. In the context of congressional elections, possible challengers might be unsure of an incumbent's willingness to commit resources in a reelection battle beyond the apparent value of the office. By engaging in excessive amounts of constituency service, the incumbent signals his intention to fight a challenge to the bitter end. Conceivably, acquiring such a reputation would deter the entry of strong challengers so that, in the end, the incumbent would avoid a costly challenge. (1989, 22)

As these passages attest, the notion that the district-oriented activities of MCs could be aimed at other elites and potential challengers is scarcely new. But neither these authors nor anyone else has given serious consideration to the possibility that impressing other elites with their ability to get grants and their prowess as campaigners may be the most important things MCs do. Could it be that this is the main explanation for incumbency advantage?

An argument that stresses the importance of campaigning among local elites can, as the passage from Jacobson indicates, make full use of what is known about how MCs deploy the perquisites of office in their campaigns. The same can be said for Fiorina's (1989) emphasis on how MCs have learned to capitalize on being the local representative of a far-away but powerful establishment. If anything, local elites and activists might be more aware of and impressed by district-specific benefits than ordinary constituents, in part because they can often share in the credit-claiming for them.

The increase in travel allowance in the 1960s may be especially important, since it enables MCs to overcome the effects of longer congressional sessions and larger and more-distended districts. With it, MCs can, like other territorial animals, patrol their turf on a regular basis, marking trees, so to speak, in every corner of the district. The message they leave may always be, as Fenno says, "Trust me," but the twist, especially in unfriendly territory, might be something like, "Trust me, you can't beat me—and you don't even need to try, because we can do business with one another to our mutual advantage." And when the MCs themselves cannot be present in the district, their enlarged staffs can be, looking for ways to be helpful to, and thereby co-opt, activists and local officeholders, including officeholders from the opposition party. Thus, challengers who might otherwise be able to build support among activists and officeholders with no reason to care what the MC thought of them can find few local elites with nothing to lose from angering the incumbent.

In short, the new perquisites of congressional office have given MCs both the means to reach and a currency for dealing with opposition elites that they did not previously possess, and this, perhaps more than anything that the masses of voters ever find out, might explain why, as in the districts Fiorina (1989) visited in the 1970s, the local opposition had lost its will to resist. The whole Fenno-Fiorina-Jacobson story about trust may be exactly right except for one detail—the primary audience of the reelection effort.

This argument fully accommodates the findings of Levitt and Snyder (1997), who, as noted earlier, found that MC efforts to win federal grants for their districts are associated with higher vote margins. Their paper is the only study to demonstrate wide-scale effects of MC activity on electoral safety, and—notably—it does so without making any claims about what individual voters know or do not know.[30]

Electoral Selection

In a seminar at UCLA in 1988, Douglas Rivers formally proved that, in an idealized world in which there were no aging effects and in which challengers always had to beat incumbents in order to gain office, the quality of incumbents would continually be ratcheted upward, until all incumbents would win reelection with a probability of one (Rivers 1988). More recently, two senior scholars of congressional elections, Robert Erikson and Gerald Wright, have observed that

> the first thing one notices about district-level House races is that when incumbents seek reelection they almost always win. . . . Although several factors account for incumbents' electoral success, attention tends to focus on one specific reason: incumbents exploiting their "advantages of incumbency" over potential opponents. . . . One simple but sometimes overlooked reason incumbents win is that incumbency status must be earned at the ballot box. . . . Strong candidates tend to win and by winning become incumbents. Upon winning they survive until they falter or lose to even stronger candidates. . . . The process of electoral selection is independent of any incumbency advantage [due to exploiting the status or resources of office], but the two factors may reinforce each other. (1993, 99–100)

The existence of electoral selection has been recognized by these and other scholars for some years (Gelman and King 1990; Jacobson 1992, 45–46), but except for an unpublished paper by W. Phillips Shively (1995), it has never to my knowledge been systematically investigated.[31] As I argue below, the "overlooked" factor of electoral selection is, like elite co-optation, a sufficient explanation for the observed data on incumbency advantage.[32] And like the co-optation model, the electoral selection model makes no assumptions about voter loyalty to MCs.

At the core of this argument is a comparison of the careers of MCs and professional boxers. What makes this comparison illuminating is this similarity: world heavyweight champions, like MCs, compete in a sequence of contests in which the winner continues for as long as possible to fight new challengers, most of whom have never previously been champions. Incumbent champions in both professions are thus a much more select group than their opponents. This structural similarity creates a likelihood that the champions, whether boxers or MCs, will be, in some general sense, "better" competitors than most challengers and may seem to enjoy a special incumbency advantage for this reason alone.

Let me begin the analysis with figure 6.6, which shows the number of lifetime title victories by each of the twenty-two men who became the world heavyweight champion between 1930 and 1994. The tally of career victories begins at the point at which the boxer first wins an undisputed world championship and continues for the rest of his career.[33] Each time a boxer wins a title fight, whether as a challenger or as the defender of a title he currently holds, he gets credit for another career victory.

As the figure shows, there is a right-hand skew to the distribution of career title victories, with a few "superchampions" at the far right and a larger number who have won one or just a few title fights at the left. The two cases at the far right are Joe Louis, who won 26 title fights without a loss, and Mohammed Ali, who suffered setbacks but won a total of 21 title fights.

It is interesting that, although the modal champion is a "mediocre champ" who wins one championship and is unable to defend his title even once (27 percent of all individual cases), a large majority of title bouts are contested by notable champions. In particular, the 21 title fights won by Ali and the 26 title fights won by Louis constitute 37 percent of the 126 title fights from 1930 to 1994. If these title fights were elections, we would say that 37 percent of all "heavyweight" elections since 1930 were won by just two superchampions, Ali and Louis. Consider also the career of another extraordinary champion, Rocky Marciano. He won 42 fights without a loss as a light heavyweight; graduated to the heavyweight class, in which he won 7 world heavyweight title fights; and finally retired with a lifetime professional record of 49–0. From the data in figure 6.6, it can be calculated that 72 percent of all heavyweight title fights were won by someone at the level of Rocky Marciano or greater, often by knockouts.

What this means is that if one were to drop into a randomly chosen heavyweight title fight sometime in the last fifty years, there would be a 72 percent chance of encountering a champion at the level of Rocky Marciano or higher. Watching such champions fight, one might suspect that the incumbent had some sort of special advantage—or at least many political analysts might so sus-

Figure 6.6 Number of Career Title Fights Won of Heavyweight Boxing Champions, 1930–1994 ($N = 22$)

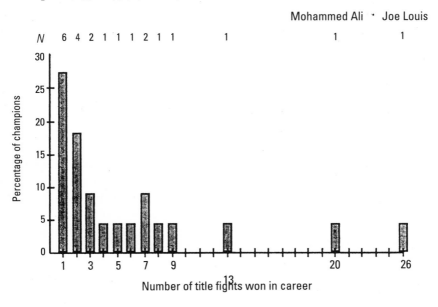

pect. But the main reason that superchampions like Louis, Ali, and Marciano won so many fights is that they were simply better than their opponents, usually a lot better. Why, one must wonder, doesn't each of the 435 congressional districts in the U.S. constitute a microcosm of the boxing world in which "heavyweight" politicians compete for the title of member of Congress, with superchampions dominating the competition for years at a time just because they are better than most of their opponents?

Let me acknowledge certain important, but I hope not fatally important, differences between the two professions: In boxing, potential challengers have every incentive to fight reigning champions, even if they expect to lose. Their supporting cast of managers and financiers have similar incentives, since everyone makes money if a title fight occurs. This virtually guarantees that the strongest opponents will seek to fight the champion. Champions, for their part, have a right to choose whom to fight and sometimes choose to avoid strong opponents. But the boxing federations, at least until recently, would strip the titles of champions who avoided strong opponents. Hence, although there may be some delay, boxing champions must fairly quickly fight the strongest potential opponents (see appendix).

In the case of MCs, by contrast, losing efforts by strong challengers are costly. The challenger must often give up a lucrative post elsewhere; backers must donate money and effort; and even neutral onlookers, as pointed out in the last section, may have to bear some costs. Hence, strong potential opponents routinely fail to enter the lists against incumbent MCs. But this argument applies in full force only to candidates who would expect to lose; it does not apply to the strongest challengers, who would still be expected to mount serious challenges whenever they judged themselves to have a good chance. They may pick their time carefully (Jacobson and Kernell 1981), but there is little reason to hold back from a fight they think they can win. Thus, the incentives of the strongest challengers—those who might actually beat an incumbent MC—are such as to make the dynamics of title defense in politics more similar, in this important respect, to the case of boxing than they might at first seem.[34] Strong challenges may be more carefully timed than in boxing, but they do come.

Yet how often do really strong challengers lack adequate funding? Certainly, one can point to many cases, in both professions, in which challengers are hopelessly outspent and lose badly. But many of these challengers would be likely to lose in any case, simply because they aren't very good. And, at the same time, there are also many cases in which a challenger has essentially as much as the incumbent to spend on the contest, in the form of training or advertising. This has been especially well documented in the case of congressional elections, in which it has been repeatedly shown that anything that predicts challenger quality also predicts how much money the challenger will be able to raise (Jacobson

1997b). The claim is not that incumbent MCs have no real spending advantage over even strong challengers but, rather, that this advantage is much smaller than it appears to be at first glance and, as I now suggest, quite possibly within the range of the advantage in training that an incumbent boxing champion enjoys over his strongest challengers. My argument, then, is that strong challengers emerge in congressional politics whenever they see an opportunity to win, that when they do they are able to command the resources necessary to mount serious fights, and that, in consequence, incumbent MCs, like incumbent boxing champions, cannot survive in office much longer than their personal skills warrant.

On this general premise, I now proceed with the analysis. Let us look first at the lifetime victory records of MCs—that is, the total number of congressional elections that were won—who departed the House between 1982 and 1996 (figure 6.7). These career data are presented in the same general form as the boxing career data[35] and bear a clear resemblance to them. The single most common type of MC career is, as in the case of the boxing champions, a short one, but some contestants nonetheless manage long careers, thereby creating a strong skew in the data. From casual inspection, the data from MCs do not suggest any more incumbency advantage than boxers enjoy.

Figure 6.7 Consecutive Congressional Elections Won by Nonsouthern MCs at Time of Defeat or Retirement, 1982–1996 ($N = 247$)

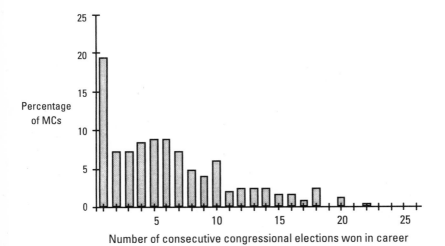

The strong skew in both the boxing and MC data merits a moment's reflection. If, as I have been suggesting, success in boxing and politics depends on skill, and if, as seems inevitable, skills of any sort have a unimodal or peaked distribution, then the distribution of skill levels of the individuals who become champions ought to resemble the right-hand tail of a peaked distribution. If, further, the number of total career victories is an indication of skill, then the distribution of career victories ought perhaps to resemble the right-hand tail of a peaked distribution—as, in fact, appears to be the case in figures 6.6 and 6.7. I say "perhaps" because this line of argument turns out to be faulty, but it is worth keeping in mind.

The similarity in career patterns between boxers and MCs masks a difference between the two groups: though some boxers end their careers by retiring, most end through defeat, whereas for MCs it is the reverse—a few are defeated and most voluntarily retire. In order for career length to reveal anything about the skill of MCs, we must assume that most MCs, like most boxing champs, would like to hold onto their office as long as possible and therefore could not last in office much longer than they do.[36] Given this strong assumption, career length is a rough indicator of skill, because the greater an MC's skill, the more victories he or she will be able to achieve before skill or interest fall below the threshold necessary to remain a champion.[37]

The notion that most MCs want to stay in office as long as possible does not apply very well to Republicans in the 1980s and early 1990s. With opportunities for political careers in the House limited by Democratic control, many Republicans retired after relatively short careers (Ansolabehere and Gerber 1997). For such persons, length of career provides little information about skill. For Democratic MCs, on the other hand, there was every incentive to stay around as long as possible, and many certainly tried to do so. For Democrats, therefore, career length may be taken as a rough indicator of skill. Reflecting this, figure 6.8 presents data on the careers of Democratic MCs alone. These data are broken out separately for the period 1982 to 1990, a time of unusual electoral tranquillity in Congress, and the period 1992 to 1996, a time of much more volatility. Because of oddities associated with southern politics in both decades, I have collected career data for nonsouthern Democrats only.

From the upper panel of figure 6.8, we see that the distribution of Democratic careers in the 1980s is quite different from the career patterns of champion boxers. Nearly 40 percent of Democrats leaving the House in this period had been there through ten elections or more—compared with just 14 percent of boxers (Larry Holmes, Ali, and Louis) who won more than ten title fights. There are also comparatively few one-term MCs. Altogether, then, the MC data are much less skewed than the boxing data and bear little resemblance to the right-

Figure 6.8 Length of Careers among Nonsouthern Democrats, 1982–1990 ($N = 46$) and 1992–1996 ($N = 82$)

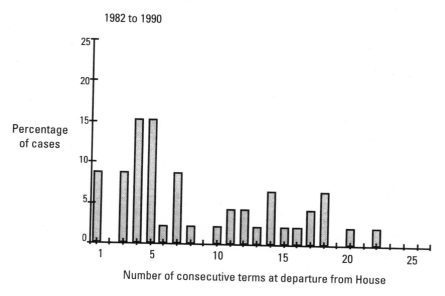

1982 to 1990

Percentage of cases

Number of consecutive terms at departure from House

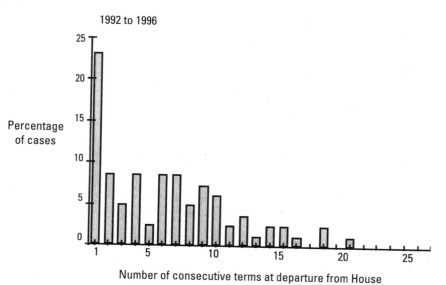

1992 to 1996

Percentage of cases

Number of consecutive terms at departure from House

hand tail of a peaked distribution. If we take the careers of boxers as the standard for what careers look like in a regime of intense electoral selection, we might conclude from these data that Democratic MCs in the 1980s faced little real competitive pressure, perhaps because of the extra boost that incumbency gave them.

This conclusion seems strengthened by examination of Democratic career patterns in the 1990s, as shown in the lower panel of figure 6.8. In a period in which incumbency and even pork-barrel politics came into some disrepute—a time, therefore, in which individual political skill was perhaps more important to survival in office—the career patterns of Democratic MCs look much more like those of the boxers and also more like the right-hand tail of a peaked distribution. It is still the case in the 1990s that departing MCs have a good deal of seniority—23 percent of the departees have been in the House for ten or more terms—but these long careers were mostly made in the 1970s and 1980s. One can readily imagine that the "instantaneous" career patterns of Democratic incumbents in the 1990s were even more similar to those of the boxers than they appear to be. Perhaps, then, the 1980s were a regime of incumbency advantage and the 1990s were a regime of political skill.

One more comparison between boxing and MC data needs to be drawn. As we have seen, House careers in the 1980s were characterized by a strong Sophomore Surge. There is, as it happens, a strong Sophomore Surge among boxers as well, but with a big difference: it runs in reverse. That is, boxing champions tend to have closer contests in their first title defense than in the fight in which they first won the title. After that—and in another contrast to the MCs of the 1980s, who, as we saw, acquire most of their incumbency advantage at the time of their first reelection—senior boxers win by greater and greater margins with each additional fight (i.e., they achieve more knockouts in a smaller number of rounds).[38] (Details of the estimation of Sophomore Surge and term-by-term effects among boxers are presented in the appendix.)

It thus appears that the careers of boxers resemble those of MCs in some respects and for some time periods, but not all. In an attempt to understand more clearly the process that has generated these career data, including both similarities and differences across groups and periods, I turn now to computer simulation. I turn, that is, to a stylized model of the competitive process by which boxers and MCs win and maintain their positions. The key event is the assignment of "skill" and "luck" scores to each player through random draws from a lottery. The competitor with the higher net score of skill and luck wins the contest and then goes on to take on new challengers, each of whom gets a fresh draw from the skill lottery. The skill levels that winners draw at the time of their first elections stay with them throughout their careers, but there is a fresh draw of luck for each new contest. Individuals go on winning as long as they can, up to a "term limit," whereupon they retire and open-seat elections occur in their districts. The patterns of wins and losses in many thousands of such computer-run election contests constitutes the simulation. By analyzing these patterns and the "careers" they generate, it is possible to learn about the dynamics of the stylized electoral process I have described, which can in turn cast light on the actual electoral process.

More specifically, I conduct the simulation as follows:

1. I assume that the skill necessary to become a champion boxer or politician has a unimodal or peaked distribution. The first step in the simulation, then, is to assign "political skill" scores to candidates on the basis of random draws from such a distribution. In the simulations that follow I used the right-hand tail of a $(0, 1)$ normal distribution, with a threshold of $z > 2$. Limited investigation indicated that the simulation was not sensitive to particular cutoff points; in test runs, I got essentially the same results using cutoffs of 3, 1, and even -2.

2. Each general election involves a luck factor, which is drawn from a normal distribution with a mean equal to zero. Positive luck scores aid the incumbent and negative ones aid the challenger. Luck can be almost any nonskill factor, from an off night in boxing to a partisan tide in congressional elections. Since I am not sure how important luck is in relation to skill, I vary the amount of luck in the simulations from none to little to high (as I explain in detail below). Differences in the amount of luck have a large effect on career patterns. As would be expected, incumbency domination is much greater when skill rather than luck predominates.

3. Elections are created by matching the skill and luck of two candidates. Incumbents win when their skill minus challenger's skill plus luck (which may be positive or negative) sums to a positive number. The winning candidate goes on to the next election, keeping the same level of skill but drawing a new luck factor and an opponent with a fresh draw of skill.

4. Winning incumbents are forced to "retire" after a specified number of terms, whereupon open-seat contests occur in their districts. The term limit I use is seventeen. There was, of course, no term limit in the period in which my actual data were generated, but no MC can stay in office forever. In the actual data, one MC stays in office for twenty-two terms, but most begin retiring earlier. In the 1980s, only 15 percent of nonsouthern Democratic MCs left office after seventeen terms or more. A limit of seventeen is something like a practical maximum—the highest level that most MCs can hope to achieve.

5. For open-seat contests, the competing candidates are chosen by means of a party "primary," whereby each party selects the most able of three contenders,

each of whose abilities comes from a random draw from the same talent distribution as other candidates. There is no luck factor in the primaries beyond
the random draw of ability scores.

6. The simulation runs for a hundred elections in each of fifty districts. To
eliminate start-up effects and allow an equilibrium to establish itself, I throw
out the first thirty elections, using the rest as a basis of inference about equilibrium conditions in the system.[39]

In reporting the results of the simulations, I begin with an electoral regime
in which there is no luck factor and then proceed to regimes with increasing
amounts of luck. Figure 6.9 presents the first set of results, in which the luck factor is zero. The data from the Democratic MCs in the 1980s have been truncated
at more than seventeen elections, to make them comparable with results from
the simulation, which forces retirement after seventeen elections.

The main point to notice in figure 6.9 is that the distribution of career lengths
in the simulation fails to reproduce the right-hand tail of a normal distribution,
from which the skill scores driving the simulation were drawn. Rather, the simulation produces a distinctly bimodal distribution of careers, with one node at
one or two elections and the other at the term limit, which is seventeen elections. This bimodal distribution is not an artifact of the particular term limit I
chose, nor is it dependent on the particular z-score cutoff used in the random
assignment of skill. As other simulations (not presented here) show, a bimodal
distribution of career lengths arises for a wide range of z-score cutoffs and for
any plausible term limit.

The lesson learned from this initial simulation, then, is that electoral selection
in a regime of all skill and no luck leads to a situation in which most incumbents
enjoy very long careers. Viewed in this light, the actual careers of Democratic
incumbents in the 1980s, despite initial appearances, are not too long to be consistent with electoral selection on the basis of skill alone. Indeed, the career
lengths of Democrats from the 1980s fall somewhat short of what might be
expected. The reason for this shortfall is not clear from the data. It could be
that many Democratic MCs were simply not interested in staying in office for
seventeen or more terms and hence retired after a "mere" ten or fifteen terms;
or, alternatively, it could be that, even in the tranquil 1980s, the pressures of electoral competition were driving many Democratic MCs from office, usually in
the form of "strategic retirements" to avoid impending defeat, perhaps in a primary (see Jacobson and Dimock 1994); or, more likely, a combination of both
processes was at work. This is the first of several indications we shall encounter
that the most senior MCs do not have the staying power that a model of electoral selection, which takes no account of possible life cycle effects, expects of

them. But whatever the reason for the shortfall, the key point is that the long careers enjoyed by Democratic incumbents in the 1980s seem to be well within the range of what can be explained by a model of electoral selection on the basis of skill.

Having examined congressional careers in a regime of pure skill, let us now see what happens when luck intrudes on the electoral process. Table 6.4 shows results from seven sets of simulations with varying amounts of luck. These simulations are reported in the first seven columns of the table. Columns 8 through 11 present parallel data from the real world of boxing and congressional elections.

As indicated, the seven sets of simulations differ in the amount of luck in the election process. In the first simulation, shown in column 1, there is no luck at all. Figure 6.9 shows the full distribution of career lengths produced by this simulation, but the first column of table 6.4 provides additional information about it. The second column shows results when a small amount of luck is factored in. Luck scores for the simulation in column 2 have been drawn from a

Figure 6.9 Actual and Simulated Congressional Careers

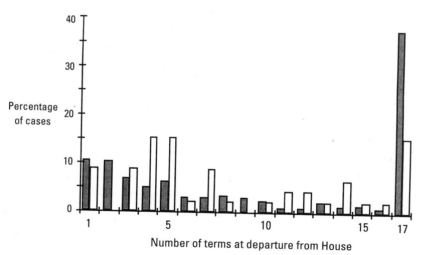

Number of terms at departure from House

■ Simulated careers
□ Nonsouthern congressional careers, 1982–90

Table 6.4 Simulated and Actual Effects of Electoral Selection

	(1)	(2)	(3)	(4)	(5)	(6)	(7)	(8)	(9)	(10)	(11)
	Simulation under Specified Ratio of "Luck" to "Skill"							MCs 1982–1990	Swing Districts 1982–1990	MCs 1992–1996	Boxing Champ-ions
	No Luck	1/8	1/4	1/2	1/1	2/1	4/1				
First term reelection rate (percent)	90.0	83.4	80.0	79.6	71.4	61.0	54.3	93.2	84.1 (N = 63)	85.6	67
Overall reelection rate (percent)	92.9	92.2	90.5	88.7	85.6	76.4	67.4	96.5	94.2 (N = 382)	88.9	81
Departees who reached 10+ terms (percent)	47	45	37	32	26	12	7	39[a]	—	23[a]	14
Departees who reached 17+ terms (percent)	35	33	27	22	17	7	3	15[a]	—	4[a]	9
Sophomore Surge (coefficient)	.25	.23	.19	.18	.01	-.21	-.47	10.8[b] ($p < .01$)	—	7.20[c] ($p < .01$)	-.84[d] ($p < .01$)
Term effect (coefficient)	.023	.025	.030	.031	.050	.070	.080	.070[b] (n.s.)	—	.475[c] ($p < .01$)	.060 ($p < .01$)

[a] Based on departures from office among nonsouthern Democrats only, because of early retirements among Republicans.
[b] Based on 1990 only. [c] Based on 1996 only. [d] See table 6.A1 for calculation of regression coefficients for surge and year-to-year gains.

normal distribution with mean of zero and a variance equal to one-eighth the variance in the distribution of skill;[40] in the third column, luck scores have come from a distribution having one-fourth the variance in skill. Moving from left to right, each column increases the amount of luck in the electoral process, until, in the seventh column, the variance in luck is four times greater than the variance in skill. Thus, the simulations show the effects of electoral selection in a range of conditions, from a regime of pure skill in column 1 to a regime of mostly but not entirely luck in column 7.

The reason for simulating a range of luck conditions is that, as indicated, no one really knows how much luck exists in political life. For example, a ratio of luck variance to skill variance of four to one is high but not obviously implausible for congressional elections. Recall that incumbents, especially senior incumbents, are, virtually by definition, a highly selected group. Hence, variation among them in political skill will probably be small, at least compared with variance in political skill in the population at large. But the selection process for chance factors in election contests is likely to be less severe. Incumbents try to foresee and guard against chance factors, such as electoral tides, but their ability to do so is imperfect. Hence, incumbents may have to withstand a fairly large portion of the natural variance in luck factors, whatever that natural variance may be.

I turn now to the results of the simulations, beginning with sophomore reelection rate. These rates are quite high in a regime of pure skill (90 percent), as shown in column 1 of table 6.4, but only somewhat better than chance (54.3 percent) in the regime in which chance variance is four times greater than skill variance, as shown in column 7.[41] As figure 6.10 shows, however, reelection rates improve with each subsequent reelection, approaching plateaus around 95 percent. It should be noted that this improvement has nothing to do with any "experience" MCs might gain from their earlier elections, since experience is not represented in the model. The explanation is purely selection: as the weaker incumbents are gradually weeded out, the surviving group is stronger and hence collectively more successful.

Overall reelection rates—combining results from all cohorts in whatever proportions they occur in the population—are shown in the second row of table 6.4. They range from 92.9 percent in a regime of pure skill to 67.4 percent in a regime of mostly luck. Yet as long as skill is more important than luck, incumbents do pretty well, and even when luck variance equals skill variance (column 5), the overall reelection rate for incumbents is 85.6 percent.

That such a high rate of reelection can occur in a regime in which luck is equal to skill is both notable and surprising. The result comes about because, even though the sophomore reelection rate is only 71.4 percent in this regime, stronger incumbents survive longer than weaker ones, thereby dominating the calculation of incumbent reelection rates. An 85.6 percent reelection rate in contests involving so much luck feeds the impression that incumbents have some special advantage, but there is none. It is all a matter of selection.

Given high rates of reelection in simulations in which there is some but not an overwhelming amount of luck, many incumbents enjoy long careers. In the "no luck" regime, 47 percent survive in office for ten or more terms, and 38 percent make the mandatory retirement limit of seventeen elections. When luck is equal to skill, 26 percent last ten or more terms, and 17 percent reach the limit of seventeen elections. Again, these rates are notably high. When luck is low or nonexistent, more than a third of all MCs can, if they wish, stay in office for the mandatory retirement age of thirty-four years in office, solely on the basis of superior skill.

The final two rows of table 6.4 are especially important but require some explanation. The entries are regression coefficients and are intended to capture

Figure 6.10 Simulated Effect of Luck and Prior Terms on Reelection Rate

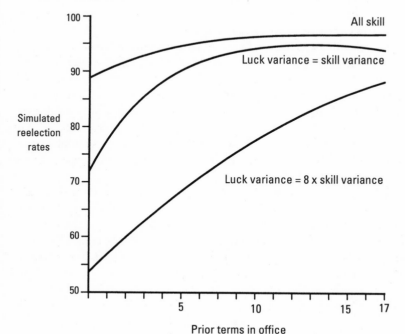

the effects of prior election on margin of victory, where victory margins are computed by subtracting the challenger's skill from the incumbent's skill and adding in luck. I use two variables to capture the effects of prior elections: a Sophomore Surge variable that takes the value of zero in an MC's first election and the value of one in all reelection contests and a Term variable, which counts the number of prior elections and ranges from zero to sixteen.

Thus, to be clear, I have run regressions in which margin of victory is the dependent variable and Surge and Term are the two independent variables. Coefficients for the Surge and Term variables, as estimated for each set of simulations, are reported in the bottom two rows of table 6.4.

The notable feature of these results is the effect of luck on the Sophomore Surge and Term coefficients. In the regime of pure skill (column 1), the Surge coefficient has more impact in one election (.25) than the Term coefficient has in ten elections (.023 × 10 = .23). But as luck increases, the Surge coefficient diminishes and eventually turns hugely negative, while the Term coefficient becomes steadily larger.

It is essential to understand why these opposing trends occur. I begin with the effect of term. With each election, selection weeds out the weaker incumbents, leaving the survivors a stronger group that then tends to win by larger margins. The Term coefficient captures this selection effect.

The Sophomore Surge, which is positive at low luck and negative at high luck, is driven by two opposing forces. The first is a selection effect. A candidate's first election is fought against either a reigning incumbent or the winner of a party primary, so that, in either case, the opponent is likely to be very good. But all reelections, including the first, are fought against candidates who are each merely "the best of one" draw from the skill lottery. Opponents in the first election are thus a more select group than opponents in the first reelection. Given this, MCs are likely to have a greater skill advantage in the first reelection than in their first election, and this skill advantage should, all else being equal, boost their margin of victory at the time of their first reelection. "Regression to the mean" is the second, countervailing part of the surge dynamic: all else being equal, first-time winners are likely to have better-than-average luck, since luck is part of what has enabled them to win. Their skill (whatever it is) carries over to their first reelection, but their luck does not, tending to "regress" to zero and thereby lowering their victory margin at the time of first reelection. As the luck variance becomes greater, the (negative) regression effect becomes greater too, gradually catching and surpassing the (positive) selection effect, leading to a net negative surge, or sophomore slump.[42]

But this is all simulation. Let us now compare the simulations to actual data, beginning with reelection rates for MCs, as shown in columns 8, 9, and 10. Reelection rates in table 6.4 are based on all incumbents who seek reelection. They also include primary election defeats, which may be considered the real elections in districts in which there are one-sided partisan majorities. They do not, however, include incumbents who were defeated in 1982 by virtue of having been paired against another incumbent, which is a factor outside the simulation.[43]

The first point to notice is that the reelection rate in Congress in the period 1982 to 1990 is 96.4 percent, which is higher than what the selection model can explain, even in a regime of pure skill. The sophomore reelection rate, 95.2, is also too high for the simulation to explain. These results could be seen as an embarrassment to the model, but only if primary elections are considered a fully adequate substitute for general elections in cases in which districts have lopsided partisan majorities. Yet it would be hard to argue that this is the case. Because party elites like to avoid attacks on their own incumbents, even in safe districts, primary elections are at best a partial substitute for general elections.

What this suggests is that if we want a clean test of the effects of electoral selection, we must look to districts in which the partisan balance is roughly even. In such districts, the skill of incumbents will be at least intermittently tested by the best challengers the other party can put up.[44]

To make this test, I have calculated House reelection rates in the period 1982 to 1990, controlling for the underlying partisanship of the district. The control is the average of the district vote for Democratic candidates in five federal elections, the three presidential contests of the 1980s and two Senate elections (per district) in the period 1978 through 1982.[45] The average of the Democratic vote across these elections was 48.7. Because, however, this estimate is based in part on two Reagan landslides and a big Bush victory, it understates the true level of Democratic partisanship in the country and in most districts.[46] To correct for this tilt, I have added 4.3 points to each district vote, thereby bringing average partisanship to 53 percent Democratic, which seems to me a plausible value. I then calculated reelection rates for MCs in districts that were, by this adjusted measure, between 47 percent and 53 percent Democratic in their underlying partisanship. The results are shown in column 9 of table 6.4.

Note, first of all, how high the MC reelection rates remain even in districts in which there is essentially no underlying partisan advantage—94.2 percent overall and 84.1 percent in sophomore reelections. These figures are quite notable in themselves. But of the two, the latter figure should be considered the more valid indicator of incumbent success, for this reason: the overall reelection rate undoubtedly misses some strategic retirements among senior incumbents, which would lead to an upward bias. Since, by contrast, scarcely any incumbents ever strategically retire prior to their sophomore reelections, the sophomore reelection rate suffers no such bias. It is also well within range of my simulation.[47]

It would obviously be useful to estimate the rate of strategic retirement among more senior MCs rather than, as I have done, simply assert that it probably occurs with enough frequency to cover the shortfall in my simulation. Consider, in this regard, the following argument: Jacobson and Dimock (1994) report that of the 27 MCs who had 200 or more overdrafts in 1992, 33 percent retired;[48] this compared with a 15 percent retirement rate among those 20 MCs who had 100–199 overdrafts, an 11.9 percent retirement rate among those 219 with 1–99 overdrafts, and an 8.9 percent retirement rate among those 168 with no overdrafts. The difference between an 8.9 percent retirement rate in the no-overdraft group and the retirement rates in the overdraft groups amounts to fourteen individuals, or 3.2 percent of the House membership who showed up as retirements but could well be considered defeats. This level of strategic retirement, though not especially high, is high enough to bring the "real defeat rate" among MCs—that is, the rate that would be observed if incumbents did not retire strategically—into range of my simulations. In another study, Peters and Welch (1980) find that, in the period 1968 to 1978, incumbents faced with scandal also tended to retire at slightly elevated rates. Paul Herrnson (1997, 32) also maintains that senior incumbents retire strategically in order to avoid defeat, but he does not provide a numerical estimate.

My point here is not simply that scandals lead to a certain amount of strategic retirement, since scandals are too rare to have much effect on overall election statistics. The point is more general: that some incumbents facing a high danger of defeat decide to quit rather than fight. Scandals are important to this argument only because they constitute a reliable way of identifying a few cases of severe threat for the sake of observing the effect of such threat. By far the greatest number of strategic retirements undoubtedly occur in response to threats not so readily detectable, at least from my academic distance. But such retirements may nonetheless occur regularly, perhaps taking the form of what seem like open-seat victories by "quality" or "experienced" challengers who have, in reality, scared a senior incumbent into strategic retirement.

If, then, we return to the sophomore reelection rate and take it as the most valid currently available estimate of electoral risk, an examination of table 6.4 suggests that the risk faced by incumbents in marginal districts is roughly what would be expected in an electoral regime in which the variance in luck is perhaps a little less than an eighth of the variance in skill (column 2).[49]

The data in table 6.4 on the actual percentage of MCs who serve ten or more terms (39 percent, as shown in column 8) also look reasonably similar to what would be expected in a regime in which luck variance is one eighth of skill variance (45 percent, as shown in column 2). The simulation and the actual data are, however, far apart for the percentage of MCs who serve seventeen terms—a repetition of the earlier observation of underperformance by very senior MCs.

Partisan tides in the elections from 1982 to 1990 were within the normal range. Not so in the elections of 1992, 1994, and 1996, which included an unusually disruptive reapportionment and the so-called revolution of 1994. Thus, as column 10 of table 6.4 shows, reelection rates for MCs in these elections are notably lower than in the earlier set—88.9 percent overall and 85.6 percent in sophomore elections. As column 11 further shows, the successful title defense (reelection) rate for boxers is still lower: 81 percent overall and 67 percent in "sophomore reelections"—that is, the first title defense bout. These lower rates are not, in themselves, illuminating, but they do create the conditions for a challenging test of the selection model: lower reelection rates indicate higher levels of luck, and higher levels of luck indicate, in turn, a decrease in the magnitude of the Surge coefficient and an increase in the magnitude of the Term coefficient, as explained above. The expectation, then, is that the Surge coefficient should be larger for MCs in 1990 than in 1996, and that the Term coefficient should be smaller among MCs in 1990 than in 1996. The model further implies that the Surge coefficient among boxers should be lower than among MCs, and possibly negative. And finally, the model implies that the Term coefficient should be larger among the boxers than among the MCs. As table 6.4 shows, the first three of these implications is supported by the data, while the last cannot be easily evaluated, owing to differences in the scaling of the dependent variables.

This pattern of effects, especially the negative Surge coefficient among boxers, seems to me strong support for the electoral selection model. The support is not, however, unblemished. I should add that, in conducting the regressions just described, I did not include a variable for terms squared, even though I did include this variable in my earlier analysis of the effect of terms of service on vote margin (see table 6.2). The reason is that, in the earlier analysis, I had a clear theoretical reason for including terms squared, while in the present analysis, I do not. Nonetheless, and in contrast to data from the 1980 and 1990 elections, the 1996 data exhibit pronounced nonmonotonicity, such that a Terms Squared variable attracts a significant negative coefficient if included in the analysis.

Why nonmonotonicity might exist in the electorally turbulent 1990s but not in the more tranquil 1980s is not clear. Perhaps it reflects Fenno's (1978) observation that, late in their careers, MCs become Washington oriented and hence more electorally vulnerable. Or, even more simply, it may indicate that incumbents are less energetic or skillful near the end of their careers. This vulnerability remains invisible in politically tranquil times, such as the 1980s, but appears in more turbulent times, when strong challengers are emboldened to take them on.

I should also note that, as shown in figure 6.3, there is essentially no term-by-term increase in margins of victory by incumbents in the "low luck" period of the 1980s, despite the existence of a skill-driven selection process that, as I claim, is quite relentless. This virtually flat trend in the data is thus something of a puzzle, not only for my argument on electoral selection but for the standard argument that MCs build voter support at least during their first several terms in office. Putting these two arguments somewhat inelegantly together, however, can render intelligible the data from the 1980s: If, over time, incumbents become increasingly oriented toward Washington work at the expense of district work and are also an increasingly selected group, the effects of these opposing processes could yield a flat trend in electoral support, as observed.

These explanations all invoke factors outside the model of electoral selection—essentially, some sort of life-cycle-related diminution of political skill—to account for weaker-than-expected showings by the most senior MCs in both the 1980s and 1990s. The need to do so points up a real shortcoming of the model and an area where modification might prove fruitful. But the limitation is not so great as to undermine the main implications of the model, which are that electoral selection is a more powerful mechanism than has generally been recognized and, furthermore, that in combination with district partisanship, the model can provide a sufficient if general account of many important aggregate features of the data on congressional careers, most especially the misleading appearance of special incumbency advantage.

Conclusion

The interaction of luck and skill can explain the most salient aspects of congressional career data. Such an argument is admirably general, yet it risks, despite its ability to explain important details, being overly abstract. What, after all, are "luck" and "skill," as theorized in the selection model? And how do they relate to existing literature on congressional elections?

A simple answer to the latter question is that, while most congressional scholars have focused on what MCs do to insure reelection, my argument focuses on how well they do it. The omitted question in conventional scholarship is: But how well do MCs do what they do? And the omitted question in my argument is: But what do MCs do well?

Let me, then, discuss my omitted question. Unlike the existing literature, which focuses on a handful of district-specific MC behaviors, my model, because it is so general, is open to the possibility that what MCs do to get themselves reelected is a wide variety of things: they raise campaign contributions, take stands on issues with a view to how constituents will respond, develop ties to interest groups, create TV ads, give speeches at citizen assemblies, impress potential challengers and other elites with their political skill—and, finally, they provide particularistic services of many types to individual citizens and to the district as a whole. Although such particularistic service certainly has some importance, the claim that it is more important than the other activities in which MCs engage is by no means established. As recent work shows, many congressional representatives achieve electoral success without making district work their main selling point, probably because many constituencies are not primarily interested in particularistic services (Sellers 1997). In view of this, little seems lost by neglecting the specific activities that MCs undertake and focusing instead on how well they perform a broad range of activities whose details are entirely open.

The conception of skill implicit in my model follows directly from this argument: Political skill, like many other kinds of ability, is probably not any one thing. It is many different skills, which different individuals possess in different amounts and combinations. One politician is good at casework, another is good with donors, another with local party officials, another at making TV ads, another at the art of bamboozlement. What exactly counts as political skill probably varies by district, depending on local interests and culture, as Sellers (1997) suggests. It probably also varies by historical era. But political skill, though variable in content across place and time, would tend to have a set and definite distribution in each particular place and time—some individuals would have a lot, some very little, and so on—and this would give rise to a distribution of skills within each district, as hypothesized in my simulation.

It is hard to say what exactly the shape of the distribution of political skill would be. My initial intuition was that political skill is formed from the sum of numerous discrete and somewhat independent talents. If so, the Central Limit Theorem would suggest that the overall distribution of talents in nature would be normal, which would justify my use of the right-hand tail of a normal distribution as the foundation of my simulations. However, my colleague, James DeNardo, points out that a politician who was deficient in any important aspect of political skill would tend to fall abruptly out of the competitive game, in which case the distribution of political talent in nature might be more like a log normal distribution. In view of this uncertainty, I am pleased to be able to report that simulations do not seem to be very sensitive to this issue, since I have obtained similar results doing runs with the whole normal distribution.

In sum, political skill is a type of ability and, as such, it is most appropriately conceptualized as an aggregate (whether additive or multiplicative) of numerous, somewhat discrete talents. This implicit conception articulates well with Jacobson's (1997b) account of the multiple activities in which MCs routinely engage. It also fits well with Jacobson and Kernell's work (1981; see also Jacobson 1989) on the importance of challenger quality and with Gary Cox and Jonathan Katz's (1996) finding that increases in the importance of candidate quality have been the key reason for the increase in incumbency advantage since the late 1960s.

This last point bears amplification. As Cox and Katz argue, the massive redistricting forced by the Supreme Court's "One person, one vote" rulings of the 1960s was unusually disruptive to congressional politics. When the new, often oddly shaped but always equal-population districts came into existence in the late 1960s, they rendered party organizations that were organized along county lines useless for contesting many congressional elections. As a result, individual candidates who once relied on the parties to run their campaigns were suddenly forced into the business of campaign management. This, in turn, put a greater premium on candidate "quality" than had previously existed, and it was at this point that incumbency advantage suddenly took on heightened importance. An argument that stresses candidate quality as the basis of incumbency advantage is obviously a very close fit with my own.

My argument would, of course, be stronger if I could make "political skill" more concrete and measure its effect in relation to the effect of incumbency, independent of skill. It is, as it happens, possible to do something like this for a special sample of cases. Between 1982 and 1996, there were forty-three pairs of elections in which the same candidates faced each other in successive elections and in which one of the candidates was a nonincumbent in the first election and an incumbent in the second.[50] For these pairs, the difference between the loser's vote in the first election and his or her vote in the second is a measure of the power of incumbency, controlling for the skill of the opponents. The results are that repeaters win 44.1 percent of the vote in the first race in the pair and 43.0 percent in the second, for a mean shift of −1.1 percent. These results are nearly identical with those of Peverill Squire and Eric R. A. N. Smith (1984), who found a mean difference of −1.3 percent for thirty-eight comparable pairs between 1962 and 1980. Thus, the effect of incumbency, controlling for the skill of the opponents, seems to be small. One can imagine important factors that might bias this test either way, so I do not place great emphasis on it.[51] But the results seem worth reporting nonetheless.

A last point about the nature of political skill: Although political skill is, as I have stressed, probably a composite of many small skills, it seems likely that a good number of these skills bear in some fairly direct way on electioneering, since, as seems likely, most constituents are too disengaged from congressional politics to give MCs much credit for activities that never become issues in the electoral arena. Given the infrequency of strongly contested House elections, it may be difficult to learn much about electoral skill from them, but senatorial, gubernatorial, and other state-level contests would seem to offer excellent opportunities (Alvarez 1997).[52]

The conception of luck implicit in my simulation of electoral selection is any kind of randomly occurring event that helps or hurts a candidate. National partisan swings are probably the most important form of luck—tides that sweep otherwise weak candidates into office and defeat even strong ones. An MC may also be lucky enough to be able to claim credit for bringing scheduled airline service to a regional airport, or unlucky enough to have a spouse divorce him or her in a media extravaganza. In boxing, a great champion is one who is good enough to survive even off nights and biased judges, and the same is presumably true of champion politicians. Example: In 1992 Senator Arlen Specter, a proven champion, defeats Lynn Yeakel, a novice, even in the Year of the Woman and despite Specter's questioning of Anita Hill in the Clarence Thomas hearings.

One final but important point. Although my empirical analysis emphasizes the limited attention of voters to MC activities and my theoretical analysis of electoral selection focuses entirely on candidates and their skills, it does not follow that voters are irrelevant to the dynamics of congressional elections. To the contrary, voters drive the whole process: Political skill, more elaborately stated, is really skill at finding out what voters want and convincing them that you have given it to them. Voters do not need to follow everything politicians do on a day-to-day basis in order to choose the better politicians; they need only pay attention at election time to what the incumbent has done and what the challenger promises to do.

Thus, what candidates do and promise to do—whether the provision of particularistic service, issue representation, or some other bundle of services—is by no means irrelevant to understanding the politics of congressional elections. But it is not what candidates do that explains incumbency advantage; it is, rather, how well they do it.

Appendix: Trends in Careers of Heavyweight Boxers

This appendix describes the estimation of the effect of "incumbency" on the margin of victory for heavyweight boxing champions, as reported in table 6.4. I constructed three indicators of victory margin. The first, called KNOCKOUT, takes into account whether a knockout has occurred. A knockout by the champion is scored as +2, a judge's decision for the champion as +1, a decision against the champion as −1, and a knockout of the champion as −2. In the second, more elaborate measure, I take account of how long it took for a knockout to occur. A first-round knockout in a fifteen-round fight is scored as +16 for the victor, a second-round knockout as +15, and so on, down to a fifteenth-round knockout as +2 and a victory by decision as +1. Losses by a champion are given corresponding negative values; thus, a first-round knockout of the champion by a challenger is scored as −16 and a loss by decision as −1. This variable is called ROUNDS. Finally, to accommodate nonlinearity, I created a compressed version of ROUNDS by taking logs. This variable is called LOGROUNDS.

In most cases, fighters have only one run as champion, such that if they lose, they never win again. But a few had two separate runs, and Mohammed Ali had two runs of ten fights and a third title victory besides. In my scoring of the Term variable, I count each string of victories as a separate career, including its own Surge term. Fights in which a champion is defeated are counted twice, once as the last fight in the string of the outgoing champion and once as the first fight in the string of the new champion.

Results for each form of the dependent variable are shown in table 6.A1. A negative Surge coefficient and a positive Term coefficient are obtained for each scoring rule, though results are considerably stronger for the simplest form of the scale. Given the results of the simulation, I report one-tailed significance tests, all six of which exceed the .05 level. Table 6.A2 shows the data on which these calculations were made.

The boxing career data through 1986 were taken from *The World Sports Record Atlas* (Emery and Greenberg 1986). For title fights from 1986 through

Table 6.A1 Title Fight Wins and Victory Margin among Heavyweight Boxing Champions ($N = 149$)

	KNOCKOUT (−2 to +2)	ROUNDS (−16 to +16)	LOGROUNDS (−1.2 to +1.2)
Sophomore Surge (range 0–1)	−.84 (.29)	−2.92 (1.74)	−.29 (.15)
Number of title fights (terms) won (range 1 to 26)	.06 (.02)	.26 (.12)	.028 (.01)
Intercept	1.61	6.71	.60
Adjusted r-square	.06	.02	.03

Note: Standard errors appear in parentheses. Measures described in the appendix.

Table 6.A2   Careers of Heavyweight Boxing Champions

Champion	Opponent	Date	Consec-utive Prior Title Wins	Total Prior Titles	Total Rounds	KO	Win	Case
Schmeling	Sharkey	6/12/30	0	0	4	No	Yes[a]	1
	Stibling	7/3/31	1	1	15	Yes	Yes	2
	Sharkey	6/21/32	2	2	15	No	No	3
Sharkey	Schmeling	6/21/32	0	0	15	No	Yes	4
	Carnera	6/29/33	1	1	6	Yes	No	5
Carnera	Sharkey	6/29/33	0	0	6	Yes	Yes	6
	Uzcudun	10/22/33	1	1	15	No	Yes	7
	Loughran	3/1/34	2	2	15	No	Yes	8
	Baer	6/14/34	3	3	11	Yes	No	9
Baer	Carnera	6/14/34	0	0	11	Yes	Yes	10
	Braddock	6/13/35	1	1	15	No	No	11
Braddock	Baer	6/13/35	0	0	15	No	Yes	12
	Louis	6/22/37	1	1	8	Yes	No	13
Louis	Braddock	6/22/37	0	0	8	Yes	Yes	14
	Farr	8/30/37	1	1	15	No	Yes	15
	Mann	2/23/38	2	2	3	Yes	Yes	16[b]
	Thomas	4/1/38	3	3	5	Yes	Yes	17
	Schmeling	6/22/38	4	4	1	Yes	Yes	18
	Lewis	6/25/39	5	5	1	Yes	Yes	19
	Roper	4/17/39	6	6	1	Yes	Yes	20
	Galento	6/28/39	7	7	4	Yes	Yes	21
	Pastor	9/20/39	8	8	11	Yes	Yes	22
	Godoy	2/9/40	9	9	15	No	Yes	23
	Paycheck	3/29/40	10	10	2	Yes	Yes	24
	Godoy	6/20/40	11	11	8	Yes	Yes	25
	McCoy	12/16/40	12	12	6	Yes	Yes	26
	Burman	1/1/41	13	13	5	Yes	Yes	27
	Dorazio	2/17/41	14	14	2	Yes	Yes	28
	Simon	3/21/41	15	15	13	Yes	Yes	29
	Musto	4/8/41	16	16	9	Yes	Yes	30
	Baer	5/23/41	17	17	7	Yes	Yes	31
	Conn	6/18/41	18	18	13	Yes	Yes	32
	Nova	9/29/41	19	19	6	Yes	Yes	33
	Baer	1/9/42	20	20	1	Yes	Yes	34
	Simon	3/27/42	21	21	6	Yes	Yes	35
	Conn	6/19/46	22	22	8	Yes	Yes	36
	Mauriello	9/18/46	23	23	1	Yes	Yes	37
	Walcott	12/5/47	24	24	15	No	Yes	38
	Walcott	6/25/48	25	25	11	Yes	Yes	39[b]

Table 6.A2. (*continued*)

Champion	Opponent	Date	Consec-utive Prior Title Wins	Total Prior Titles	Total Rounds	KO	Win	Case
Charles	Walcott	6/22/49	0	0	15	No	Yes	40
	Lesnevich	8/10/49	1	1	7	Yes	Yes	41
	Valentino	10/14/49	2	2	8	Yes	Yes	42
	Beshore	8/15/50	3	3	14	Yes	Yes	43
	Louis	9/27/50	4	4	15	No	Yes	44
	Barone	12/5/50	5	5	11	Yes	Yes	45
	Oma	1/12/51	6	6	10	Yes	Yes	46
	Walcott	3/7/51	7	7	15	No	Yes	47
	Maxim	5/30/51	8	8	15	No	Yes	48
	Walcott	7/18/51	9	9	7	Yes	No	49
Walcott	Charles	7/18/51	0	0	7	Yes	Yes	50
	Charles	6/5/52	1	1	15	No	Yes	51
	Marciano	9/23/52	2	2	13	Yes	No	52
Marciano	Walcott	9/23/52	0	0	13	Yes	Yes	53
	Walcott	5/15/53	1	1	1	Yes	Yes	54
	LaStarza	9/24/53	2	2	11	Yes	Yes	55
	Charles	6/17/54	3	3	15	No	Yes	56
	Charles	9/17/54	4	4	8	Yes	Yes	57
	Cockell	5/16/55	5	5	9	Yes	Yes	58
	Moore	9/21/55	6	6	9	Yes	Yes	59[c]
Patterson	Moore	11/30/56	0	0	5	Yes	Yes	60
	Jackson	7/29/57	1	1	10	Yes	Yes	61
	Rademacher	8/22/57	2	2	6	Yes	Yes	62
	Harris	8/18/58	3	3	12	Yes	Yes	63
	London	5/1/59	4	4	11	Yes	Yes	64
	Johansson	6/26/59	5	5	3	Yes	No	65
Johansson	Patterson	6/26/59	0	0	3	Yes	Yes	66
	Patterson	6/20/60	1	1	5	Yes	No	67
Patterson	Johansson	6/20/60	0	5	5	Yes	Yes	68
	Johansson	3/13/61	1	6	6	Yes	Yes	69
	McNeeley	12/4/61	2	7	4	Yes	Yes	70
	Liston	9/25/62	3	8	1	Yes	No	71
Liston	Patterson	9/25/62	0	0	1	Yes	Yes	72
	Patterson	7/22/63	1	1	1	Yes	Yes	73
	Ali	2/25/64	2	2	6	Yes	No[d]	74
Ali	Liston	2/25/64	0	0	6	Yes	Yes	75
	Liston	5/25/65	1	1	1	Yes	Yes	76
	Patterson	11/22/65	2	2	12	Yes	Yes	77
	Chuvalo	3/29/66	3	3	15	No	Yes	78
	Cooper	5/21/66	4	4	6	Yes	Yes	79

Table 6.A2. (*continued*)

Champion	Opponent	Date	Consecutive Prior Title Wins	Total Prior Titles	Total Rounds	KO	Win	Case
	London	8/6/66	5	5	3	Yes	Yes	8
	Mildenberger	9/19/66	6	6	12	Yes	Yes	8
	Williams	11/14/66	7	7	3	Yes	Yes	8
	Terrell	2/6/67	8	8	15	No	Yes	8
	Folley	3/22/67	9	9	7	Yes	Yes	8
Frazier	Ellis	2/16/70	0	0	4	Yes	Yes	8
	Ali	3/8/71	1	1	15	No	Yes	8
	Foster	11/18/71	2	2	2	Yes	Yes	8
	Daniels	1/15/72	3	3	4	Yes	Yes	8
	Strander	5/25/72	4	4	4	Yes	Yes	8
	Foreman	1/22/73	5	5	2	Yes	No	9
Foreman	Frazier	1/22/73	0	0	2	Yes	Yes	9
	Roman	9/1/73	1	1	1	Yes	Yes	9
	Norton	3/3/74	2	2	2	Yes	Yes	9
	Ali	10/30/74	3	3	8	Yes	No	9
Ali	Foreman	10/30/74	0	10	8	Yes	Yes	9
	Wepner	3/24/75	1	11	15	Yes	Yes	9
	Lyle	5/16/75	2	12	11	Yes	Yes	9
	Bugner	7/1/75	3	13	15	No	Yes	9
	Frazier	10/1/75	4	14	14	Yes	Yes	9
	Coopman	2/20/76	5	15	5	Yes	Yes	1
	Young	4/30/76	6	16	15	No	Yes	1
	Dunn	5/24/76	7	17	5	Yes	Yes	1
	Norton	9/28/76	8	18	15	No	Yes	1
	Evangelista	5/16/77	9	19	15	No	Yes	1
	Spinks	2/15/78	10	20	15	No	No	1
Spinks	Ali	2/15/78	0	0	15	No	Yes	1
	Ali	9/15/78	1	1	15	No	No	1
Ali	Spinks	9/15/78	0	20	15	No	Yes	1
	Holmes	10/2/80	1	21	10	Yes	No	1
Holmes	Ali	10/2/80	0	0^g	10	Yes	Yes	1
	Berbick	4/11/81	1	1	15	No	Yes	1
	Spinks	6/12/81	2	2	3	Yes	Yes	1
	Snipes	11/6/81	3	3	11	Yes	Yes	1
	Cooney	6/14/82	4	4	13	Yes	Yes	1
	Cobb	11/25/82	5	5	15	No	Yes	1
	Rodriquez	3/27/83	6	6	12	No	Yes	1
	Witherspoon	5/20/83	7	7	15	No	Yes	1
	Frank	9/10/83	8	8	5	Yes	Yes	1

Table 6.A2. (*continued*)

Champion	Opponent	Date	Consecutive Prior Title Wins	Total Prior Titles	Total Rounds	KO	Win	Case
	Frazier	11/25/83	9	9	1	Yes	Yes	119
	Smith	11/9/84	10	10	12	Yes	Yes	120
	Bey	3/15/85	11	11	10	Yes	Yes	121
	Williams	5/20/85	12	12	15	No	Yes	122
	Spinks	9/20/85	13	13	15	No	No	123
Spinks	Holmes	9/20/85	0	1	15	No	Yes	124
	Holmes	4/19/86	1	2	15	No	Yes	125[h]
Tyson	Tucker	8/1/87	0	0	12	No	Yes	126
	Biggs	10/16/87	1	1	7	Yes	Yes	127
	Holmes	1/22/88	2	2	4	Yes	Yes	128
	Tubbs	3/20/88	3	3	2	Yes	Yes	129
	Spinks	6/27/88	4	4	1	Yes	Yes	130
	Bruno	2/25/89	5	5	5	Yes	Yes	131
	Williams	7/21/89	6	6	1	Yes	Yes	132
	Douglas	2/10/90	7	7	6	Yes	No	133
Douglas	Tyson	2/10/90	0	0	6	Yes	Yes	134
	Holyfield	10/25/90	1	1	3	Yes	No	135
Holyfield	Douglas	10/25/90	0	0	3	Yes	Yes	136
	Foreman	4/19/91	1	1	12	No	Yes	137
	Cooper	11/24/91	2	2	7	Yes	Yes	138
	Holmes	6/19/92	3	3	12	No	Yes	139
	Bowe	11/13/92	4	4	12	No	No	140
Bowe	Holyfield	11/13/92	0	0	12	No	Yes	141
	Dokes	2/6/93	1	1	1	Yes	Yes	142
	Ferguson	5/22/93	2	2	2	Yes	Yes	143
	Holyfield	11/6/93	3	3	12	No	No	144
Holyfield	Bowe	11/6/93	0	5	12	No	Yes	145
	Moorer	4/22/94	1	6	12	No	No	146
Moorer	Holyfield	4/22/94	0	0	12	No	Yes	147
	Foreman	11/5/94	1	1	10	Yes	No	148
Foreman	Moorer	11/5/94	0	3	10	Yes	Yes	149

[a] Sharkey disqualified in fourth round for foul.

[b] Louis retired undefeated as champion.

[c] Marciano retired undefeated as champion.

[d] Liston listed as having "retired" from fight—he failed to answer the bell for the seventh round.

[e] Ali stripped of title by WBA and New York State Athletic Commission for refusal to submit to draft process.

Table 6.A2. (*continued*)

[f] Stander failed to answer the bell for the fifth round.
[g] Holmes had won eight fights under WBC banner, but I don't count him as champion until he beats Ali.
[h] Spinks stripped of title in February 1987 for failing to defend within six months; subsequent fight with Cooney not counted as title fight.

1994, my research assistant, Mark Hunt, consulted newspapers. In cases of disputed titles, the rule was to recognize the most important champion. After 1994, feuding among competing confederations made it impossible to specify who the champion was.

Notes

This chapter has benefited enormously from comments by Doug Arnold, Kathy Bawn, Jack Citrin, Barbara Geddes, John Geer, Gary Jacobson, Gary King, Jon Krasno, Dan Lowenstein, David Mayhew, Tom Schwartz, Barbara Sinclair, Raymond Zaller, and an anonymous reviewer for the Johns Hopkins University Press. Jim DeNardo was especially helpful and encouraging. I also particularly thank Mo Fiorina and Doug Rivers for friendly advice on how to improve a paper that disagrees with some of their work. Having saved me from many errors, none of these individuals has any responsibility for those that remain. Special thanks to Gary Jacobson for kindly making available to me his contextual data on candidate status and electoral history. I am also extremely grateful for research assistance from Mark Hunt and Scott Desposato, whose timely help made section 3 of this chapter possible. The survey data used in this chapter were collected by the American National Election Studies under a grant from the National Science Foundation, and made available through the Inter-University Consortium for Social and Political Research at the University of Michigan. A grant from the National Science Foundation (Ref: SES-9210742) enabled me to collect some of the data used in the study. (These data are publicly available at www.umich.edu/~nes/.) Finally, much of the work for the chapter was conducted while I was a fellow at the Center for Advanced Study in Behavioral Sciences in Palo Alto.

1. George Sera (1994) finds similar evidence: a special sample of respondents, supplied by an MC after staff had done casework for them, have more favorable attitudes toward the MC than randomly selected respondents who had not had casework done for them. There are, however, three questions about such studies. The first is scale. Sera reports that the staff of the MC who cooperated with him handled about thirty-five casework requests per week. At the rate of thirty-five constituents per week for ten years, an MC would reach about 4 percent of the adults (circa four hundred thousand) in a typical congressional district. Of course, MCs engage in many other kinds of activities, but the question of scale remains. Second is the question of memory. Sera reports having to discard about 10 percent of cases because of either incomplete interviews or a discrepancy

between the MC list and the constituent's recollection that service had been rendered. This suggests the existence of a significant amount of forgetting or inventing or both. A third concern is selection bias: are the respondents who contact an MC with a problem a random sample of constituents or a group that has a favorable impression of the MC and seeks help for that reason? The Cover and Brumberg study (1982) does not have the third problem, but it does have the other two, especially the first.

2. Jacobson 1997b, 32–33, and associated notes. See Fiorina's summary (1989, ch. 10).

3. The N's for these percentages are 59 (1980) and 31 (1982); Jacobson 1992, table 5.17.

4. Yet, a person shaking hands with as many people as Pressler did had to be pretty indiscriminate, contacting them at factories, shopping centers, and wherever people congregate. If so, the bias in favor of meeting actual voters might not have been very great.

5. It might be argued that some people claiming to have met a candidate may have seen the candidate at an event and so be reporting an actual behavior. This would seem reasonable if respondents were given no other opportunity to indicate that they had seen the MC or candidate at a meeting. But they are given this opportunity, and quite clearly so. Measurement of contact with the MC is as follows: Respondents are given a seven-item show card listing various forms of contact and asked whether they learned about the person "in any of these ways." Those answering yes are then asked to indicate which types of contact they have had. "Met [X] personally" is listed first on the show card, followed by "attended a meeting or gathering where [X] spoke." Thus, respondents are well able, if they wish to do so, to indicate that they only saw the candidate at a meeting.

6. Jonathan Krasno (1994) shows that in states with populations of five million or more—i.e., ten times the size of a congressional district—voters report less contact with their senator. But in other states, they report equal or more contact with their senator than with their MC.

7. The 1994 survey contains some panel respondents, but the effect does not show up in the panel segment of the data. It is driven by respondents outside the panel segment. Panel respondents are, of course, included in the base from which figure 6.1 has been calculated.

8. Because of reapportionment in 1982 and 1992, some respondents in those years had different incumbents than in the previous election. In light of this, I omitted from the analysis losses suffered in the 1982 and 1992 elections. However, the 1982 and 1994 elections are used as T1 (baseline) elections for assessing losses at the time of the 1984 and 1994 elections.

9. The expected effect of electoral duress shows up in five of six elections in table 6.1. The chance of getting five successes in six independent trials under the null hypothesis is .12. The exception occurred in the 1984–86 election sequence.

10. I also ran a regression in which reported meeting with the MC was the dependent variable, and in which the independent variables were election difficulty (0–1, by the criteria described in the text), the standard NES item on following public affairs (the four-point, uncollapsed scale), and the interaction of following public affairs and election difficulty. The interaction term was just statistically significant at $t = .05$ on a one-tailed test.

11. The one-sided p-value was .35 overall and .22, .19, and .30 for interactions terms of the form described in the preceding footnote. See note 15 below.

12. See note 15 below.

13. My sense of the cutpoints that would serve these competing considerations was primarily based on my prior experience with the 1978–80 data set. In light of this, I later reran table 6.1 with the 1978–80 cases excluded. To my surprise, the effect was to increase the effect of electoral duress slightly (to −4.3 percent, from −3.5 percent in table 6.1) and to improve the *p*-value of the difference slightly as well, to .08.

14. See Bartels 1997 for a consciousness-raising and illuminating discussion of how to do meaningful tests of statistical significance when essential features of one's hypothesis cannot be specified a priori. My response to Bartels' essay was to scrap my initial data exploration and to conduct a single, new hypothesis test on data with which I was mostly unfamiliar. Happily, there was enough such data to make this approach possible.

15. This is a weaker claim than I made in earlier versions of this chapter, which found evidence that the principal variables used in the Rivers-Fiorina analysis were prey to the same effects of electoral duress as the "ever personally met" item. That evidence, from the 1978 and 1980 NES studies, showed that survey respondents were less likely to report having "ever contacted" their MC's office when the MC came under electoral duress, which is the same pattern as shown in figure 6.1 and table 6.1, above. For the 1978–80 and 1982–84 election sequences, the overall *t*-value on that effect is 1.79. (The 1980–82 sequence is omitted because of reapportionment.) However, I have discovered that in each pair of elections since 1984, the effect runs the other way, with respondents more likely to report having "ever contacted" MCs when their MCs get into electoral duress. The reversal of the earlier trend is large and highly statistically significant ($t = 3.02$, two-tailed $p = .002$, for the overall difference in the period 1986 to 1994, excluding the reapportionment set of elections). Tested with time as a continuous variable in a regression model, the relevant interaction term (time $\times$ electoral duress) is significant at $p = .02$ on a two-tailed test.

What could have caused such an apparent reversal? My hunch was that the rise of political activism on the part of the Christian Right might be responsible, such that those claiming to have contacted politically weakened MCs might be disproportionately members of conservative denominations who were mobilized by their ministers. At least in 1994, there was both NES survey and newspaper evidence that this was the case. Furthermore, it turns out that, although the "ever contacted" variable very strongly predicts support for incumbents in easy races since 1986 ($t = 3.2$), the relation reverses in hard races ($t = -.94$), which tends to support the hunch that increased contact in hard races comes from mobilized opponents. Thus, the "ever contacted" item may be as endogenous as the "ever personally met" item, though in a way I had not expected. Pursuing this line of evidence would be too much of a digression in the current essay.

As should be obvious, the results reported in this note are based on thorough exploration of the data rather than one-shot hypothesis tests. As an aside, I suggest that the approach I am taking here—explicit distinction between results that reflect a more-or-less straight hypothesis test as against thorough exploration of the data—may be a partial solution to the problem noted by Bartels (1997), at least for cases in which the approach he proposes is not feasible.

16. Despite a mean difference in Sophomore Surge, graphical representations based on either election are quite similar. In fact, my entire argument would stand using either set of results alone. See also note 17.

17. Concerning substantive accuracy, I note that my results are quite similar to the far more extensive analysis by John Hibbing (1991, 35, figure 2.3). They are also consistent with the analysis of Alford and Brady (1993), which is based on district-by-district pairings and proves essentially my conclusion by showing that the Sophomore Surge is nearly equal in magnitude to the "retirement slump." Sophomore Surge would not be comparable in magnitude to retirement slump if MCs went on increasing their vote margin year after year. Finally, my result for 1980 alone is 6.1 points (based on a separate regression not shown in table 6.2), which is predictably short of but still reasonably close to the Gelman-King estimate of incumbency advantage of about 8 points (1990, 1158). My estimate for 1990 alone is 10.6 points, which, surprisingly, is above the Gelman-King estimate of 8 points, as reported by Jacobson (1997b, figure 3.3). Thus, my average for 1980 and 1990 is almost exactly the average of the Gelman-King estimates for these same two years.

18. These are the only years for which I have seniority codes for all House members, including those not in NES samples.

19. The sophomore slump in spending is larger in 1990 than in 1980; this is expected, since the Sophomore Surge in MC vote share is also larger in 1990.

20. Spending data from 1980 substantiate the same general point, though less dramatically. Median opposition spending levels in open-seat and first reelection (sophomore) contests in that year were $120,000 and $50,000, respectively; median spending for MCs in their first elections and first reelections in 1980 were about $230,000 and $190,000, respectively.

21. Two types of cases are excluded from the analysis. On grounds of conceptual ambiguity, I excluded cases in which a member had come into office by special election since the last regularly scheduled election. Also, owing to the small number of districts represented in each cohort of each survey, I sought, to the extent possible, to make comparisons across the same districts. Accordingly, I excluded winning candidates and first-term MCs whose cohorts were not included in an adjacent sample. This meant excluding first-time winners from 1980 and 1990 (since I could not follow their constituents into 1982 and 1992) and first-term incumbents in 1978 and 1986 (since I did not have constituents from their open-seat contests in 1976 and 1984). This adjustment only slightly affected the results.

22. The mean thermometer score for all incumbents in this period was 63.3.

23. The 1993 Pilot Study (*American National Election Studies* 1993) was based on a reinterview of 746 respondents who had long-form interviews in the 1992 NES study; interviews were conducted from September to November 1993. Of those selected for reinterview, 74 percent agreed to be interviewed, 10 percent refused to be interviewed, and the remainder were never contacted for this wave of the survey, most often because they could not be reached at the phone address interviewers had to work with.

24. Parenthetically, I note that a question that begins by asking respondents whether they remember who ran for Congress in the last election might be a poor way of probing for information about MCs who rarely or never face a serious reelection contest, and it is surely a poor way of probing name recall a year after the election has passed. To put it the other way around, it is likely that the level of incumbent-name recall would be higher if respondents were asked directly, "Do you happen to know the name of the congressional representative in this district?" There is probably nothing that can be done

about this in midterm NES studies, but in general elections, one might ask a direct recall question on the preelection survey. See, however, Jacobson 1997a.

25. It should be noted that the baseline data for newly elected members in 1992 are, by the standards of figures 6.3, 6.4, and 6.5, unusually low. Name recall, in particular, is only 18 percent, compared with a recall rate of 34 percent for winning candidates in figure 6.3. A possible explanation is compositional. The 1993 freshman class contains more minority MCs than usual, and such MCs tend to come from urban districts in which congressional politics are ignored by the local media, television advertising is expensive, and races are lopsided and hence boring. All of these factors could contribute both to low initial levels of citizen awareness and affect and to difficulty in improving on the initially low scores.

26. The overreport is concentrated among voters who can remember neither candidate's name—which is about 53 percent of self-reported voters between 1978 and 1990 (Jacobson and Rivers 1993, table 6). In the old question format, this type of voter underreported in favor of the incumbent, according to Jacobson and Rivers. The NES Board of Overseers has struggled for years over how to accurately measure vote choice in congressional elections, with no solution yet in sight.

27. Jacobson also shows sharp gains in voter knowledge of MCs during the election. Beside the modest gains shown in Table 6.3, this underscores the relative unimportance of inter-election learning, as I argue throughout.

28. As Jacobson points out, the preelection interview may increase the sensitivity of voters to the ensuing campaign, or it may simply teach them the names of the candidates without doing anything else. Either way, my point holds.

29. Incumbency advantage, though tarnished in the 1990s, remains intact, according to Jacobson 1997b, 24.

30. It may also be significant that Levitt and Snyder explain average vote margin rather than probability of reelection, which, as Jacobson (1997b, 26, table 3.2) has shown, are not the same thing. Opposition elites, thus, may refrain from supporting hopeless challengers while still supporting strong ones when they come along.

31. Shively seeks to measure the "quality" advantage of individual MCs and show their effects. Gelman and King examine a form of electoral selection in their discussion of incumbency advantage, which they define as a compound of advantage due to incumbency per se and advantage "gained by a party because its candidate is of higher quality than the typical open seat candidate" (1990, 1153). However, they do not empirically investigate the effects of selection on candidate quality.

32. Jacobson (1992, 45–46) also suggests that an important selection effect may operate in congressional elections, though it is one based on willingness to exploit the resources of incumbency rather than, as I propose, on general political skill.

33. Because disputes do arise in some cases, and because champs are sometimes stripped of their titles without losing a fight, some cases might be coded differently. The appendix contains a list of the cases used in the analysis as well as notes about difficult ones.

34. Because, for the reason just given, strong challengers are likely to appear in intermittent waves, someone wishing to get an accurate measure of incumbent reelection rates, as I will need to do, must examine a sequence of elections long enough to include some years propitious to challengers. See notes 44 and 49, below.

35. There is a single exception: in the boxing data, all fights won are counted, whether won consecutively or not. Counting by consecutive wins, Mohammed Ali would have two careers, each ten fights long, plus a third, one-win career. A few other cases are affected, but not in a way that alters the visual impact of figure 6.6. It would have been best to count MC careers in the same way as the boxing careers, but I did not have the resources to do so, and I do not think it would make an important difference if I did.

36. In light of this assumption, it is notable that when Joe Louis returned to boxing just two years after voluntary retirement, he was beaten by the new champion, a man few now remember.

37. It is difficult to say exactly how strong this assumption is. Roderick Kiewiet and Langche Zeng are certainly impressed by the tenacity of incumbents, for whom neither narrow election margins nor being redistricted out of a seat nor getting plum leadership posts much affects the calculus on whether to quit politics (1993, 935). On the other hand, Jacobson and Dimock (1994) show that strategic retirements do occur, sometimes on a large scale, as I discuss below. I would like to have it both ways on this point: to believe that most MCs hang on as long as they can but then, when their time is up, sometimes retire strategically in order to avoid defeat.

38. This, however, is due mostly to selection: among champions who have won seven or more fights, there is only a small tendency to improve with experience or age during the first seven fights.

39. Some of the defeats and retirements in elections 31 through 100 involve careers that began in the earlier set of elections. In one set of experiments, I used elections 36 through 40 from each of 320 districts (rather than using elections 31 through 100 from each of 50 districts). These results showed the same trends as in my main simulations, except with more chance (because of the smaller number of cases) and greater trouble (more cases wasted reaching equilibrium in each district before any results were counted). The computer program necessary to run this simulation was written in XLISP and SPSS by Scott Desposato, a graduate student at UCLA. They are available on my website homepage. Other information necessary to replicate Table 4, including raw output from the XLISP simulations, are also on the webpage. The address is www.sscnet.ucla.edu/polisci/faculty/zaller/.

40. The variance of the ability scores, as determined empirically from random draws from the right-hand tail of a normal distribution for $z > 2$, is about .12. Variances for the distributions from which luck scores are drawn are set as multiples of this figure. The specific SD values used in columns one to seven of Table 4 are 0, .12, .17, .243, .34, .485, .68.

41. There is some chance instability in these figures. I did not attempt to estimate it, but my impression from watching many simulations is that the standard error of these figures is about 1 or 2 percent.

42. This regression effect is the same as the one identified by Gelman and King (1990) as the bias inherent in many measures of incumbency advantage.

43. Reelection rates do, however, include cases in which incumbents were thrown into uncongenial districts as part of the reapportionment, which seems to me a type of (bad) electoral luck and hence within the simulation.

44. "Intermittently" is an important qualifier here. Talented challengers do not contest incumbents randomly but choose their time to capitalize on partisan tides and other

nonskill—in my terms, luck—factors, such as reapportionment and economic climate, ·
as Jacobson and Kernell (1981) and Jacobson (1989) have shown. Hence, to get an accurate idea of the amount of competition incumbents face, one must take care to include
at least some elections in which the luck factors are such that the best potential challengers are willing to come forth and do battle with the reigning champion. This problem does not arise in boxing, where the nonskill factors that affect outcomes are not national tides that can be forecast months before the contest. See note 34, above.

45. The Senate vote totals and the 1980 presidential election results are based on constant districts—that is, the population base that became the House districts of the 1980s
after the 1982 reapportionment—as reported in *Congressional Districts in the 1980s* (1983).

46. For example, the average Democratic vote in nonsouthern districts in 1980 was
44.7 percent, which is a clear underestimate of Democratic partisanship at the subpres-
idential level.

47. If I adjust underlying district partisanship to 52 percent Democratic rather than
53 percent (by adding 3.3 points rather than 4.3 points to the average vote in five federal
elections), the overall and sophomore reelection rates are 95.3 percent and 85.5 percent,
respectively. If I adjust instead to 54 percent Democratic, these rates are 93.6 percent and
88.5 percent, respectively.

A caveat: The overall reelection rate in the simulations is somewhat sensitive to the
specific value of the term limit, which is a parameter in the model. The reelection rate is
higher with higher term limits, since high term limits permit the strongest incumbents
to stay in the game longer, thus driving up the overall reelection rate. Hence, if I raise the
term limit from seventeen elections to twenty-two elections in a regime in which luck
variance is one-eighth of skill variance, the overall reelection rate rises slightly, to 93.1
percent from 92.4 percent. If I lower the term limit to twelve elections, the overall reelection rate falls to 90.6 percent. Sophomore reelection rates are unaffected by this manipulation.

48. Thirty-nine percent of the rest (7/18) were defeated in the primary or general election.

49. I would like at this point to acknowledge a discrepancy between the simulation
and the data. I do so in a footnote because I judge the discrepancy to be, despite appearances, an unimportant one.

Reelection rates vary by party, by year, and by decade. The most important variations
are the reelection rates for Democrats in the 1980s, which are 96.5 percent overall and
93.2 percent in sophomore elections. Both figures—especially the former, which is probably inflated by strategic retirement—are notably above what even a model of pure skill
can explain. If, however, there were any partisan tides (luck) that favored the Democrats
in the 1980s, both figures would be within range of the simulation. This is because the
simulation, as presented, assumes that luck has a mean of zero in all cases; if there were
a group (Democrats in the 1980s or Republicans in the 1990s) for which luck was generally positive for an election or series of elections, reelection rates would be higher in
those groups. But because the simulation estimates reelection rates for all cases, not sub-
sets of cases for which luck seems to be positive, its estimates ought to be evaluated in
light of overall reelection rates.

But suppose that the high reelection rates of Democrats in the 1980s cannot be satis-
fyingly explained in this way. How much too high, then, would the actual rates be? For

districts, such as the ones we are considering, in which underlying partisanship is virtually even, the expected reelection rate ought to be around 50 percent. Hence, anything much above this level requires special explanation. According to column 2 of table 6.4, a simulation involving mostly skill but some luck can explain why the overall reelection rate in such districts might be as high as 92.2 percent and the sophomore rate might be as high as 83.4 percent. As indicated, these actual rates for Democratic incumbents in the 1980s are 97 percent and 93 percent, respectively. The difference might be attributed to other factors, including the special value of incumbency. Although, as I argue in the first two sections of this chapter, there is little strong evidence that the value of incumbency is large, it may not be zero, either.

But the first argument is, I think, the more important: results of the simulation ought to be evaluated in light of reelection rates for the population as a whole, not rates for subgroups known to be doing especially well in a particular period. This argument would lose force if the advantaged group seemed to enjoy a permanent edge, but experience in the 1990s suggests that this is not the case.

50. This data is available upon request.

51. Repeat challengers might be a more determined group than average, which would bias the test against finding an incumbency effect. On the other hand, repeat challengers, having lost once, might find it more difficult to raise money for a second try, which would bias the test in favor of finding an incumbency effect. The latter confound could, in principle, be controlled for, along with other factors, such as partisan tides. I have not been able to do this analysis.

52. Among the most neglected aspects of MC activity in the agenda-setting literature is use of the mass media, both within and between elections. Fenno's (1978) classic study mentions it only incidentally, focusing instead on meetings between MCs and relatively small groups. The mass media, to the extent they are noted, are often simply the name for a variable in a regression model. An exception is Mark Westlye (1991), who emphasizes the importance of media decisions to cover or ignore challenges to incumbents. See also Cook 1989.

References

Alford, John R., and David W. Brady. 1993. "Personal and Partisan Advantage in U.S. Congressional Elections, 1846–1990." In *Congress Reconsidered*, ed, Lawrence C. Dodd and Bruce I. Oppenheimer. Washington, D.C.: Congressional Quarterly Press.

Alvarez, R. Michael. 1997. "Why Study Only Presidential Campaigns? Statewide Races as a Laboratory for Campaign Analysis." Paper presented at Conference on Capturing Campaign Effects, University of British Columbia, June 21–22.

American National Election Studies, 1948–1994. 1995. CD-ROM issued in May. Available through the Inter-University Consortium for Political and Social Research, University of Michigan, Ann Arbor.

American National Election Studies, Pilot Study. 1993. Ann Arbor: University of Michigan, Inter-University Consortium for Political and Social Research.

Ansolabehere, Stephen, and Alan Gerber. 1997. "Incumbency Advantage and the Persistence of Legislative Majorities." *Legislative Studies Quarterly* 22:161–78.

Bartels, Larry. 1997. "Specification Uncertainty and Model Averaging." *American Journal of Political Science* 41:641–73.

Cain, Bruce, John Ferejohn, and Morris Fiorina. 1987. *The Personal Vote.* Cambridge: Harvard University Press.

Congressional Districts in the 1980s. 1983. Washington, D.C.: Congressional Quarterly Press.

Cook, Timothy. 1989. *Making Laws and Making News.* Washington, D.C.: Brookings Institution Press.

Cover, Albert D., and Bruce S. Brumberg. 1982. "Baby Books and Ballots: The Impact of Congressional Mail on Constituency Opinion." *American Political Science Review* 76:347–59.

Cox, Gary, and Jonathan N. Katz. 1996. "Why Did Incumbency Advantage in U.S. House Elections Grow?" *American Journal of Political Science* 40:478–97.

Emery, David, and Stan Greenberg. 1986. *The World Sports Record Atlas.* New York: Facts on File.

Erikson, Robert. 1971. "The Advantage of Incumbency in Congressional Elections." *Polity* 3:395–405.

Erikson, Robert S., and Gerald C. Wright. 1993. "Voters, Candidates, and Issues in Congressional Elections." In *Congress Reconsidered,* ed. Lawrence C. Dodd and Bruce I. Oppenheimer. Washington, D.C.: Congressional Quarterly Press.

Eubank, Robert, and David John Gow. 1993. "The Pro-Incumbent Bias in the 1978 and 1980 National Election Studies." *American Journal of Political Science* 27:122–39.

Fenno, Richard F. 1978. *Homestyle.* New York: HarperCollins.

Fiorina, Morris P. 1981. "Some Problems in Studying the Effects of Resource Allocation in Congressional Elections." *American Journal of Political Science* 25:543–67.

———. 1989. *Congress: Keystone of the Washington Establishment.* 2d ed. New Haven: Yale University Press.

Gelman, Andrew, and Gary King. 1990. "Measuring Incumbency without Bias." *American Journal of Political Science* 34:1142–64.

Herrnson, Paul. 1997. *Congressional Elections: Campaign at Home and in Washington.* Washington, D.C.: Congressional Quarterly Press.

Hibbing, John. 1991. *Congressional Careers: Contours of Life in the U.S. House of Representatives.* Chapel Hill: University of North Carolina Press.

Jacobson, Gary C. 1989. "Strategic Politicians and the Dynamics of House Elections, 1946–1986." *American Political Science Review* 83:773–93.

———. 1992. *The Politics of Congressional Elections.* 3d ed. New York: HarperCollins.

———. 1997a. "Measuring Campaign Spending Effects in U.S. House Elections." Paper presented at Conference on Capturing Campaign Effects, University of British Columbia, June 21–22.

———. 1997b. *The Politics of Congressional Elections.* 4th ed. New York: Longman.

Jacobson, Gary C., and Michael A. Dimock. 1994. "Checking Out: The Effects of Bank Overdrafts on the 1992 House Elections." *American Journal of Political Science* 38:601–24.

Jacobson, Gary C. and Sam Kernell 1981. *Strategy and Choice in Congressional Elections.* New Haven: Yale University Press.

Jacobson, Gary C., and Douglas Rivers. 1993. "Explaining Overreport of Vote for Incumbents in the National Election Studies." Paper presented at the annual meeting of Western Political Science Association, Pasadena, Calif., March 18–20.

Kiewiet, D. Roderick, and Langche Zeng. 1993. "An Analysis of Congressional Career Decisions, 1947–1986." *American Political Science Review* 87:928–48.

Krasno, Jonathan S. 1994. *Challengers, Competition, and Reelection: Comparing Senate and House Elections.* New Haven: Yale University Press.

Levitt, Steven, and James M. Snyder Jr. 1997. "The Impact of Federal Spending on House Election Outcomes." *Journal of Political Economy* 105:30–53.

Lowenstein, Daniel Hays. 1992. "Incumbency and Electoral Competition." Manuscript, UCLA Law School.

Mann, Thomas E. 1978. *Unsafe at Any Margin: Interpreting Congressional Elections.* Washington, D.C.: Brookings Institution Press.

Mann, Thomas E., and Raymond E. Wolfinger. 1980. "Candidates and Parties in Congressional Elections." *American Political Science Review* 74:617–32.

Mayhew, David R. 1974. "Congressional Elections: The Case of the Vanishing Marginals." *Polity* 6:295–317.

McAdams, John C., and John R. Johannes. 1981. "Does Casework Matter? A Reply to Professor Fiorina." *American Journal of Political Science* 25:581–604.

Peters, John G., and Susan Welch. 1980. "The Effects of Charges of Corruption on Voting Behavior in Congressional Elections." *American Political Science Review* 74:697–708.

Rivers, Douglas. 1988. "Partisan Representation in Congress." Paper presented at Seminar on Congressional Elections, University of California, Los Angeles.

Rivers, Douglas, and Morris Fiorina. 1989. "Consistency Service, Reputation, and the Incumbency Advantage." In *Home Style and Washington Work,* ed. Morris Fiorina and David W. Rohde. Ann Arbor: University of Michigan Press.

Romero, David W. 1996. "The Case of the Missing Reciprocal Influence: Incumbent Reputation and the Vote." *Journal of Politics* 58:1198–1207.

Sellers, Patrick. 1997. "Fiscal Consistency and Federal District Spending in Congressional Elections." *American Journal of Political Science* 41:1024–41.

Sera, George. 1994. "What's in It for Me? The Impact of Congressional Casework on Incumbent Evaluation." *American Politics Quarterly* 22:403–20.

Shively, W. Phillips. 1995. "Electoral Screening in Congressional Elections." Unpublished manuscript, Department of Political Science, University of Minnesota.

Squire, Peverill, and Eric R. A. N. Smith. 1984. "Repeat Challengers in Congressional Elections." *American Politics Quarterly* 12:51–70.

Vermeer, Jan P. 1987. *For Immediate Release.* Westport, Conn.: Greenwood.

Westlye, Mark. 1991. *Senate Elections and Campaign Intensity.* Baltimore: Johns Hopkins University Press.

Wright, Gerald C. 1993. "Errors in Measuring Vote Choice in the National Election Studies." *Journal of Politics* 37:291–316.

CHAPTER 7

Campaigns, Party Competition, and Political Advertising

John G. Geer

$\mathbf{P}$olitical scientists place great faith in the ability of competition to shape desirable outcomes. An excellent example involves our theories of representative democracy, which usually pit two (or more) political parties against each other in a series of free elections. Joseph Schumpeter surely expressed the greatest confidence in the ability of competition to promote the public good, but other scholars, ranging from E. E. Schattschneider to Morris Fiorina, have rested much on its benefits. The usual story is that when at least two parties battle for control of government, the parties will try to respond to the wishes of the public—with the winner of the struggle being the set of leaders that best meets the needs of the citizenry. And as long as politicians desire elective office, we should have a government that is responsive to the public's preferences, allowing "democracy" to reign.

Because of the central place of competition in our theories of representative democracy, we need to focus attention on the electoral campaign. It is during the months prior to election day that candidates take their case to the electorate. Stanley Kelley once observed that the campaign is the "principal institution" that links politicians and the electorate (1956, 3). We often forget, however, the importance of this institution for democratic government. Instead, observers tend to associate campaigns with dirty politics where contenders make unwarranted attacks on the opposition while overstating their own qualifications for office. Although the conduct of campaigns rarely meets our normative ideals, this institution, nonetheless, provides a critical link between citizens and government. William Riker perhaps puts it best, observing that campaigns are a distinguishing feature, worldwide, of modern representative democracies. For most citizens in most polities, campaigns provide a compelling incentive to think about government. So campaigns thus are a, perhaps the, main point of contact between officials and the populace over matters of public policy. If, as democratic theorists postulate, rulers are responsible to the ruled, the nexus of responsibility, the time and place we impose on it, is during campaigns and the elections in which they culminate. (1989, 1)

Yet in the vast amount of research, both theoretical and empirical, on party competition, little attention has been paid to the actual campaign.[1] For instance, the bulk of research on party competition has relied on analyses of platforms as the empirical base to assess how parties seek the electorate's support (e.g., Pomper 1980; Budge, Robertson, and Hearl 1987; Klingemann, Hofferbert, and Budge 1994). Yet these documents are crafted prior to the campaign. Our theories of electoral competition reflect the same sort of bias. Consider the idea of issue ownership that paints the competition between candidates as a product of long-standing differences that exist between the parties (e.g., Robertson 1976; Petrocik 1991, 1996). That theory has many merits, but it gives little importance to how the dynamics of the campaign might shape competition in elections.

The purpose of this chapter is to close this gap by integrating the campaign explicitly into our understanding of party competition. This particular endeavor has three parts. First, I offer a way to think about how candidates compete for votes that gives a more prominent role to the dynamics of the campaign than the typical account of party competition. Second, I introduce a new data set specifically designed to assess how presidential aspirants compete for the mass electorate's support. Although the analysis represents just a first cut at the data, the results underscore the need to include the campaign in our models of party competition. Finally, I suggest that the logic of competition in campaigns may work in ways that preclude a full discussion of the important issues confronting the nation. If so, our assumptions about the ability of competitive elections to promote democracy may be in need of revision.

Searching for Differences

To the outside observer, presidential campaigns often appear chaotic. Candidates scramble from state to state, while their aides try to ensure that the scheduled events produce good footage for the evening news. This whirlwind of activity does, however, have a central and shared objective: to win the election. That fundamental goal has provided the basis for political scientists to think more theoretically and systematically about these great democratic spectacles.

Scholars have, of course, developed a number of theories about how candidates seek votes in elections. But they usually play down the campaign. For instance, spatial models tend to describe competition in elections as largely the product of the positions candidates take on issues, often ignoring the strategic decisions made by candidates in the weeks prior to the casting of ballots. On the other hand, cleavage theory or issue ownership suggests that candidates compete in elections by stressing the divisions that have long separated the parties. So Democrats talk about social security, because they have a reputation with the public as a party able to handle that issue. The Republicans, in contrast, focus on taxes. The political maneuvers by candidates during the campaign are not part of this approach. Yet we know that the partisan appeals made by presidential contenders are not nearly so stable. In 1988, for example, George Bush tried to co-opt classic Democratic issues by telling voters that he would be the "education" and "environmental" president.

To give the campaign a more prominent role, I argue that candidates use the weeks prior to the election to search for a set of differences between themselves and their opposition that maximizes their chance for victory. We know that candidates jockey for position, offering claims and counterclaims in an effort to secure enough votes to win the upcoming election. But those activities can be usefully thought of as a "search for differences." So when Bush issued a plea in 1992 for a return to "family values" on the heels of the Republican convention, he was trying to find a wedge issue that might rally the electorate to his side. Robert Dole's attacks on Bill Clinton's character in the early stages of the 1996 election represented an effort to distinguish himself from the president.

This idea of searching for differences builds upon existing theories of party competition, such as cleavage theory and issue ownership (Robertson 1976; Lipset and Rokkan 1967; Petrocik 1991, 1996). As mentioned earlier, these perspectives view competition between candidates largely as a by-product of existing cleavages between the parties. John Petrocik (1991), for example, claims that parties stress those issues for which they have credibility. The perspective offered in this chapter extends this view. Parties have certain reputations, but so do individual candidates. Although the reputation of candidates will have much in common with those of their party, there can be important differences. If Colin Powell, rather than Robert Dole, had been the Republican nominee in 1996, Clinton would have handled such matters as experience, affirmative action, and abortion very differently. In short, the types of appeals that are most rational for candidates to promote are a function not only of the parties' strengths and weaknesses but also of candidates' personal qualifications and those of their opposition.

In addition, the reputations of parties are not fixed. They move over time, as events and politicians reshape them. For instance, the GOP lost a great deal of credibility on economic issues following the Great Depression. But since the 1950s, the GOP has shed that reputation. In the same way, the Democrats were not viewed as the party of fiscal responsibility, but with the deficits during the 1980s and the trimming of the debt under Clinton, the Democrats now fare much better on such issues. This approach allows the strengths and weaknesses of parties and candidates to change and at the same time allows candidates to define themselves in relation to the strengths and weaknesses of the opposition, as well.

The search for differences also builds upon Anthony Downs' *An Economic Theory of Democracy* (1957). In that influential book, Downs contends that office-seeking candidates will generally converge toward the center of public opinion.[2] But from a candidate's perspective, this insight is only partially correct. Although it is true that candidates, by positioning themselves near the midpoint of public opinion, can maximize their electoral support, victory-seeking candidates actually want to control the median position. That is, rational candidates want no other contenders near them, stealing their thunder. For if an opposing politician offers a comparable view on an issue, the electoral power of that issue wanes. Thus, politicians do not want to offer similar views on issues; rather, they want to differentiate themselves from the opposition—but only when that differentiation puts them in a favorable light.

The relevance of this modified goal becomes even clearer within the context of Downs' original model. In the simplest of spatial worlds, there are two candidates and only one issue in the election. Using all the restrictive assumptions, rational contenders move to the median position, offering identical views on the single issue.[3] But if we push the logic further, a problem arises. Although adopting the median position maximizes votes, that strategy does not produce a victory for either candidate. The election, instead, ends in a tie, because the electorate, under this simple scenario, splits its vote evenly between the two candidates.

Thus, offering the median position in this restricted model is rational when we assume that politicians seek to maximize votes. But if we, instead, assume that politicians want to win elections, which is their ultimate goal, then they face a rationality crisis. If a candidate moves away from the median position, the opposition will seize it and win the election. On the other hand, staying at the median position yields only a tie. Hence, neither choice is optimal for the politician who wants to emerge the victor.[4]

Consequently, contenders who want to win elections will try to alter this situation. They will pursue strategies that will provide them opportunities to win the battle. They accomplish this task by searching for and establishing differences between themselves and their rivals.[5] This search takes place during the campaign.

This approach is consistent with how candidates and their staffs think about elections—something that counts strongly in its favor. Consider, for instance, that one of the central objectives of then-president Gerald Ford's 1976 advertising strategy was to "portray the important differences between" him and Jimmy Carter.[6] Lawrence Jacobs and Robert Shapiro report that in the 1960 campaign, "Kennedy's aides repeatedly urged their candidate to emphasize the differences on the issues" (1992, 32). One can also turn to the 1992 presidential campaign, where Bush often talked about the "fundamental differences" between him and the governor from Arkansas, or to Clinton's frequent references to the "clear choice" facing the electorate in 1992. Candidates spend a great deal of time trying to differentiate themselves from others in a way that makes them look good and their opponents bad.

If one accepts this idea that rational candidates want to establish favorable differences between themselves and their opponents, a different picture of how candidates compete for votes arises. No longer does it appear that candidates just adopt median positions on issues or make appeals on those issues that traditionally favor their party. Instead, in the weeks prior to the actual voting, contenders fight to get their issues on center stage. This argument gives the agenda a more prominent role in the campaign, which has been increasingly viewed as critical to understanding political competition (see Riker 1982, 1986, 1993; Budge, Robertson, and Hearl 1987; Semetko et al. 1991; Klingemann, Hofferbert, and Budge 1994; Simon 1997).

This approach also provides an explicit role for negative campaigning. In the traditional spatial theory, for instance, attacks on one's opponent were not part of the story. But one way to establish differences is to attack the opposition. And given the frequency of negative appeals in today's campaigns, it is important that we offer theories that make room for that kind of behavior. In the same spirit, this theory does not limit competition for votes to matters of policy. The personal traits of candidates, too, can serve as a way for candidates to establish differences. Furthermore, the argument advanced here is not limited to competition in the general election. It can also be applied to the nomination process, where presidential aspirants battle for control of the party. The theory of issue ownership, for example, has little to say about intraparty contests, since it relies on interparty divisions to explain the behavior of candidates.[7]

As a final point, this argument provides an explanation for why candidates do not always offer median positions on issues. Because contenders look for those issues they can claim to be their own, this process will yield some differences between them. And if a difference emerges, the candidate in the nonmedian position may prefer to raise a new issue or attack the opposition rather than change position on that issue and risk the charge of "flip-flopping." But the strategic moves of candidates do suggest that candidates try to put themselves at the median on some issues—as Downs wrote years ago. Candidates accomplish this goal by raising those issues that favor them—not by adopting the median positions on all issues. Thus, the election may still be a struggle over the center. That struggle, however, is largely over the agenda, as opposed to the positions on such things as the so-called liberal-conservative spectrum.

Evidence

During the course of a campaign, candidates flood the market with a variety of propaganda. To determine whether politicians do, indeed, search for differences, we need to gather evidence about how candidates compete for the public's support during the campaign. This requirement restricts the kind of propaganda that can be used to test this argument. Party platforms, which have been a linchpin in previous work on partisan competition, are a problematic choice. These documents are written prior to the campaign. In addition, platforms are suppose to represent the party's views on issues, which means they not only tend to ignore the traits of the presidential hopefuls but also contain fewer attacks on the opposition than are witnessed during the campaign.[8] Bob Dole, in fact, claimed during the 1996 campaign that he did not even read the GOP platform, underscoring the point that platforms may not serve as a good indication for how candidates seek votes during the campaign.

Another possible source of evidence is speeches candidates make during the campaign. Benjamin Page (1978) and Stanley Kelley (1966) have, for instance, made good use of speeches in analyzing elections. These data have a number of assets, such as representing direct statements from the candidates on matters of policy during the campaign. One practical problem, however, is that there are only a handful of cases where a complete set of speeches exists for both candidates (Page 1978). But, more importantly, speeches usually do not reach the public directly. The news media may use small parts of speeches in their coverage of the campaign, making them important parts of it. But as a result, what voters see is a function of the news media's, not the candidates', decisions. The journalistic filter limits the value of such data to assess the framework presented here.

One source of data that should be able to shed a great deal of light on the workings of competition is the paid television advertising of the presidential candidates. Spots aired on TV reach the mass audience directly and serve as a central part of candidates' controlled, and hence strategic, efforts to win elections. As Frank Luntz, a prominent political consultant, observes, "Candidates have come to accept paid advertising as the primary mode of interaction with the electorate" (1988, 73). Luntz's claim is borne out by the enormous amount of money presidential aspirants spend on political advertising (Devlin 1987; West 1993). The Dole campaign planned to spend 64 percent of their campaign war chest on paid political advertising, while Clinton kicked in 69 percent (Goldstein 1997). Spots, in short, represent a critical component of the candidates' attempts to convince voters to support them, allowing these bits of propaganda to shed much light on how candidates compete for the public's support.

Fortunately, the University of Oklahoma has an impressive archive of political advertisements from presidential campaigns. Julian Kanter, its founder, cannot claim that the archive has every campaign commercial run since 1960, but he has close to a complete set in most cases and a complete set in some.[9] These data, therefore, should provide a good account of the kinds of appeals candidates have made to the public over the last thirty years.[10] Toward that end, I have undertaken a detailed content analysis of presidential advertisements aired on TV from 1960 to 1992. To expand the scope of inquiry, I also analyzed the spots from the 1980, 1984, 1988, and 1992 Democratic and Republican primaries and caucuses.[11]

For details on the content analysis, one should turn to the appendix. But let me provide a brief overview. To begin, three basic types of appeals were examined: traits, values, and issues.[12] Within each category, I attempted to gather as much detail as possible about the concerns raised in the presidential advertisements. So, for example, I did not just code whether the spot addressed economic policy. Instead, the number of references to specific issues like inflation or unemployment were counted. It was then recorded whether the appeal was positive or negative. That is, did the candidate talk about how he had lowered (or would lower) inflation or how his opponent had generated (or would generate) rampant inflation? Because of this coding scheme, more than nine hundred different categories were used for issues alone. For traits, I employed nearly two hundred unique codes, for references ranging from the candidate's sense of humor to the fact that his opposition "flip-flopped" on some issue. These data, in short, should provide a representation of the specific appeals the presidential aspirants made to voters during the course of the campaign.

Before proceeding to the results, let me make one final comment. Some may think of the spot as the unit of analysis in this data set, but that is usually not the case. Sixty-second spots, which dominated the airwaves in the 1960s, contain many more appeals, on average, than the thirty-second variety, which are now king. To make these two eras comparable, I summed these appeals across all spots for a particular candidate. This decision makes the unit of analysis the appeal within an advertisement. It also allows the full set of messages to be examined, as opposed to pigeonholing an entire advertisement as a "trait" or an "issue" spot.

Advertising versus Platforms

Earlier, I argued that the campaign has been ignored in previous accounts of how candidates compete for the support of the electorate. Some will take issue with this claim, noting that the analysis of platforms has provided a good basis for understanding partisan competition (see Budge, Robertson, and Hearl 1987; Pomper 1980; Robertson 1976; Ginsberg 1976; Klingemann, Hofferbert, and Budge 1994). Alan Monroe, in fact, argues that "platforms almost always represent the policy preferences of the eventual nominee" and provide "a virtual preview of the campaigns that followed" (1995, 15). To see if there are, as I hypothesize, differences between what is said in platforms and in the subsequent campaign, I compared the substantive policy issues raised in platforms with that of ads.[13] Given that these documents are rarely concerned with the personalities of the candidates, attention was restricted to issues to provide the most favorable comparison for these party manifestos. This test, therefore, is a conservative one.

For this analysis, I focused on eight different sets of general concerns: economic issues (e.g., jobs, inflation, taxes), the management of government (e.g., spending, deficits, efficiency), New Deal issues (e.g., agriculture, health care, social security and the aged, education, poverty, welfare), racial issues (e.g., civil rights, discrimination, quotas), social issues (e.g., crime, busing, abortion, drugs), foreign policy (e.g., war and peace, dealings with the USSR), defense policy (e.g., military spending, nuclear arms), and "other domestic" issues (e.g., energy, urban affairs, the environment). There are, of course, other ways to organize these issues.[14] But I chose these categories because they represent most of the concerns parties have fought about over the last thirty years (see, for instance, Carmines and Stimson 1989; Sundquist 1983; Kelley 1988).

Table 7.1 gives the issue areas most frequently cited in the presidential election campaigns from 1960 to 1992. Merely by scanning the raw frequencies, we can see that the content of the two forms of propaganda differ. As the table shows, the issue that drew most attention in the party's platform often differed from that stressed in the candidate's political advertising. In only four of the eighteen cases (22 percent) did the platforms and the ads agree on what was the most important issue. I also calculated the average difference between the issue agenda in the ads and the platforms. The mean was just below nine percentage points, with a standard deviation also near nine. These results demonstrate that sizable differences exist between the content of ads and that of platforms.

Within these differences, another pattern emerges: candidates during the campaign focus on fewer issues than are represented in party platforms. Since the platform seeks to placate the interests of various activists, the document must address a vast array of issues in an effort to satisfy the many supporters

Table 7.1 Most-Cited Theme in Ads and Platforms, 1960–1992 (percentage)

	Democrats		Republicans	
	Ads	Platforms	Ads	Platforms
1960	47 (New Deal)	25 (New Deal)	57 (Foreign Policy)	26 (New Deal)
1964	53 (New Deal)	27 (Foreign Policy)	44 (Foreign Policy)	38 (Foreign Policy)
1968	36 (New Deal)	26 (Foreign Policy)	33 (Social)	29 (Foreign Policy)
1972	29 (Economic)	23 (New Deal)	39 (Foreign Policy)	22 (Foreign Policy)
1976	33 (Economic)	23 (Foreign Policy)	33 (Economic)	29 (Foreign Policy)
1980	27 (Foreign Policy)	28 (Foreign Policy)	56 (Economic)	25 (Foreign Policy)
1984	31 (Defense)	30 (Foreign Policy)	60 (Economic)	25 (Foreign Policy)
1988	26 (Social)	26 (Foreign Policy)	36 (Economic)	29 (Foreign Policy)
1992	70 (Economic)	24 (New Deal)	40 (Economic)	17 (New Deal)
Mean	39	26	44	27
Overall Mean:		Ads 42	Platforms 26	

Note: The phrase (or word) in parentheses is the general theme that was given the most attention in either the ads or the platform.

of the party. But when campaigning for the public's support, candidates have an incentive to concentrate their fire, not disperse it. Data confirm this hypothesis. In 1992, for instance, Clinton's ads highlighted the now famous phrase, "It's the Economy, Stupid": 70 percent of all appeals concerning substantive issues dealt with the economy. Yet in the Democratic platform, only 24 percent of all appeals on issues concerned such matters. Four years earlier, the GOP platform only briefly mentioned crime (1 percent). But Bush's ads focused heavily on it (15 percent). To look at the Democratic platform in 1964, one would not have thought social security would have been a central issue in the campaign. Yet nearly one quarter of Lyndon Johnson's appeals dealt with this matter. On average, nearly 42 percent of the appeals in the ads across the eighteen campaigns dealt with just one of the eight issues. The comparable figure for platforms falls to about 26 percent. This sixteen-point gap highlights the tendency of candidates to concentrate their attention on fewer issues than what the platforms suggest.

Do Candidates Search for Differences?

That the content of political ads differs significantly from that of platforms underscores the need to focus on the messages candidates send to the public during the campaign. Those findings, however, represent only the first step. We now need to see whether the "searching for differences" perspective provides a useful way to understand how candidates seek votes.

But before testing a few hypotheses that flow from this argument, I want to describe a couple of important features of the data. As suggested earlier, candidates do more than just discuss the issues that favor them in their struggle for votes during the campaign. About 27 percent of all appeals from 1960 to 1992 concerned the personal traits of presidential candidates. It varied from a low of 11 percent for Richard Nixon in 1968 to a high of 45 percent for Jimmy Carter in 1980. Issues, on the other hand, comprised 52 percent of all appeals. Of those issues, 30 percent represented attacks on the opposition. Of ads directed at personality traits of the opposition, 35 percent were negative. Over the last four decades, there has been a general increase in negativity (see Finkel and Geer 1998).[15] These findings, while hardly shocking, demonstrate the importance of making room for such empirical regularities in our theories of partisan competition.

As a first test, I examine whether candidates alter their appeals during the campaign. A traditional Downsian account of party competition gives us little reason to expect candidates to alter their agendas. Instead, the struggle is over the optimal position on issues that matter to the public. The claim that parties own certain issues (see, for instance, Petrocik 1991, 1996; Robertson 1976) predicts that nominees will highlight those issues that have long favored the party. But because those issues are part of a partisan tradition, instability is again not an explicit part of the story. The notion of searching, however, suggests a more dynamic process whereby candidates look for those topics that permit them to gain support in the electorate. Hence, one simple test of this approach is to see whether the content of appeals changes between August and November.

It is fair to say that candidates do shift their appeals with much frequency during the course of a campaign. A crude indicator can be found in the changes between candidates' agendas (from 1976 to 1992) from the first part of the campaign to the last part.[16] There was, on average, a shift of about eight percentage points in the attention paid to the eight sets of issues. For the five general types of trait appeals (experience, leadership, integrity, compassion, and personal characteristics), the mean change was more than eleven percentage points.[17] The standard deviations were also large, 7.0 and 9.6, respectively. Michael Dukakis, for example, started his general election campaign by stressing the theme of leadership. But as November drew near, he shifted course and focused attention on compassion and caring as an important personal trait. In the latter stages of his campaign, Walter Mondale talked a lot about "Star Wars" and defense policy. This focus came on the heels of his concern with government management and the deficit. Ronald Reagan largely ignored foreign policy in the early stages of his 1980 bid for the presidency. But as October rolled around, he gave the topic much more attention.

This search for differences will not, however, work in the same way for all candidates. My argument predicts that candidates behind in the polls will behave differently than those ahead. That is, the "losers" should be expected to change their appeals more frequently than the "winners," because the former have an incentive to inject new issues into the campaign in an effort to attract additional support. In contrast, politicians who have found a winning theme, so to speak, should tend to keep with it during the course of the campaign.

To test this hypothesis, I examined the relationship between candidates' support in the Gallup Poll at the start of the campaign and the number of ads I coded from the archive (see appendix).[18] In only one election since 1960 did a candidate who trailed in the polls at the start of the campaign air fewer spots than the front-runner.[19] That was George Bush in 1992. By regressing the candidate's Gallup Poll standing on his share of spots, we can secure a more systematic reading of this relationship. The results are as follows (the sample size is eighteen, the adjusted r-squared is .26; standard errors are reported in the parentheses):[20]

$$s = 84 - .67g,$$
$$(13) \ (.25)$$

where

s is the percentage of spots aired by candidate, and
g is the candidate's support in the Gallup Poll.

These estimates confirm the hypothesis. For every ten percentage point gain in the Gallup Poll, a candidate can be expected to air seven percentage points fewer ads than the opposition. So, for instance, a candidate who leads with 60 percent of the vote at the beginning of the campaign is predicted to air only 38 percent of the ads that year.

As a further test of the behavior of candidates ahead and behind in the polls,

I have reanalyzed some data presented earlier. Specifically, I examined whether stressing a single theme is correlated with the actual share of the vote a candidate receives in the election. If this argument is correct, there should be a positive relationship between being single-minded in one's ads and the actual share of the vote. Regressing the data from table 7.1 onto the share of the vote that a candidate garnered in the election yields the following results (the sample size is eighteen, the adjusted r-squared is .22; standard errors are reported in the parentheses):

$$v = 38.2 - .28i,$$
$$\quad (5) \quad (.12)$$

where

v is the percentage of two-party vote a candidate receives, and
i is the percentage of attention given to the candidate's most-stressed issue.

These results show that for every additional four percentage points in attention paid to the most cited issue, a candidate's vote increases by one percentage point. I am not arguing that a causal connection exists. Instead, the finding simply shows that candidates who win elections do so, in part, because they have a core theme that they can build their campaign on. Clinton's almost single-minded focus on the economy is a case in point.

If the candidates do search for differences that favor them, their quest should also lead the nominees to stress different agendas. Since presidential aspirants will spend much of their time trying to put their own spins on issues and raising other concerns that favor them, contenders will end up "talking past each other." This idea has been floating around for some time. Over a century ago, James Bryce noted that each party "pummels, not his true enemy, but a stuffed figure set up to represent that enemy" (1895, 214). Others, too, have noted that parties will talk past each other (e.g., Petrocik 1991; Kelley 1992; Simon 1997).

To test this claim, I have looked at the statistical relationship between ads from the Democratic and Republican nominees for the eight sets of issues across the past nine elections. The two agendas yield a correlation of .34, suggesting that while they do not completely ignore each other, there is, at least, some disagreement.[21] But one still might counter that it is unclear whether that particular correlation supports or refutes the hypothesis. Perhaps .34 is a high level of agreement. To provide a benchmark, I compared the parties' agendas in the platforms for the same issues and elections. The correlation between the Democratic and Republican platforms was .88, indicating much more similar agendas than found in the ads.[22] These findings confirm that when the campaign starts, candidates often head in different directions (as suggested by the lower correlation), leading them to talk past each other.[23]

Granted that differences exist between the appeals the two candidates make, does this framework help us understand the specific differences? Table 7.2 documents the relative attention the candidates gave to eight broad themes in presidential ads from 1960 to 1992. Not surprisingly, Democratic nominees stress New Deal issues more than Republicans.[24] Since 1960, 28 percent of all issues in each Democratic campaign dealt with New Deal policies. In contrast, only 10 percent of appeals from the GOP contenders fell into this category. When looking at foreign policy and economic matters, the Republican nominees take the lead.

The findings that Democratic and Republican nominees offer different issues is consistent with other perspectives, such as cleavage theory (Lipset and Rokkan 1967) or issue ownership (Petrocik 1991, 1996).[25] According to these theories, Republicans are unlikely to make social security a centerpiece of their campaign against the Democrats. At the same time, the Democrats have little incentive to talk about crime as a reason to vote for them instead of Republicans. Thus, the choice of agendas will follow the same kind of pattern documented here.

Although this argument has much in common with previous theories, my approach provides some additional advantages. First, the search for differences does not rely solely on the "fixed" traditions of the parties to predict what candidates will talk about in campaigns. In 1988, for instance, according to the theory of issue ownership we would not expect Bush to raise the environment as an issue at the outset of his campaign. But understanding that this concern favored Dukakis, Bush attacked his Democratic rival to minimize the impact of that issue—behavior consistent with the argument of this chapter. Moreover, in 1984 Mondale's heavy emphasis on defense and foreign policy reflected the fact that those concerns represented one of Reagan's few vulnerabilities at the time. The theory of issue ownership would not predict such a focus, given the usual GOP hold on such matters. Also, as table 7.2 documents, Bush gave a fair amount of attention to New Deal issues in 1992. The decision to do so was made not because of traditional links the GOP has with those sets of concerns but rather because of Bush's effort to find issues that could separate him from the then-governor from Arkansas.

Second, this perspective provides insights into how candidates will use personal traits in their attempt to gain votes. For example, incumbent candidates, on average, should make greater use of traits than nominees from the out-party. Having been in office for the last fours years allows these contenders to tout their experience.[26] Previous theories have little to say about such matters. Table 7.3 tests this hypothesis. As the table shows, Democratic and Republican nominees talk about traits and issues at the same rate. But in-party nominees focus more on traits (33 percent of the total) than the out-party standard-bearers (23

Table 7.2 Issue Agenda of Candidates in General Election Ads (percentage)

	1960–1992 Presidential Elections			1992 General Election Only		
	Republican Nominees	Democratic Nominees	Difference[a]	Bush	Clinton	Difference
Economic issues	30	24	+6	40	70	–30
Government management	9	6	+3	14	3	+11
New Deal policies	10	28	–18	23	20	+3
Racial issues	1	2	–1	0	0	0
Social issues	9	6	+3	7	2	+5
Foreign policy	24	11	+13	7	0	+7
Defense policy	8	8	0	3	0	+3
Other domestic issues	5	15	–10	3	5	–2

[a] Difference is calculated by subtracting the proportion for Democratic nominees from that of their Republican counterparts.

percent). When looking at the specific content of trait appeals, the hypothesis gains even further support. Across all references to personal traits, 47 percent of appeals to traits by the in-party nominee focused on matters related to experience. That proportion shrinks to 25 percent for the out-party nominees.

Table 7.3 Comparison of Values, Issues, and Traits in General Election Ads, 1960–1992 (percentage)

	All Ads	Demo-cratic Ads	GOP Ads	In-Party Ads	Out-Party Ads
Values	21	20	21	20	21
Issues	52	52	52	47	56
Traits	27	28	27	33	23
N	7,333	3,717	3,162	2,979	3,900

The third advantage of the search for differences argument is that it offers a way to understand the behavior of candidates in presidential primaries and caucuses—an arena about which, again, previous theories have had little to say. In contests for the party's nominations, this argument predicts that candidates will have to offer different kinds of appeals from those they offer in the general election. Since these struggles are intraparty affairs, candidates will, on average, have fewer differences on issues than in the general election campaign, forcing them to search for new ways to secure votes. One hypothesis, then, is that candidates in primaries and caucuses will turn more to traits as a way to distinguish themselves from their opponents than they do in the general election. This claim is counterintuitive. Many scholars view primaries as a competition for votes among a more ideologically charged electorate, leading candidates to stake out a more issue-oriented agenda (Polsby 1983; Lengle 1981). But this argument suggests such a strategy will not be pursued frequently, because candidates in primaries and caucuses often have similar ideological leanings, forcing them to compete on other grounds.

The data in table 7.4 provide a simple proportional breakdown of the use of issues, traits, and values in ads aired during general elections and during primaries and caucuses.[27] The proportions support the hypothesis offered above: issues play a bigger role in general elections than in primaries, while traits become more important in contests for the nomination.

A related hypothesis is that issues raised in ads aired during primaries and caucuses are different from those aired in the general election. Specifically, we

Table 7.4 Comparison of Values, Issues, and Traits in Primary and General
Election Ads, 1980–1992 (percentage)

	General Election Ads	Ads in Primaries and Caucuses
Values	21	20
Issues	50	42
Traits	29	38
N	4,177	1,860

should see some inversion in the agendas of campaigns for the nomination from
those in the general election. So, for instance, while Dukakis might talk about
social security in an attempt to lure votes from George Bush, that strategy is not
as likely to work against fellow Democrats who, like Dukakis, probably have a
history of supporting programs for the elderly. Consequently, we should see Democrats competing for the nomination by moving away from classic New Deal
issues and perhaps turning to foreign policy concerns or social issues. On the
other side, Republicans may be more willing to tackle New Deal concerns during primaries, because these issues provide a way for candidates to sort themselves out. At the same time, discussions about the (former) Soviet threat should
play a less significant role in the GOP primaries and caucuses, since most candidates will have credibility on these matters.

Table 7.5 presents a breakdown of issues for Democratic and Republican primaries. As predicted, New Deal concerns do play a bigger role in their ads during GOP primaries than in those during the general election. Democratic candidates focus less on New Deal concerns in their caucuses and primaries,
moving more toward foreign policy. In short, the differences work in the expected directions.

These tests not only lend support to this theoretical perspective; they also
show the need to include the campaign in our accounts of party competition.
By so doing we develop a richer theoretical account of competition between
candidates and, as well, map a process that is closer to what we observe during
the weeks prior to the November balloting.

Concluding Thoughts

Conventional wisdom tells us that when candidates compete for the public's
votes, they discuss the kinds of issues that will allow the citizenry to make good
choices on election day. If one side ignores an important issue, the other side

Table 7.5   Issue Agenda of Candidates' Ads in Presidential Primaries and
Caucuses, 1980–1992 (percentage)

	Republicans	Democrats
Economics issues	29 (−1)	35 (+11)
Government management	9 (0)	7 (+1)
New Deal issues	18 (8)	20 (−8)
Racial issues	0 (−1)	1 (−1)
Social issues	5 (−4)	4 (−2)
Foreign policy	13 (−11)	13 (+2)
Defense policy	6 (−2)	8 (0)
Other domestic issues	13 (+8)	10 (−5)

Note: Figures in parentheses represent the difference from general election proportions.
Difference is calculated by subtracting the proportion in the general election ads reported in table 7.3 from the proportion in primary and caucus ads.

The mean proportion is calculated using those candidates with more than 30 appeals
on issues, making the sample size 12 for Republicans and 16 for Democrats.

References to viability and other strategic concerns make up a small proportion of
appeals in primaries. I have not reported them here since there are almost no such appeals made in the general election.

will raise it in a quest for votes. This competitive process forces the candidates
to be responsive to the needs of the electorate.

But if the battle between candidates and their parties in fact turns on establishing differences, that process may not lead to a discussion of the most pressing issues of the day. Rather, the debate during campaigns will center on the
often unique combination of the strengths and weaknesses of the candidates involved. So, for example, in 1988 Bush talked about flag factories and patriotism
rather than the large federal deficit. Why? Was it because that patriotism was
more important to the electorate than deficits? Or was it because the Bush campaign felt Dukakis was more vulnerable to the issue of patriotism than to a serious discussion of deficits that had tripled during the Reagan years? The obvious counter is that Dukakis should have raised the deficit as an issue. But for
a governor of a liberal, "tax-and-spend" state, such an appeal was unlikely to
be successful. Hence, an important issue was largely left on the sidelines, despite
the fierce competition between these two individuals. Such biases in two-can-

didate competition are a source of concern, especially given political scientists' faith in the ability of competitive struggles to shape good outcomes.

Figure 7.1 seeks to illustrate this general process, albeit in crude form. By assuming that any given issue or trait is either a strength or a weakness for a candidate or party, I can construct a simple two-by-two table that captures the possible outcomes. Clearly, there is, on average, more incentive to duck issues than to address them.[28] Little attention will be paid to those issues, such as the deficit, that pose problems for both sides. By comparison, those concerns that are assets for both parties will be discussed. But since those concerns do not really cut for either side, they are unlikely to be a hallmark of either campaign. Instead, competition will center on the two remaining boxes. But even here there is little direct confrontation between candidates on the issue, since one side has good reason to duck it. The end result of this competition may look more like professional wrestling than a heavyweight bout.[29]

Without genuine competition on the important issues from both camps, the picture painted for the electorate is unlikely to be a fair representation of the

Figure 7.1 Potential Biases of Partisan Competition

	Candidate A	
	Issue is a Strength	*Issue is a Weakness*
Candidate B *Issue is a Weakness*	*A* will talk some, *B* will talk some	*A* will duck, *B* will talk a lot
Candidate B *Issue is a Strength*	*A* will talk a lot, *B* will duck	*A* will duck, *B* will duck

debate. Candidates can only be counted on to provide their side of the story. Propaganda is not supposed to be an even-handed discussion of the matter. Hence, the quality of information the electorate receives may not be of the type that would permit an informed decision.

To compound matters, it is unlikely that the pressing issues of the day will fall randomly into these four boxes, introducing an even greater tendency to duck the important issues than just suggested above. Any issue that is a strength of both sides is unlikely to be a burning concern for the public. The fact that it is an asset for both suggests that the problem has been solved or that both sides seem well equipped to deal with it. As a result, the problems of this country, as viewed by the electorate, are likely to fall disproportionately in the other three boxes. If so, salient issues will, on average, receive even less attention by the competitors.

Because of these potential biases, this chapter raises questions about our assumptions concerning the merits of competition and also casts doubt on the optimism of previous empirical work on party competition. Scholars have shown a sizable empirical connection between what parties say in platforms and what they do in office (Pomper 1980; Monroe 1979; Klingemann, Hofferbert, and Budge 1994). But there are important differences between the appeals candidates make in their ads and what parties say in their platforms. While platforms tell us much about the parties' thinking on many issues, they apparently tell us far less about what appeals candidates actually make to the electorate during the campaign. And it is the latter that provide important clues about the competition between candidates for elective office.

The results of this study cast a shadow over some of the conclusions made about "party competition." The link that others have found between what parties say and what governments do may need some modification. It may be that ads, too, are good predictors of governmental actions—perhaps even better predictors. The opposite, of course, may also be true, especially since campaigns, as shown here, tend to focus on fewer issues than would be predicted by the content of party platforms. If that is the case, the information that voters come across during a campaign may not be good indicators of future action by elected leaders. That possibility is especially unnerving and demands further investigation.

Much more, of course, needs to be said about these matters. But the end result of this chapter, I hope, is a better understanding (or, at least, appreciation) of the workings of competition during campaigns. As a discipline, we have hinged a lot of our theories on the perceived benefits of competition. But before we can be sure that that faith is warranted, we need to unlock the many puzzles of how candidates compete for support in the weeks prior to the actual balloting. Otherwise, we may risk misunderstanding how elections work. It is perhaps for these reasons that we need to take the campaign more seriously as an institution when studying the operation of democratic governments.

Appendix

The Data

At least 90 percent of the presidential ads in the Julian P. Kanter Archives are not more than a minute long. In the content analysis, I chose to focus on these shorter ads, since they constitute the bulk of the contenders' advertising campaign.[30] This focus should allow me to capture the major campaign themes of the nominees. Moreover, in recent years, there has been a greater emphasis on the shorter spot, making this choice even more reasonable.

Besides the length of the ads, I had a number of other criteria concerning which ads to code. For instance, I coded only those ads aired by the candidates. The archive possessed a handful of spots that the candidates' campaigns created but decided not to run. Since I am interested in only those appeals presented to the electorate, I did not include these ads in the analysis. In addition, I did not code ads that were near duplicates of earlier spots. In recent elections, there have been a number of very similar ads. With technological advances, it is easier to make one or two small changes in a spot. For example, Dukakis ran a series of ads under the title, "The Packaging of George Bush." One of these spots implied that the Japanese might someday buy the White House—a negative comment about the amount of foreign investment in the country. Two days later, a new version of the ad was produced by the Dukakis camp, and the only change was that the ad referred to "foreign interests" rather than to Japan specifically. This difference, while an interesting story, did not affect my coding of the ad. Hence, I analyzed only one ad, so as to avoid double-counting of themes. If the change, however, introduced an important new idea, then an effort was made to include that new appeal into my results.

Besides near-duplicate ads, some thirty-second or twenty-second spots are simply shortened versions of longer sixty-second spots. Reagan's campaigns in 1980 and 1984, for instance, cut a number of their sixty-second spots into thirty-second editions. In these cases, I coded only the sixty-second spot. As with the near duplicates mentioned above, there is no reason to double count the topics in these spots.

A third criterion was that I excluded any spot directed at a specific state for the general election. (I did not use this criterion in selecting ads from campaigns for the presidential nominations, since campaigns are conducted by state). I wanted to tap the appeals candidates were making in their national campaigns, limiting the value of specific appeals to specific states. There were not a lot of these ads, but occasionally a well-known politician from a state might be used to endorse a particular candidate. In addition, I did not code ads in Spanish, since I do not know the language. But this decision, dictated by my own ignorance, turns out not be to a serious problem. Many ads aimed at Latino audiences are often Spanish-language versions of existing spots (Subervi-Velez, Herrera, and Begay 1987).

Some commercials, however, clearly had an apparent regional appeal, such as ads focusing on farmers. I did, however, include them in the analysis. The reason is that these spots can cover a huge area of the country, like the Midwest or parts of California. Moreover, I have no data about when and where ads were actually shown, forcing me to guess about the actual target of the ad.[31] As a result, only in cases where I knew for sure the ad was aimed at a local or state audience did I bump it from the analysis.

Finally, I limited my attention to spots authorized by the candidate's campaign committee. Occasionally, a group aired an ad either attacking or supporting a particular candidate. But since I am concerned with how candidates compete with one another, these ads fell outside the bounds of this project. Because of this rule, perhaps the most famous ad of recent times—the Willie Horton spot—is not included in the analysis. One might worry about the absence of such ads. But for the most part, this was not a common occurrence. And in the particular case of Bush's ads, the themes of the Willie Horton ad appeared in other spots authorized by the vice president's campaign, making this omission not as troubling as one might first think.

Table 7.A1 shows the number of sixty-second (or shorter) spots aired in the general election that were available at the archive and the number I actually coded. Table 7.A2 gives the same information for ads in primaries and caucuses.

The Content Analysis

The actual content analysis of these ads involved a code sheet of fifteen pages, covering topics ranging from the traits of the candidates to the slogan at the end of the commercial. One immediate question with any content analysis concerns reliability of the coding. Before going to Oklahoma, I obtained a set of ads from the archive for the 1968 and 1988 presidential elections. I coded these ads ahead of time to help develop the coding sheet and to test for reliability. While I did not check the reliability of all the ads I coded from 1968 and 1988, a research assistant coded a random sample of 20 from the nearly 140 ads from the 1968 and 1988 campaigns. In this sample, our codings agreed 91 percent of the time,

Table 7.A1   Available versus Coded Political Commercials in General Elections, 1960–1992

	Coded Spots	Spots Available[a]
1960		
Kennedy	44	54
Nixon	31	40
1964		
Johnson	17	18
Goldwater	26	31
1968		
Humphrey	27	29
Nixon	15	24
1972		
McGovern	31	32
Nixon	18	19
1976		
Carter	33	37
Ford	39	73
1980		
Carter	60	84
Reagan	80	136
1984		
Mondale	38	40
Reagan	27	40
1988		
Dukakis	75	126
Bush	26	36
1992		
Clinton	29	39
Bush	18	30
Perot (3d party)	15	18
Wallace (3d party)	4	8
Anderson (3d party)	2	2

[a] Number of spots available was determined by the lists of possible ads from each campaign, supplied by Julian Kanter.

Table 7.A2   Available versus Coded Political Commercials in Primaries and Caucuses, 1980–1992

	Coded Spots	Available Spots
1980 Democrats		
Carter	40	50
Kennedy	29	41
1980 Republicans		
Bush	21	21
Anderson	21	23
Connally	21	27
Reagan	14	18
Baker	13	17
Dole	5	5
1984 Democrats		
Hart	49	50
Mondale	43	58
Glenn	22	25
Cranston	6	6
Askew	4	4
Hollings	1	1
1988 Republicans		
Bush	18	22
Dole	16	23
Robertson	14	24
Kemp	12	15
du Pont	6	10
Haig	3	5
1988 Democrats		
Gore	29	33
Dukakis	27	35
Gephardt	14	24
Jackson	12	15
Babbitt	9	9
Simon	9	9
Hart	3	3

Table 7.A2 (*continued*)

	Coded Spots	Available Spots
1992 Republicans		
Buchanan	16	24
Bush	12	19
1992 Democrats		
Clinton	43	61
Tsongas	17	18
Kerrey	15	18
Harkin	13	14
Brown	11	13

Source: Data from Julian P. Kanter Political Commercial Archives, University of Oklahoma.

providing me sufficient confidence to proceed with the analysis.[32] I also tested for whether, as time unfolded, my coding changed. It was possible that I might be "learning" how to code, which would interfere with the comparability of the results. During my stay in Oklahoma, I recoded a set of ads I had examined three days earlier. The agreement in this case was over 93 percent. As a final test, I compared my coding of ads prior to my visit at the archive and after my return. Here, the reliability was 91 percent.[33]

The actual coding sheet reflected an effort to gather as much information as possible about the ads. For instance, great care was given to create a set of codes that tapped general themes and values in the ads. If the "spirit of America" was mentioned, that comment was coded. If prosperity was discussed, that too was coded separately. "Hard work," "hope," "change," and the "future" were all included explicitly in the code sheet. Overall, there were ninety-eight different possible statements of values or general themes in the ads. The result is fewer judgment calls about what theme fits where, increasing the accuracy of this scheme.

A separate section was also created for coding the personal traits of the candidates. In these ads, nearly two hundred different traits (both positive and negative) were coded. Some of the codes included were "good leader," "trustworthy," "experienced," "cares about people like you," and "tough." The flip side of these traits were separately coded when presidential nominees attacked the opposition.

The core of the analysis represented an attempt to capture in detail the substantive issues raised by the presidential contenders. Using the American National Election Studies' (NES) open-ended codes for the Like/Dislike questions as a starting point, I developed over nine hundred different themes candidates might mention. The topics ranged from concerns about unemployment to worries over states' rights. In each case, the detail of the appeal was captured. If taxes were mentioned, was it an appeal to lower taxes? to raise the taxes of the wealthy? or to promote tax reform? When education was discussed, did the candidate talk about a general concern for the issue? Or did the nominee call for an increase in federal funding? In this way, we can look at the different basis of the appeals candidates make to the public.

One final point about the analysis is that I focused primarily on the spoken and written word.[34] Originally, I attempted to code the visual aspects of the ads, but I could not attain a reasonable level of reliability. The visual aspects of the commercials apparently play differently with different people, as perhaps intended by their producers. Only when the visual was central to the purpose of the ad did I code it. For these exceptions, there was reliability. Perhaps the best example of this would be the famous "Daisy" spot from the 1964 Johnson campaign. The nuclear explosion in the ad was coded, for instance, as a reference to nuclear war.

Some may find this focus on the spoken and written word a problem. Clearly, lots of important messages are communicated with the pictures in the ads. Being unable to ensure reliability of interpretation, I saw little point in proceeding. As far as I can tell, the visual side usually did not contain different messages from the audio. At some point in the future, however, I hope to conduct some experimental studies comparing people's reactions to the audio messages alone with their responses to audiovisual ads. The comparison may provide a better handle on this important matter.

Notes

I thank Tracy Jarvis, Bruce I. Oppenheimer, Thomas R. Rochon, and Donald E. Stokes for comments on an earlier version of this chapter. I also acknowledge the kind help of Julian Kanter and the Political Commercial Archives at the University of Oklahoma.

1. For notable exceptions, see Enelow and Hinich 1984, Ferejohn and Noll 1978, Page 1978, and Simon 1997.

2. This idea, of course, has attracted much scholarly attention, which has resulted in extending and improving Downs' highly simplified theory. Over the years, scholars have developed models more consistent with what we observe empirically. Some have, for in-

stance, introduced additional dimensions to reflect the fact that elections are battles over numerous issues (e.g., Aldrich 1983b; Enelow and Hinich 1984). Others have included nonspatial concerns, like traits, in these models (Enelow and Hinich 1982). Scholars have also allowed candidates to pursue goals other than just winning elections (Schlesinger 1975; Wittman 1973, 1983; Chappell and Keech 1986; Herrera 1989). A few have even turned their attention to how voters behave, showing that candidates may be able to maximize votes by offering nonmedian positions (Rabinowitz and Macdonald 1989). And finally, political scientists have brought other actors into play, such as party activists (Aldrich 1983a; Aldrich and McGinnis 1989).

3. Anthony Downs (1957) did not argue that parties (or candidates) would adopt the exact same position. But if one sticks with the simple model, rational candidates must take the same position. To do otherwise would allow the opposition to grab the median position and win the election.

4. It is, of course, true that a politician prefers a tie to a loss. But the assumption underlying most rational actor models is that politicians want to win elections, not that they want to avoid losing them. One might, nonetheless, argue that in an uncertain world with lots of voters, a candidate will end up winning the election by chance. While surely true, it will not be clear before the election who will win. Thus, candidates will still be left with choices that do not permit them to pursue their goal.

5. This argument, incidentally, also helps voters out of their rationality crisis, since candidates will provide them enough differences to make a rational decision.

6. This quote comes from the preliminary media plan issued by Bailey and Deardourff, Ford's advertising team. See Jamieson (1992, 346), for a fuller discussion of this matter.

7. The Downsian framework has been used to examine the behavior of candidates in primaries. See Brams (1978) for an excellent example.

8. As an example, in 1992, about 15 percent of the issues in both the Democratic and Republican platforms represented an attack on the opposition. Yet nearly 45 percent of the issue appeals in Bush's and Clinton's spots were negative.

9. Kanter correctly claims that no one can be sure of the true population of presidential ads. Even the candidates themselves usually do not keep good records on the matter. Nonetheless, Kanter feels confident that the archive has, at minimum, a representative sample of spots.

10. Darrell West (1993; 1997) has undertaken an analysis of political advertisements in an attempt to test the effect of spots on voters' attitudes. My focus, in contrast, is on how candidates compete for votes. This difference in focus leads us to employ different samples of spots and to devise alternative coding strategies.

11. I chose these contests because the archive had only a few spots from earlier campaigns for the nomination, limiting the value of any generalizations from those cases.

12. There is, of course, overlap between traits, values, and issues. The appendix provides some clues about how I defined these three items. The actual code sheet for these data probably provides the best handle on the differences between these concepts. It is available upon request.

13. I completed a content analysis of all party platforms from 1960 to 1992. I used the same system of coding for the platforms as for the ads, making the results comparable.

The intercoder reliability was greater than 90 percent for the platforms, providing confidence in these data. I also compared the results, where possible, with Pomper's analysis. The relevant proportions correlated at .91.

14. I examined the data using a number of different coding schemes, and in no instance did the basic results change.

15. The extent of this trend depends heavily on how one interprets the 1960 election. The 1960 election was the most positive among those elections studied. If the Kennedy-Nixon battle is viewed as typical of races prior to 1960, then the trend toward negativity is steep and unmistakable. But if 1960 is viewed as the outlier, then the trend toward negativity has been unfolding in a more gradual and uneven pattern. For example, the 1964 contest is one of the most negative in the data set, with the 1992 election holding that dubious honor.

16. I can only analyze the campaigns from 1976 to 1992, since prior to 1976 the data set does not include the date the ad was created for both nominees. The "first part" of the campaign was defined as July, August, and September, the "last part" as October and very early November.

17. There were nearly two hundred different codes for the personal traits of the candidates. In an effort to simplify these data, I merged the work by Arthur Miller, Martin Wattenberg, and Oksana Malanchuk (1986) and Donald Kinder (1986), showing that the public's reaction to traits can be broken down into five different categories: experience, integrity, leadership, caring, and personal matters. Thus, the many codes were organized under these five general themes, which, in turn, provided the basis for assessing change in the pattern of traits talked about by the candidates. As it turned out, the many detailed codes easily fit within the five categories that were developed by Kinder and Miller and colleagues—evidence of the usefulness of their scheme.

18. The actual date of the Gallup Poll varied across the twenty-eight-year time frame. I chose the first available trial heat of the campaign following each party's convention. The dates of these polls ranged from mid-August to early September.

"Coded" ads were used, since the content analysis included only new spots, not repeats of old ones or thirty-second versions of sixty-second spots. This variable, therefore, should capture reasonably well the number of new messages. To control for the variation in the raw number of ads aired in particular years (see table 7.A1), we divided the number of ads for a given candidate by the total number of both GOP and Democratic spots. This calculation yields the proportion of ads a contender aired in a particular campaign, making comparisons possible across the years.

19. In two elections (1960 and 1980), the two major-party candidates were in a dead heat at the start of the campaign.

20. The proportion used here ignores third-party candidates and the share of undecideds.

21. One can look at more specific issues. The problem, however, is that in many cases, like abortion or race, the topic is never mentioned in either candidate's ads, which artificially inflates the correlation. Nevertheless, the correlation did not reach .50. The sample size for the correlation reported above is seventy-two.

22. At first, I was surprised by this high correlation for platforms. To confirm these

findings, Gerald Pomper's work was examined (1980, 138–39). His content analysis of platforms leads to a similar correlation between the agendas of the two parties, lending additional support to these results.

23. I also calculated the average difference between the two parties' agendas in ads and platforms. The results confirm the patterns indicated by the correlations. For platforms, the parties differed by three percentage points across the eight issues, with a standard deviation of 2.7. In contrast, the ads generated an eleven-point gap, with a standard deviation of nearly 12.

24. "New Deal issues" includes such concerns as agricultural policy, education, day care, health care, housing, job training, minimum wage, welfare policy, and unemployment compensation. For a more compete definition of New Deal issues, see Kelley (1988).

25. Ian Budge, David Robertson, and Derek Hearl (1987) also refer to parties "owning" issues. And even earlier, John Kingdon noted that the party of the candidate structures "the type of issue appeal he makes in his campaign" (1968, 122).

26. Since 1960, the in-party nominees have either been sitting presidents or sitting vice presidents. Those positions allow them to talk about their "experience" in the Oval Office.

27. When comparing the share of traits and issues in ads from the primaries and caucuses, I cut the data in a number of ways to test rival hypotheses. For example, I used only March, April, and May advertisements to eliminate the initial spots that tend to introduce the candidate to the public. These introductions usually stress a large number of traits of the candidates. Such ads might bias the results. To avoid that problem, I examined ads that were created once the battle for delegates was in full swing. I also examined the general election ads that were created in October and November to see if later ads focused more on issues as the campaign unfolded. There was a slight difference, but it was hardly significant. Issues constituted 51 percent of all appeals, and traits made up another 27 percent.

28. I do not want to suggest that when candidates duck an issue they ignore it completely. It is likely that they will give lip service to the issue, especially if the other side is attacking them on it. My point is a statement not of absolute rules of behavior but of a general tendency.

29. It should be noted that this general observation about the potential problems with two-party competition is not new. Scholars ranging from James Bryce to Stanley Kelley have made this very point. But all too often these concerns have been drowned out by those who believe that competition does work. Hence, my objective is to give new life to these long-standing concerns. Also, see Simon (1997) for an interesting attempt not only to examine the biases of competition in campaigns but also to see how various tactics may influence the views of citizens toward the candidates.

30. Although the bulk of ads under study are not more than 60 seconds long, in the 1960s some ads ran the odd time of 61 or 62 seconds. I included them in the analysis. Also, in 1960, I coded a two-minute ad from John Kennedy's campaign. As one may recall, the "Catholic" issue was an important issue in that campaign. In the archive, the only "Catholic ad" was a 120-second spot. Given the importance of this issue, I made an exception for fear of misrepresenting Kennedy's appeals. Finally, I included a five-

minute spot of John Anderson's, since it was one of the few direct appeals he offered to the American public. His limited war chest prevented a large assault in the paid media.

31. Ideally, I would know where the ads were aired and how frequently. Such information could be of great use when trying to measure the set of appeals candidates make to the public. The absence of these variables may not be a serious problem, however. First, the relation between the importance of an ad and the frequency with which it is aired is unclear. Consider that the famous "Daisy" spot from 1964 appeared on TV just once and that the Willie Horton ad was only aired a few times in the Midwest; yet these ads are viewed as critical to those elections. Second, candidates do not seem to be tailoring appeals for particular regions of the country. For instance, no significant differences in the appeals are found between the ads created for the New Hampshire primary and those for all subsequent primaries. Third, West and colleagues (1995) have collected data on ad buys by presidential candidates in 1992. Their data present the frequency of airing and also note whether the spot was aired locally or nationally. I have tried to use their results to weight my data from 1992. Early indications are that the weighting does not make much difference in the distribution of appeals across issues or traits for 1992.

Kenneth Goldstein (1997) is making progress on solving this problem by using a new technology, "Polaris Ad Detector," that counts the frequency of ads being aired in campaigns. His work is still in the early stages, but it holds much promise.

32. The 91 percent refers to the proportion of agreement across all items in the code sheet. In general, the coding for issues yielded the highest reliability, whereas the coding of values was less successful (about 84 percent).

33. There are additional reasons to think my coding was accurate. First, a recent article by Lynda Lee Kaid and Anne Johnston (1991) reports the results of a content analysis of presidential ads from 1960 to 1988. While their analysis is different in many ways, the one comparable item (proportion of negative advertising) produced similar results. Second, John Kessel was kind enough to share some of the marginals from data on campaign managers. My content analysis, if valid, should match well with what these activists thought the message of the campaign was. As before, there is a strong positive correlation between these data sets. These findings add further confidence to the results presented here.

34. For instance, I coded all slogans at the end of the spots and any other written material that appeared during the ad.

References

Aldrich, John H. 1983a. "A Downsian Model with Party Activism." *American Political Science Review* 77:974–90.
———. 1983b. "A Spatial Model with Party Activists: Implications for Electoral Dynamics." *Public Choice* 41:63–99.
Aldrich, John H., and Michael D. McGinnis. 1989. "A Model of Constraints on Optimal Candidate Positions." *Mathematical Computer Modeling* 12:437–50.
Brams, Steve. 1978. *The Presidential Election Game.* New Haven: Yale University Press.
Bryce, James. 1895. *The American Commonwealth.* New York: Macmillan.

Budge, Ian, David Robertson, and Derek Hearl. 1987. *Ideology, Strategy, and Party Change: Spatial Analyses of Post-War Election Programmes in Nineteen Democracies.* New York: Cambridge University Press.

Carmines, Edward G., and James A. Stimson. 1989. *Issue Evolution.* Princeton: Princeton University Press.

Chappell, Henry W., and William R. Keech. 1986. "Policy Motivation and Party Differences in a Dynamic Spatial Model of Party Competition." *American Political Science Review* 80:881–900.

Devlin, L. Patrick. 1987. "Campaign Commercials." In *Political Persuasion in Presidential Campaigns,* ed. L. Patrick Devlin. New Brunswick, N.J.: Transaction Books.

Downs, Anthony. 1957. *An Economic Theory of Democracy.* New York: Harper and Row.

Enelow, James M., and Melvin J. Hinich. 1982. "Nonspatial Candidate Characteristics and Electoral Competition." *Journal of Politics* 44:115–30.

———. 1984. *The Spatial Theory of Voting: An Introduction.* New York: Cambridge University Press.

Ferejohn, John A., and Roger G. Noll. 1978. "Uncertainty and Formal Theory of Political Campaigns." *American Political Science Review* 72:492–505.

Finkel, Steven, and John G. Geer. 1998. "Spot Check: Casting Doubt on the Demobilizing Effect of Attack Advertising." *American Journal of Political Science* 42:573–95.

Ginsberg, Benjamin. 1976. "Elections and Public Policy." *American Political Science Review* 70:41–49.

Goldstein, Kenneth M. 1997. "What Did They See and When Did They See It?" Unpublished paper, Department of Political Science, Arizona State University.

Herrera, Richard. 1989. "Party Goals and Party Behavior: An Examination of Ideology as a Party Goal." Paper presented at the annual meeting of the American Political Science Association, Atlanta, Aug. 31–Sept. 3.

Jacobs, Lawrence R., and Robert Y. Shapiro. 1992. "Public Decisions, Private Polls: John F. Kennedy's Presidency." Paper presented at the annual meeting of the Midwest Political Science Association, Chicago, Sept. 3–6.

Jamieson, Kathleen. 1992. *Packaging the Presidency.* 2d ed. New York: Oxford University Press.

Kaid, Lynda Lee, and Anne Johnston. 1991. "Negative versus Positive Television Advertising in U.S. Presidential Campaigns, 1960–1988." *Journal of Communication* 41:53–64.

Kelley, Stanley, Jr. 1956. *Professional Public Relations and Political Power.* Baltimore: Johns Hopkins University Press.

———. 1966. "The Presidential Campaign." In *The National Election of 1964,* ed. Milton Cummings. Washington, D.C.: Brookings Institution Press.

———. 1988. "Democracy and the New Deal Party System." In *Democracy and the Welfare State,* ed. Amy Guttman. Princeton: Princeton University Press.

———. 1992. "Party Politics and Democratic Government." Unpublished manuscript, Department of Politics, Princeton University.

Kinder, Donald R. 1986. "Presidential Character Revisited." In *Political Cognition,* ed. Richard R. Lau and David O. Sears. Hillsdale, N.J.: Lawrence Erlbaum.

Kingdon, John W. 1968. *Candidates for Office: Beliefs and Strategies*. New York: Random House.

Klingemann, Hans-Dieter, Richard I. Hofferbert, and Ian Budge. 1994. *Parties, Policies, and Democracy*. Boulder, Colo.: Westview.

Lengle, James I. 1981. *Representation and Presidential Primaries*. Westport, Conn.: Greenwood.

Lipset, Seymour M., and Stein Rokkan. 1967. *Party Systems and Voter Alignments*. New York: Free Press.

Luntz, Frank. 1988. *Candidates, Consultants, and Campaigns*. New York: Blackwell.

Miller, Arthur H., Martin P. Wattenberg, and Oksana Malanchuk. 1986. "Schematic Assessments of Presidential Candidates." *American Political Science Review* 80:521–40.

Monroe, Alan D. 1979. "Consistency between Public Preferences and National Policy Decisions." *American Politics Quarterly* 7:3–18.

———. 1995. "Public Opinion, Party Platforms, and Public Policy: 1984 and 1988." Paper presented at the annual meeting of the American Political Science Association, Chicago, Aug.31–Sept. 3.

Page, Benjamin. 1978. *Choices and Echoes in Presidential Elections*. Chicago: University of Chicago Press.

Petrocik, John R. 1991. "Divided Government: Is It All in the Campaigns?" In *The Politics of Divided Government*, ed. Gary W. Cox and Samuel Kernell. Boulder, Colo.: Westview.

———. 1996. "Issue Ownership in Presidential Elections, with a 1980 Case Study." *American Journal of Political Science* 40:825–50.

Polsby, Nelson W. 1983. *Consequences of Party Reform*. New York: Oxford University Press.

Pomper, Gerald M. 1980. *Elections in America*. 2d ed. New York: Longman.

Rabinowitz, George, and Stuart Elaine Macdonald. 1989. "A Directional Theory of Issue Voting." *American Political Science Review* 83:93–122.

Riker, William H. 1982. *Liberalism against Populism*. San Francisco: W. H. Freeman.

———. 1986. *The Art of Political Manipulation*. New Haven: Yale University Press.

———. 1989. "Why Negative Campaigning Is Rational." Paper presented at the annual meeting of the American Political Science Association, Atlanta, Sept.3–6.

———. 1993. *Agenda Formation*. Ann Arbor: University of Michigan Press.

Robertson, David. 1976. *A Theory of Party Competition*. New York: Wiley.

Schlesinger, Joseph A. 1975. "The Primary Goals of Political Parties: A Clarification of Positive Theory." *American Political Science Review* 69:840–49.

Semetko, Holli A., Jay Blumler, Michael Gurevitch, and David Weaver. 1991. *The Formation of Campaign Agendas*. London: Lawrence Erlbaum.

Simon, Adam. 1997. "The Winning Message? Candidate Behavior and Democracy." Ph.D. diss., University of California, Los Angeles.

Subervi-Velez, Frederico A., Richard Herrera, and Michael Begay. 1987. "Toward an Understanding of the Role of the Mass Media in Latino Political Life." *Social Science Quarterly* 68:185–96.

Sundquist, James L. 1983. *Dynamics of the Party System.* Washington, D.C.: Brookings Institution Press.

West, Darrell. 1993. *Air Wars.* Washington, D.C.: Congressional Quarterly Press.

———. 1997. *Air Wars.* 2d ed. Washington, D.C.: Congressional Quarterly Press.

West, Darrell, Montague Kern, Dean Alger, and Janice Goggin. 1995. "Ad Buys in Presidential Campaigns." *Political Communication* 12:275–90.

Wittman, Donald A. 1973. "Parties as Utility Maximizers." *American Political Science Review* 67:490–98.

———. 1983. "Candidate Motivation: A Synthesis of Alternative Theories." *American Political Science Review* 77:142–57.

CHAPTER 8

Interpreting the 1994 Elections

Jonathan S. Krasno

By any measure, the 1994 elections were a tremendous success for the Republican Party. Republicans seemingly won every race in sight, picking up hundreds of state legislative seats and eleven governorships formerly held by Democrats and gaining control of the U.S. Senate. Perhaps most spectacular, the GOP also won a majority of seats in the U.S. House of Representatives for the first time in forty years, ending the longest such drought for a major party in U.S. history. Republicans picked up fifty-three House seats, defeating thirty-five Democratic incumbents, including such stalwarts as Speaker Tom Foley (Wash.), Judiciary Chairman Jack Brooks (Tex.), and former Ways and Means Chairman Dan Rostenkowski (Ill.). The election made a star of the new Speaker of the House, Newt Gingrich (R-Ga.), at least among Republicans convinced of his political genius, and made the House of Representatives the focal point of the GOP policy agenda in 1995.

Even before the dust had settled, politicians and the media immediately applied themselves to the question that follows each election: what did it mean? Elections are widely believed to offer messages to the government about what the people want. But exactly what that message is is usually not very clear. Even 1994, with its seemingly decisive results, is subject to a variety of interpretations, particularly from the newly elected or defeated.

For members of the new Republican majority in the House, much of the media, and more than a few Democrats, 1994 was a clear endorsement of conservatism. Republicans argued that they won so many elections because they had campaigned to roll back big government, the welfare state, the Great Society, parts of the New Deal, and anything associated with Bill Clinton. What is more, they appeared to genuinely believe this explanation, for they moved with remarkable unanimity on a series of bills to change radically the nature of the federal government, along the way voting to repeal a series of popular programs, including a few championed by past Republican presidents. In part, their view of the election stemmed from the perceived success of Gingrich's Contract with America. As Mike Collins, deputy communications director of the National Republican Congressional Committee, put it, the Contract "turned the 1994 election into the most ideologically based election in history. It turned what is typically a local election into an ideological struggle" (quoted in Gruenwald 1995, 3361).

Democrats, of course, were not without their own explanations for 1994. President Bill Clinton was a favorite scapegoat, and in the aftermath of the election many House Democrats spoke about what he had cost them on election day. The Republicans capitalized on the association, and many ran television advertisements showing their opponent's face "morphing" into Clinton's. Acting on the belief that the president was a liability, Democratic House leaders took pains to declare their independence from the White House following the November election. Naturally, Clinton himself saw things differently. In his post-election press conference he continually referred to people's desire for "change" and their sense that it was not happening fast enough, never conceding the point that the change he envisioned might be unpopular. Clinton's explanation was reminiscent of V. O. Key's argument that the public rewards successful results and punishes failure, not ideology or partisanship (Key 1966).

> Last night the voters not only voted for sweeping changes, they demanded [that] a more equally divided Congress work more closely with the president for the interest of the American people. . . . Last night [the voters] said that they were not satisfied with the progress we had made. They said the Democrats had been in control of the White House and Congress. They said they were going to make a change, and they did make a change. But they still want the same goal as before. ("Presidential News Conference" 1994, 3293–94)

Divining the electorate's message in the Republican victory, then, is not easy, but it is important. How politicians themselves, and to a lesser extent the media and the public, interpret the election returns may have major consequences for the laws that come out of Washington. That is why politicians are so eager to put their own spin on things. Of course, it is no surprise that politicians should not be counted on to explain their own victories and defeats. Even if they were able to perceive things accurately, they have many incentives to find a self-serving meaning in the election returns.

The question is how scholars might do better. There are, of course, many ways of analyzing voting behavior. In this chapter I utilize one, the approach introduced by Stanley Kelley in his 1974 article, "The Simple Act of Voting" (with Thad W. Mirer), and expanded on in his 1983 book, *Interpreting Elections*. Kelley's method is appropriate here because his goals are the same as mine—to try to discover the themes that motivated people on election day, the true message, if any, that the electorate is delivering to Washington. To do this I use the same style of analysis to examine the 1994 American National Election Study (NES). In addition, to provide a basis for comparison I also examine NES surveys from two earlier midterm elections—1982, a smaller landslide where the Democrats added twenty-six seats to their already healthy majority, and 1990, a less eventful year in which the Democrats gained just nine seats.

The results show there was no simple message in the 1994 election returns. We already know that voters preferred Republican candidates; the survey shows that they preferred Republican policies, too. Yet, the findings offer several cautionary notes to the GOP. First, their victory in the House was far from decisive; it was, rather, what might be termed a "close landslide" (Kelley 1983). Second, on most matters of public policy a sizable minority definitely preferred the Democrats. The GOP agenda seems to have had little appeal beyond those who supported Republican candidates in 1994, and even among these voters its attractiveness was often underwhelming. In short, the results of the 1994 elections offered only general encouragement to the GOP to pursue its policies, not a mandate to remake the federal government.

Interpreting Elections

The hallmark of Kelley's analysis of elections is his use of open-ended questions about the parties and the candidates. Since 1952, the National Election Studies have included a series of such questions—asking respondents to name any feature they particularly liked or disliked about either of the parties and the presidential candidates and recording up to five responses for each question. But aside from Philip Converse and the other authors of *The American Voter* (Campbell et al. 1960), relatively few analysts have made much use of these data.[1] Instead, most have relied on the scores of closed-ended items in each NES survey, questions about specific issues that ask respondents to choose from a list of answers.

Kelley, of course, is a notable exception. In his view, asking people to state in their own words what they like and dislike about the parties and candidates is the surest way to measure what is in their heads when they think about these political actors.[2] The responses to the likes and dislikes questions are labeled "considerations," and they form the raw material fueling the "Voter's Decision Rule," which describes the way in which voters make up their minds:

> The voter canvasses his likes and dislikes of the leading candidates and major parties involved in an election. Weighing each like and dislike equally, he votes for the candidate toward whom he has the greatest net number of favorable attitudes, if there is such a candidate. If no candidate has such an advantage, the

voter votes consistently with his party identification, if he has one. If his attitudes do not incline him toward one candidate or another, and if he does not identify with one of the major parties, the voter reaches a null decision. (Kelley and Mirer 1974, 574)

Voters perform a simple calculation by adding the number of things they like about the Democrats (the party and the candidate) and the number of things they dislike about the Republicans; from this number they then subtract the number of things they dislike about the Democrats and the number they like about the Republicans.[3] One useful product of this approach is that it creates a scale of net scores, allowing us to distinguish between respondents who are enthusiastic about a particular candidate and those whose support is lukewarm. Citizens with the most favorable set of considerations toward a party and its candidate are most likely to vote for that candidate, whereas turnout and level of support is lower among respondents with weaker attachments. For all voters, the rule is a quite accurate predictor of behavior. Kelley reports that it correctly estimates the vote for 84.4 percent of NES respondents between 1952 and 1980 (1983, 16). In a sense, these forecasts are true predictions, though they are calculated long after the election, because they are based on questionnaires administered before the election.

The Voters' Decision Rule was developed to interpret presidential elections. House contests, however, are a different story, for several reasons. First and foremost, there are 435 such contests, not just one. In 1994, the NES interviewed 1,795 respondents, including 937 House voters, living in 190 different congressional districts. Thus, in half the questions that form the basis of the Voters' Decision Rule, respondents were asked about different candidates. Combining answers to items about candidate X, a Republican incumbent, with candidate Y, a Republican challenger in a district a thousand miles away, is obviously a matter of concern; individual circumstances in their respective districts may vary so widely that the search for common themes could be a fool's errand.[4] Yet, the notion that there is a common theme in both districts is behind almost all of the interpretations of the 1994 elections; their certainty that a national tide had swept over the electorate inspired the policy agenda of House Republicans. Nevertheless, because of the large number of House candidates, we might expect the Voters' Decision Rule to work less well for congressional elections than for presidential ones.

On the other hand, one factor suggests it might work better: in contrast to its procedure for presidential elections, the NES conducts no preelection interviews in midterm years. Instead, in these years people are asked what they like and dislike about the parties and candidates only after the election has taken place, after the media and politicians have had the opportunity to digest the results and offer their spin. As a result, we might expect positive feelings toward the Republican Party and candidates to swell in the wave of favorable publicity that winners usually enjoy. We know, for instance, that postelection surveys usually exaggerate winners' share of the vote, though in 1994 the percentage of NES respondents who reported voting for a Republican (54 percent) is nearly identical with Republicans' actual share of the two-party vote nationwide (52.7 percent).[5] In addition, we might expect the themes that have been emphasized by politicians and the media since the election—the publicity accorded to the Contract with America and the ascendancy of conservatism—to become more common in people's thoughts about the parties and the candidates. These concerns are common to all analyses of congressional elections, since nearly all NES questions about these races have been included in postelection instruments.

In fact, the Voters' Decision Rule accounts for NES respondents' choices for the House of Representatives almost as well as it does for presidential contests. In 1994 the rule accurately "predicts" the votes of 83.6 percent of respondents; in 1990, 85.4 percent; and in 1982, 82.2 percent. These are fairly impressive numbers, especially when one considers the role incumbency plays in House elections; for instance, more than half of the errors in 1994 were the result of people supporting incumbents in the face of a more favorable mix of considerations about the opposing candidate and party. And, as in presidential elections, respondents who express the most positive views about a party and its candidates are the ones most likely to support it, while those with weaker preferences are more often defectors.

One difference between congressional and presidential elections worth noting, however, is that people have less to say about House candidates than they do about presidential contenders. For instance, the 1994 NES survey included 759 respondents who had also been part of the 1992 survey. In 1992 these people reported an average of 6.0 considerations about the two candidates, Bill Clinton and George Bush, but about the House candidates two years later they reported 1.6, fewer than a third as many considerations. Political parties were as salient as in 1992; in fact, the mean number of responses per respondent about the parties grew slightly, from 3.8 to 4.2.[6] Presidential candidates attract much more attention than their House counterparts, even in a historic year like 1994. The relative lack of likes and dislikes about House candidates in midterm years makes them harder to study but, as I show below, not impossible.

The Decisiveness of the GOP Victory

While there is complete agreement that the GOP won smashing victories in 1994 House contests, questions remain about exactly how smashing their victory actually was. For instance, which statistic is most telling about the House elections of 1994—the GOP's 53-seat gain, the largest since 1948? the fact that the Republican's election total of 231 seats was the smallest majority since 1955 (the last time the GOP controlled the House)? or perhaps the Republican's percentage of the vote in all congressional districts nationwide, a bare 52.7 percent? Obviously, these figures suggest different conclusions about the decisiveness of the GOP's win, but, worst of all, none of them really provides any insight on the depth of the public's attachment to Republican congressional candidates. It is possible, after all, that support for Republicans was "a mile wide but an inch deep," that many of the people who voted for them barely preferred them to Democrats. In fact, we might wonder whether people actually liked them at all, or whether they merely disliked them less than they disliked the Democrats. Aversion to both parties, of course, was behind much of the speculation about the surprising popularity of third parties and independent candidates in 1992 and 1994. Election returns alone cannot provide any insight on these points.

What can? The sheer number of things that people have to say about the parties and candidates is a start, being in a sense a measure of the salience of the election itself. We know that people had less to say about the parties and candidates in the 1994 election than in 1992, but what about other midterms? By this measure there is a clear dividing line between 1994 and the previous midterm election in 1990, a low-key year. Respondents in 1994 averaged 5.5 considerations compared with just 2.8 in 1990 (see table 8.1). And, more than twice as many people (42 percent) had nothing whatever to say about the parties and candidates in 1990 as in 1994 (20 percent). How does 1994 compare with another midterm "landslide," the 1982 election? As table 8.1 shows, respondents in both years had virtually identical numbers of considerations about the parties and

Table 8.1   Salience of Three Midterm Elections

	1994	1990	1982
Mean number of considerations			
All respondents	5.5	2.8	5.1
Voters	7.4	4.0	6.7
Percentage expressing no views			
All respondents	20	42	18
Voters	8	25	7
	1,795	2,000	1,418
N (voters)	937	802	711

Source: Data from American National Election Studies 1995.

candidates. Clearly, there was more interest and excitement about politics in tl
two landslide years than in 1990.

There are other standards by which we might gauge the decisiveness of tl
1994 elections. Table 8.2, which presents the scale created by calculating r
spondents' net number of favorable attitudes, allows us to consider the dep
of support for the various candidates. We can distinguish, for instance, betwe
an individual whose views are the most uniformly pro-Republican (−20) ar
those whose comments only slightly favor the GOP (−1). Not surprisingly, tl
net scores show that 1994 was a good year for the Republicans; it is the only ele
tion of the three where the average score for all voters (−.67) favors the GOP, a
beit by a small margin.

This figure, however, combines Republican and Democratic voters. In fac
the average scores of members of each group are quite distinct; Republican vo

Table 8.2 Strength of Voters' Attachments in Three Midterm Elections (net
scores in parentheses)

	1994	1990	1982
Avid Democrat (7 to 20)	8%	6%	9%
Solid Democrat (4 to 6)	13%	12%	17%
Leans Democratic (1 to 3)	19%	28%	25%
Uncommitted (0)	13%	28%	14%
Leans Republican (−1 to −3)	20%	18%	19%
Solid Republican (−4 to −6)	14%	5%	10%
Avid Republican (−7 to −20)	15%	2%	5%
Mean			
all voters	−.67	.90	.80
Dem voters	2.88	2.37	3.31
Rep voters	−3.84	−1.73	−2.57
N (respondents)	937	802	711

Source: Data from *American National Election Studies* 1995.

ers averaged −3.84 and Democratic voters 2.88, making 1994 the most polar-
ized of the three elections I examine here by a modest margin. As table 8.2
shows, the main reason for any difference between 1994 and the 1982 landslide
is that the percentage of voters with extremely pro-Republican scores (15 percent) is about twice as high as the percentage of avid Democrats in their banner year (9 percent). Still, a majority of voters in both years can be labeled as
weakly committed, having scores between −3 and 3. In this respect, 1994 is only
a little different from 1982.

Finally, we might ask whether a favorable set of considerations toward either the Republicans or Democrats was actually a sign of confidence in that
party. Because of the way the Voters' Decision Rule is calculated, voters may have
fairly strong preferences on the negative basis of their distaste for the other party
and candidate. Did people really like the Republicans in 1994, or did they simply dislike the Democrats more? The first possibility was encouraging for the
GOP, but the second disturbing, since it means that the public is less attached
to the Republicans than they liked to think. Kelley (1983) introduces "credit ratings" to address this question. Credit ratings are computed by adding the likes
and dislikes of each party and its candidates separately in order to determine
how people felt about them without taking their opponents into account.[7]
These figures allow us to tell whether 1994 was a victory for the GOP or a defeat
for the Democrats.

The results in table 8.3 provide little comfort for Republicans. Certainly, Republicans improved tremendously from their position in previous midterms;
in 1994, 38 percent of voters had a positive impression of them and not the Democrats, compared with 26 percent in 1982 and just 19 percent in 1990. Still, that

Table 8.3 Parties' Credit Ratings among Voters in Three Midterm Elections
(percentage)

	1994	1990	1982
Likes neither party	7	3	4
Likes both parties	8	4	12
Likes only Democrats	31	41	41
Likes only Republicans	38	19	26
Neutral on both parties	18	34	17
N	937	802	711

Source: Data from American National Election Studies 1995.

is far short of a majority. Even adding the 8 percent of the public who liked both parties leaves the GOP with just 46 percent of voters with more good things to say about them than bad. The Democrats did better in 1982 and almost as well in 1990. These figures suggest a definite lack of enthusiasm for the GOP and its candidates in 1994 but even less enthusiasm for Democrats, who fell to their lowest point in the three elections. Still, it should be noted that, even in losing, the Democrats enjoyed higher credit ratings than did the GOP in 1990 or 1982. By this measure the Republicans' win in 1994 was slimmer than the Democrats' previous victories.

Issues in 1994

Thus far I have only counted the considerations expressed by respondents; I have not considered the content of their remarks. The ability to examine what people say about the parties and candidates is one of the most attractive aspects of working with the open-ended questions. By grouping the NES's coding of respondents' statements into a workable number of categories reflecting the political themes of the day, it is possible to discern the message contained in the choices of the millions of voters on election day. If we were to find, for instance, that people often mentioned the GOP Contract with America as a reason to like (or dislike) the Republican Party or its candidates, it would be powerful evidence that the Contract really was as important as Collins and other Republicans believed (see Gruenwald 1995).

Coding individuals' responses to open-ended questions is a difficult task. Fortunately, the NES does the lion's share of the work by grouping responses into several hundred different categories that it has developed over time. It is from the short descriptions of these categories, not the full text of their remarks, that I work. Kelley (183) provides a full account of his coding scheme for the 1964 and 1972 elections; the NES still uses the same system from 1972, so I was not forced to start from scratch. Still, there are several differences between my classification and Kelley's. I ignored several of his categories, like "relations with the USSR," that no longer seem relevant, and I created some new ones, such as "health care," that have become a part of current politics. I made health care a New Deal issue, something not in Kelley's original coding. I also rearranged two of his categories by creating a separate category for abortion (previously part of "amnesty, abortion, and acid," the GOP's characterization of George McGovern's platform) and making his "social issue" category into "family values" so that it refers only to the agenda items of social conservatives, like abortion and gay rights. The appendix to this chapter provides a full account of the NES data codes in each category. Obviously, creating a system of classification such as this one relies on many judgement calls; others may disagree with the choices I have made.

From these groupings I created several different measures, following Kelley's lead. The most basic is the "aggregate salience" of an issue, defined as the percentage of respondents who mention the issue at least once in response to any of the questions. Because individuals may mention several different considerations (and most do) and because some of the categories overlap (abortion, for one, is both a separate category and a family value), aggregate salience across all issues does not sum to 100 percent.

It is also possible to determine which side respondents find most and least appealing on a given issue—its "bias"—by comparing the number of likes and dislikes. For example, a respondent who states more things that he or she likes about the Democrats (including dislikes of the GOP) on an issue than about the Republicans (see note 3) favors the Democrats on that issue. Bias is measured only by the responses from the percentage of people who find an issue salient and favor one of the parties on it, not those from all respondents (i.e., responses from neutral respondents are not included). The combination of the salience of a set of considerations and its bias can be used to gauge the amount that an issue helped a candidate, or its *pull* (aggregate salience multiplied by bias). Thus, a domain where the Republicans are favored by a substantial margin might not have as large an impact on voters as a more salient issue where the bias is closer to even.

Table 8.4 shows the results of these calculations for the three elections. The 1994 election clearly stands out from the others. Most noteworthy is the change in Democratic bias in almost every category; the proportion of voters for whom a given issue favors the Democrats is reduced almost across the board. Some of the declines were spectacular. For instance, in 1990, 64 percent of respondents who mentioned military matters favored the Democrats; just 26 percent did so in 1994. Democrats also suffered an equally large reversal among those who saw health care as favoring one party or another, along with fairly dramatic losses elsewhere. The failure of the health care issue to help Democrats is not a surprise in the wake of Clinton's disastrous foray into this area. Of the twenty-nine sets of concerns I examined, only four—the environment, race, the personal qualities of the candidate, and relations to big business and the common man— worked to the Democrats' advantage (i.e., the bias scores exceeded 50 percent) in 1994.[8] Democrats' losses, of course, were Republicans' gains.

Bias is only part of the story. For an issue to have a major impact on the election it also must be salient to a large portion of the electorate, or else its pull is negligible. Thus, in areas like big government or military preparedness, where the Democratic bias is lowest (and the corresponding Republican bias is high-

Table 8.4   Considerations of Voters in Three Midterm Elections (percentage)

| | 1994 | | 1990 | | 1982 | |
Issues	Salience	Bias	Salience	Bias	Salience	Bias
Foreign policy	11	33	5	65	17	48
Military preparedness	7	26	3	64	12	53
New Deal issues	74	46	44	69	79	64
Economic issues	34	29	17	45	35	50
Big government	13	9	3	31	9	12
Taxes	20	27	11	43	9	55
Economic impact of election	9	50	3	52	17	78
Ideological stance	50	34	20	53	43	43
Liberalism, conservatism	28	25	10	31	19	33
Welfare	23	38	7	47	17	22
Social security	4	50	4	74	14	74
Health care	14	48	2	88	4	89
Relations to big business, common man	30	82	23	91	46	92
Law and order	13	40	1	44	2	15
Guns	8	40	1	33	1	22
Family values	26	40	9	47	6	45
Abortion	19	45	7	47	4	41
Other social issues:						
Environment	5	63	7	87	2	93
Race	2	58	2	72	2	82
Competence	37	39	32	54	44	38
Candidates' record	8	48	7	59	11	58
Candidates' other traits	26	53	25	61	30	50
Integrity	14	48	13	67	17	50
Quality of stewardship	18	48	11	51	13	44
Corruption	5	34	2	50	3	38
Partisanship	23	47	11	57	21	53
Campaign conduct	16	48	10	58	18	59
Contract with America	2	23	—	—	—	—
Clinton	6	27	—	—	—	—
N	937	802	711			

Source: American National Election Studies 1995.

Note: "Salience" is the percentage of voters who mention an issue in connection with either of the parties or candidates. "Bias" is Democratic bias, the percentage of voters who find a given issue salient and favor the Democrats on that issue.

est), the boon to the GOP is limited, since relatively few people mentioned these things as a reason to dislike either party or candidate. Democrats were in worse shape, however, because two of their best issues, environment and race, so rarely came up in people's responses. What concerns were highly salient in 1994? The first column of table 8.4 provides the answer. Five issues were mentioned by at least 30 percent of the public as a reason to like or dislike the parties and candidates—New Deal issues (mostly a compendium of narrower considerations), economic issues, ideological stance, relations to big business and the common man, and competence of the candidates. Republicans were favored in four of the five areas, particularly in ideological stance and economic issues.

A different version of the question about the salience of various issues in 1994 is to ask which categories showed the biggest growth. Issues constantly fluctuate in their importance to the public—just ask George Bush about the staying power of the Gulf War. One message that elections may send is some insight into what the voters are thinking about at a given time. Voters' concerns stem from many different sources, of course, including the deliberate efforts of the candidates to sell their own messages. Campaigns are, after all, partly attempts to set the political agenda; in the process of convincing voters that theirs is the best candidate, campaigns often try to establish the standards by which the candidate might be judged. Who is tougher on criminals, more determined to cut taxes, or a better environmentalist are only important questions if the voters care about them. What issues gained and lost ground in 1994?

The short answer is that traditional GOP themes became more salient. Taxes, law and order, welfare, social issues, guns, and liberalism/conservatism are areas where the public has consistently favored Republicans. All were more frequently cited as reasons to like and dislike the parties and candidates in 1994 than in the two previous elections. Of course, there were very few issues where the public favored the Democrats in 1994, and none were more salient than they had been in the past. The public was clearly more attuned to the GOP agenda in 1994 than to the Democratic one, or perhaps the Republicans did a better job marketing their issues.

One thing they did not manage to sell very well was the Contract with America. Just 2 percent of the public mentioned the Contract at all—this is in the months after the election, when it was receiving so much publicity in the wake of the Republicans' victory—although three-quarters of those who did mention it favored the GOP. Of course, issues that were part of the Contract—taxes, welfare, law and order, the military, and so on—achieved greater prominence, and 1994 did generate more references to ideology than had 1990 or 1982. (It is not true, however, that local issues, at least as measured by likes and dislikes toward the candidates, became less salient.) Nevertheless, as a brand name, the Contract with America was a failure. As Gary Jacobson put it, "the Contract itself had far more influence on Republican candidates (before and after the election) than on voters" (1995, 6).

Similarly, despite the widespread impression that the 1994 elections were a referendum on President Bill Clinton, just 6 percent of voters mentioned his name when discussing the parties and candidates (see Brady, Cogan, and Rivers 1995). Most of the references were negative. Doubtless, his performance affected the Democrats in other areas—health care is an obvious example—but the paucity of comments about him is surprising for a number of reasons. For one thing, while many Republican candidates grew mum on the Contract after the hoopla of its unveiling in Washington, by most accounts Clinton remained a popular weapon with which to attack Democrats. And the media certainly shared the interpretation of the election as a referendum on Clinton, giving much coverage to the nation's anti-Clinton mood in the wake of the election. Finally, the lack of references to Clinton is astonishing because of the ease of making such a statement; Clinton, as the leading Democrat and most identifiable political figure, could be expected to be one of the first things to come to mind about the Democratic Party. This pattern suggests that the Democratic Party's problems extend beyond Clinton. Clinton may have been right: the Democrats were punished as a team for their perceived failures as a team.

Despite this gloomy picture for the Democrats, it is important to remember that they still received the support of 46 percent of NES respondents. This fact suggests that the analysis above may overlook some variation between respondents by looking at all voters at once. Table 8.5 shows the aggregate salience and Democratic bias of these same issues separately for Democratic and Republican voters. One thing is clear: most voters had very good reasons to chose the candidates they supported. There is a clear pro-Democratic bias among Democratic voters and, if anything, an even clearer pro-Republican bias among those who supported GOP candidates. For example, 80 percent of Democratic voters felt that New Deal issues favored the Democrats, while Republican voters felt that these issues favored their party by an equally large margin. There were also differences in salience: Republican voters mentioned economic issues (especially big government), ideology, abortion, and other social issues more often than Democratic voters, while the latter were far more concerned about the parties and candidates' relationship to big business and the common man than were Republicans. What does this mean? For one thing, it means that the GOP agenda does not have much support outside those who voted for Republican candidates in 1994. That is bad news for Republicans who dream of expanding their base in the future, and for the present it suggests the opposition of a sizable minority of voters to the Republican agenda.

Table 8.5 Considerations of Voters, 1994, by Party (percent)

Issues	Democratic Salience	Democratic Bias	Republican Salience	Republican Bias
Foreign policy	10	49	12	22
Military preparedness	4	50	9	16
New Deal issues	72	80	77	18
Economic issues	29	56	39	11
Big government	8	29	18	1
Taxes	16	59	24	9
Economic impact of election	8	73	9	33
Ideological stance	42	69	58	12
Liberalism, conservatism	19	55	35	11
Welfare	20	65	25	19
Social security	4	73	5	33
Health care	12	75	16	30
Relations to big business, common man	42	94	19	58
Law and order	12	69	14	19
Guns	7	67	9	23
Family values	19	73	33	24
Abortion	14	84	25	27
Other social issues:				
Environment	5	86	5	41
Race	2	82	2	25
Competence	32	74	42	16
Candidates' record	6	96	10	22
Candidates' other traits	26	88	25	18
Integrity	15	79	14	18
Quality of stewardship	17	60	18	37
Corruption	5	48	6	24
Partisanship	25	65	22	29
Campaign conduct	15	78	17	23
Contract with America	1	66	3	14
Clinton	6	38	6	18

Source: *American National Election Studies* 1995.

Note: "Salience" is the percentage of voters who mention an issue in connection with either of the parties or candidates. "Bias" is Democratic bias, the percentage of voters who find a given issue salient and favor the Democrats on that issue.

Conclusion

What is the bottom line about the 1994 House elections? Was the election a sweeping endorsement of the Republican Party and their brand of conservatism, a repudiation of Bill Clinton, or something else? I have presented a variety of evidence about the decisiveness of the Republicans' victory and the issue assessments of the voters. Unfortunately—or perhaps not, depending on one's politics—a clear picture has not emerged. The results of 1994 were too complex to represent a single, straightforward message from the voters. That point alone is bad news for the Republicans, who sought to draw this sort of clear-cut interpretation from the election.

To begin, the results of this analysis show that the Republicans' victory was a narrow one. Calculations for the Voter's Decision Rule show a definite preference for the GOP and its candidates, but not by a particularly large margin and certainly not by a historic one, unless 1982 was also a historic election. Worse, much of this partiality reflected the weakness of the Democrats rather than the strength of Republicans; fewer than half of voters had more positive than negative things to say about the Republican Party and its House candidates. The Republicans' secret weapon was that the Democrats were in even worse shape. This is far from the pro-Republican surge depicted by the Republicans themselves, much of the media, and a few Democrats.

On the other hand, examining responses to the likes and dislikes questions shows that the GOP has some claim on a conservative mandate from 1994. The election was more ideological than past midterms; ideology, whether specific references to liberals and conservatives or broader statements, came up more often and strongly favored the Republicans. Republicans were also preferred on a wide variety of other issues, including a handful formerly "owned" by the Democrats. To the extent that the GOP can claim the mantle of America's conservative party, their conservatism did play some role in their victory.

This conclusion must be tempered, however, by the knowledge that these views were not shared by all voters. In fact, Democrats received 47.3 percent of the all House votes cast for a major-party candidate in 1994. The NES shows why: Democratic voters were markedly less conservative than Republican voters, and they preferred the Democrats on many other issues, as well. Republican voters were even more favorably disposed toward the Republican Party and its candidates, and they slightly outnumbered Democrats. But there was no conservative tide that swept beyond, or far beyond, the slim majority who supported Republican candidates.

Nor do these survey results tell us in any detail exactly what respondents wanted the government to do. We know that voters, at least slightly more than half of them, expressed some preference for more conservative policies, but what policies? It is easy to see, for example, how respondents who favored the GOP on taxes or abortion might be satisfied by their actions, but what of those concerned about welfare, the economy, or even big government? The GOP certainly had good political reasons to pursue these issues. However, what path they should have followed or how far they should have gone is not certain from these survey results. It may be that Republican voters really did expect the sort of broad, "revolutionary" assault against so many familiar features of government that the GOP attempted for much of the 104th Congress, though that is far from a sure thing. In short, it is not clear that the GOP ever had a mandate from its own voters to do all of the things it tried to do, let alone from the rest of the electorate. Given the weak preferences of many voters (on both sides) and the GOP's low credit rating, it is most likely that they did not. That made their self-styled "radical" agenda a dangerous strategy for their party, though Newt Gingrich and other Republican leaders could argue that they are responding to *potential* public opinion, not just to where the public is today or to where it was immediately following the election (e.g., Arnold 1990). That is still high-risk politics.

Finally, it is also possible that local factors played a role in the Republicans' victory, something that is more unwelcome news to those searching for a sweeping mandate in these results. For example, Carol Swain (1995) emphasizes the importance of redistricting, especially in the South, and Jacobson (1995) discusses challenger quality, maintaining that most familiar patterns of congressional elections held true, despite the unfamiliar results (see also Rosenbaum 1994). My own preliminary explorations support Jacobson's view; by my count, the Republicans nominated their best crop of challengers in more than ten years, and it was their best candidates who won most frequently (see Krasno 1994, 173–74). All of this discussion, of course, is for the future, because future elections will surely allow us to place 1994 in more accurate perspective.

Appendix: Definitions of Issues (NES Data Codes)

1. Military preparedness: 1106, 1107, 1110–12, 1170–72, 1184

2. Foreign policy: military preparedness plus 1155–66, 1175–77, 1123–32, 1190–95, 1104, 1105

3. Big government (government spending): 605, 606

4. Taxes: 929–33

5. Election's economic impact: 934–41

6. Economic issues: big government, taxes, and economic impact of election plus 605, 606, 901, 926–28

7. Liberalism, conservatism: 531–36, 815, 816, 817, 162–65

8. Ideological stance: liberalism, conservatism plus 805–14, 818–38, 902–4

9. Welfare: 905, 906, 907, 1219, 1220

10. Social security, the aged, and workers' welfare programs: 908–13, 1221, 1222

11. Health care: 1001–3, 1025–27

12. Environment: 962–64, 1004–6

13. Relations to big business and the common man: 1201, 1202, 1205, 1206, 1209, 1210, 1233, 1234

14. New Deal issues: economic issues, ideological stance, welfare, social security, health care, and relations to big business and the common man plus 952–58, 1207, 1208, 942–45, 1215, 1216, 920–22, 959–61, 1001–3, 1025–27

15. Guns: 988–90

16. Law and order: guns plus 968–78, 982–84

17. Abortion: 985–87

18. Race-related issues: 405, 406, 946–48, 970, 975, 991–93, 1217, 1218

19. Family values: abortion plus 423, 424, 979–81, 1223, 1224, 982–84, 847–49, 1022–24

20. Candidate's record or experience: 211, 212, 215–21, 297, 429

21. Competence of candidates: candidate's record plus 303–8, 311, 312, 413–18, 53, 54, 309, 310, 317–20, 407, 408, 419–22, 601, 602, 431, 432, 707, 708, 213, 214, 437, 438, 448, 450–54, 425, 609

22. Integrity, sincerity: 313, 401–4

23. Candidate's other traits: integrity plus 445, 446, 449, 315, 316, 502, 503, 301, 302, 314, 411, 412, 423, 424, 426–28, 433–36, 439–44, 705, 706, 709, 710

24. Governmental corruption: 720, 603, 604, 1198, 1199

25. Quality of stewardship: corruption plus 121, 122, 709, 710

26. Partisanship: 101, 102, 111, 112, 151, 161, 500, 501, 502, 506, 507, 509–20, 131, 132

27. Contract with America: 608

28. Conduct of the campaign: Contract with America plus 628, 407, 505, 804, 951

29. Clinton: 17, 18

Notes

The data utilized in this chapter were made available by the University of Michigan's Inter-University Consortium for Political and Social Research, on a CD-ROM entitled *American National Election Studies, 1948–1994*, issued in May 1995. Neither the collectors of the original data nor the Consortium bears any responsibility for the analyses or the interpretations presented here.

1. See Converse 1964 and Campbell et al. 1960.

2. There are several possible objections to this view. For one thing, the use of open-ended questions penalizes the inarticulate, the people who have a hard time verbalizing their political views. Of course, many of the responses to these items are not exactly eloquent, though some individuals may be inhibited about expressing themselves poorly or may not be able to achieve even that standard. There may also be problems due to faulty memories. What happens if someone does not recall a consideration that had impressed them earlier? Finally, for a discussion about whether responses to open-ended questions constitute a justification for a respondent's actions or a cause for them, see Rahn, Krosnick, and Breuning 1994. These shortcomings should not rule out open-ended questions, but they do raise caution about viewing them as the solution to all the problems that plague more traditional survey items.

3. Kelley's formula for calculating a voter's "net score" is $(D^+ - D^-) - (R^+ - R^-)$ where D^+ is the number of likes about the Democratic Party and its candidates, D^- is the number of dislikes about the Democrats, R^+ is the number of likes about the Republicans, and R^- is the number of dislikes. Up to five comments are usually recorded for each of the eight likes and dislikes questions, resulting in a scale that ranges from −20, the set of considerations most favorable to Republicans, to +20, the most strongly Democratic, with zero being the neutral point. In 1982, however, the NES lists only four responses to the questions about the House candidates, reducing the range of the scale from −18 to +18. This change made little difference, since no more than 3 percent of respondents had as many as four likes or dislikes about either of the candidates.

4. For that reason I also looked separately at responses to questions about the parties, since, despite some regional differences, there is only one Democratic or Republican Party nationwide. None of the results reported below is appreciably changed if likes and dislikes of the candidates are excluded from the analysis.

5. See Eubank and Gow 1983 and Gow and Eubank 1984.

6. Respondents had many more things that they liked or disliked about the political parties in the two landslide years, 1994 and 1982, than in 1990; the mean number of considerations for the full sample of respondents in each year is 4.0 in 1994, 3.6 in 1982, and just 1.6 in 1990.

7. The Democratic credit rating is positive when $(D^+ - D^-)$ is greater than zero; the Republican, when $(R^+ - R^-)$ is greater than zero.

8. The category "relations to big business and the common man" also includes references to "special interests," a favorite term in current politics whose meaning is vague. As a result, some of the people who cited this consideration might have been thinking

not of the divide between big business and the common man but about other groups that have been called "special interests."

References

American National Election Studies, 1948–1994. 1995. CD-ROM issued in May. Available through the Inter-University Consortium for Political and Social Research, University of Michigan, Ann Arbor.

Arnold, R. Douglas. 1990. *The Logic of Congressional Action.* New Haven: Yale University Press.

Brady, David W., John F. Cogan, and Douglas Rivers. 1995. *How the Republicans Captured the House: An Assessment of the 1994 Midterm Elections.* Palo Alto, Calif.: Hoover Institution Press.

Campbell, Angus, Philip E. Converse, Warren E. Miller, and Donald Stokes. 1960. *The American Voter.* New York: Wiley and Sons.

Converse, Philip E. 1964. "The Nature of Belief Systems in Mass Publics." In *Ideology and Discontent,* ed. David Apter. New York: Free Press.

Eubank, Robert B., and David John Gow. 1983. "The Pro-Incumbent Bias in the 1978 and 1980 National Election Studies." *American Journal of Political Science* 27:122–39.

Gow, David John, and Robert B. Eubank. 1984. "The Pro-Incumbent Bias in the 1982 National Election Study." *American Journal of Political Science* 28:224–30.

Gruenwald, Juliana. 1995. "Shallow Tactics or Deep Issues: Fathoming the GOP 'Contract'." *Congressional Quarterly Weekly Report* 52:3361–62.

Jacobson, Gary C. 1995. "The 1994 House Elections in Perspective." Paper presented at the annual meeting of the Midwest Political Science Association, Chicago, Apr. 6–8.

Kelley, Stanley, Jr. 1983. *Interpreting Elections.* Princeton: Princeton University Press.

Kelley, Stanley, Jr., and Thad W. Mirer. 1974. "The Simple Act of Voting." *American Political Science Review* 68:572–91.

Key, V. O., Jr., with Milton Cummings. 1966. *The Responsible Electorate.* Cambridge: Harvard University Press.

Krasno, Jonathan S. 1994. *Challengers, Competition, and Reelection: Comparing Senate and House Elections.* New Haven: Yale University Press.

"Presidential News Conference: Clinton Reaches Out to GOP, Assesses Voters' Message." 1994. *Congressional Quarterly Weekly Report* 52.

Rahn, Wendy M., Jon A. Krosnick, and Marijke Breuning. 1994. "Rationalization and Derivation Processes in Survey Studies of Political Candidate Evaluation." *American Journal of Political Science* 38:582–600.

Rosenbaum, David. 1994. "GOP Unleashes Its New Weapon: Winning Candidates." *New York Times,* Nov. 13.

Swain, Carol M. 1995. *Black Faces, Black Interests: The Representation of African Americans in Congress.* 2d ed. Cambridge: Harvard University Press.

Part III

Governing

CHAPTER 9

Myth of the Presidential Mandate

Robert A. Dahl

On election night in 1980, vice-president-elect George Bush enthusiastically informed the country that Ronald Reagan's triumph was

> not simply a mandate for a change but a mandate for peace and freedom; a mandate for prosperity; a mandate for opportunity for all Americans regardless of race, sex, or creed; a mandate for leadership that is both strong and compassionate . . . a mandate to make government the servant of the people in the way our founding fathers intended; a mandate for hope; a mandate for hope for the fulfillment of the great dream that President-elect Reagan has worked for all his life. (Kelley 1983, 217)

I suppose there are no limits to permissible exaggeration in the elation of victory, especially by a vice-president-elect. He may, therefore, be excused for failing to note, as did many others who made comments in a similar vein in the weeks and months that followed, that Reagan's lofty mandate was provided by 50.9 percent of the voters. A decade later it is much more evident, as it should have been then, that what was widely interpreted as Reagan's mandate, not only by supporters but by opponents, was more myth that reality.

In claiming that the outcome of the election provided a mandate to the president from the American people to bring about the policies, programs, emphases, and new direction presented during the campaign by the winning candidate and his supporters, the vice-president-elect was, like other commentators, echoing a familiar theory.

Origin and Development

A history of the theory of the presidential mandate has not been written, and I have no intention of supplying one here. However, if anyone could be said to have created the myth of the presidential mandate, surely it would be Andrew

Jackson. Although, as far as I know, he never used the word "mandate," he was the first American president to claim not only that the president is uniquely representative of all the people but that his election confers on him a mandate from the people in support of his policy. Jackson's claim was a fateful step in the democratization of the constitutional system of the United States—or, rather, what I prefer to call the *pseudodemocratization* of the presidency.

As Leonard White has observed, it was Jackson's "settled conviction" that the president was "an immediate and direct representative of the people" (1954, 23). Presumably as a result of his defeat in 1824 in both the electoral college and the House of Representatives, Jackson, in his first presidential message to Congress, proposed that the Constitution be amended to provide for the direct election of the president, in order that "as few impediments as possible should exist to the free operation of the public will" (ibid.). "To the people," he said, "belongs the right of electing their Chief Magistrate: it was never designed that their choice should, in any case, be defeated, either by the intervention of electoral colleges or by . . . the House of Representatives" (quoted in Ceaser 1979, 160). His great issue of policy was the Bank of the United States, which he unwaveringly believed was harmful to the general good. Acting on this conviction, in 1832 he vetoed the bill to renew the bank's charter. Like his predecessors, he justified the veto as a protection against unconstitutional legislation; but unlike his predecessors in their comparatively infrequent use of the veto, he also justified it as a defense of his or his party's policies.

Following his veto of its charter, the bank became the main issue in the presidential election of 1832. As a consequence, Jackson's reelection was widely regarded, even among his opponents (in private, at least), as amounting to "something like a popular ratification" of his policy (White 1954, 23). When, in order to speed the demise of the bank, Jackson found it necessary to fire his treasury secretary, he justified his action on the ground, among others, that "the President is the direct representative of the American people, but the Secretaries are not" (quoted in White 1954, 23).

Innovative though it was, Jackson's theory of the presidential mandate was less robust than it was to became in the hands of his successors. In 1848 James Polk explicitly formulated the claim, in a defense of his use of the veto on the matters of policy, that as a representative of the people the president was, if not more representative than the Congress, at any rate equally so. "The people, by the constitution, have commanded the President, as much as they have commanded the legislative branch of the Government, to execute their will. . . . The President represents in the executive department the whole people of the United States, as each member of the legislative department represents portions of them." The president is responsible "not only to an enlightened public opinion, but to the people of the whole Union, who elected him, as the representative in the legislative branches . . . are responsible to the people of particular States or districts" (quoted in White 1954, 24).

Notice that in Jackson's and Polk's views, the president, both constitutionally and as the representative of the people, is on a par with Congress. They did not claim that in either respect the president is superior to Congress. It was Woodrow Wilson who took the further step in the evolution of the theory by asserting that in representing the people the president is not merely equal to Congress but actually superior to it.

Earlier Views

Because the theory of the presidential mandate espoused by Jackson and Polk has become an integral part of our present-day conception of the presidency, it may be hard for us to grasp how sharply that notion diverged from the views of the earlier presidents. As James Ceaser (1979) has shown, the framers of the Constitution designed the presidential election process as a means of improving the chances of electing a national figure who would enjoy majority support. They hoped their contrivance would avoid not only the populistic competition among candidates dependent on "the popular arts," which they rightly believed would occur if the president were elected by the people, but also what they believed would necessarily be a factional choice if the president were chosen by the Congress, particularly by the House.[1]

In adopting an electoral college as the solution, however, the framers seriously underestimated the extent to which the strong impulse toward democratization that was already clearly evident among Americans—particularly among their opponents, the Anti-Federalists—would subvert and alter their carefully contrived constitutional structure. Since this is a theme I pick up later, I want now to mention only two such failures that bear closely on the theory of the presidential mandate. First, the Founding Fathers did not foresee the developments of political parties, nor did they comprehend how a two-party system might achieve their goal of insuring the election of a figure of national rather than merely local renown. Second, as Ceaser remarks, although the founders recognized "the need for a popular judgement of the performances of an incumbent" and designed a method for selecting the president that would, they thought, provide that opportunity, they "did not see elections as performing the role of instituting decisive changes in policy in response to popular demands" (84). In short, the theory of the presidential mandate not only cannot be found in the framers' conception of the Constitution; it almost certainly violates that conception.

No president prior to Jackson challenged the view that Congress was the legitimate representative of the people. Even Thomas Jefferson, who adeptly employed the emerging role of party leader to gain congressional support for his policies and decisions, "was more Whig than . . . the British Whigs themselves in subordinating [the executive power] to the supreme legislative power." The tone of his messages is uniformly deferential to Congress. His first one closes with these words: "Nothing shall be wanting on my part to inform, as far as [is] in my power, the legislative judgement, nor to carry that judgement into faithful execution" (quoted in Corwin 1948, 20).

James Madison, demonstrating that a great constitutional theorist and an adept leader in Congress could be decidedly less than a great president, deferred so greatly to Congress that in his communications to that body his extreme caution rendered him "almost unintelligible" (Binkley 1947, 56)—a quality we would hardly expect from one who had been a master of lucid exposition at the Constitutional Convention. His successor, James Monroe, was so convinced that Congress should decide domestic issues without presidential influence that throughout the debates in Congress on "the greatest political issue of his day . . . the admission of Missouri and the status of slavery in the Louisiana Territory," he remained utterly silent (White 1951, 31).

Madison and Monroe serve not as examples of how presidents should behave but as evidence of how early presidents thought they should behave. Considering the constitutional views and the behavior of Jackson's predecessors, it is not hard to see why his opponents called themselves Whigs in order to emphasize his dereliction from the earlier and presumably constitutional view of the presidency.

Woodrow Wilson

The long and almost unbroken succession of mediocrities who succeeded to the presidency between Polk and Wilson for the most part subscribed to the Whig view of the office and seem to have laid no claim to a popular mandate for their policies—when they had any. Even Abraham Lincoln, in justifying the unprecedented scope of presidential power he believed he needed in order to meet secession and civil war, rested his case on constitutional grounds and not on a mandate from the people.[2] Indeed, since he distinctly failed to gain a majority of votes in the election of 1860, any claim to a popular mandate would have been dubious at best. Like Lincoln, Theodore Roosevelt also had a rather unrestricted view of presidential power; he expressed the view then emerging among Progressives that chief executives were also representatives of the people. Yet the stewardship he claimed for the presidency was ostensibly drawn— rather freely drawn, I must say—from the Constitution, not from the mystique of the mandate.[3]

Woodrow Wilson, more as political scientist than as president, brought the mandate theory to what now appears to be its canonical form. His formulation was influenced by his admiration for the British system of cabinet government. In 1879, while still a senior at Princeton, he published an essay recommending the adoption of cabinet government in the United States (Wilson [1879] 1947). He provided little indication as to how this change was to be brought about, however, and soon abandoned the idea without yet having found an alternative solution.[4] Nevertheless, he continued to contrast the American system of congressional government, in which Congress was all powerful but lacked executive leadership, with British cabinet government, in which Parliament, though all powerful, was firmly led by the prime minister and his cabinet. Since Americans were not likely to adopt the British cabinet system, however, he began to consider the alternative of more powerful presidential leadership.[5] In his *Congressional Government,* he acknowledged that "the representatives of the people are the proper ultimate authority in all matters of government, and that administration is merely the clerical part of government" (Wilson [1885] 1956, 181). Congress is, "unquestionably, the predominant and controlling force, the center and source of all motive and of all regulative power" (31). Yet a discussion of policy that goes beyond "special pleas for special privilege" is simply impossible in the House, "a disintegrate mass of jarring elements" (72–73), while the Senate is no more than "a small, select, and leisurely House of Representatives" (145).

By 1908, when *Constitutional Government in the United States* was published, Wilson had arrived at strong presidential leadership as a feasible solution. He faulted the earlier presidents who had adopted the Whig theory of the Constitution.

> The makers of the constitution were not enacting Whig theory. . . . The President is at liberty, both in law and conscience, to be as big a man as he can. His capacity will set the limit; and if Congress be overborne by him, it will be no fault of the makers of the Constitution—it will be from no lack of constitutional power on its part, but only because the President has the nation behind him, and Congress has not. He has no means of compelling Congress except through public opinion. . . . The early Whig theory of political dynamics . . . is far from being a democratic theory. . . . It is particularly intended to prevent the will of the people as a whole from having at any moment an unobstructed sweep and ascendancy.

And he contrasted the president with Congress in terms that would become common among later generations of commentators, including political scientists:

Members of the House and Senate are representatives of localities, are voted for only by sections of voters, or by local bodies of electors like the members of the state legislatures.[6] There is no national party choice expect that of President. No one else represents the people as a whole, exercising a national choice. . . . The nation as a whole has chosen him, and is conscious that it has no other political spokesman. His is the only national voice in affairs. . . . He is the representative of no constituency, but of the whole people. When he speaks in his true character, he speaks for no special interest. . . . There is but one national voice in the country, and that is the voice of the President. (Wilson 1908, 72–74, 126–29, 168)

Since Wilson, it has become commonplace for presidents and commentators alike to argue that by virtue of his election the president has received a mandate for his aims and policies from the people of the United States. The myth of the mandate is now a standard weapon in the arsenal of persuasive symbols all presidents exploit. For example, as the Watergate scandals emerged in mid-1973, Patrick Buchanan, then an aide in the Nixon White House, suggested that the president should accuse his accusers of "seeking to destroy the democratic mandate of 1972." Three weeks later, in an address to the country, Richard Nixon said: "Last November, the American people were given the clearest choice of this century. Your votes were a mandate, which I accepted, to complete the initiatives we began in my first term and to fulfill the promises I made for my second term" (quoted in Kelley 1983, 99). If the spurious nature of Nixon's claim now seems self-evident, the dubious grounds for all such pretensions are perhaps less obvious.[7]

Critique of the Theory

What does a president's claim to mandate amount to? The meaning of the term itself is not altogether clear.[8] Fortunately, however, in his excellent book *Interpreting Elections*, Stanley Kelley has "piece[d] together a coherent statement of the theory":

Its first element is the belief that elections carry messages about problems, policies, and programs—messages plain to all and specific enough to be directive. . . . Second, the theory holds that certain of these messages must be treated as authoritative commands . . . either to the victorious candidate or to the candidate and his party. . . . To qualify as mandates, messages about policies and programs must reflect the *stable* views both of individual voters and of the electorate. . . . In the electorate as a whole, the numbers of those for or against a policy or program matter. To suggest that a mandate exists for a particular policy is to suggest that more than a bare majority of those voting are agreed upon it. The common view holds that landslide victories are more likely to involve mandates than are narrow ones. . . . The final element of the theory is a negative imperative: governments should not undertake major innovations in policy or procedure, except in emergencies, unless the electorate has had an opportunity to consider them in an election and thus to express its views. (1983, 126–28)

To bring out the central problems more clearly, let me extract what might be called the primitive theory of the popular presidential mandate. According to this theory, a presidential election can accomplish four things. First, it confers constitutional and legal authority on the victor. Second, at the same time, it also conveys information. At a minimum it reveals the first preferences for president of a plurality of votes. Third, according to the primitive theory, the election, at least under the conditions Kelley describes, conveys further information: namely, that a clear majority of voters prefer the winner because they prefer his policies and wish him to pursue his policies. Finally, because the president's policies reflect the wishes of a majority of voters, when conflicts over policy arise between president and Congress, the president's policies ought to prevail.

While we can readily accept the first two propositions, the third, which is pivotal to the theory, might be false. But if the third is false, then so is the fourth. So the question arises: Beyond revealing the first preferences of a plurality of voters, do presidential elections also reveal the additional information that a plurality (or a majority) of voters prefer the policies of the winner and wish the winner to pursue those policies?

In appraising the theory I want to distinguish between two different kinds of criticisms. First, some critics contend that even when the wishes of constituents can be known, they should not be regarded as in any way binding on a legislator. I have in mind, for example, Edmund Burke's famous argument that he would not sacrifice to public opinion his independent judgment of how well a policy would serve his constituents' interests and the argument suggested by Hanna Pitkin that representatives bound by instructions would be prevented from entering into the compromises that legislation usually requires (Kelley 1983, 133).

Second, some critics may hold that when the wishes of constituents on matters of policy can be clearly discerned, they ought to be given great and perhaps even decisive weight. But, these critics contend, constituents' wishes usually cannot be known, at least when the constituency is large and diverse, as in presidential elections. In expressing his doubts on the matter in 1913, A. Lawrence Lowell quoted Sir Henry Maine: "The devotee of democracy is much in the same position as the Greeks with their oracles. All agreed that the voice of an oracle was the voice of god, but everybody allowed that when he spoke he was not as intelligible as might be desired" (quoted in Kelley 1983, 134).

It is exclusively the second kind of criticism that I want now to consider. Here again I am indebted to Stanley Kelley for his succinct summary of the main criticisms: "Critics allege that (1) some particular claim of a mandate is unsupported by adequate evidence; (2) most claims of mandates are unsupported by adequate evidence; (3) most claims of mandates are politically self-serving; or (4) it is not possible in principle to make a valid claim of mandate, since it is impossible to sort out voters' intentions" (1983, 136).

Kelley goes on to say that while the first three criticisms may well be valid, the fourth has been outdated by the sample survey, which "has again given us the ability to discover the grounds of voters' choices." In effect, then, Kelley rejects the primitive theory and advances the possibility of a more sophisticated mandate theory according to which the information about policies is conveyed not by the election outcome but by opinion surveys. Thus, the two functions are cleanly split: presidential elections are for electing a president, opinion surveys provide information about the opinions, attitudes, and judgments that account for the outcome. However, I would propose a fifth proposition, which I believe is also implicit in Kelley's analysis: While it may not be strictly impossible *in principle* to make a reasoned and well-grounded claim to a presidential mandate, to do so *in practice* requires a complex analysis that in the end may not yield much support for presidential claims.

But if we reject the primitive theory of the mandate and adopt the more sophisticated theory, then it follows that prior to the introduction of scientific sample surveys, no president could reasonably have defended his claim to a mandate. To put a precise date on the proposition, let us remember that the first presidential election in which scientific surveys formed the basis of an extended and systematic analysis was in 1940 (Lazarsfeld, Berelson, and Gaudet 1948). I do not mean to say that no election before 1940 permits us to draw the conclusion that a president's major policies were supported by a substantial majority of the electorate. But I do mean that for most presidential elections before 1940 a valid reconstruction of the policy views of the electorate is impossible or enormously difficult, even with the aid of aggregate data and other indirect indicators of voters' views. When we consider that presidents ordinarily assert their claims to mandates soon after their elections, well before historians and social scientists have sifted through the reams of indirect evidence, then we must conclude that before 1940 no contemporary claim to a presidential mandate could have been supported by the evidence available at the time.

While the absence of surveys undermines validation of presidential claims to a mandate before 1940, the existence of surveys since then would not necessarily have supported such claims. Ignoring all other shortcomings of the early election studies, the analysis of the 1940 election I just mentioned was not published until 1948. While that interval between the election and the analysis may have set a record, the systematic analysis of survey evidence that is necessary (though perhaps not sufficient) to interpret what a presidential election means always comes well after presidents and commentators have already told the world, on wholly inadequate evidence, what the election means.[9] Perhaps the most famous voting study to date, *The American Voter*, which draws primarily on interviews conducted in 1952 and 1956, appeared in 1960. Stanley Kelley's book on the elections of 1964, 1972, and 1980, *Interpreting Elections*, on which I draw freely here, appeared in 1983.

A backward glance quickly reveals how empty the claims to a presidential mandate have been in recent elections. Take 1960. If more than a bare majority is essential to a mandate, then surely Kennedy could have received no mandate, since he gained less than 50 percent of the total popular vote by the official count—just how much less by the unofficial count varies with the counter. Yet "on the day after election, and every day thereafter," Theodore Sorenson tells us, "he rejected the argument that the country had given him no mandate. Every election has a winner and a loser, he said in effect. There may be difficulties with the Congress, but a margin of only one vote would still be a mandate" (quoted in Safire 1978, 398).

By contrast, 1964 was a landslide election, as was 1972. From his analysis, however, Kelley concludes that "Johnson's and Nixon's specific claims of meaningful mandates do not stand up well when confronted by evidence" (1983, 139). To be sure, in both elections some of the major policies of the winners were supported by large majorities among those to whom these issues were salient. Yet "none of these policies was cited by more than 21 percent of respondents as a reason to like Johnson, Nixon, or their parties" (140).

In 1968, Richard Nixon gained office with only 43 percent of the popular vote. No mandate there. Likewise in 1976, Jimmy Carter won with a bare 50.1 percent. Once again, no mandate there.

When Ronald Reagan won in 1980, a more sophisticated understanding of what that election meant no longer had to depend on the academic analyses that would follow some years later, thanks to the much higher quality of surveys undertaken by the media. Nonetheless, many commentators, bemused as they so often are by the arithmetical peculiarities of the electoral college, immediately proclaimed both a landslide and a mandate for Reagan's policies. What they often failed to note was that Reagan gained just under 51 percent of the popular vote. Despite the claims of the vice-president-elect, surely we can find no mandate there. Our doubts are strengthened by the fact that in the elections to the House, Democratic candidates won just over 50 percent of the popular vote and a bare majority of seats. However, they lost control of the Senate. No Democratic mandate there, either.

These clear and immediate signs that the elections of 1980 failed to confer a mandate on the president or his Democratic opponents were, however, largely ignored. For it was so widely asserted as to be commonplace that Reagan's election reflected a profound shift of opinion away from New Deal programs and toward the new conservatism. However, from this analysis of the survey evidence, Kelley concludes that the commitment of voters to candidates was weak; a substantial proportion of Reagan voters were more interested in voting against Carter than for Reagan; and despite claims by journalists and others, the New Deal coalition did not really collapse. Nor was there any profound shift toward conservatism. "The evidence from press surveys . . . contradicts the claims that voters shifted toward conservatism and that this ideological shift elected Reagan" (1983, 185). In any case, the relation between ideological location and policy preferences was "of a relatively modest magnitude" (quoted in Kelley 1983, 187).

In winning by a landslide of popular votes in 1984, Reagan achieved one prerequisite to a mandate. Yet in that same election, Democratic candidates for the House won 52 percent of the popular vote. Two years earlier, they had won 55 percent of the vote. On the face of it, surely the 1984 elections gave no mandate to Reagan.

Before the end of 1986, when the Democrats had once again won a majority of popular votes in elections to the House and had once again won a majority of seats in the Senate, it should have been clear, and it should be even clearer now, that the major social and economic policies for which Reagan and his supporters had claimed a mandate have persistently failed to gain majority support. Indeed, the major domestic policies and programs established during the thirty years preceding Reagan's arrival in the White House have not been overturned in the grand revolution of policy that his election was supposed to have ushered in. For eight years, what Reagan and his supporters claimed as a mandate to reverse those policies was regularly rejected by means of the only legitimate and constitutional processes we Americans have for determining what the policies of the United States government should be.

What are we to make of this long history of unsupported claims to a presidential mandate? The myth of the mandate would be less important if it were not one element on the larger process of the pseudodemocratization of the presidency—the creation of a type of chief executive that in my view should have no proper place in a democratic republic.

Yet even if we consider it in isolation from the larger development of the presidency, the myth is harmful to American political life. By portraying the president as the only representative of the whole people and Congress as merely representing narrow, special, and parochial interests, the myth of the mandate elevates the president to an exalted position in our constitutional system at the expense of Congress. The myth of the mandate fosters the belief that the particular interests of the diverse human beings who form the citizen body in a large, complex, and pluralistic country like ours constitute no legitimate element in the general good. The myth confers on the aims of the groups who benefit from presidential policies an aura of national interest and public good to which they are no more entitled than the groups whose interests are reflected in the policies that gain support by congressional majorities. Because the myth is almost always employed to support deceptive, misleading, and manipulative interpretations, it is harmful to the political understanding of citizens.

It is, I imagine, now too deeply rooted in American political life and too useful a part of the political arsenal of presidents to be abandoned. Perhaps the most we can hope for is that commentators on public affairs in the media and in academic pursuits will dismiss claims to a presidential mandate with the scorn they usually deserve.

While a presidential election does not confer a popular mandate on the president—nor, for that matter, on congressional majorities—it confers the legitimate authority, right, and opportunity on a president to try to gain the adoption by constitutional means of the policies the president supports. In the same way, elections to Congress confer on a member the authority, right, and opportunity to try to gain the adoption by constitutional means of the policies he or she supports. Each may reasonably contend that a particular policy is for the public good or in the public interest and, moreover, is supported by a majority of citizens.

I do not say that whatever policy is finally adopted following discussion, debate, and constitutional processes necessarily reflects what a majority of citizens would prefer or what would be for the public good in any other sense. What I do say is that no elected leader, including the president, is uniquely privileged to say what an election means—nor to claim that the election has conferred on the president a mandate to enact the particular policies the president supports.

The Democratization of the Presidency

It was inevitable that the executive branch designed by the framers of the Constitution would be fundamentally altered in response to the powerful influence of democratizing impulses. If they had intended a chief executive whose election and capacity for governing would not require him (or her) to compete for popular approval and who therefore would not depend on "the popular arts" of winning public support (Ceaser 1979, 47), they seriously underestimated both the strength of the democratic impulses among their fellow citizens and its effects on the presidency. Nothing reveals this more clearly than the amazing speed with which the framers' design for the executive was replaced by a presidency dependent on popular election and popular approval.

The consequences of democratization were evident almost at once and gained strength with the passage of time. I have already described one aspect of this process of democratization in some detail: the invention of the theory of the presidential mandate. Jackson's invention was, however, preceded by decades of democratization that gave plausibility to the theory.

By Jackson's time the presidency had long since become an office sought by partisan candidates in popular elections. Although political parties had existed in Britain and Sweden as elite organizations in systems with a severely limited suffrage, under the leadership of Jefferson and Madison the Republican Party became an instrument by which popular majorities could be organized, mobilized, and made effective in influencing the conduct of government. Henceforth, a president would combine his role as a presumably nonpartisan chief executive with his role as a national leader of a partisan organization with a partisan following.[10]

If the presidential office was to be attained by partisan contestation, then in order to reach that office a serious presidential candidate would ordinarily need to gain the endorsement and support of a political party. Although the story of the evolution of the presidential nominating process has often been told, it so vividly reveals the impact of democratizing impulses that I want to summarize it briefly.

The Nominating Process

The first organized system for nominating candidates for president and vice president was the congressional caucus, which both the Republicans and the Federalists introduced in 1800 (Cunningham 1957, 163–65). Yet given the emerging strength of democratic ideology, a system so obtrusively closed to participation by any but a small group of congressional politicians was clearly vulnerable. Democratic sentiments we would find familiar in our own time were expressed in a resolution passed in the Ohio legislature in 1823: "The time has now arrived when the machinations of the *few* to dictate to the *many* . . . will be met . . . by a people jealous of their rights. . . . The only unexceptional source from which nominations can proceed is the people themselves. To them belongs the right of choosing; and they alone can with propriety take any previous steps" (quoted in Ostrogorski 1926, 12).

By 1824, when the candidate of the congressional caucus of Democratic Republicans trailed a bad fourth in the election behind Jackson, John Quincy

Adams, and Henry Clay, who all ran without benefit of a blessing by the caucus, the outrage to democratic sentiments was easily exploited, most notably by Jackson and his supporters. The congressional nominating caucus came to an end.[11] In 1831 and 1832, in an obvious extension of democratic ideas, which by then had thoroughly assimilated the concept of representation, the nominating convention came into existence. But in due time, "just as once the democratic passion of the people were roused against the Congressional caucus, so now they were turned against the convention system. . . . Away therefore with the delegates, who can never be trusted, and back to the people!" (Ostrogorski 1926, 342).

In a further obvious extension of democratic ideas to the nominating process, from 1901 onward the direct primary was introduced, initially for state and congressional nominations and soon for presidential candidates. The presidential primary system was in turn subjected to the democratizing impulse. "By the election of 1972," Ceaser remarks, "the election process had been transformed into what is essentially a plebiscitary system" (1979, 213).[12]

Reducing Intermediate Forces

The democratization of the nominating process is instructive for many reasons —among others because after almost two centuries of trials employing three major forms with many variations, a sensible method of nominating presidential candidates still seems beyond the reach of Americans. The present system has its defenders no doubt, but their number seems to be rapidly diminishing.

The democratization of the nominating process is also instructive because it shows how the relations between the public and presidents or presidential candidates have become increasingly direct. Jeffrey Tulis (1987) has described the enormous change that has taken place in the way presidents address the public—presidential speech, if you like. The view that prevailed during the early years of the republic, and for much of the nineteenth century, tended to follow "two general prescriptions for presidential speech." First, proposals for laws and policies would be fashioned and directed principally to Congress; although public, they would be fashioned for congressional needs and not necessarily for general public understanding or approval. Second, when presidential speech was directed primarily to the people at large, it would address general principles rather than specific issues. "The inaugural address, for example, developed along lines that emphasized popular instruction in constitutional principle and the articulation of the general tenor and direction of presidential policy, while tending to avoid discussion of the merits of particular policy proposals" (46–47).

Presidents rarely directly addressed the general public, except possibly on official occasions. From George Washington through Andrew Jackson, no president gave more than five speeches a year to the general public, a total that was not exceeded by half the presidents from Washington through William McKinley. When they did address the general public, the early presidents rarely employed popular rhetoric or discussed their policies (Tulis 1987, 64, 66). The great exception was Andrew Johnson, who, however, scarcely served as a model for his successors (ibid., 87). Moreover, Gil Troy has recently discovered that until Woodrow Wilson no president had ever "stumped on his own behalf." Until the 1830s, even presidential candidates did not make stump speeches. "Such behavior," Troy writes, "was thought undignified—and unwise. Presidential candidates, especially after nomination, were supposed to stand, not run, for election" (Troy 1988).

What we now take as normal presidential behavior is a product of this century. The innovators were Theodore Roosevelt and, to an even greater extent, Woodrow Wilson (see Tulis 1987). Since their day, and particularly in recent decades, the task of shaping presidential speech to influence and manipulate public opinion—if necessary by appealing over the heads of Congress in order to induce the Congress to support the president's policies—has become a central element in the art and science of presidential conduct.

The President and the Constitutional System

Thus the presidency has developed into an office that is the very embodiment of the kind of executive the framers, so far as we can discern their intentions, strove to avoid. They did not wish for an executive who would be a tribune of the people, a champion of popular majorities; who would gain office by popular election; who, as a consequence of his popular election, would claim a mandate for his policies; who, in order to mobilize popular support for his policies, would appeal directly to the people; who would shape the language, style, and delivery of his appeals so as best to create a public opinion favorable to his ambitions; and who, whenever it seemed expedient, would bypass the members of the deliberative body in order to mobilize public opinion and thereby induce a reluctant Congress to enact his policies. That is, however, a fair description of the presidency that emerged out of the intersections of the framers' design with the strongly democratic ideology that came to prevail among politically active Americans.

One response to this kind of presidency is to argue that these developments are, on the whole, good. They are good, it might be said, because democracy is good, more democracy is better than less democracy, and a more democratized presidency is better than a less democratized presidency. In the immortal cliché of the 1970 McGovern-Fraser Commission, "the cure for the ills of democracy is more democracy" (quoted in Ceaser 1979, 275). Yet this response does not seem to quiet the fears of a growing number of critics. In Arthur Schlesinger's now popular term, the presidency was transformed into the "imperial presidency" (1973). James Ceaser (1979), Theodore Lowi (1985), and others have referred to development of the plebiscitary presidency. Lowi has also dubbed it the "personal presidency," remarking that "the new politics of the president-centered Second Republic can best be described as a plebiscitary republic with a personal presidency" (1985, xi). Jeffrey Tulis (1987) calls the presidency that was seeded by Wilson and cultivated by his successors the "rhetorical presidency."

I want to distinguish several different perspectives in the criticisms of the modern presidency. From one, what is lamentable is the break with the doctrines, intentions, and designs of the founders. A rather different perspective, one more pragmatic and functional, emphasizes that the presidency is simply no longer working satisfactorily in its existing constitutional setting. For example, a president claiming a mandate for his policies may be blocked in one or both houses of Congress by a majority of members who in effect also claim a mandate for their policies. The result is not constructive compromise but deadlock or contradictions in policies. Examples are the recent conflicts over the deficit and over American policies in Central America.

From a third perspective, however, the presidency has come to endanger the operation of democratic processes. It is this perspective that I want to emphasize here.

I have alluded to the developments over the past two centuries as the *pseudodemocratization* of the presidency. I have no wish to add to the other epithets another even more cumbersome and more ugly; but the term does speak directly to my concerns. By *pseudodemocratization* I mean change taken with the ostensible and perhaps even actual purpose of enhancing the democratic process that in practice retains the aura of its democratic justification and yet has the effect, intended or unintended, of weakening the democratic process.

In the case of the presidency, I have two adverse consequences in mind. One, the more obvious, is a loss of popular and congressional control, direct and indirect, over the policies and decisions of the president. A president endowed with the mystique of a mandate—which may sometimes be deepened in a democratic country by the majesty and mystery generated by his popularity and his capacity to evoke and reflect popular feelings, yearnings, and hopes—may encounter resistance to a particular policy in Congress, perhaps even in the public. The president exploits all the resources of his office to overcome that resistance: his rhetorical resources, his unique capacity to influence or even manipulate public opinion, and all the power and authority derived properly or factitiously from the Constitution—including his power as commander in chief, his unique authority over foreign affairs, his right or claim to executive privilege and secrecy, and his authority and influence over officials in the executive branch, over the objectives they are obliged or induced to seek, and over the moneys and other resources necessary to reach those objectives. Whatever term we may wish to apply to an executive like this, we can hardly call it democratic.

The other consequence, though more elusive and not wholly independent of the first, is equally important. According to one view—which I would describe as either simplistic or hostile—democracy means rule by public opinion. This view is mistaken, both historically and theoretically. Democracy cannot be justified, and its advocates have rarely sought to justify it, as no more than the triumph of raw will. It can be and is justified because more than any feasible alternative it provides ordinary people with the opportunities to discover what public policies and activities are best for themselves and for others and to insure that collective decisions conform with—or at least do not persistently and fundamentally violate—the policies they believe best for themselves and for others.

I cannot undertake to explicate the complexities in the notion of discovering what is best for themselves and for others, nor do I need to. For it is obvious that discovering what is best for oneself or others requires far more than announcing one's raw will or surface preferences. Imagine this extreme situation. Suppose we were called upon to vote in a national plebiscite on a proposed treaty governing nuclear weapons that had been secretly negotiated between the president and the leader of Russia. Suppose further that the plebiscite is to be held one day after the agreement between the two leaders and that we are to vote yes or no. The very perversity of this example serves to emphasize the crucial importance of opportunities for *understanding* as a requirement in the democratic process and illustrates why in the absence of such opportunities we should speak instead of a "pseudodemocratic" process.

Many writers have stressed the importance of deliberation. While some associate it with classical republicanism, deliberation is surely central to the idea of democratic decision making. What I have referred to elsewhere as enlightened understanding is an essential criterion for the democratic process. Deliberation is one crucial means, though I think not the only means, to enlightened understanding. Others include systematic research and analysis, experimentation, consultation with experts, orderly discussion, daydreaming, and self-inquiry.

The modern presidency all too often impairs not only deliberation but also other means to a more enlightened understanding by citizens and the Congress. Nelson Polsby's conclusion about the presidential selection process should be extended to the presidency as a whole (1983, 170–72). The increasing directness of relationships between a candidate or president and the public means that the traditional "intermediation processes," to use his term, have become less effective (1983, 134). Face-to-face groups, political parties, and interest groups are less autonomous and now rely heavily on the mass media. For example, some careful experiments have recently shown that in assessing the relative importance of different issues, citizens are strongly influenced by television news (Iyengar and Kinder 1987). I share Polsby's judgement that not only are deliberative processes weak in the general public's consideration of candidates and presidents, but they are also insufficiently subject to extensive review and appraisal by their peers. I also share his judgment that "the directness of direct democracy in a very large scale society seems . . . illusory" (147).

Conclusion

How serious a matter is the pseudodemocratization of the presidency? What, if anything, can and should we do about it? To answer those questions responsibly would obviously take us far beyond the slender limits of this chapter. Among friends and colleagues I think I detect rather sharply different perspectives. Let me list several.

First, the problem is not serious.

Second, though the problem is serious, the solution is to elect one more great president.

Third, the problem is serious but there isn't much we can do about it.

Fourth, the problem is serious but can be corrected by fairly modest incremental changes, possibly including a constitutional amendment, one, for example, providing for an American equivalent to the question hour in the British or Canadian Parliaments.

Last, the problem is so profoundly built into the interaction between the constitutional framework and democratic ideology that it cannot be solved without a fundamental alteration in one or the other. This is the conclusion to which I find myself increasingly drawn.

However, given that conclusion, a solution—assuming one is attainable—could require that Americans either transform their constitutional framework or give up their democratic beliefs. I think some critics may hope that Americans will reject their democratic ideology in favor of what these critics believe to be eighteenth-century republican doctrines that would restore the Constitution to its pristine condition in the form the framers presumably intended. I think this alternative is not only morally wrong but politically and historically illusory.

A goal more suitable to the democratic beliefs of Americans would be to begin the arduous task of rethinking constitutional needs in order to determine whether they may not design a form of government better adapted to the requirements of democracy and less conducive to pseudodemocratization.

Among other rethinking, Americans need to consider how to create better opportunities for deliberation and other means by which citizens might gain a
more enlightened understanding of their political goals.

To achieve the daunting goal of rethinking the Constitution will not be easy,
and no one should believe that, properly done, it can be accomplished quickly.
But begun now, it might be achieved before this century is over. It would be an
appropriate undertaking to commence now that the bicentennial of the American Constitution is behind us.

Notes

This essay is reprinted with the permission of *Political Science Quarterly* and the author.

1. Although James Madison and Alexander Hamilton opposed the contingent solution of a House election in the event that no candidate received a majority of electoral
votes, Gouverneur Morris and James Wilson accepted it as not too great a concession
(Ceaser 1979, 80–81).

2. Lincoln drew primarily on the war he created in uniting the president's constitutional obligation "to take care that the laws be faithfully executed" with his power as commander in chief. He interpreted the war power as a veritable cornucopia of implicit constitutional authority for the extraordinary emergency measures he undertook during an
extraordinary national crisis (Corwin 1948, 277).

3. "Every executive officer, in particular the President, Roosevelt maintained, 'was a
steward of the people bound actively and affirmatively to do all he could for the people. . . .' He held therefore that, unless specifically forbidden by the Constitution or by
law, the President had 'to do anything that the needs of the nation demanded. . . . Under
this interpretation of executive power,' he recalled, 'I did and caused to be done many
things not previously done. . . . I did not usurp power, but I did greatly broaden the use
of executive power'" (Blum 1954, 108).

4. "He seems not to have paid much attention to the practical question of how so radical an alteration was to be brought about. As far as I know, Wilson's only published
words on how to initiate the English system are in the article, *Committee of Cabinet Government*, which appeared in the *Overland Monthly* for January, 1884." His solution was
to amend section 6 of Article 1 of the Constitution to permit members of Congress to
hold offices as members of the cabinet and to extend the terms of the president and representatives (see Lippmann 1956, 14–15).

5. Wilson's unfavorable comparative judgment is particularly clear in *Congressional
Government* ([1885] 1956, 181). Just as Jackson had proposed the direct election of the
president, in his first annual message Wilson proposed that a system of direct national
primaries be adopted (Ceaser 1979, 173).

6. The Seventeenth Amendment requiring direct election of senators was not adopted until 1913.

7. For other examples of claims to a presidential mandate resulting from the election, see Safire 1978, 398, and Kelley 1983, 72–74, 126–29, 168.

8. See *mandate* in the *Oxford English Dictionary* (Oxford, England: Oxford University Press, 1971, compact ed.), Safire 1978, 398, Plano and Greenburg 1979, 130, Gould and Kolb 1964, 404, Sharfritz 1988, 340.

9. The early election studies are summarized in Berelson, Lazarsfeld, and McPhee 1954, 331.

10. As Ceaser remarks, "The nonpartisan selection system established by the Founders barely survived a decade. By the election of 1796, traces of partisanship were already clearly in evidence, and by 1800 the contest was being fought on strictly partisan lines" (1979, 88). Like many other innovations, Jefferson's had unintended consequences. "Jefferson . . . had an abiding distrust of national elections and, except in the case of his own election, never regarded them as the proper forum for making decisive changes. . . . The paradox of Jefferson's election in 1800 was that while he was chosen for partisan reasons, he did not intend to institute a system of permanent party competition" (ibid., 90).

11. Though Jackson gained more votes than Adams, both popular and electoral, he was denied victory in the House of Representatives.

12. Ceaser describes three phases in the evolution of the presidential selection process since the introduction of the primaries: from 1912 to 1920, a period of the expansion of the primaries and the "plebiscitary model"; from 1920 to the 1960s, which saw the decline of primaries and the resurgence of parties; and the period since 1972.

References

Berelson, Bernard, Paul F. Lazarsfeld, and William McPhee. 1954. *Voting.* Chicago: University of Chicago Press.

Binkley, Wilfred E. 1947. *President and Congress.* New York: Alfred A. Knopf.

Blum, John Morton. 1954. *The Republican Roosevelt.* New York: Atheneum.

Ceaser, James W. 1979. *Presidential Selection: Theory and Development.* Princeton: Princeton University Press.

Corwin, Edward S. 1948. *The President: Offices and Powers, 1789–1948.* 3d ed. New York: New York University Press.

Cunningham, Noble E., Jr. 1957. *The Jeffersonian Republicans: The Formation of Party Organizations, 1789–1801.* Chapel Hill: University of North Carolina Press.

Gould, Julius, and William L. Kolb. 1964. *A Dictionary of the Social Sciences.* New York: Free Press.

Iyengar, Shanto, and Donald R. Kinder. 1987. *News That Matters: Television and American Opinion.* Chicago: University of Chicago Press.

Kelley, Stanley, Jr. 1983. *Interpreting Elections.* Princeton: Princeton University Press.

Lazarsfeld, Paul F., Bernard Berelson, and Hazel Gaudet. 1948. *The People's Choice.* New York: Columbia University Press.

Lippmann, Walter. 1956. *Introduction to Congressional Government*. New York: Meridian Books.

Lowi, Theodore J. 1985. *The Personal President: Power Invested, Promise Unfulfilled*. Ithaca: Cornell University Press.

Ostrogorski, M. 1926. *Democracy and the Party System in the United States*. New York: Macmillan.

Plano, Jack C., and Milton Greenburg. 1979. *The American Political Dictionary*. New York: Holt, Rinehart and Winston.

Polsby, Nelson W. 1983. *Consequences of Party Reform*. New York: Oxford University Press.

Safire, William. 1978. *Safire's Political Dictionary*. New York: Random House.

Schlesinger, Arthur, Jr. 1973. *The Imperial Presidency*. Boston: Houghton Mifflin.

Sharfritz, Jay M. 1988. *The Dorsey Dictionary of American Government and Politics*. Chicago: Dorsey Press.

Troy, Gil. 1988. *New York Times*, Jan. 17.

Tulis, Jeffrey K. 1987. *The Rhetorical Presidency*. Princeton: Princeton University Press.

White, Leonard D. 1951. *The Jeffersonians: A Study in Administrative History, 1801–1829*. New York: Free Press.

———. 1954. *The Jacksonians: A Study in Administrative History, 1829–1861*. New York: Free Press.

Wilson, Woodrow. [1879] 1947. *Cabinet Government in the United States*. Stamford, Conn.: Overbrook Press.

———. [1885] 1956. *Congressional Government: A Study in American Politics*. New York: Meridian Books.

———. 1908. *Constitutional Government in the United States*. New York: Columbia University Press.

CHAPTER 10

Clinton, the 103d Congress, and Unified Party Control
What Are the Lessons?

David R. Mayhew

Divided government is not working," David S. Broder wrote in the summer of 1992. "Only the voters can fix this mess." In November of that year, the voters performed on cue by trading in George Bush for Bill Clinton, keeping solid Democratic majorities in the House and Senate, and consequently opting for single-party control of the U.S. government for the first time since 1977–80, under Jimmy Carter. It was a "dramatic shift," notes Richard E. Cohen, "from a divided government stuck in neutral to one in which a single party was operating the vehicle and had well-defined goals" (1994, 2). At hand was a test of whether unified party control could overcome gridlock and make the system work (Brady 1993). At stake, from the standpoint of part 3 of this volume, was the role of American parties in governing.

Once Clinton took office in 1993, things went quite well on Capitol Hill, as the president pressed his ambitious budget plan and then the North American Free Trade Agreement (NAFTA). Congress, according to one late-1993 assessment, had generated "a spate of new laws, as Democratic policies and programs . . . flowed freely down the legislative sluice for the first time in more than a decade" (Hook 1993, 3355). Using roll-call data, *Congressional Quarterly* reported in September 1993 that Clinton had scored "the highest success rate in Congress of any first-year president since Dwight D. Eisenhower" (Langdon 1993).[1]

But no one was voicing any such claims a year later, after the downfall of Clinton's health care plan and numerous other Democratic aims. "This will go into the record books as perhaps the worst Congress—least effective, most destructive, nastiest—in 50 years," declared the *Washington Post* (1994). "It's back to gridlock, or so it has seemed lately—but of a nasty, internecine kind that makes the Bush administration seem like a checkers game by comparison" (*Washington Post National Weekly Edition* 1994, 24). Also judging thumbs-down was the *New York Times* (1994), which argued that "Bill Clinton and the Democrats have failed to persuade the American people that they can govern as a party" and pointed to "rising public frustration at the majority party's inability to govern even when it has the keys to the Capitol and the White House." In a national opinion poll reported in September 1994, only 19 percent of respondents said that Congress had accomplished more than it does in a typical two-year period; 52 percent thought it had accomplished less (Clymer 1994d; Toner 1994).

How does the 103d Congress of 1993–94 stack up when examined more closely and placed in historical perspective? I pursue that question here in an analysis that dwells on the enactment of laws and on possible differences between unified and divided party control. The analysis feeds off and extends my 1991 work, *Divided We Govern*, which covers Congresses from 1946 through 1990.[2]

Volume and Direction of Lawmaking

This discussion is organized under ten general "claims" that I believe are backed up by the record of the 103d Congress. All ten deal directly or indirectly with unified versus divided party control. Some are framed as historical generalizations about the U.S. regime (at least since World War II); others, implicitly hedged in by understandings about background conditions, are framed as propositions of universalistic form.

Claim 1: The volume of important laws enacted by Congress does not vary significantly between conditions of divided as opposed to unified party control. On average, that is, the number of major laws passed by Congresses under unified party control (where one party holds the presidency, House, and Senate) does not differ significantly from the number passed by Congresses under divided control (where one party holds two of the three institutions but not the third). This is the central claim of *Divided We Govern* and is given prime attention here. The legislative record of 1993–94 is juxtaposed to those of the twenty-three preceding postwar Congresses of 1947–48 through 1991–92.

Is this a direct probe for the existence of gridlock as opposed to its absence? It is not. "Gridlock" implies proposals not passed—failures that could have been successes. Thus, any search for whether gridlock exists or not seems to call for some kind of ratio measure—a numerator comprising laws successfully passed over a denominator comprising all proposals that might have passed (whether they did or not). An obvious supply of such ratio measures appears in presidential "support scores" or "success scores" of various kinds. But for anyone studying the legislative output of the U.S. regime—and particularly anyone examining how that output may vary under conditions of divided as opposed to unified party control—presidential scores have dubious merit.[3] The president is not the only elected official who has legislative powers and an agenda. As an analogy, it would make little sense to investigate the decision outputs of families by looking only at whether mothers get what they want.

This is not just a quibble. Yes, President Clinton did largely set the legislative agenda for the 103d Congress, but right after that, who set the Contract with America agenda for the 104th? Also, proposals for laws often bubble up from the congressional ranks one by one rather than descend as a packaged program from the White House or a Newt Gingrich-like party leadership. Any realistic, committed conservative knows about the subleadership route to success that produced such major measures as the McCarran Internal Security Act of 1950, the McCarran-Walter Immigration Act of 1952, the so-called Hyde amendments to curb government support of abortion, and the Gramm-Rudman-Hollings antideficit act of 1985. On the liberal side, in the decades after the White House became Republican in 1968, various blocs and entrepreneurs crafted a legislative art form in maneuvering to enactment such initiatives as Senator Edmund Muskie's Water Pollution Control Act of 1972, the War Powers Act of 1973, the Federal Election Campaign Act of 1974, South Africa sanctions in 1986, and the Family Support Act of 1988. In fact, Capitol Hill is a swirl of legislative options that emerge endlessly from all corners and sides—not just from the White House (Lindblom 1965). That makes it hard to isolate a useful "legislative agenda" for a Congress.

My substitute solution in *Divided We Govern* was, in effect, to count the full-grown oaks but ignore the acorns—to try to compile two-year lists of important laws that actually did pass but to ignore any underlying agendas or denominators. This way, we could at least try to see whether levels of successful legislative volume or motion differ under conditions of unified as opposed to divided party control. What are the levels of legislative production? That might be the best answerable question. Accommodated by this course is one plausible theoretical viewpoint about denominators indexing legislative proposals—namely, that they always should be set at infinity, regardless of conditions of party control. In principle, acorns exist without end (Krehbiel 1996). What politicians could propose under specified circumstances is limitless; what they do propose is secondary and, at any rate, likely to be affected by the circumstances.

To canvass for important enactments in *Divided We Govern*, I conducted two independent sweeps through the history of all post–World War II Congresses (Mayhew 1991, ch. 3). By "important" items, I meant in principle ones that were both innovative and consequential—or at least believed likely, at the time of passage, to be consequential. My first sweep relied on contemporary accounts, chiefly a series of stylized end-of-session "wrap-up" stories written by *New York Times* and *Washington Post* journalists, that cited enactments evidently thought by the Washington community to be major initiatives. The test was this: Did the writers seem to think a new law was particularly important or not? The second sweep relied on judgments by specialists in forty-three policy areas, writing mainly in the 1980s, regarding which laws enacted in their areas during the preceding decades had proved to be major measures. This two-pronged methodology has many difficulties, including ones associated with coding elusive materials (Mayhew 1991, 6–7, 34–50, 74–80, 90–91; Mayhew 1993b), but it has the strength of offering cross-time appraisals by two sets of arguably relevant witnesses. The wrap-up journalists, like the policy experts, really do try to place lawmaking in absolute or historical perspective. A quick reality test of this, for example, is that the wrap-up sweep for Lyndon B. Johnson's historic Great Society Congress of 1965–66 yielded nineteen major laws, whereas the one for Eisenhower's last Congress of 1959–60—a model of meager performance for many historians and political scientists—yielded just four major laws.

All statutes netted by either sweep added up to 274 items for the Congresses of 1947–48 through 1991–92—and now another 11 for 1993–94. The second column of table 10.1 presents the number of laws passed by each Congress. In parentheses just to the right are figures for a small number of laws (already included in the larger counts) that seemed to stand out to contemporary witnesses in the first sweep as historically important. Included are the Marshall Plan in 1948, Medicare in 1965, the Voting Rights Act of 1965, Reagan's two budgetary instruments in 1981, and Bush's and Clinton's deficit reduction acts of 1990 and 1993.[4]

Evident in the second column of table 10.1 is a bulge of lawmaking from the early 1960s through the mid-1970s. I believe the bulge is real—not some methodological fluke (see also Cameron et al. 1996, 22–24; Davidson 1988, 351–54). It indexes the immense expansion of the U.S. domestic state through increased expenditure and regulation that took place under John Kennedy, Lyndon Johnson, Richard Nixon, and Gerald Ford (Mayhew 1991, ch. 4; Sundquist 1968; Vogel 1981; Skocpol 1987, 364–65). Lawmaking really did surge, perform at a high rate, and decline. Since that time, however, the falloff in law counts does owe partly to two artifactual considerations. First, Congress switched, around 1980, to large comprehensive or omnibus bills—notably, budgetary instruments—as vehicles of choice for many legislative items that once would have passed as free-standing laws. No doubt this cut down a bit on the number of documentable "major laws" for more recent times. The most embarrassing con-

Table 10.1 Analysis of Laws Passed by Congress, 1947–94

Congress	Total Number of Laws[a]	Part of Presidential Term		Party Control	
		1st Half	2d Half	Unified	Divided
1947–48	10 (2)	——	10	——	10
1949–50	12 (2)	12	——	12	——
1951–52	6	——	6	6	——
1953–54	9	9	——	9	——
1955–56	6	——	6	——	6
1957–58	11 (1)	11	——	——	11
1959–60	5	——	5	——	5
1961–62	15 (1)	15	——	15	——
1963–64	13 (4)	——	13	13	——
1965–66	22 (3)	22	——	22	——
1967–68	16 (1)	——	16	16	——
1969–70	22	22	——	——	22
1971–72	16	——	16	——	16
1973–74	22 (1)	22	——	——	22
1975–76	14	——	14	——	14
1977–78	12	12	——	12	——
1979–80	10	——	10	10	——
1981–82	9 (2)	9	——	——	9
1983–84	7	——	7	——	7
1985–86	9 (1)	9	——	——	9
1987–88	12	——	12	——	12
1989–90	9 (1)	9	——	——	9
1991–92	7	——	7	——	7
1993–94	11 (2)	11	——	11	——
Mean	11.9	13.6	10.2	12.6	11.4

[a] Figures in parentheses represent the number of laws that were considered to be of particular historical importance at the time of their passage.

sequence for this study is the confinement of the 1981 "Reagan revolution" to just two statutes—the president's tax cut (the largest in U.S. history) and the so-called Gramm-Latta II (or OBRA—the Omnibus Budget Act) package of expenditure cuts (Mayhew 1991, 43, 69, 76). Second, my second sweep through the works of "policy experts"—an independent source of listable laws—faltered in the early 1980s and came to a complete halt in 1986. Those writers' works could not be consulted for events occurring after their publication dates. A result is that my methodology, now reduced to the wrap-up stories of the first sweep, has probably grown both stingier and less sound when applied to very recent Congresses. Almost certainly it skips a few additional laws that a continued second sweep would have netted, and it loses the sensibility of policy experts as a useful complement to that of journalists.

This having been said, the middle columns of table 10.1 document one solid generalization: More major laws pass during the first half of a presidential term than during the second half. The only exception is Reagan's second term, when Democratic House Speaker Jim Wright ushered through a considerable program in 1987–88 (Mayhew 1991, 118–19). (After the 1994 midterm, of course, congressional Republicans aimed for a second exception during 1995–96.) But the right hand columns of table 10.1, which test for any difference in legislative productivity between conditions of unified (UNI) and divided party control (DIV), show close to a wash. On average, unified control scores a bit higher in volume, but even that slight edge may owe to the fact that the recent use of omnibus measures has cut down on law counts chiefly during the Republican divided-control presidencies of 1981–92. Overall, for legislative productivity, divided as opposed to unified party control seems to be a minor factor at best (Mayhew 1991, 76, 175–78; Cameron et al. 1996, 21–22).

Now for the Clinton era's opening contributions. The list that follows presents eleven enactments of Clinton's first Congress of 1993–94.[5] Two of them, the 1993 budget package and NAFTA, were billed by the media as extraordinarily important.[6] In addition, the wrap-up discussions at the close of the 1993 legislative year contributed another four items—the family leave act, the "motor voter" act, Clinton's national service plan, and the Brady bill, which orders a waiting period in the purchase of handguns. These were relatively easy choices.[7] The late-1994 wrap-ups added on three more items unproblematically—that year's omnibus crime bill, the soon-to-be-ratified GATT (General Agreement on Tariffs and Trade) accord, and a California desert protection plan that surprisingly stayed alive in October 1994 when just about every other initiative was dying. Beyond that, the 1994 sources become harder to read, as they discuss education reforms without always identifying particular bills. I ended up listing the Goals 2000 education measure of 1994 as well as a belatedly dwelt-on reform of college-loan financing that had passed back in 1993. This last is the shakiest of the eleven listed choices. My overall result for 1993–94 corresponds particularly well to the 1994 *Washington Post* and *Boston Globe* wrap-ups.[8]

• OMNIBUS DEFICIT REDUCTION ACT. Clinton's centerpiece. A claimed $496 billion in savings over five years including $220 billion in tax hikes; top income-tax bracket rate to go from 31 percent to 36 percent, plus a 10 percent surcharge on the exceptionally wealthy. Expansion of the Earned Income Tax Credit (EITC).

• NORTH AMERICAN FREE TRADE AGREEMENT (NAFTA) APPROVED. Bush-Clinton plan for free-trade zone encompassing the United States, Canada, and Mexico.

• Family and Medical Leave Act of 1993. Employers required to allow twelve weeks of unpaid leave for family medical emergencies.

• Motor Voter Act of 1993. States required to provide voter registration forms in motor vehicle offices, military recruiting stations, and welfare offices.

• National Service Act of 1993. Clinton's "AmeriCorps" plan to offer college educational grants in exchange for community service work.

• Reform of college-student loan financing. Deprivatization; government to provide money directly rather than through banks. (A provision of the omnibus budget act.)

• Brady bill. Requires a five-day waiting period for purchase of handguns.

• Goals 2000. Establishes national education goals for all students and schools.

• Omnibus crime act. Ban on assault weapons; expansion of the death penalty; $30 billion to finance prison construction, hiring of 100,000 new police officers, and prevention programs.

• California desert protection. Creates largest wilderness area outside Alaska. Dianne Feinstein's bill.

• General Agreement on Tariffs and Trade (GATT) accord approved. Lowers tariffs among 124 nations and creates World Trade Organization.

The closest also-rans were a revision of the Hatch Act in 1993, which drew marginal interest in the 1993 wrap-ups but faded in 1994; a new injection of aid to the ex-Soviet republics; the killing of the supercollider in 1993; and a measure outlawing blockades of abortion clinics. One or more of these items could surface in any future "policy experts" search in the style of my second sweep. An excellent prospect for such status is a 1994 banking reform unlisted here that authorized interstate branch networks (Bradsher 1994). This key bipartisan measure evidently was not controversial enough to intrude into session-closing wrap-up accounts dominated by Clinton's agenda. So there exist misses that look as if they might have been hits. It is a hazard of the methodology for all Congresses, particularly all recent ones, not just the 103d.

Recently, at least three other political scientists have independently compiled their own lists of major laws for a Bush or Clinton Congress (see also Gettinger 1994). The results are shown in table 10.2.[9] For the 101st Congress, Timothy J. Conlan (1993) uses the same methodology as mine. Charles O. Jones makes his own overall assessments for the 102d and 103d Congresses (1994, 145; 1995), though he may have aimed for an importance cutoff point something like mine, since he refers to my lists for pre-1990 Congresses. For the 103d Congress, Bruce I. Oppenheimer (1996) uses end-of-session appraisals by *Congressional Quarterly Weekly Report*. In general, Conlan's and Jones' lists match mine pretty well in both length and content.[10] Oppenheimer's list for the 103d Congress is longer, but evidently that is because he uses *Congressional Quarterly*, which, unlike the mass-audience newspapers, seems to aim for completeness rather than summary judgments. That is its unique virtue. When I tried to use *Congressional Quarterly Weekly Report* for 1947–90 I ended up with lists that were quite long, and I couldn't tell when to stop counting.[11]

Referring back to table 10.1 for long-term comparisons, we see that the record of 1993–94 looks like those of most other pre-Kennedy or post-Nixon Congresses held during the opening half of a presidential term—regardless of conditions of party control. It is nothing special. The 103d arguably belongs in a range with, for example, Truman's Congress of 1949–50 (UNI), which likewise featured one big domestic and one big foreign item—the landmark Housing Act of 1949 and the NATO treaty; or Carter's Congress of 1977–78 (UNI), which addressed surface mining, food stamps, clean air, clean water, the minimum wage, Social Security financing, the tax code, civil service reform, energy, the Panama Canal treaties, and airline deregulation.

I invite readers to examine table 10.2, consult their memories, and see if they think that Clinton's first Congress of 1993–94 (UNI) really proved to be more productive than Bush's first one of 1989–90 (DIV).[12] For "party government" enthusiasts this may be a cruel comparison, but note the 1989–90 items—a deficit reduction package just as prodigious as Clinton's (more about that below), immigration reform, child care, a minimum wage hike, the $50 billion savings-and-loan bailout of 1989, the Americans with Disabilities Act of 1990, and the crowning achievement of Senator George Mitchell's career—the telephone-book-sized Clean Air Act of 1990.[13]

Certain other Congresses are in a higher league. The 103d came nowhere near the Great Society Congress of 1965–66 (UNI), and in my view it fell well short

Table 10.2   Major Laws for Recent Congresses, according to Four Political Scientists

Congress	D. R. Mayhew	T. J. Conlan	C. O. Jones	B. I. Oppenheimer
101st (1989–90)	$N = 9$ minimum wage	$N = 9$ minimum wage		
	S & L bailout	S & L bailout		
	DEFICIT REDUCTION	DEFICIT REDUCTION		
	disabilities	disabilities		
	clean air	clean air		
	child care	child care		
	immigration	immigration		
	housing	housing		
	agriculture			
		kill catastrophic		
102d (1991–92)	$N = 7$ transportation		$N = 9$ transportation	
	civil rights		civil rights	
	energy		energy	
	arms treaty			
	Russian aid		Russian aid	
	cable TV		cable TV	
	California water			
			Gulf resolution	
			banking	
			unemployment benefits	
			JTPA amendments	

Table 10.2 (*continued*)

Congress	D. R. Mayhew	T. J. Conlan	C. O. Jones	B. I. Oppenheimer
103d (1993–94)	$N = 11$		$N = 12$	$N = 18$
	DEFICIT REDUCTION		DEFICIT REDUCTION	DEFICIT REDUCTION
	NAFTA		NAFTA	NAFTA
	family leave		family leave	family leave
	motor voter		motor voter	motor voter
	national service		national service	national service
	college loans			
	Brady bill		Brady bill	Brady bill
	Goals 2000		Goals 2000	Goals 2000
	omnibus crime		omnibus crime	omnibus crime
	California desert			
	GATT accord		GATT accord	GATT accord
			amend Hatch Act	
			supercollider	
			banking	banking
				economic stimulus
				S & L fund
				foreign aid
				NIH reauthorization
				DOD authorization
				abortion clinics
				independent counsel
				DOA reorganization

Source: Data from Conlan 1993; Jones 1994, 145; 1995; Mayhew 1991, chap. 3; 1993, 200; and Oppenheimer 1995.

of the "Reagan revolution" Congress of 1981–82 (DIV), whose significance is uniquely underindexed in table 10.1. (We might ask ourselves whether, even now, Reagan's budget of 1981 leaves more of a trace in U.S. finances, programmatic options, and political discourse than does Clinton's budget of 1993.)

Again, this is an analysis innocent of agendas or denominators. To bring those up is to confront the outsized ambitions adopted by Democrats after the 1992 election. For lawmaking, it was expected to be 1933 or 1965 all over again. But it did not turn out that way. Legislative drives ensued and failed on Clinton's BTU energy tax, his economic stimulus plan (Clymer 1993b), a "freedom of choice" charter for women (Clymer 1993a), statehood for the District of Columbia (Ayres 1993), welfare reform, labor's goal to bar replacement of strikers (Manegold 1994), campaign finance reform (Rosenbaum 1994), lobbying reform (Clymer 1994a), a range of environmental bills addressing clean water, safe drinking water, pesticides, hazardous wastes, Superfund overhaul, mining law, endangered species, and cabinet status for the Environmental Protection Agency (Kenworthy and Lee 1994; *USA Today*, Oct. 6, 1994, 4A; Cushman 1994), and, of course, health care (Clymer 1994c; Priest and Weisskopf 1994; Clymer, Pear, and Toner 1994; Rovner 1995; Johnson and Broder 1996, chs. 14–20). Most or all of these items might have been expected to succeed, given the new Democratic hegemony. There were other agendas in 1993–94. Drives not so clearly partisan failed in the areas of product liability, telecommunications (Andrews 1994), and congressional accountability (that is, a move to make regulatory laws that apply to everyone else apply to Congress, too). Conservatives auditioned for 1995 with unsuccessful drives for term limits, a balanced budget amendment, a line-item veto, a curb on unfunded federal mandates, and the so-called "A to Z" and Penny-Kasich expenditure cuts. In the 103d, there was plenty of failure to go around.

Claim 2: The ideological direction of lawmaking does not vary with patterns of party control as much as we ordinarily think. A simple, paint-palette model of U.S. policy making would have it that we receive one bright shade of ideological result when the Democrats control the government, another bright shade when the Republicans do, and a blend (if any policies are made at all) when party control is divided. Call it red, blue, and purple.

Obviously, there is a good deal of truth to this model. To contrast certain Congresses with their immediate predecessors, for example, Truman's Congress of 1949–50 (D-UNI) and Kennedy's of 1961–62 (D-UNI) moved lawmaking policy in a red direction, and the Taft-led Congress of 1947–48 (DIV), the Reagan-led Congress of 1981–82 (DIV), and the Gingrich-led Republican Congress of 1995 (DIV) moved it in a blue direction. The results flashed bright red during the first two years of Lyndon Johnson's presidency (D-UNI). Both the general point and the details are as well known as any lore about American politics.

But that model is far from the whole story. Try the following experiment: (1) Disregard all actual election returns, party labels and holdings, roll call scores, and other such paraphernalia we ordinarily rely on. (2) With an eye for ideological direction, look at just the results of lawmaking for each Congress since World War II (as in, for example, Mayhew 1991, table 4.1). (3) Assume that Democrats are liberals (red) and Republicans are conservatives (blue). (4) Guess which party ran the government during each postwar Congress (assume for the moment no divided party control). No peeking at the actual party holdings. Here is a good bet for a guess: The Republicans governed until 1960, the Democrats from 1961 through roughly 1977, and the Republicans have been in control since then. In a census of statutes, you would notice, for example, the anti-Communist laws enacted under Truman (D-UNI) and Eisenhower (R-UNI) from 1950 through 1954 (Mayhew 1991, 43–44, 173–74); the sequence of welfare state expansions from roughly 1964 through 1975—not just food stamps, Medicare, and Medicaid under Johnson (D-UNI) but also Social Security indexing and Supplementary Security Income (SSI) under Nixon (DIV) and the Earned Income Tax Credit (EITC) under Ford (DIV). You would notice the regulatory explosion under Nixon[14] and the deregulation of securities, railroads, airlines, natural gas, trucking, and banking from 1975 through 1982, chiefly under Carter (D-UNI).[15] Clearly, there exist prominent lawmaking tendencies not explainable by the usual party-based lore; the bents of eras can override those of parties.[16]

Clinton's Congress of 1993–94 bears out the conventional party logic but also, strikingly, its override. On the one hand, yes, as in 1949 and 1961 the new Democratic ascendancy brought successes for the left. The family leave, motor voter, and national service acts of 1993 would almost certainly never have passed in a renewed Bush presidency. Nor would top-bracket income taxes have been raised to the degree they were in the deficit reduction act of 1993—from 31 percent up to 36 percent, with an extra 10 percent surcharge on income over $250,000. These were prize achievements for the liberal side.

But on the other hand, if placed more generally in a context with preceding Congresses, the 1993–94 record looks a lot like more of the same. Future historians will probably make that judgment. Even family leave, from one perspective, was just one more of a miniseries of strenuous moves to regulate industry that passed starting in 1990. It joined the Americans with Disabilities Act of 1990, the Clean Air Act of 1990, and the Civil Rights Act of 1991 (Weidenbaum 1991). In the trade area, NAFTA and GATT had been Bush projects. Also, the nonactions during 1993–94 came to look surprisingly like those under Bush: the thwarted aims of one side or another on health care, freedom of choice, striker replacement, the environment, campaign finance, term limits, the line-item veto, and the balanced budget amendment. Clinton lost an economic stimulus proposal in 1993, but so had Bush lost one in 1992 (Stein 1993).

And the 1993 Clinton budget package, once Congress had stripped away much of its "investment" and other new ideas, comfortably joined a class of high-aim deficit reduction measures extending back over a decade—those of 1982, 1984, 1987, 1990, and now 1993 (Birnbaum 1993). Republicans charged that the Clinton measure set a record for new tax revenue. That was false: in constant dollars, the 1982 plan had raised more. Clinton himself claimed authorship of "the largest deficit reduction package in history" (Pear 1995). That was false too: the bipartisan act of 1990 had taken a five-year $482 billion bite; given inflation, the 1993 act would have needed a $532 billion bite to match that mark, but in fact it ended up somewhere between $432 and $477 billion.[17] In general, the 1993 package strikingly resembled the now-orphaned one of 1990 (no one was claiming credit for the earlier deal any more). The 1990 act had already raised the top-bracket income tax rate from 28 percent to 31 percent. (In retrospect, it seems clear that the historically low 28 percent rate proudly achieved by the Tax Reform Act of 1986 was just sitting there as a target; it survived only four years of real political life.) The 1993 act, like the 1990 one, relied heavily on post–Cold War defense cuts, placed caps on congressional discretionary spending, slashed Medicare payments to providers (though not beneficiaries), raised the gas tax (up 4.3 cents, as opposed to a 5.0 cent increase in 1990), and went out of its way to include social welfare sweeteners—notably, a new five-year $20.8 billion hike in the Earned Income Tax Credit that topped the $12.4 billion hike in the credit in 1990 (Hager 1993c; Wessel 1993; Yang 1993; *New York Times* 1993).[18] "It tells you a lot about the politics of deficit reduction," remarked former Congressional Budgetary Office director Rudolph G. Penner in mid-1993. "Regardless of who controls the government, you are pushed in the same direction" (quoted in Hager 1993c).

As the Democratic 103d Congress adjourned, several commentators marveled at its surprising friendliness to business and hostility to unions—what with, among other things, the wins on NAFTA and GATT and the losses on health care and striker replacement (Broder and Weisskopf 1994; Birnbaum 1994; Gigot 1994). To the political director of the Sierra Club, the 103d had turned out to be "the worst environmental Congress since the first Earth Day in 1970" (Kenworthy and Lee 1994, 14). In the mix of laws actually passed, the chief themes were arguably deficit reduction, free trade, and crime control. Clearly, much was going on in these two years beyond the reach of the conventional party paint-palette.

Why the Results Even Out

The gist of the two claims given above is that, both in volume and ideological direction, U.S. lawmaking seems to "even out" across conditions of party control. Why this evening out might occur is taken up briefly in the following four claims.[19]

Claim 3: "National moods" help to override conditions of party control (that is, as the U.S. system varies among conditions of party control, "moods" can cut down on the kinds of differences in legislative volume or ideological direction, or both, that conventional "party government" wisdom would lead us to predict). This elusive though arguably basic explanation can only be touched on here (see Mayhew 1991, 142–74). It addresses both volume and ideology. During the Civil War and the Reconstruction era, the Progressive era, the New Deal era, and the 1960s through the early 1970s, the argument goes, an intense public activism drove up the volume of ambitious lawmaking and tilted its product to the left. At other times, less has been undertaken, and on average its tenor has been more conservative. In recent decades, at least, the up-and-down pattern has not corresponded all that well to conditions of party control.

It would be hard to find a better exhibit for this case than Clinton's first Congress. Notwithstanding Democratic Party control in 1993–94, the lions in the background environment were Ross Perot and Rush Limbaugh, not, as with a generation earlier, liberal mobilizers like Ralph Nader and Martin Luther King Jr. No liberal cause of the 1990s—including health care—seemed to draw anywhere near the intense public support given to term limits and other antigovernment causes. For Democrats, it was a jungle out there. First-term congressman Don Johnson (D-Ga.), fresh from voting for the president's allegedly big-government budget, returned home in 1993 to face picketing, demands for his recall, and "a raucous town-hall meeting with 350 people in the small community of Grovetown, during which he was repeatedly booed and shouted down with catcalls" (Cohen 1994, 221).[20] This climate evidently made it very rough for Democrats on Capitol Hill— especially in 1994. "Despite their minority status," observed a reporter late that year, "the Republicans have virtually controlled the legislative agenda since they stalled the crime bill in July" (Seelye 1994). The tactics associated with that stall included a remarkably effective GOP case—it seemed to echo through a receptive public—that the crime measure was loaded with "social pork" (Boyer 1994; Johnson and Broder 1996, 482–86). (A revised crime package later passed.) In this and other areas, intense or whipped-up conservative opinion seemed to override party labels. Grassroots communications to Congress surged on the conservative side during 1993–94 (Goldstein 1995).[21]

A good analogy to the 103d is Truman's Congress of 1949–50. Democrats at that time, excited by their 1948 election triumph, also aimed for a replay of the New Deal and scored a few victories (notably in housing) but soon bogged down in a nasty, stalemate politics in which most of their program—including national health insurance—died and a surge of intense conservatism (then of an anti-Communist variety) prevailed. The McCarran Internal Security Act of 1950 was one landmark result. For liberal Democratic legislators, it was a deadly environment.

Claim 4: Crosscutting opinion cleavages help to override conditions of party control. In certain issue areas, the electorate divides intensely and lastingly along lines that do not match party identification. As a result, whether laws pass or not can bear little relation to congressional party holdings (Mayhew 1991, 139–42). Thus, since abortion divides the public the way it complicatedly does, the strong "freedom of choice" initiative could founder in a 1993 House populated by 258 Democrats. As another example, issues of basic labor-management relations tend to unite Republicans but divide Democrats—and also, possibly because business outspends and outlobbies labor, to stiffen Republicans and de-energize Democrats—with the result that Republican Senate filibusters can succeed. It is a complex combination, but the 103d Congress, with the failure of striker replacement, took its place as one more high-tide Democratic one in which labor unions tried hard but could not get their way. (The others since the New Deal have been Truman's Congress of 1949–50, Johnson's of 1965–66, and Carter's of 1977–78. See Mayhew 1991, 78, 140n.)

During 1993–94, however, Exhibit A for the crosscut theory is NAFTA. A new, intense opinion cleavage over free trade versus protectionism seems to have emerged in the 1990s that crosses party lines. One result is the eye-catching 1993 roll-call pattern on NAFTA, a Clinton priority: majorities of Republicans in both houses voted for it, but majorities of Democrats in both houses voted against it (Black 1994). (Of the 285 major post–World War II laws discussed earlier, only 2 others bore a Republicans-over-Democrats enactment profile like that—the Twenty-second Amendment curbing presidential terms in 1947 and the Gramm-Rudman-Hollings antideficit act of 1985). Could a reelected Bush have maneuvered NAFTA through a Democratic Congress? My guess is yes. Since he largely lacked other priorities, he could have pressed it during his honeymoon period of early 1993 when White House influence would have been high.

5: Lack of easy majority processes helps to override conditions of party control. Even under unified party control, that is, Capitol Hill processes can be tortuous and sometimes nonmajoritarian (Mayhew 1991, 119–35). Laws do not "flow freely down the legislative sluice." In 1993–94, for example, disagreements between Senate and House figured in the demise of reforms of mining law and for provision of safe drinking water (Cushman 1994; Clymer 1994d). Also, telecommunications reform, a consensus winner in the House, "collapsed . . . in the Senate amid feuding between rival industry groups" (Andrews 1994). On show here was a kind of politics in which one segment of an industry—in this case, the regional Bells—could pull a log out of a tall pile and bring it down.

As Keith Krehbiel (1996) argues, a notably effective equalizer across conditions of party control is the Senate cloture rule, which erects a 60 percent hurdle for enactments under unified control that can rival the 67 percent hurdle allowed by presidential vetoes under divided control. In effect, President Bush the law blocker in 1991–92 could give way to Minority Leader Dole the law blocker in 1993–94.[22] In at least five instances—Clinton's economic stimulus bill, product liability, striker replacement, lobbying reform, and campaign-finance reform—Senate filibustering was at least the proximate cause of a major bill's defeat in 1993–94, and other bills sagged before such threats (Clymer 1994b; Wirls 1995).

Still, the filibuster weapon needs to be kept in perspective. Many defeats in 1993–94 owed little or nothing to real or anticipated Senate filibusters. Certain of the Democrats' environmental initiatives were dogged by appealing, hard-to-beat amendments that raised questions of unfunded mandates, property rights, or risk assessment—all perspectives that came of age in the succeeding 104th Congress. Welfare reform sank in committee. District of Columbia statehood and "freedom of choice" foundered for lack of House votes. On health care, so far as we know, never at any time was there a House floor majority for any plan the Democrats wished to advance.[23] "There wasn't anything out there they wanted to vote for. We weren't close to a majority on any specific health care plan," Speaker Tom Foley later recalled (Johnson and Broder 1996, 509). Also, a proximate cause of defeat is often just part of the story, as is suggested later in a discussion of campaign finance.

Claim 6: Something like "reason of state" can help to override conditions of party control. Political scientists delight in models that posit individuals or societal groups whose fixed, distinctive preferences vector toward and explain policy outcomes. Nothing is more basic to the discipline.

But policy making does not always work that way. There seems to exist a class of policy areas in which, over time, outcomes are constant but the coalitions that support them vary. More specifically, an elite "reason of state" view seems to override customary party or district preferences on certain subjects where whoever holds power dutifully takes unpopular actions thought to be necessary. It is a root-canal style of politics. Thus, for example, foreign aid bills enjoyed support only from Democrats under Truman, but once Eisenhower took office in 1953 the roll-call backing for them shifted to bipartisan (Kesselman 1961). Another example is the raising of the national debt limit, which needs to be done occasionally even though it is unpopular back home. To cite one span of congressional history, majorities of both Democrats and Republicans tended to back debt-ceiling hikes under Eisenhower, only Democrats would do so under Kennedy and Johnson, but both Democrats and Republicans did so again under Nixon (*Congress and the Nation, 1945–1964*, 393–95, *1965–68*, 127–40, *1969–72*, 64–75; *Congressional Quarterly Almanac*, *1966*, 714, 886, 953, *1967*, 316–22, 38 H, 48 H, 7 S, 8 S, 28 S, *1970*, 293–95, 30 H, 32 S). Particularly for Republicans, much depended on which party held which office.

A good analogue to these instances is deficit reduction from 1982 through 1993. Senate Republicans took the policy lead through 1986, during which time they controlled that chamber (Hager 1993b). In 1990, under Bush, deficit reduction had a bipartisan coalitional base: the White House and Senate Minority Leader Dole finally struck a deal with House and Senate Democrats. But in 1993, as they had with foreign aid and the debt ceiling at earlier times of unified party control, the ruling Democrats had to act all by themselves. Republican support vanished. This is not to say that exactly the same result occurred in 1993 as earlier or that what happened was inevitable, but in fact a very similar result accrued even though it owed to a very different coalition. The idea of constant outcomes based on varying coalitions could use more study; it might open a window into "state autonomy."

First-Year versus Second-Year of Congresses

A finer-grained analysis can be obtained from examining the 1993–94 Congress. When Clinton pursued deficit reduction and NAFTA in 1993 but put off health care, many of us asked certain questions. Can this work? How long can a president keep pressing successfully? What is the likely legislative rhythm of a president's first Congress? Below are some suggestive patterns.

Claim 7: In Congresses just after presidential elections, major laws tend to pass during the first year if party control is unified, but during the second year if it is divided. Here, finally, is a straightforward difference between unified and divided control. Table 10.3 divides post–World War II Congresses into four categories—the result of crosscutting a distinction of unified- versus divided-control Congresses against a distinction of the first-half versus the second-half of a presidential term. Within each of the four categories, the number of major laws passed by each Congress is broken down according to whether it was passed in the first or the second year.[24] Thus, in Clinton's case, NAFTA is a first-year enactment, and GATT is a second-year one.

The top tier in table 10.3 presents data on initial Congresses under unified party control. This is the milieu of freshly elected Democratic presidents (Eisenhower is the outlier) who claim mandates for their domestic programs, unfold "hundred days" scenarios, and prod Congress to act fast (Kelley 1983; Dahl 1990; Hershey 1992). In fact, lawmaking under these conditions has tilted toward the first year—by an average of 7.3 as opposed to 6.2 major enactments. Clinton's first-year tilt looks like those under Kennedy in 1961–62, Johnson in 1965–66, and Carter in 1977–78. The general relation here is arguably better than it looks. Under Truman, three of the 1950 measures involved the just-begun Korean War. And 1953–54 is a stark, genuine exception. For lawmaking, Eisenhower's first year in office, 1953, stands out as the leanest of all the fifty or so years since World

Table 10.3   Comparison of Number of Laws Passed in First and Second Year of Congress

Presidency	Years	First Year	Second Year
Unified party control: 1st Congress of presidential term			
Truman	1949–50	5 (2)	7
Eisenhower	1953–54	1	8
Kennedy	1961–62	9	6 (1)
Johnson	1965–66	15 (3)	7
Carter	1977–78	7	5
Clinton	1993–94	7 (2)	4
Mean		7.3	6.2
Divided party control: 1st Congress of presidential term			
Eisenhower	1957–58	2 (1)	9
Nixon	1969–70	6	16
Nixon/Ford	1973–74	11 (1)	11
Reagan	1981–82	2 (2)	7
Reagan	1985–86	2	7 (1)
Bush	1989–90	2	7 (1)
Mean		4.2	9.5

War II, because the new president did not have a legislative program at all in 1953. (Once he swung into gear in 1954, Eisenhower successfully promoted a sizable program: tax code revision, Social Security expansion, flexible farm prices, Food for Peace, urban renewal, authorization of an atomic energy industry, the St. Lawrence Seaway.)[25]

The second tier in table 10.3 lists the data for initial Congresses under divided party control. Once again, the Congress of 1981–82 requires a warning label: the count of laws for 1981 greatly understates their significance. Notably, this first Reagan Congress is the only one in the category where a president vigorously pursued an early-days mandate strategy. That having been said, the story for this set of Congresses is that lawmaking tends to be backloaded rather than frontloaded—there is an average of 9.5 measures in the second year versus 4.2 in the first. As for the post-midterm Congresses (see the right half of table 10.3),

Table 10.3 (*continued*)

Presidency	Years	First Year	Second Year
Unified party control: 2d Congress of presidential term			
Truman	1951–52	3	3
Kennedy/Johnson	1963–64	6 (1)	7 (3)
Johnson	1967–68	6	10 (1)
Carter	1979–80	3	7
Mean		4.5	6.8
Divided party control: 2d Congress of presidential term			
Truman	1947–48	6 (1)	4 (1)
Eisenhower	1955–56	2	4
Eisenhower	1959–60	3	2
Nixon	1971–72	5	11
Ford	1975–76	6	8
Reagan	1983–84	3	4
Reagan	1987–88	5	7
Bush	1991–92	2	5
Mean		4.0	5.6

Source: Data from Mayhew 1991, 52–73; 1993a, 200.

lawmaking tilts slightly toward the second year under both conditions of party control.

Some inferences can be drawn from all the data: (1) For whatever reasons, an upfront mandate appeal does seem to work for newly elected presidents operating under unified party control. Only in this circumstance (with due respect to Reagan) does the lawmaking volume of the first year tend to dominate that of the second. (2) With a newly elected president operating under divided party control, lawmaking takes an especially long time. Ordinarily, there exists no mandate claim to help things along; yet the president, who was, after all, just elected, may insist on getting his way; the needed cross-party deals may be especially hard to make. Consider this contrast: it took eight months—until August 1993—to enact Clinton's deficit reduction plan, yet it took twenty-two months—until October 1990—to arrange one under Bush. (3) Nevertheless, although pre-midterm Congresses tend to vary according to party control in their timing profiles, they do not vary according to party control in their overall lawmaking volume. Different balance, same mass. Of course, under divided party control the final product does not so clearly reflect presidential tastes.

Bruce I. Oppenheimer (1996, 129–32, tables 6 and 7) confirms the idea that lawmaking takes longer under divided party control—at least in Congresses convening just after presidential elections. He examines the initial Congresses under Carter (1977–78), Reagan (1981–82 and 1985–86), Bush (1989–90), and Clinton (1993–94) and reports this result: budget resolutions and appropriations bills are much more likely to meet their deadlines (or at least come close) under unified control than under divided control. The pattern is nearly perfect. One way to look at it is that, on these budgetary matters, expeditiousness trades off against inclusiveness; under divided control, the coalitions need to be larger, and that takes longer.

Claim 8: Among presidents who have pressed ambitious domestic legislative programs (successfully or not) during their first year after winning election, none has ever had much luck pressing one also during his second year. This is another wrinkle on first year versus second year. (It introduces exactly the kind of ratio thinking I sidestepped earlier, but here the emphasis is on presidential success, not on the system's legislative output.) With health care in 1994, on the heels of deficit reduction in 1993, was Clinton trying to do something that none of his predecessors had ever pulled off? Surprisingly, perhaps, the answer seems to be yes. I arrived at this answer by reading secondary sources to try to get a general sense of past Congresses.

Here is an arguably complete list of twentieth-century presidents who have undertaken ambitious domestic legislative drives during their first postelection year: Wilson in 1913 (the New Freedom), Franklin Roosevelt in 1933 (his "hundred days"), Roosevelt in 1937 (court packing, executive reorganization, etc.), Truman in 1949 (the Fair Deal), Kennedy in 1961 (the New Frontier), Johnson in 1965 (the Great Society), Carter in 1977 (his energy plan), Reagan in 1981 (his budget package), and Clinton in 1993 (his budget package).

These drives enjoyed varying degrees of success. But never has a drive by the same president in a follow-up second year enjoyed notable success.[26] Reagan in 1982 and, it is probably fair to say, FDR in 1934 did not conduct ambitious second-year drives. Although Wilson won some victories in 1914, nonetheless, "the weakening of the administration's antitrust program was only the first sign of a general reaction that began to set in around the beginning of 1914 and increasingly affected the administration and the president" (Link 1954, 75). Johnson in 1966, then receding into conducting the Vietnam War, scored some successes on Capitol Hill but lost out on D.C. home rule, unemployment compensation, open housing, and a Taft-Hartley rollback (Evans and Novak 1966, 499–500, 558–61; *Congressional Quarterly Almanac, 1966*, 69–88). Kennedy won some middle-sized items in 1962 but suffered a drawn-out, dramatic defeat on Medicare (Koenig 1962; Bernstein 1991, ch. 8; *Congressional Quarterly Almanac, 1962*, 62–74). FDR in 1938, though victorious in advancing economic pump priming and the country's first nationwide minimum wage law, suffered a decisive loss on executive reorganization and had to live with a business-oriented congressional tax package he would not sign (Davis 1993, ch. 6; Patterson 1967, ch. 7). Carter in 1978 saw his energy program unravel in the Senate and, like FDR, was confronted with an unwanted probusiness tax package; he signed it (Kaufman 1993, chs. 5, 6, 8). Truman had a disastrous year in 1950, what with the onset of McCarthyism and the loss of virtually all his legislative priorities (Truman 1959, ch. 2; Gosnell 1980, ch. 34; Hamby 1973, ch. 15; McCoy 1984, ch. 8).

Clinton, in short, joined good company with his health care loss in 1994. Second-year success on a project of that scale would have broken all precedent. If this historical analysis is correct, here is a guess about what drives the trend: a president, on becoming the beneficiary of an act of public authorization (ordinarily a presidential election), gets a shot at one season of legislative leeway; that is it. It seems to be a matter of leadership license and public attention span.

This account is compatible with a few odd cases of legislative drives conducted at times other than first years of presidential terms. Eisenhower saved his shot until his second year, but it was still available. FDR conducted a textbook legislative campaign during his third year in office—the "Second New Deal" of 1935. But that benefited from a unique authorizing event—the 1934 midterm that gave his ruling party an unprecedented gain in congressional seats. And Lyndon Johnson did in fact conduct successful legislative drives during back-to-back years—in 1965 following his election landslide but also before that, between November 1963 and November 1964. From the standpoint of lawmaking, that earlier twelve-month span was arguably the most eventful season since 1935: it yielded food stamps, aid to higher education, the countercyclical Kennedy tax cut, Johnson's antipoverty program, the Wilderness Act of 1964, the landmark Civil Rights Act of 1964, and, to boot, the Tonkin Gulf resolution that paved the way for the Vietnam War. Behind these results, though, seems to have been another kind of authorizing act—the assassination of President Kennedy, which by way of a complex public psychology seems to have awarded his successor great temporary leeway (Mayhew 1991, 90, 182).[27] The implication of all this for 1994 is that Clinton pushed up against the envelope and the envelope held. His ambition was out of line.

Of Partisanship and Indicators

All else aside, wasn't the 103d Congress at least a triumph for political scientists? Didn't "party voting" and related pleasing indicators find their day? Here, the answer is yes.

Claim 9: "Party voting" reached a new high in final passage of major laws by the 103d Congress. There is no doubt about it. Table 10.4 presents roll-call data on final passage for the eleven major enactments of 1993–94 listed earlier. The figures are broken down by party and chamber. In nine of the eleven instances, "party votes" carried the measures in both House and Senate—that is, a majority of Democrats voted one way and a majority of Republicans the other. A near miss is the California desert protection bill, which in fact Republican senators tried to block but finally gave in on. Only GATT drew support from most members of both parties. To look at the results another way, only two of the eleven measures—Goals 2000 and the California desert protection act—drew backing from at least two-thirds of the members of both houses (though GATT and family leave earned that distinction in one house).

No previous postwar Congress had performed anything like this. No previous Congress had enacted more than a quarter of its major laws by "party votes" in both houses or by narrow (less than two-thirds) majorities in both houses.[28] In these regards the 103d stands out as an extreme exception. This is not to say it came as a complete surprise, however; according to other evidence, it was more like a culmination. David W. Rohde (1991, chs. 1, 3, 5) and others have documented rises dating to the 1980s in party cohesion indexes, party loyalty scores, overall party voting, and other such congressional indicators.

Much might be said about the accentuated partisanship of the 103d Congress, but I make just one brief argument here. On current evidence, the kind of partisanship indexed by "party voting" does not seem to contribute to legislative productivity.[29] It might do so under some specifiable conditions, and it might do so in the future—certainly that is one vision of "party government" doctrine. But it does not seem to have done so to date. Indeed, particularly in light of the programmatic meltdown of the summer of 1994, at least as good a case seems to exist that, in the U.S. constitutional setting today, high partisanship contributes instead to inaction—even under unified party control. The opposition digs in, ugly wrangling ensues, the atmosphere sours, the public loses confidence and turns off, and measures die.

Claim 10: Certain indicators of government performance can be misleading. If partisanship bears an uncertain relation to legislative productivity, so too does an especially well known statistic currently relied on to index government performance.[30] That is *Congressional Quarterly*'s "presidential support score," which presents for each year the proportion of House and Senate roll calls on which the president's side won, from among those on which the White House took a position. It is by this standard that Clinton, as of September 1993, was said to be doing better than any first-year president since Eisenhower in 1953 (Langdon 1993). For 1994, the index reading is a very high 86.4 percent, which

Table 10.4 Final Passage Votes on Major Enactments, 1993–1994

	House			Senate		
Bill	Dem	GOP	Total[a]	Dem	GOP	Total[b]
1993						
DEFICIT-REDUCTION	217–41	0–175	218–216	50–6	0–44	51–50
NAFTA	102–156	132–43	234–200	27–28	34–10	61–38
Family leave	210–29	36–123	247–152	55–2	16–25	71–27
Motor voter	237–14	21–146	259–160	57–0	5–37	62–37
National service	248–5	26–147	275–152	51–4	6–36	57–40
College loans[c]	217–41	0–175	218–216	50–6	0–44	51–50
Brady bill	184–69	54–119	238–189	47–8	16–28	63–36
1994						
Goals 2000	246–6	59–115	306–121	53–1	10–21	63–22
Crime	188–64	46–131	235–195	54–2	7–36	61–38
California desert	244–6	53–122	298–128		voice vote	
GATT accord	167–89	121–56	288–146	41–13	35–11	76–24

[a] House totals include votes cast by Bernard Sanders (Socialist-Vt.).
[b] Vice President Gore broke a 50-50 Senate tie on deficit reduction.
[c] College loan reform passed as part of the deficit reduction act.

ranks that year among the reputed Everests of presidential success—1953 under
Eisenhower, 1963 through 1965 under Kennedy and Johnson, and, yes, 1993
under Clinton (Langdon 1994).[31]

I argued earlier that it is dubious in principle to accept "presidential support
scores" as a guide to overall system performance, since the White House's agenda
is not the only one.[32] But here the problem goes deeper. The score is not measuring presidential success very well. We were invited to compare 1993 with 1953,
when, as it happens, Eisenhower did not have a legislative program. Should that
not have counted somehow? That was bad enough, but the 1994 result seems
to me to be worse. In fact, given Clinton's health care and lesser defeats, the interesting question arises: How could such a poor year earn such a high score?
Here is a guess: congressional Democrats, by the early 1990s, had grown orga-
nizationally strong enough to make themselves look good on the floor. Their
leaders, by manipulating agendas and rules, could largely detour the party's internal antagonisms away from roll-call processes. But the party was not necessarily strong enough to carry its bills. The disparity became plain in 1994. A
tip-off is that health care, which dominated that year's news, politics, and policy processes, eventually figured in no roll calls at all in the House—it never
came up—and in only four minor ones in the Senate. For 1994, we are looking at a "presidential support score" that leaves out health care. Little more
needs to be said.

But how about presidential vetoes? (This is a standard student question.)
Bush cast many vetoes and made them stick; Clinton cast none during the 103d
Congress. Surely that disparity somehow indexes legislative productivity? Well,
no. An absence of vetoes does not necessarily mean full-throttle lawmaking. Let
me proceed by anecdote, using the subject of campaign-finance reform. In the
102d Congress (DIV), the Democrats served up a bill, and Bush vetoed it. In the
103d Congress (UNI), the two houses passed differing bills in 1993, but House
Democrats stalled off a compromise until September 29, 1994—apparently because deep down many of them were not eager for any action at all (they had
been no more eager under Bush, but they knew he would veto)—and Senate
Republicans finished things off with an end-of-session filibuster the next day,
on September 30, 1994. These are the bare facts with a spice of motivation
(Donovan 1994; "Legislative Summary" 1994). Note the pattern: identical results
in the two Congresses—nothing at all passed—but the smoking gun of a veto
only under Bush. There is more than one way to kill a bill.

Not the least of lessons available from the 103d Congress is a caveat about
indicators. Only with an awareness of context should they be consulted at all.

**Bonus claim: High-publicity congressional investigations of the executive
branch occur just as often under unified party control as under divided con-**

trol. And yes, investigations. "Democrats in Congress won't investigate a Democratic administration," Senator Dole asserted in January 1994, voicing the conventional wisdom of that time as the Whitewater controversy unfolded ("Dole Calls for Whitewater Answers" 1994). But it kept unfolding; nervousness set in among Capitol Hill Democrats who started switching to an "it's best to get the facts out" posture, hearings came to look inevitable, the Democratic leadership signed on to them, and once again a Congress did investigate an administration of its own party.

In fact, at least since World War II, investigations of the executive branch that have drawn high media attention have occurred as often against one background of party control as the other (Mayhew 1991, ch. 2). Table 10.5 lists all probes conducted under Carter, Reagan, Bush, and Clinton that figured in front-page stories of the *New York Times* for at least twenty days. These last four presidents offer a recent illuminating comparison.

In the Whitewater hearings of the summer of 1994, party loyalist Henry B. Gonzalez, chair of the House Banking Committee, caused the Clinton administration little trouble. But the Senate Banking Committee, chaired by Donald W. Riegle Jr., caused a great deal. Roger C. Altman, deputy secretary of the treas-

Table 10.5 High-Publicity Congressional Investigations of the Executive Branch under the Last Four Presidents

Congress	President	Party Control	Subject	Number of Days on Front Page of *New York Times*
1977–78	Carter	UNI	Bert Lance bank deals	26
1979–80	Carter	UNI	Billy Carter/Libya	21
1981–82	Reagan	DIV	none	——
1983–84	Reagan	DIV	EPA favoritism	28
1985–86	Reagan	DIV	none	——
1987–88	Reagan	DIV	Iran/Contra	95
1989–90	Bush	DIV	Dept. of Housing and Urban Development	23
1991–92	Bush	DIV	none	——
1993–94	Clinton	UNI	Whitewater	22

ury, had to resign after testifying, and the spectacle came at a bad time for a White House still trying to keep stride in its health care march. A year later, in 1995, Republican-run committees took up Whitewater too, but they found it hard to exact as much political damage as Riegle and his committee had done in 1994.

The 103d Congress is receding into history, and now, of course, it has to compete with fresher recollections of the Republican Congress of 1995–96 (DIV). The record of those Gingrich-driven years is a story for another time. Suffice it to say that they brought a lawmaking disaster rivaling Clinton's health care debacle—the Republicans' shut-down-the-government budget drive that derailed in the winter of 1995–96—but it also yielded, if actual enactments are considered, a surprisingly large harvest of legislation. Included were significant new laws addressing unfunded mandates, congressional responsibility, lobbying reform, securities stockholder suits, telecommunications, agriculture deregulation, the line-item veto, antiterrorism, pesticides, safe drinking water, welfare reform, health insurance portability, the minimum wage, and immigration. Adam Clymer, fresh from covering both the 103d and 104th Congresses for the *New York Times*, reflected in late 1996: "As for the Congress of 1993–94, in which Democrats ran both the House and the Senate, it did less than its successor" (Clymer 1996).

Notes

For their critiques of earlier versions of this work, I would like to thank R. Douglas Arnold, Fred Greenstein, Rogan Kersh, Keith Krehbiel, Eric Schickler, and Ian Shapiro.

1. To that date, Clinton's side had prevailed on 88.6 percent of House and Senate roll calls on which the White House had taken a position. Like a successful rumor, this *Congressional Quarterly* report of presidential success traveled through the politics of ensuing months and improved as it traveled. Thus, "It's *the most productive first year* of any president since President Eisenhower's first term," said Senate Majority Leader George Mitchell on "Meet the Press" (as reported in Calmes and Harwood 1993; italics added). And, "Democrats *steered more legislation through Congress* in Clinton's first year as president than at any other similar time since Dwight D. Eisenhower was president" (Zuckman and Farrell 1994; italics added).

2. The Congress of 1991–92 is addressed in Mayhew 1993a, 200.

3. This is not to deny that whether presidents get what they want is an interesting question in its own right. On this subject, see notably Edwards 1980.

4. The other acts appearing in parentheses in table 10.1 are the Taft-Hartley Act of 1947, the Housing Act of 1949, the NATO Treaty (1949), the Civil Rights Acts of 1957, 1964, and

1968, the Trade Expansion Act of 1962, the Test Ban Treaty (1963), the Anti-Poverty Act of 1964, the Kennedy tax cut of 1964, the Elementary and Secondary Education Act of 1965, the War Powers Act of 1973, the Tax Reform Act of 1986, and NAFTA (1993). These highlighted acts appear in capital letters in Mayhew (1991, 51–74, 91n). This list is reported here with misgivings. More than any other data set used here, its contents can owe to media hype, and such hype is routinely given to presidents deploying a mandate script for their major aims under conditions of unified party control. In fact, in terms of real long-term impact, it is questionable whether Kennedy's trade act or Soviet treaty outranked similar measures under later Republican presidents. (These latter appear in the longer list of 285 laws.) Not on the short list of twenty-one laws are the highly consequential Highway Act of 1956 and the Clean Air Act of 1970, which were enacted without great fanfare during Eisenhower's and Nixon's presidencies under conditions of divided party control. On the general problem, see Mayhew 1991, 90–91.

5. Full books have been written about three of the 1993 items: Cohen 1994 on Clinton's budget, Elving 1995 on family leave, and Waldman 1995 on national service.

6. If an official or customary title of an act proved to be available, brief, and to the point, it was used in this list. The form for these is "Family and Medical Leave Act of 1993." Otherwise, items take a form such as "Omnibus crime act." Laws judged by sources to be of exceptional importance are presented at the beginning of the list and are capitalized.

7. For recent Congresses, I have not been able to resist reaching beyond the *Washington Post* and the *New York Times* to incorporate other journalistic wrap-ups that seem to follow similar standards in discussing achievements, weighing evidence, presenting material hierarchically according to importance, as journalists will, and implicitly or explicitly imposing cutoff points. I give primary attention to the prose discussions in such pieces and much less to the boxes with enactment checklists of varying length that sometimes appear alongside. For 1993, a model wrap-up piece is Church 1993, which gives attention to all six laws discussed above in the text for 1993 and to no others, though it does question the significance of national service ("applies to so few people that it is really only tokenism") and the Brady bill ("has some loose ends") (33). The other sources from late 1993 are Dewar and Cooper 1993; Clymer 1993c; Calmes and Harwood 1993.

8. The *Washington Post*'s writers discuss nine enactments from 1993–94 and also refer summarily to "several education bills" from 1994. Nine of my listings are the same as theirs, if Goals 2000 can serve for the education bills. I have two items they lack (college loans, motor voter), and they have one that I lack (the killing of the supercollider in 1993). The *Boston Globe* writers discuss eleven enactments for 1993–94 plus "significant reforms in primary and secondary education." If Goals 2000 can serve for those reforms, I have one item they lack (California desert protection), and they have two that I lack (aid to the ex-Soviet republics in 1993, which I thought offered little new over 1992; and a 1994 measure outlawing blockades of abortion clinics, which is referred to just briefly in the *Globe* discussion and not taken up in anyone else's wrap-up account). The 1994 *New York Times* wrap-up does not do a good job of incorporating enactments from 1993; NAFTA and deficit reduction are discussed but not family leave, motor voter, national service, or the Brady bill. Otherwise, the *Times* discusses five items (1993 college loans,

crime, Goals 2000, California desert protection, and GATT) that are on my list, plus another education measure that is not. The 1994 sources are Dewar and Cooper 1994; Clymer 1994d; Zuckman and Farrell 1994.

9. For space reasons, some of the entries in table 10.2 for particular laws are cryptic. In the 101st Congress, "disabilities" means the Americans with Disabilities Act. "Kill catastrophic" means repeal of the Medicare Catastrophic Coverage Act of 1988. In the 102d Congress, "Gulf resolution" means the resolution authorizing the Persian Gulf war in early 1991. In Oppenheimer's (1995) list for the 103d Congress, "S&L fund" means a new deposit insurance fund for the savings and loan bailout; "foreign aid" means an authorization that included aid for Russia; "NIH reauthorization" included money for family planning and counseling; "DOD authorization" covered "Star Wars" cuts and gays in the military.

The alert reader of table 10.2 may wonder about two particular sources of bias inherent in my reliance on journalistic wrap-up sources or in the way I interpret those sources. First, note that my lists, compared with the others, "miss" the repeal of catastrophic insurance in 1989–90 and the killing of the supercollider in 1993–94. My guess is that the wrap-up methodology, as I employ it, underplays somewhat the deaths of laws and programs (as opposed to their births) throughout the post–World War II era. One reason is that terminations tend to slip out of focus by occurring as parts of larger bills. On the methodology's missing of "appropriations erosion," see Mayhew 1991, 41. On the politicians' logic of hiding, so to speak, stiff programmatic budgeting cuts in larger bills, see Arnold 1990, 105. Second, note that my lists, unlike the others, include an overhaul of California water policy in 1991–92 and the California desert protection plan of 1993–94. In both cases, these bills caused a stir just before congressional adjournments. No doubt, they were fresh in journalists' minds as the wrap-up stories took shape. Throughout the post–World War II era, the wrap-up methodology probably overplays a bit such end-of-session success stories.

10. Jones's list for the 102d Congress is closer to mine than it looks, if we take into account his inclusion of the 1991 Persian Gulf resolution; I have not counted such resolutions, even if they are important (as that one surely was). See Mayhew 1991, 40–42.

11. Of the last nine entries in the Oppenheimer list, three are referred to only cursorily in the 1993 and 1994 newspaper wrap-up discussions, and six are not referred to at all.

12. An October 1994 assessment: "Bush's legacy is having a dramatic impact on how Washington operates in the Clinton era because many of the programs implemented by the Republican president, from defense cuts to budget rules to environmental regulations, are only now taking effect. . . . The greatest irony is that the interparty gridlock of the Bush era does not look so intractable in comparison with the sometimes-stalemate of the Clinton era. Bush's accommodation with Democrats resulted in legislation that appears in many ways more activist than Clinton has been able to achieve" (Kranish 1994).

13. The Clean Air Act of 1990 "produced the comprehensive revision (after nearly a decade of deadlock) of one of the most important statutes ever enacted by Congress [that is, the Clean Air Act of 1970—also enacted under divided party control]. It also

serves as proof that divided government can work" (Bryner 1993, xi). See also Cohen 1995.

14. "ATF, CPSC, DEA, the Endangered Species Act, EPA, LSC, NHTSA, NOAA, OSHA—all had their origin during the Nixon administration. In addition, affirmative action and wage and price controls were introduced" (Friedman 1995). See also Vogel 1981.

15. On the conservative shift under Carter, see Mayhew 1991, 93–94, 166–69, 172–73.

16. The most familiar epicycle to a party-based model of U.S. lawmaking involves the "conservative coalition" of Republicans and southern Democrats. That is, Democrats, even if formally in power, cannot flash bright red because of their Dixie wing (and Republican congressional ranks are augmented by that wing). But this line of argument does not help to explain the liberal lawmaking results under Nixon or the shift to relatively conservative results under Carter.

17. Data are from the Congressional Budgetary Office (CBO) (Hager 1993a). At its time of passage, the 1993 measure was advertised as offering a $496 billion bite, but that figure declined after later CBO calculations. A range, rather than a single value, is offered for 1993 because of alternative assumptions about whether certain savings specified earlier in 1990 were now being double counted. See also Rosenbaum 1993.

18. In loose talk, Clinton supporters sometimes claimed credit for EITC, period. That idea turned up in, for example, a Molly Ivins (1994) column: "Another contender for Most Significant [Legacy] is the earned-income tax credit—the most important part of the first budget package."

19. Discussions of the first three of these explanations appear in Mayhew 1991, chs. 5, 6. (Of the six arguments presented in those chapters, the three taken up here seem to be the most illuminating with regard to 1993–94.)

20. For an account of the abuse heaped on the White House's cross-country bus caravan staged to rally support for health care reform in the summer of 1994, see Johnson and Broder 1996, ch. 18.

21. That public opinion in general shifted in a conservative direction during 1993–94 is reported in Ferejohn, Gaines, and Rivers 1996, 11–18. See also Johnson and Broder 1996, 447–49.

22. Dole usually served as aggregator of the opposition in 1993–94, but he needed forty allies to block a measure. Technically, in any instance, the least "anti" of forty-one naysayers was the pivotal Senate voter.

23. "No postmortems, what-ifs, or finger-pointing can change the fact that the overhaul of the nation's health care system lacked majority support with the American public and in Congress" (Schick 1995, 227). "A whip count in the House showed that the *Democratic* votes weren't there. The Senate was in much the same situation" (Moynihan 1995, 39).

24. The source for the breakdowns through 1990 is Mayhew 1991, 52–73; for the breakdowns from 1991 and 1992, see Mayhew 1993a. Strictly speaking, the year cited for each enactment is the one in which it formally became law (usually through a president's signature). A measure signed, for example, in January of an even year might have received most or all of its congressional treatment during the preceding odd year—though, in

fact, the typical pattern for laws listed here as passing in even years was to pass Congress during a late-season crush of the even year. In table 10.3, the figures in parentheses refer to the twenty-one earlier-mentioned measures that were thought by the media to be historically important; these are already included here as ordinary single items in the larger counts, and they do not play any extra role in the calculations of the averages.

25. For 1953, only the tidelands oil act, a conservative congressional favorite held over from 1952, made the list of 285 postwar enactments. On Eisenhower's presenting a program in 1954 but not in 1953, see Reichard 1975, chs. 5–7; Neustadt 1955.

26. Paul C. Light writes of a "cycle of decreasing influence" that induces newly elected presidents to introduce and fight for their proposals just after taking office (1982, ch. 2).

27. I have avoided discussing the instance of Theodore Roosevelt in 1905–7. Roosevelt certainly advanced an ambitious program then, but the old legislative calendar before the ratification of the Twentieth Amendment makes it difficult to talk about a first versus a second legislative year. Wilson solved this problem, so to speak, in 1913, as did FDR in 1933, by calling a special first session of the incoming Congress for March just after his election. Also unaddressed here is Wilson's successful legislative drive of 1916.

28. See Mayhew 1991, 121–22 for data on 1947 through 1990. In the second Bush Congress of 1991–92, six of the seven allegedly major enactments (all but cable-TV reform) passed with bipartisan support in both houses; six (all but aid to Russia) passed with better than two-thirds majorities in both houses.

29. To make a broader statement, the ups and downs in the standard annual "party voting" index based on all congressional roll calls since World War II do not seem to match the ups and downs in any dimension of government performance worth attending to—including the volume of major lawmaking and the level of White House success in passing programs. See the argument in Mayhew 1991, 126.

30. For another discussion of this subject, see Jones 1994, ch. 6.

31. Langdon is quite aware of the difficulty the index runs into in 1994.

32. Among the troughs in the "presidential support score" series are 1973 and 1987–88, when Nixon and Reagan respectively were on the ropes politically and lacked influence on Capitol Hill. Nevertheless, the overall system's legislative production was quite heavy both times. The year 1973 brought CETA jobs (through the Comprehensive Employment and Training Act), D.C. home rule, a Social Security hike, the Trans-Alaska pipeline, Conrail, HMOs, the War Powers Act, and a landmark foreign aid measure. In 1987–88, Speaker Jim Wright presided over the enactment of a Democratic program.

References

Andrews, Edmund L. 1994. "Bill to Revamp Communications Dies in Congress." *New York Times*, Sept. 24.

Arnold, R. Douglas. 1990. *The Logic of Congressional Action.* New Haven: Yale University Press.

Ayres, B. Drummond, Jr. 1993. "House Soundly Defeats a Proposal on District of Columbia Statehood." *New York Times*, Nov. 22.

Bernstein, Irving. 1991. *Promises Kept: John F. Kennedy's New Frontier.* New York: Oxford University Press.

Birnbaum, Jeffrey H. 1993. "Clinton Follows Predecessors' Path in Wrestling with the Demon Deficit." *Wall Street Journal*, May 21.

———. 1994. "As Clinton Is Derided as Flaming Liberal by GOP, His Achievements Look Centrist and Pro-Business." *Wall Street Journal*, Oct. 7.

Black, Gordon L. 1994. "NAFTA—Clinton's Victory, Organized Labor's Loss." *Political Geography* 13:377–84.

Boyer, Peter J. 1994. "Whip Cracker." *New Yorker*, Sept. 5, 38–54.

Bradsher, Keith. 1994. "Interstate-Banking Bill Gets Final Approval in Congress." *New York Times*, Sept. 14.

Brady, David W. 1993. "The Causes and Consequences of Divided Government: Toward a New Theory of American Politics?" *American Political Science Review* 87:189–94.

Broder, David S. 1992. "Wreckage of Divided Government." *Washington Post*, Aug. 30.

Broder, David S., and Michael Weisskopf. 1994. "Business Prospered in 103d Congress: Despite Democratic Leadership, Labor Had a Sparse Two Years on Hill." *Washington Post*, Sept. 25.

Bryner, Gary. 1993. *Blue Skies, Green Politics: The Clean Air Act of 1990.* Washington, D.C.: Congressional Quarterly Press.

Calmes, Jackie, and John Harwood. 1993. "Congress Rushes to Close Book on One Busy Year, But Clinton Promises to Apply the Spurs in Next." *Wall Street Journal*, Nov. 22.

Cameron, Charles, William Howell, Scott Adler, and Charles Riemann. 1996. "Measuring the Institutional Performance of Congress in the Postwar Era." Unpublished manuscript, Department of Political Science, Columbia University.

Church, George J. 1993. "The Gridlock Breakers: Passage of the Brady Bill Caps a Solid Season for the 103d Congress." *Time*, Dec. 6, 32–33.

Clymer, Adam. 1993a. "Bill to Prohibit State Restrictions on Abortion Appears to Be Dead." *New York Times*, Sept. 16.

———. 1993b. "GOP Senators Prevail, Sinking Clinton's Economic Stimulus Bill." *New York Times*, Apr. 22.

———. 1993c. "Sour End to Strong Year." *New York Times*, Nov. 24.

———. 1994a. "GOP Filibuster Deals a Setback to Lobbying Bill." *New York Times*, Oct. 7.

———. 1994b. "Having 'Done Enough Harm,' Senate Inches to Adjournment." *New York Times*, Oct. 5.

———. 1994c. "National Health Program, President's Greatest Goal, Declared Dead in Congress." *New York Times*, Sept. 27.

———. 1994d. "Rancor Leaves Its Mark on 103d Congress." *New York Times*, Oct. 9.

———. 1996. "Clinton and Congress: Partnership of Self-Interest." *New York Times*, Oct. 2.

Clymer, Adam, Robert Pear, and Robin Toner. 1994. "For Health Care, Time Was a Killer." *New York Times*, Aug. 29.

Cohen, Richard E. 1994. *Changing Course in Washington: Clinton and the New Congress.* New York: Macmillan.

———. 1995. *Washington at Work: Back Rooms and Clean Air.* Boston: Allyn and Bacon.

Congress and the Nation, 1945–1964, 1965–1968, 1969–1972. Washington, D.C.: Congressional Quarterly Service, 1965, 1969, 1973.

Congressional Quarterly Almanac, 1962, 1966, 1967, 1970. Washington, D.C.: Congressional Quarterly Service, 1963, 1967, 1968, 1971.

Conlan, Timothy J. 1993. "Intergovernmental Regulatory Enactments in the 1980s." In U.S. Advisory Commission on Intergovernmental Relations, *Federal Regulation of State and Local Governments: The Mixed Record of the 1980s*, A-126. Washington, D.C.: U.S. Government Printing Office.

Cushman, John H., Jr. 1994. "Congress Drops Effort to Curb Public-Land Mining." *New York Times*, Sept. 30.

Dahl, Robert A. 1990. "Myth of the Presidential Mandate." *Political Science Quarterly* 105:355–72.

Davidson, Roger H. 1988. "The New Centralization on Capitol Hill." *Review of Politics* 50:345–64.

Davis, Kenneth S. 1993. *FDR: Into the Storm, 1937–1940: A History.* New York: Random House.

Dewar, Helen, and Kenneth J. Cooper. 1993. "Dust Clears on a Fruitful Legislative Year." *Washington Post*, Nov. 28.

———. 1994. "103d Congress Started Fast but Collapsed at Finish Line." *Washington Post*, Oct. 9.

"Dole Calls for Whitewater Answers." 1994. *Washington Post*, Jan. 17.

Donovan, Beth. 1994. "Democrats' Overhaul Bill Dies on Senate Procedural Votes." *Congressional Quarterly Weekly Report* 52 (Oct. 1): 2757–58.

Edwards, George C., III. 1980. *Presidential Influence in Congress.* San Francisco: W. H. Freeman.

Elving, Ronald D. 1995. *Conflict and Compromise: How Congress Makes the Laws.* New York: Simon and Schuster.

Evans, Rowland, and Robert Novak. 1966. *Lyndon B. Johnson and the Exercise of Power.* New York: New American Library.

Ferejohn, John A., Brian J. Gaines, and Douglas Rivers. 1996. "The Failure of Incumbency: Why the Democrats Lost the House in 1994." Unpublished manuscript, Department of Political Science, Stanford University.

Friedman, Milton. 1995. "Getting Back to Real Growth." *Wall Street Journal*, Aug. 1.

Gettinger, Stephen. 1994. "View from the Ivory Tower More Rosy than Media's." 1994. *Congressional Quarterly Weekly Report* 52 (Oct. 8): 2850–51.

Gigot, Paul A. 1994. "103d Congress: Pass the Balloons and Party Hats." *Wall Street Journal*, Oct. 7.

Goldstein, Kenneth M. 1995. "Tremors before the Earthquake: Grass Roots Communications to Congress before the 1994 Election." Paper presented at the annual conference of the American Political Science Association, Chicago, Aug. 31–Sept. 3.

Gosnell, Harold F. 1980. *Truman's Crises: A Political Biography of Harry S. Truman.* Westport, Conn.: Greenwood Press.

Hager, George. 1993a. "Latest CBO Figures Support Clinton Deficit Projection: But Forecasters Deflate Reduction Package Total, Warn That Sustained Economic Health Is a Must." *Congressional Quarterly Weekly Report* 51 (Sept. 11): 2376–77.

———. 1993b. "1985 All Over Again?" *Congressional Quarterly Weekly Report* 51 (July 24): 1936.

———. 1993c. "1993 Deal: Remembrance of Things Past: With Democratic Congresses and Limited Options, New Package Is Similar to 1990 Version." *Congressional Quarterly Weekly Report* 51 (Aug. 7): 2130–31.

Hamby, Alonzo L. 1973. *Beyond the New Deal: Harry S. Truman and American Liberalism*. New York: Columbia University Press.

Hershey, Marjorie Randon. 1992. "The Constructed Explanation: Interpreting Election Results in the 1984 Presidential Race." *Journal of Politics* 54:943–76.

Hook, Janet, and the *Congressional Quarterly* staff. 1993. "Democrats Hail 'Productivity,' But Image Problems Remain." *Congressional Quarterly Weekly Report* 51 (Dec. 11): 3355–57.

Ivins, Molly. 1994. "Even Though No One's Looking at the Scoreboard." *Boston Globe*, Nov. 20.

Johnson, Haynes, and David S. Broder. 1996. *The System: The American Way of Politics at the Breaking Point*. Boston: Little, Brown.

Jones, Charles O. 1994. *The Presidency in a Separated System*. Washington, D.C.: Brookings Institution Press.

———. 1995. Personal communication with author, via E-mail.

Kaufman, Burton I. 1993. *The Presidency of James Earl Carter Jr*. Lawrence: University Press of Kansas.

Kelley, Stanley, Jr. 1983. *Interpreting Elections*. Princeton: Princeton University Press.

Kenworthy, Tom, and Gary Lee. 1994. "The Green Gridlock: Hopes for a Flowering of Environmental Laws Are Falling Flat." *Washington Post National Weekly Edition*, Sep. 26–Oct. 2, 14.

Kesselman, Mark. 1961. "Presidential Leadership in Congress on Foreign Policy." *Midwest Journal of Political Science* 5:284–89.

Koenig, Louis W. 1962. "Kennedy and the 87th Congress." In *American Government Annual, 1962–1963*, ed. Ivan Hinderaker. New York: Holt, Rinehart and Winston.

Kranish, Michael. 1994. "Legacy of the Bush Years Blooming in the Clinton Era." *Boston Globe*, Oct.23.

Krehbiel, Keith. 1996. "Institutional and Partisan Sources of Gridlock: A Theory of Divided and Unified Government." *Journal of Theoretical Politics* 8:7–40.

Langdon, Steve. 1993. "Clinton Prevails on Capitol Hill despite Poor Showing in Polls." *Congressional Quarterly Weekly Report* 51 (Sept. 25): 2527.

———. 1994. "Clinton's High Victory Rate Conceals Disappointments." *Congressional Quarterly Weekly Report* 52 (Dec. 31): 3619–20.

"Legislative Summary." 1994. *Congressional Quarterly Weekly Report* 52 (Nov. 5): 3148–49.

Light, Paul C. 1982. *The President's Agenda: Domestic Policy Choice from Kennedy to Carter (with Notes on Ronald Reagan)*. Baltimore: Johns Hopkins University Press.

Lindblom, Charles E. 1965. *The Intelligence of Democracy: Decision Making through Mutual Adjustment*. New York: Free Press.

Link, Arthur S. 1954. *Woodrow Wilson and the Progressive Era, 1910–1917*. New York: Harper and Brothers.

Manegold, Catherine S. 1994. "Senate Republicans Deal a Major Defeat to Labor." *New York Times*, July 13.

Mayhew, David R. 1991. *Divided We Govern: Lawmaking, Investigations, and Party Control, 1946–1990.* New Haven: Yale University Press.

———. 1993a. *Divided We Govern: Lawmaking, Investigations, and Party Control, 1946–1990.* Rev. ed. New Haven: Yale University Press.

———. 1993b. "Let's Stick with the Longer List." *Polity* 25:485–88.

McCoy, Donald R. 1984. *The Presidency of Harry S. Truman.* Lawrence: University Press of Kansas.

Moynihan, Daniel Patrick. 1995. "The Professionalization of Reform II." *The Public Interest*, no. 121:39.

Neustadt, Richard E. 1955. "Presidency and Legislation: Planning the President's Program." *American Political Science Review* 49:980–1021.

New York Times. 1993. Editorial, July 26.

———. 1994. Editorial, Oct. 9.

Oppenheimer, Bruce I. 1996. "The Importance of Elections in a Strong Congressional Party Era: The Effect of Unified versus Divided Government." In *Do Elections Matter?* ed. Benjamin Ginsberg and Alan Stone, 3d ed. Armonk, N.Y.: M. E. Sharpe.

Patterson, James T. 1967. *Congressional Conservatism and the New Deal.* Lexington: University Press of Kentucky.

Pear, Robert. 1995. "Clinton Decides to Control, but Not Cut, the Deficit." *New York Times*, Feb. 5.

Priest, Dana, and Michael Weisskopf. 1994. "Death from a Thousand Cuts: White House Mistakes and Rabid Washington Partisanship Killed Health Care Reform." *Washington Post National Weekly Edition*, Oct. 17–23, 9–10.

Reichard, Gary W. 1975. *The Reaffirmation of Republicanism: Eisenhower and the Eighty-third Congress.* Knoxville: University of Tennessee Press.

Rohde, David W. 1991. *Parties and Leaders in the Postreform House.* Chicago: University of Chicago Press.

Rosenbaum, David E. 1993. "Beyond the Superlatives: Budget Bill Is Neither Biggest Deficit Cutter Nor the Biggest Tax Rise in Recent Years." *New York Times*, Aug. 5.

———. 1994. "Bill to Revamp Financing of Campaigns Fails Again." *New York Times*, Oct. 1.

Rovner, Julie. 1995. "Congress and Health Care Reform 1993–1994." In *Intensive Care: How Congress Shapes Health Policy,* ed. Thomas E. Mann and Norman J. Ornstein. Washington, D.C.: American Enterprise Institute and Brookings Institution Press.

Schick, Allen. 1995. "How a Bill Did Not Become a Law." In *Intensive Care: How Congress Shapes Health Policy,* ed. Thomas E. Mann and Norman J. Ornstein. Washington, D.C.: American Enterprise Institute and Brookings Institution Press.

Seelye, Katharine Q. 1994. "Clinton and Allies Rediscover Their Voice in Writing Epitaph for Congress." *New York Times*, Oct. 9.

Skocpol, Theda. 1987. "A Society without a 'State'? Political Organization, Social Conflict, and Welfare Provision in the United States." *Journal of Public Policy* 7:349–71.

Stein, Herbert. 1993. "Don't Fault D.C. for the Slow Recovery." *New York Times*, Sept. 19.

Sundquist, James S. 1968. *Politics and Policy: The Eisenhower, Kennedy, and Johnson Years*. Washington, D.C.: Brookings Institution Press.

Toner, Robin. 1994. "Health Impasse Souring Voters, New Poll Finds." *New York Times*, Sept. 13.

Truman, David B. 1959. *The Congressional Party*. New York: Wiley.

Vogel, David. 1981. "The 'New' Social Regulation in Historical and Comparative Perspective." In *Regulation in Perspective: Historical Essays*, ed. Thomas K. McCraw. Cambridge: Harvard University Press.

Waldman, Steven. 1995. *The Bill*. New York: Viking.

Washington Post. 1994. Editorial, Oct. 7, A24.

Washington Post National Weekly Edition. 1994. Editorial, Sept. 5–11, 27.

Weidenbaum, Murray. 1991. "Return of the 'R' Word: The Regulatory Assault on the Economy." *Policy Review*, no. 58:40–43.

Wessel, David. 1993. "Deficit-Cutting Bill Bears a Resemblance to 1990 Predecessor; But Differences May Be Crucial; Realistic Economic View, Increase in Taxes Are Cited." *Wall Street Journal*, Aug. 3.

Wirls, Daniel. 1995. "United Government, Divided Congress? The Senate and the Democratic Agenda in the 103d Congress." Paper presented at the annual conference of the American Political Science Association, Chicago, Aug. 31–Sept. 3.

Yang, John E. 1993. "Why Does the Budget Argument Sound So Familiar? Because We've Heard It All Before—Three Years Ago." *Washington Post National Weekly Edition*, July 26–Aug. 1, 20.

Zuckman, Jill, and John Aloysius Farrell. 1994. "Partisanship Derailed Congress's Fast Start." *Boston Globe*, Oct. 9.

CHAPTER 11

The Rise and Decline of the Congressional Black Caucus

Carol M. Swain

When the 103d Congress was seated in January 1993, the membership of the Congressional Black Caucus (CBC) had jumped from twenty-five to thirty-eight representatives, plus a delegate and a senator. With a Democrat in the White House, the CBC was poised to become a major player in the Democratic-controlled Congress. Congressional Black Caucus members were heading key committees, and they held other leadership posts, as well: nine were assistant whips, three served on the Democratic Steering and Policy Committee, and one, John Lewis (D-Ga.), was a deputy whip. In recognition of its increased stature, the Clinton administration consulted the caucus on all major political decisions.[1] The organization was more visible than it had been at any other time in its history and was a key factor in many of the important political debates that took place in Washington. From the well-documented weaknesses that characterized the CBC's early years, it had become a powerful force on Capitol Hill, a development brought about largely by the personal influence of some of its individual members and by its ability to deliver a substantial bloc of votes.[2]

As fate would have it, though, just when the organization appeared to be making a substantial difference in Congress, the Democrats lost both the House and the Senate. The 1994 elections profoundly changed the political environment in which the CBC had to operate, as its members were forced to negotiate with unsympathetic Republicans. Despite its motto, "Black people have no permanent friends, no permanent enemies, just permanent interests," the CBC throughout its existence had never functioned as more than an extension of the Democratic Party. As an interest group within the minority party, the CBC was destined to become more marginalized than ever. Though it had four times as many members in 1994 as it had at its birth in 1971, in the wake of the Democrats' defeat the caucus has exerted little power or influence.[3] To understand how the CBC has operated in the 104th Congress and where it might be headed in the future, we need to take a closer look at its historical development under both Democratic and Republican administrations.

The Republican Takeover

It is an understatement to say that most Democrats were unprepared for the 1994 Republican takeover of Congress. It had been more than forty years since the Republicans had won a majority of the House, and most Democrats in Washington were shocked and confused by their minority status. Describing the atmosphere on the Hill after the elections, Rep. Bill Richardson (D-N.M.) remarked that "it was like a funeral wake." President Bill Clinton and many of the surviving Democrats interpreted the election results as a sign that their party needed to become more centrist. Other Democrats cautioned against such a strategy. Retiring senator Howard Metzenbaum (D-Ohio), for instance, warned that "if we walk like Republicans and act like Republicans, people will want the real thing and just vote Republican. We don't need two Republican Parties."[4]

Unlike most white Democrats, however, some CBC members tried to put a positive spin on the election. Rep. Charles Rangel (D-N.Y.), for instance, asserted that CBC members were now "big fish in a little pond and should not be dictated to by losers and marginal winners."[5] Arguing that their votes might still carry considerable weight in the Republican Congress, Rangel said, "I can't tell [House Speaker] Newt Gingrich what to do, but to the extent he needs forty votes to get anything done, he should be willing to talk to anybody."[6] Rangel and former CBC chair Kweisi Mfume (D-Md.) subsequently angered white Democrats—as well as many other CBC members—by meeting secretly with Republican leaders in an attempt to forge a bipartisan coalition on issues of mutual concern. Two weeks before the elections, CBC chair-elect Donald Payne (D-N.J.) had responded confidently, in a manner similar to Rangel's, to a question about the organization's prospects in the event of a Republican majority: "We'd be able to influence policy even more. Our votes would be even more critical."[7] Payne apparently anticipated that the CBC would have greater influence if there were fewer white Democrats, since its membership would constitute a greater percentage of the Democrats on the Hill.

Mfume flirted openly with the idea of switching parties. After he had made an unsuccessful bid for the chair of the Democratic Caucus, Mfume announced that Republican leaders had approached him about joining their party. By this time three white southern Democrats had crossed the aisle, and there was talk of more defections. Mfume used the threat of his potential defection to induce congressional Democrats to create a new position for him as spokesperson for their party. The rumor that he might eventually join the Republicans was squelched when one of his aides, Dan Willson, told curious reporters, "To my knowledge nothing has changed; [Mfume] woke up a Democrat [this morning], and he will likely go to sleep as one."[8]

Any sincere hopes that CBC members entertained about negotiating with Republicans as a voting bloc were dashed after Republican leaders outlined their vision for the future, which did not include them. The Republican mission was one that CBC members found particularly hostile to their organization. Within weeks of the November elections, Republican leaders announced their plans to eliminate federal funding of 28 of 130 legislative service organizations (LSOs).[9] Among the groups affected were the CBC, the Democratic Study Group, the Republican Wednesday Group, the Caucus for Women's Issues, and the Hispanic Caucus. What these caucuses had in common was their strong reliance on membership dues paid from office allotments to support their policy-making activities.[10] Their opponents could argue, therefore, that taxpayers' money was being improperly used to support the activities of ideological groups.

Some Democrats characterized the attack on the LSOs as nothing more than ideological warfare designed to silence more liberal groups. Mfume called the move "an assault on diversity in the Congress and an attempt to disempower communities through congressional ethnic and philosophical cleansing."[11] Leaders of other caucuses agreed. Rep. Pat Schroeder (D-Colo.), of the Caucus for Women's Issues, accused the Republicans of attempting to transform congressional women into compliant "Stepford Wives." Similarly, Rep. Jose E. Serrano (D-N.Y.), speaking for the Hispanic Caucus, remarked that his LSO was punished because its members had gotten "uppity" with Republicans.[12] In reply, Republicans argued that LSOs spread propaganda and lack accountability to the public. Rep. Pat Roberts (R-Kan.), a long-time critic of LSOs, circulated a study detailing a number of abuses. Roberts reported that over a ten-year period, "7.7 million of $35 million in caucus spending [was] undocumented . . . including $20,000 in monthly tips from the California Democratic Congressional Delegation and $10,050 in petty cash expenses that the Congressional Black Caucus did not back up with receipts."[13] The elimination of federal funds cost the CBC over $200,000 in annual revenue and forced it to move its operations.[14] Since the elimination of member-funded LSOs, however, new groups have arisen on the Hill. These new groups are less organized and have considerably smaller staff, but they are powerful because some votes are close enough that they can be influenced with the defections of as few as fifteen Republicans. Among these groups are the New Federalists, the Blue Dogs, and the Lunch Bunchers.

In a single election, then, the organization had fallen from a state of considerable power and influence, which had taken the caucus almost twenty-five years to accumulate, to a relatively marginal existence. Its only formal link with House Republicans was its Republican member, Gary Franks, of Connecticut, to whom it had given a particularly hard time. Perhaps the most telling blow came from J. C. Watts of Oklahoma, who refused to join the CBC after his 1994 election and thereby became the first black ever to reject membership in the organization.

Institutional Changes on the Hill

As the new majority party, the Republicans were highly motivated to change the way the Democrats had structured the Congress over the past forty years, and they had pledged themselves to do so long before the election. Smelling victory, the Republican leaders had a transition team in place in the summer before the election. In September 1994, they had unveiled and signed on the steps of the Capitol their Contract with America, which outlined their legislative agenda. In addition to proposing sweeping changes in the administrative rules of the institution, the Contract had called for (1) a balanced budget amendment and a line-item veto; (2) tougher anticrime laws; (3) welfare reform; (4) stronger enforcement of laws governing child support, as well as more-lenient adoption requirements; (5) tax cuts for middle-class citizens; (6) increased spending on defense; (7) tax breaks for higher-income senior citizens that would repeal the Clinton administration's taxes on Social Security earnings above a certain limit; (8) a tax cut on capital gains; (9) reform of the legal system; and (10) congressional term limits.

The Republican legislative changes were swift. On the first day of the 104th Congress, Republicans and Democrats passed legislation imposing term limits on the Speaker and on committee chairs. They eliminated proxy voting, along with the practice of allowing rolling quorums on committee votes. Before the latter change was made, members could more or less vote at their convenience. Legislation guaranteeing an open-door policy to the press and public was adopted for committee proceedings. The financial records of all congressional operations were subjected to an audit, and for the first time in history, legislation passed that required members of Congress to observe the same laws and regulations as other Americans.[15] By April 10, 1995, when the first hundred days of the new session were over, all issues outlined in the Contract had been brought to the floor for a vote. Only term limits failed to pass the House. The

Republicans were able to achieve unanimity on many of their votes, and they also picked up support from Democrats, including some CBC members.

The switch in party power meant that Democrats had to relinquish their institutional leadership roles and, in many cases, become ranking minority members of committees and subcommittees they had once chaired. Prior to the Republican takeover, CBC members served on all standing committees except Natural Resources, and they held chairs of three committees and seventeen subcommittees. California's Ron Dellums chaired Armed Services, and Michigan congressman John Conyers chaired Government Operations. Missouri's Bill Clay, who chaired the Post Office and Civil Service Committee, was in line to chair the important Education and Labor Committee. New York's Charles Rangel was close to becoming chair of the powerful Ways and Means Committee. Because of seniority rules, Republican cutbacks in the size of committees meant that the most junior Democrats lost their assignments on the more prestigious committees. Among CBC members, Carrie Meeks of Florida lost her place on the Appropriations Committee, Illinois's Mel Reynolds and Louisiana's Cleo Fields lost their seats on Ways and Means, and Bobby Rush (D-Ill.) lost his seats on Banking and Financial Services and on the Science Committee.

Some CBC members charged that white racism was behind many of the Republican institutional changes that disproportionately affected their group. They cited, for example, the fact that of the three committees abolished, two had the highest percentages of blacks. The Post Office Committee was 47 percent black, and the District of Columbia Committee was 62 percent black. Furthermore, delegates from the District of Columbia, Puerto Rico, the Virgin Islands, and other U.S. possessions were stripped of their newly acquired symbolic vote, which the CBC had helped them win in the preceding Congress. Delegates had been allowed to vote in the Committee of the Whole, a House quorum, but their votes could not be used to change legislative outcomes. The facts, however, do not easily support a charge of racism. Republican leaders were able to identify Republican groups also adversely affected by their institutional changes. Moreover, undocumented LSO expenditures and staff cutbacks on committees allowed them to make a credible case that their institutional changes were designed to reduce bureaucratic inefficiency and waste. Rather than racism, ideological differences may have played a major role in how the Republican leadership treated the CBC after the elections. Why should anyone be especially surprised that the newly empowered conservatives might target for humiliation the most liberal group in the Congress, especially since the CBC, in the previous Congress, had appeared to wield considerable influence over the president?

Congressional Black Caucus Voting Patterns

Over the years, the voting of CBC members has been a source of much research and speculation—particularly the effectiveness of the caucus as a voting bloc.[16] Arthur Levy and Susan Stoudinger found that the caucus did not appear to be a major voting cue for its members. They concluded that the group served more as a social club than as an effective political organization.[17] Bruce Robeck also concluded that the organization has had little impact on legislative outcomes; consequently, it would not affect policy outcomes much if all black representatives were replaced by white northern Democrats.[18] Charles E. Jones and Augustus Adair have presented more favorable assessments of CBC achievements; but many of the issues they examined to evaluate the caucus's effectiveness were, in any case, traditional Democratic initiatives.[19]

Much of the power of the CBC has come from its potential as a cohesive voting bloc and from the individual leadership positions of its members. Using categories of general legislation, social issues, monetary issues, foreign affairs and defense, and miscellaneous legislation, Jones, and later Douglas Harris, calculated cohesion indexes for the CBC. Cohesiveness among CBC members was weakest during the 94th Congress. Between the 95th and 96th Congresses cohesion grew, except on foreign affairs and monetary issues. Cohesiveness dropped again during the 103d Congress, especially on social issues, monetary issues, and defense and foreign affairs. Harris found that it dropped 6.5 percent on social issues, the area where CBC members might be considered most likely to vote as a bloc.[20]

Since these studies were completed, the districts of CBC members have changed significantly, and the membership of the organization has more than doubled. In previous Congresses, most black representatives were representing majority-black districts located in midwestern and northeastern states. That is no longer the case. Almost half of the black representatives elected in 1992 came from southern districts, many of which had rural populations of considerable size. The most rural of these districts were in Mississippi (second district), North Carolina (first), Georgia (eleventh), and South Carolina (sixth). These districts have more white voters than have black districts of the past. During the 104th Congress, eleven black incumbents represented districts that have nonblack majorities, and eight represented districts that were barely majority-black (less than 55 percent) in their voting-age populations. Eleven others represented districts with voting-age populations that are more than 60 percent black. Given lower black registration and turnout levels, some black representatives of nonblack and barely majority-black districts had majority-white electorates on election day.[21] These district characteristics may have affected the voting of black representatives who needed the support of white voters.

David Bositis has studied voting patterns among CBC members. He examined twenty-two votes on which CBC members were heavily divided and found four distinct cluster groupings.[22] These groupings and the CBC members included in them are presented as clusters 1 to 4 in the list below.[23]

Cluster 1:
Programmatic spending
  Democratic leadership

Lucien Blackwell (Pa.)
William Clay (Mo.)
Barbara-Rose Collins (Mich.)
Cardiss Collins (Ill.)
Ronald Dellums (Calif.)
Harold Ford (Tenn.)
Earl Hilliard (Ala.)
Mel Reynolds (Ill.)
Bobby Rush (Ill.)
Louis Stokes (Ohio)
Bennie Thompson (Miss.)
Edolphus Towns (N.Y.)
Walter Tucker (Calif.)
Craig Washington (Tex.)
John Lewis (Ga.)
Major Owens (N.Y.)
Donald Payne (N.J.)
Charles Rangel (N.Y.)
Maxine Waters (Calif.)
Alan Wheat (Mo.)
Albert Wynn (Md.)

Cluster 2:
Sun Belt high-tech Clinton supporters

Sanford Bishop (Ga.)
Corrine Brown (Tex.)
Julian Dixon (Calif.)
Cleo Fields (La.)
Alcee Hastings (Fla.)
Williams Jefferson (La.)
Eddie Bernice Johnson (Tex.)
Carrie Meek (Fla.)
Robert Scott (Va.)

Cluster 3:
Priority-reordering Clinton agnostics

Eva Clayton (N.C.)
James Clyburn (S.C.)
John Conyers (Mich.)
Floyd Flake (N.Y.)
Cynthia McKinney (Ga.)
Kweisi Mfume (Md.)
Eleanor Holmes Norton (D.C.)
Melvin Watts (N.C.)

Cluster 4:
Single Member

Gary Franks (Conn.)

Cluster 1, which had twenty-one members, is described by Bositis as the "programmatic spending Democratic leadership" group. Many of its members held key leadership positions during the 103d Congress. They were considerably more likely to support the Democratic leadership than were members of the other groups. He calls the nine members of cluster 2 the "Sun Belt high-tech Clinton supporters." These members, the most conservative black Democrats, voted most unlike the members of cluster 1. Cluster 3, consisting of eight mem-

Figure 11.1 Characteristics of Cluster Members (percentage)

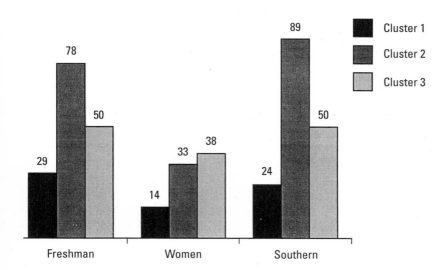

Source: Data from David Bositis, *The Congressional Black Caucus in the 103d Congress* (Washington, D.C.: University of America Press, 1994), 165.
Note: Numbers are cluster averages. Cluster 4 was omitted.

bers often voting in opposition to the president, is classified as "priority-re-ordering Clinton agnostics." These Democrats sought to reorder the priorities of government. Cluster 4 consists of Republican Gary Franks, who voted more like members of cluster 2 than the other groups. Figure 11.1 shows other characteristics of cluster members. Eighty-nine percent of the members of cluster 2 were from the South, and they were mostly freshmen.

During the first hundred days of the first session of the 104th Congress, thirty-three votes took place on the ten items that made up the Contract with America. Table 11.1 ranks black Democrats from high to low in their support of the Contract and also gives their conservative coalition scores and the percentage of blacks among the voting-age population in each representative's district. As might be expected, southern blacks are more supportive than other blacks of the Republican agenda. Georgia's Sanford Bishop (62.5%), Tennessee's Harold Ford (51.6%), and Texas's Sheila Jackson Lee (48.5%) led the pack in their support for the Contract. A similar pattern appears in conservative coalition scores. Bishop (58%), Alabama's Earl Hilliard (53%), Florida's Corrine Brown (44%), South Carolina's James Clyburn (36%), and New Jersey's Don-

Table 11.1 Black Democratic Representatives' Support for Conservative Programs and Black Voting-Age Population

Representative	Contract with America	Conservative Coalition	Black VAP[a]
Bishop (Ga.)	62.5	58	52.3
Ford (Tenn.)	51.6	17	54.1
Lee (Tex.)	48.5	2	48.6
Flelds (La.)	46.9	25	62.6
Towns (N.Y.)	46.9	11	59.4
Jefferson (La.)	46.7	28	56.2
Reynolds (Ill.)	46.4	17	66.0
Clyburn (S.C.)	45.5	36	58.3
Johnson (Tex.)	45.5	28	47.1
Dixon (Calif.)	43.8	14	39.9
Flake (N.Y.)	43.8	17	54.5
Tucker (Calif.)	43.8	22	34.2
McKinney (Ga.)	43.3	3	60.4
Clayton (N.C.)	42.4	22	53.4
Wynn (Ma.)	42.4	25	5.8
Lewis (Ga.)	40.6	6	57.5
Stokes (Ohio)	40.6	8	54.8
Rangel (N.Y.)	39.3	8	46.7
Rush (Ill.)	38.5	6	67.8
Meek (Fla.)	37.9	31	54.0
Hilliard (Ala.)	37.5	53	63.5
Brown (Fla.)	36.7	44	50.6
Clay (Mo.)	36.7	8	48.0
Mfume (Md.)	36.4	6	67.8
Payne (N.J.)	36.4	36	57.3
Thompson (Miss.)	36.4	6	58.1
Waters (Calif.)	36.4	3	44.0
Owens (N.Y.)	36.4	28	72.4
Scott (Va.)	33.3	3	61.2
Collins (Ill.)	30.0	3	59.8
Dellums (Calif.)	28.1	0	29.2
Fattah (Pa.)	28.1	2	58.4
Hastings (Fla.)	28.1	17	45.7
Watt (N.C.)	28.1	3	53.3
Collins (Mich.)	27.6	3	68.2

[a] "Black VAP" is the percentage of blacks within the district's voting-age population.

ald Payne (36%) are also among the high scorers. In contrast, Ron Dellums (D-Calif.) scored zero.

Eleven of eighteen blacks, representing districts less than 55 percent black, gave 40 percent or more of their support to Contract items. An additional six gave Contract items 28 to 38 percent of their support. These, too, represented districts less than 55 percent black. Eleven other blacks representing districts greater than 55 percent black supported the Contract to a lesser degree. Nationally, white Democrats supported the Contract items at a rate of 42 percent. Over half of the Contract items passed with more than three hundred votes, but a few pieces of legislation were close enough to be swayed by the votes of defecting Democrats.

Table 11.2 presents a regression analysis of the voting patterns of southern Democrats. It examines the influence of voters' race, rural residence, and percentage of blacks within the voting-age population on support for the Contract with America. These data show statistically significant differences between white and black southern Democrats. White Democrats were far more likely than black Democrats to support the Contract with America. Representation of a rural district was positively correlated with support for the Contract, and this, too, was statistically significant. A regression model examining only black Democrats showed no significant differences between southerners and nonsoutherners, which lends some credence to the hypothesis that racial solidarity might outweigh other factors such as region and ideology in influencing how the majority of blacks vote.[24] The extreme conservatism of many of the Contract's items dampened the likelihood of widespread support for them, even among southern blacks.

Table 11.2 Multivariate Analysis of Southern Democrats

Variables	Support of Contract	Standard Error	t = statistic
Race	−31.500[a]	8.100	−3.880
Percent rural	.369[a]	.079	3.800
Percent black	.028	.180	0.151
Constant	66.100	4.190	15.769
R-squared = .68			

Note: The regression coefficients are unstandardized. Variables are coded as follows: race (1 = black, 0 = white), Contract with America (0 to 100%), percent rural (0 to 100%), percent black (0 to 100%).
[a] $p > .01$.

Although not statistically significant, there are notable differences between southern and northern blacks. With few exceptions, the southern blacks elected in 1992 representing districts created after the 1990 census are the most politically conservative. Most of these districts have large white populations, and their borders were under legal challenge during this period. Consequently, their representatives have been engaged in a delicate balancing act in trying to serve the interests and demands of black voters while at the same time trying to win the support of more conservative white constituents. As politicians who want to be reelected, they are responding to varied demands. Another explanation, however, for their more conservative voting comes from the possibility that the newly created districts elected a different type of black politician, one more conservative than those elected in previous Congresses. Yet another possibility is that southern black Democrats are engaging in strategic voting behavior. Consider Tennessee's Harold Ford, a longtime liberal who supported 51 percent of the Contract items and who has since retired. If these same black representatives were representing safe black districts in a Democratic-controlled Congress, they might be as liberal as the northern blacks.

Does the more conservative voting behavior of southern blacks mean that they are less responsive to black interests? The answer is an unequivocal no. As former Mississippi representative Mike Espy showed with his support of the death penalty and his opposition to gun control, southerners are conservative on a number of social issues, and this includes black southerners.[25] Black southern Democrats have room to maneuver. What is most relevant for assessing black representation, however, is the legislator's support of civil rights and redistributive legislation. Black Democrats are unanimous on certain types of legislation affecting the black community, such as welfare reform. Among the legislative initiatives supported by the more conservative black Democrats were the balanced budget amendment, the measure against unfunded mandates, deportation of criminal aliens, private property rights, the omnibus regulatory overhaul, and securities litigation.

Perhaps southern Democrats have always been more conservative than northerners. Five white southern Democrats have switched political parties since the 1994 elections. Strategically, black Democrats have less latitude than white Democrats to follow white southern voting trends toward the Republican Party. Since black voters rarely support Republican candidates, there is little, if any, incentive for politicians to appeal to the black Republican vote. Some individual black politicians, however, might have conversion potential for Republicans. Republicans might profit by inducing a few black Democrats to support their more conservative agenda, and if they could persuade one or two to switch parties, this could help accelerate realignment trends in the South.

Therefore, unlike African-American voters, who, as Larry Bartels says elsewhere in this volume, "cannot credibly promise or threaten to convert to the Republicans in substantial numbers," individual black politicians may use party allegiance as a bargaining chip if they are willing to negotiate.[26]

In the Republican-controlled Congress, CBC members did not agree on strategy and as a consequence were deeply divided over how best to operate in their new environment.[27] Unable to do much else, some CBC members articulated the goal of serving as the "conscience of the Congress," and therefore they advocated a return to the earlier view of the CBC's role: "Congressmen at large for 20 million black people."[28] Other members cut deals with Republicans that were beneficial to their districts. Still others advocated a return to protest politics.

None embraced this latter strategy more enthusiastically than John Lewis, one of the "Big Six" of the civil rights movement. In January 1995, Lewis led a demonstration of nine CBC members into the Rules Committee room and demanded that its chairman, Gerald Solomon (R-N.Y.), remove a newly hung picture of Virginia segregationist Howard Smith. Several months later, Lewis led a second march, this time in Georgia, to protest cuts in the Medicare program. The group stood outside a building where Newt Gingrich (R-Ga.) was speaking and chanted "Where is Newt?"[29] Lewis charged that Gingrich had retreated on affirmative action because he feared that disruptive actions by the CBC and other liberal Democrats might bring the Congress to a halt.[30] Also, Kweisi Mfume has warned Democrats and Republicans that CBC members may abandon the legislative process and engage even more in protest politics; in the view of some, protest was the organization's strongest weapon against the Republicans.[31] Protest politics, however, was of limited value in combating the Republican agenda. White public opinion was running overwhelmingly against government support of affirmative action and against large-scale spending on social welfare programs,[32] issues of great importance to the black community.

Outlook for the Future

The CBC as a collectivity has had little to offer Republicans (or, for that matter, Democrats). As Charles Rangel reports, "We meet periodically with the president and we meet with the minority Democratic leadership—but about what? . . . We don't have the votes to win."[33] The future of the CBC depends on whether the Democrats recapture the House in the near election and on the survival rate of its current members. If the Republicans continue to hold a majority in the Congress, switching parties could enter the political calculus of a few southern black Democrats. As the price of defection, a black defector might be able to negotiate for more pork, better committee assignments, and perhaps a leadership post, which would enable that individual to enhance the substantive representation of his or her constituents. The collective strategy in which most blacks are Democrats serves to constrain the group. In the short term, a few self-interested blacks may be able to maximize the good of their white and black constituents by forming alliances with Republicans. Indeed, five black representatives with clout with the majority party could achieve more than fifty black representatives voting with the minority party.

In addition to its political problems, the CBC has suffered greatly over the past four years in another way, as criminal investigations and convictions have taken their toll on certain prominent CBC members. Two black Democrats, Mel Reynolds of Illinois and Walter Tucker of California, have resigned and are in prison, having been convicted of criminal charges. And the CBC's former vice chairwoman, Barbara Rose-Collins (D-Mich.), has been defeated and is under criminal investigation. In addition, three senior members, Mfume, Cardiss Collins (D-Ill.), and Harold Ford (D-Tenn.), have resigned to pursue other career options. Cleo Fields (D-La.) resigned after his district was invalidated by the courts as an unconstitutional gerrymander. Other black members, such as Cynthia McKinney (D-Ga.) and Sanford Bishop (D-Ga.) have been reelected in majority-white districts.

As we approach the twenty-first century, the CBC is clearly struggling to stay afloat. Over the course of decades, it has risen in power, only to lose that power in a single election. Its only hedge against elections that throw its members outside the halls of power is to strive for an organization that is hospitable to members of both parties. By doing so, the caucus might be able to protect itself from the effects of shifts in party power that are bound to occur in a two-party system. Otherwise, the marginalization of the CBC is likely to continue, and defection and discord could threaten its very existence as an organization.

Notes

1. Kenneth J. Cooper, "For Enlarged Congressional Black Caucus, a New Kind of Impact," *Washington Post*, June 10, 1993.

2. Douglas B. Harris, "On Symbolic and Material Caucus Power: The Congressional Black Caucus, 92d–103d Congresses," paper presented at meeting of the American Political Science Association, New York, Sept. 1–4, 1994.

3. Marguerite Barnett, "The Congressional Black Caucus," reprint from "Congress against the President," *Proceedings of the Academy of Political Science* 32 (1975): 35–36.

4. Quoted in Lawrence M. O'Rourke, "Divided Democrats Bickering over How To Make Comeback," *Sacramento Bee*, Dec. 11, 1994.

5. Quoted in Juan Williams, "Blacked Out in the Newt Congress: The Black Caucus Regroups as Jesse Mulls a Third-Party Bid," *Washington Post*, Nov. 20, 1994.

6. Ibid.

7. Quoted in Bob Minzesheimer, "Most Minorities' Seats Safe; Their Power Depends on Democratic Control," *USA Today*, Oct. 24, 1994.

8. Quoted in *Baltimore Sun*, Dec. 3, 1994.

9. Under the institutional rules of the House, caucuses are called legislative service organizations (LSOs). They have been positioned to wield considerable influence over the public policy process. See R. A. Champagne and Leroy N. Rieselbach, "The Evolving Congressional Black Caucus," in *Blacks in the American Political System*, ed. Huey L. Perry (Gainesville: University of Florida Press, 1995); Susan W. Hammond, "Congressional Caucuses and Party Leaders in the House of Representatives," *Political Science Quarterly* 106 (1991): 277–94; Brian A. Loomis, "Congressional Caucuses and the Politics of Representation," in *Congress Reconsidered*, ed. Lawrence Dodd and Bruce I. Oppenheimer, 2d ed. (Washington, D.C.: Congressional Quarterly Press, 1981).

10. During the 103d Congress, forty CBC members had contributed $5,000 each in annual dues, and their organization had collected an additional $1,000 each from its thirty-six white associate members. The CBC also had space in a federal office building.

11. Quoted in Kenneth J. Cooper, "Plan to Curb Caucuses Draws Plenty of Heat; House Democrats Say Advocacy Would Suffer," *Washington Post*, Dec. 8, 1994.

12. Ibid.

13. Kenneth J. Cooper, "GOP Moves to Restrict Caucus Funds; Some Women, Blacks, and Hispanics Cry Foul," *Washington Post*, Dec. 7, 1994.

14. Gabriel Kahn, "Top Ten Interest Groups, Inside Congress," *Roll Call*, Sept. 11, 1995.

15. David Cloud, "GOP, to Its Own Great Delight, Enacts House Rules Changes," *Congressional Quarterly Weekly Report* 53 (Jan. 7, 1995): 13–15.

16. Charles E. Jones, "United We Stand, Divided We Fall: An Analysis of the Congressional Black Caucus's Voting Behavior, 1975–1980," *Phylon* 48, no. 1 (1987): 26–37; Arthur Levy and Susan Stoudinger, "Sources of Voting Cues for the Congressional Black Caucus," *Journal of Black Studies* 7 (1976): 29–45.

17. Levy and Stoudinger, "Sources of Voting Cues for the Congressional Black Caucus."

18. Bruce Robeck, "The Congressional Black Caucus," paper presented at meeting of the American Political Science Association, Chicago, Aug. 29–Sept. 2, 1974, 73.

19. Charles E. Jones, "Testing a Legislative Strategy: The Congressional Black Caucus's Action-Alert Communications Network," *Legislative Studies Quarterly* (1987): 521–37; Augustus Adair, "Black Legislative Influence in Federal Policy Decisions: The Congressional Black Caucus, 1971–1975," Ph.D. diss., Johns Hopkins University, 1976.

20. Jones, "United We Stand"; Charles E. Jones and Roxanne Gile, "The Influx of African-American Congressional Representation: Implications for the Congressional Black Caucus," paper presented at the annual meeting of the Midwest Political Science Association Meeting, Chicago, Apr. 1994; Harris, "On Symbolic and Material Caucus Power."

21. Carol M. Swain, *Black Faces, Black Interests: The Representation of African Americans in Congress*, 2d ed. (Cambridge: Harvard University Press, 1995), chap. 11.

22. David Bositis, *The Congressional Black Caucus in the 103d Congress* (Washington, D.C.: University of America Press, 1994), 35–37.

23. The list is compiled from data in Bositis, *Congressional Black Caucus*, 42–44.

24. See Jones, "United We Stand"; Jones and Gile, "Influx of African-American Congressional Representation."

25. Swain, *Black Faces, Black Interests*, chap. 4.

26. Larry Bartels, "Where the Ducks Are," paper presented at the Conference Honoring Stanley Kelley, Princeton, N.J., Oct. 27–28, 1995.

27. In June 1995, the CBC Foundation sponsored a summit to think of ways to combat the Republican agenda. Their meeting ended with leaders calling for more voter registration, public education, and coalition building with middle-class whites, poor people, and the elderly. However, no blueprint for action has emerged.

28. Barnett, "Congressional Black Caucus."

29. American Political Network, "Medicare Debate I: Protesters Interrupt Gingrich Speech," Aug. 8, 1995.

30. John Lewis, telephone interview with author, Nov. 15, 1995.

31. Kenneth J. Cooper, "Affirmative Action Warning; Congressman Says Clinton, GOP Should Not Exploit the Issue," *Washington Post*, June 6, 1995.

32. Research by Paul Sniderman and Thomas Piazza shows that the great majority of white Americans consider preferential treatment of minorities to be unfair to whites (Paul M. Sniderman and Thomas Piazza, *The Scar of Race* [Cambridge: Harvard University Press, 1993]). On this issue, the Democratic Party is widely seen as out of step with most Americans.

33. Charles Rangel, quoted in *Boston Globe*, Dec. 26, 1995.

CHAPTER 12

May Constitutional Democracies "Outlaw" a Political Party?

Walter F. Murphy

Unlike the Americans who met in Philadelphia during the summer of 1787, most founders of modern constitutional democracies would insist that political parties are crucial to the functioning of a polity. Parties play critical roles in creating, organizing, and expressing public opinion, formulating public policy, and operating government. In so acting, they operate as essential elements in the constitutional order. Nevertheless, most older constitutional texts, such as that of Norway, or even younger documents, such as those of Australia, India, Ireland, and France, provide scant indication that parties exist, much less play central political roles. Indeed, many such documents fail to mention parties at all.

In contrast, a few newer charters, like those of Hungary and the Russian Federation, not only specifically recognize the right of individual citizens to form and operate political parties but also impose certain duties on them. Article 3 (1) of the Hungarian text says, "Political parties may be freely founded and may act in freedom provided they show respect for the Constitution and the statutes of constitutional law." Article 13 of Boris Yeltsin's constitutional text conveys the same message in a more prolix style: "Ideological diversity is recognized in the Russian Federation. No state or mandatory ideology may be established. Political diversity and a multiparty system are recognized in the Russian Federation. Public associations are equal before the law." The final section of this article adds a more pointed limitation than does the Hungarian document: "The creation and activity of public associations whose goals or actions are aimed at forcibly changing the foundations of the constitutional system, violating the integrity of the Russian Federation, undermining the security of the state, creating armed formations or stirring up social, racial, national, or religious discord are prohibited."[1]

The model for these younger charters is the Basic Law of the Federal Republic of Germany. On the one hand, that text recognizes a right to establish political parties and—at least as interpreted by the Federal Constitutional Court in the Socialist Reich Party Case (1952) and the Schleswig-Holstein Voters' Association Case (1952)—raises them "to the rank of constitutional institutions," making parties "integral parts of [the] constitutional structure and [the] constitutionally ordered political life." On the other hand, Article 21 of the Basic Law both obliges parties to conduct their internal operations according to principles of democratic procedure and establishes machinery to declare them unconstitutional if they "seek to impair or abolish the free democratic order or to endanger the existence of the Federal Republic of Germany."

Although particular parties may wither and die—and a few may be executed—parties as institutions flourish in constitutional democracies. Even where the basic document ignores them, their existence and operations have received constitutional protection, either, as in the United States, through general textual provisions such as those guaranteeing rights to free speech, press, assembly, and association or, as in Canada, under the British North America Act (1867), describing the political system desired. Moreover, parties typically operate within webs of governmental regulations.

This chapter looks at a fundamental problem that mixture of rights and duties generates: Can a constitutional democracy legitimately exclude from peaceful electoral competition a party that has as its goal changing that polity to a totalitarian, dictatorial, or harshly authoritarian regime? (Hereafter, for simplicity's sake, I use the term "tyrannical"[2] for such systems.) Because of exclusion's implications not only for particular elections and general party alignments but also for the nature of constitutional democracy itself, I go beyond a positivist analysis of the legitimacy of such a ban in a specific political system, such as that of Germany, where both the founders and authoritative interpreters have concluded it is constitutional, or the United States, where Congress, the president, the Supreme Court, and the electorate have agreed that such a proscription is valid, providing the policy is cloaked in euphemisms (Murphy 1993b). Instead, I want to explore the question whether barring a party whose aim is to establish a tyrannical political system is compatible with the principles that underlie constitutional democracy.

My conclusion is that, although such a proscription may be stupid, cowardly, or even corrupt, it would not violate the basic principles of constitutional democracy. In several earlier writings (Murphy 1980, 1986a, 1990, 1992a, 1992b,

1993a, 1995), I have argued that, in a constitutional democracy, a systemic change that would deny the polity's fundamental values, even if it is made with meticulous respect for existing procedural rules, is invalid. This chapter moves beyond that controversial claim and tries to give separate if not equal justification for the contention that the norms of constitutional democracy allow a polity to curtail even the peaceful electoral activities of individuals, parties, and other organizations that would, if successful at the ballot box, destroy constitutional democracy and substitute tyrannical political structures. In short, it follows from the possibility of unconstitutional change that the polity could legitimately restrict activities of individuals and parties who propose to effect such a change.

At first, this conclusion seems itself to be dangerously subversive of free government. The immediate response is simple, clear, and, on first reading, appealing: Democracy means rule by the people, and to rule rationally the people must have access to all competing views and the capacity to choose among them (Meiklejohn 1948). It would follow that a constitutional democracy cannot bar a political party or any of its functional equivalents from proposing any public policy whatsoever. In a pair of his more famous dissents, Oliver Wendell Holmes summed up this argument: The best test of "truth," he said, is "the power of the thought to get itself accepted in the competition of the market" (*Gitlow v. New York* [1925]). "Freedom for the thought we hate" (*Schwimmer* [1929]) is not merely the ideal but also the supposed constitutional rule: "If, in the long run, the beliefs expressed in the proletarian dictatorship are destined to be accepted by the dominant forces of the community, the only meaning of free speech is that they should be given their chance and have their way" (*Gitlow*).

In the 1920s, Holmes's fatalistic relativism may have reflected orthodox democratic theory and seemed to have posed only minimal risks to civil society. It could be, however, that democratic theory is more complicated than the justice believed. A decade later, in fact, many former citizens of the Weimar Republic would have good reason to judge Holmes's conception of democratic theory perilously naive, even immoral. German national elections and peaceful formation of a governing parliamentary coalition brought the leader of National Socialism to the chancellorship. That succession triggered the quick death of democratic processes associated with free speech, assembly, and association as well as of all individual rights associated with constitutionalism. It is fair, therefore, to ask whether democratic theory really requires the polity to submit passively to those who would destroy it, indeed, to accord them full opportunity to do the deed.

By definition, constitutional democracy rests on a pair of political theories, constitutionalism as well as democracy. And the two may not always speak with the same voice (Sartori 1987, chs. 11–13, 15; Murphy 1993a; Murphy, Fleming, and Barber 1995, ch. 3). For, if democratic theory demands that the people shall rule, either directly or through their freely chosen representatives, a coherent theory of constitutionalism would deny the authority of any person, persons, or institutions, whether representing the people or not, to govern in certain ways. Thus, although constitutionalism is indifferent to a wide range of political structures, it cannot, consistently with its basic principles, be indifferent to *all* kinds of political structures. It can, for example, flourish under federal or unitary governments and within parliamentary or presidential systems. It cannot, however, exist in a system in which one group, party, or set of officials has power that is limited only by its own will. To the notion that would-be dictators who would destroy individual rights "should be given their chance and have their way" providing only they can convince enough voters to abandon free government, constitutionalism shouts a resounding no.

The argument presented here is that, *pace* American memories of misuses of authority running from the Alien and Sedition Acts through Lincoln's disregard of fundamental rights to a recent past populated by Joseph McCarthy, Richard Nixon, J. Edgar Hoover, and their ilk, a constitutional democracy has no obligation to allow political freedom to parties whose goal it is to destroy that system and the ideals on which it is based. On the contrary, constitutional democracy can fulfill its duties to itself and future generations by curtailing such efforts.

Distinctions

The first distinction, perhaps too obvious to be mentioned, is that between what a government or a people may do that is consistent with their basic principles and what they can do because of the physical power they exert. Those who in fact control the might of a nation can impose their will on the country. Thus, when I speak of what a government or a people may validly do, I do not imply that they lack power to act quite differently.

The second distinction, already alluded to, is between what merely does not violate the polity's basic norms and what is wise.[3] Thus, when I argue that a constitutional democracy can curb or even proscribe political parties that try to destroy free government, I do not imply that any particular constitutional democracy should undertake such action. The norms of democratic and constitutionalist theory guide as well as restrict political choices, but neither alone nor in combination do they substitute for prudence. John Rawls has come to somewhat similar conclusions about the demands of justice. He sees the issue of "toleration of the intolerant" as involving prudence rather than basic fairness.

"Justice," he writes, "does not require that men must stand idly by while others destroy the basis of their existence" (Rawls 1971, 218–19; 1993, 58–66). For him, "the question of tolerating the intolerant is directly related to that of the stability of a well-ordered society."

A third distinction is that between the constitutional text and the larger constitution. An authoritative constitutional text forms the core of any "constitution," but that larger being typically includes an untidy collection of general understandings, specific interpretations, official practices, unofficial customs and beliefs that social scientists call cultures, normative theories (such as constitutionalism and democracy), and aspirations for the achievement of a "good society."[4] Unless otherwise indicated, I use the term "constitution" with a small "c" in Aristotle's final sense, as denoting a way of life, including the norms and aspirations the society adopts, rather than referring merely to a document so labeled.[5]

A fourth distinction is a subset of the third: What conforms to the norms of the larger constitution and what conforms to ruling constitutional law may be quite different. As Sotirios A. Barber says, constitutional law—what judges or other authoritative interpreters decree the constitutional text requires—may be unconstitutional, a fact attested to in the United States by the Supreme Court's occasionally overruling its former self (1984, 118). As I have claimed elsewhere (Murphy 1986b; Murphy, Fleming, and Barber 1995, 262–76), for any constitutional democracy the question of who interprets the constitution is as critical— and as problematic—as what that constitution includes and what functions it is supposed to perform.

The Argument

Democratic Theory

Curbing political parties that propose to destroy the very essence of constitutional democracy poses more difficult normative problems for democratic than for constitutionalist theory, for democratic theory tends to equate "correct" political results with "the will of the people" as expressed through elections. To a great extent, democratic theory embraces both positivism and moral relativism. What makes governmental decisions morally binding in a democracy is not their conformity to higher norms but their having been adopted through open political processes: The people freely choose representatives, those representatives debate and enact a policy, and they are ready to stand for reelection. "The claim [for democracy] is most persuasively put," Michael Walzer says, "not in terms of what the people know, but in terms of who they are. They are the subjects of the law, and if the law is to bind them as free men and women, they must also be its makers" (1981, 383).

But the democratic claim to legitimacy is also based on a notion of equality that partakes of substance as much as procedure. Democratic theorists, including Walzer, pretty much agree that a fundamental assumption of democracy is the equality of citizens, though precisely what equality entails is controversial. After all, "One person, one vote" was not officially recognized as a principle of American democracy until the chief justiceship of Earl Warren, somewhat late in the Republic's history.

Oliver Wendell Holmes's version of democratic theory was not only brutally simple—"a law should be called good," he wrote Felix Frankfurter, "if it reflects the will of the dominant forces of the community even if it takes us to hell" (Mennel and Compston 1996, 19)—it was also naive and incomplete. He would have violated both the basic procedural norms of democratic theory, encapsulated in the term "open political processes," and its more substantive tenet of equality. He identified democratic government with government by a single act of will or several such acts closely connected in time. These two may not have much in common after that critical act or acts have occurred. For it is quite conceivable that a people may, at a given moment, agree to abolish free government and become slaves.[6] At the very least, democratic government requires not merely a single act, but continuing acts, of will. And the latter, in turn, require continuing opportunities to renew or revoke approval of public officials' conduct in office. Adoption of a tyrannical regime ends a people's opportunities to judge official actions and peacefully renew or revoke their consent.[7]

In short, Justice Holmes's concept of democracy included no temporal dimension. He saw government's objective as merely aggregating the people's *current* preferences. But, as James March and Johan Olsen point out, "Unless a democratic system can solve the problem of representing the future, changing interests of the unborn, it violates a rather fundamental underlying premise of democracy—that those who bear the costs of decision should have their interests adequately reflected in the choice" (1989, 146–47). Omission of a temporal dimension also offends against democracy's egalitarian norms. A current majority (or super-majority) that decides to end self-government treats as less than equal not only its own future self but also all other majorities who follow. In contrast, a temporal dimension extends democracy's objectives to include integrating current preferences with those, perhaps changed, preferences the existing majority and their successors might later wish to make.

It is true that almost all choices a current generation makes, whether to wage war, incur a national debt, or pursue any long-range policy, inhibit to some degree—and often a very painful degree—future options. A decision to wage war has an enormous impact on the future, whether that war be won or lost; by wiping out some existing gene pools, it at the very least shapes later generations. Public debts, as Thomas Jefferson often lamented, impose obligations on people who had no voice in the decision; it taxes them without representation, an outcome that democratic leaders from Tom Paine to Newt Gingrich have been wont to condemn. There is, however, a qualitative difference between requiring future generations to pay heavier taxes than they would have chosen and depriving those generations of all the rights typically recognized in constitutional democracies. In short, to reduce people's disposable income is not the same as transforming them from free citizens into subservient denizens. A people may peacefully repudiate most long-range policies their predecessors have enacted, but only as long as democratic processes remain open.

At minimum, citizens acting democratically are obliged to leave to themselves as well as their successors a continuing right to self-government. Therefore, because democratic theory must conceive of its political system as stretching across time, it cannot validate the current generation's depriving itself and future generations of the right to make political choices.[8] "By means of a constitution[al text]," Stephen Holmes argues, "generation *a* can help generation *c* from being sold into slavery by generation *b*" (1988, 226). If keeping political processes free and open is essential for a viable democratic theory,[9] it is democratic for government to protect its people against private citizens who would use violence to keep some other citizens from political participation. And it is as democratic for a polity to protect its citizens against parties that would attain public office in order to use the brute force of government to close democratic processes and destroy citizens' rights to speak, assemble, and vote.

Constitutionalism

Constitutionalism's commitment to individual rights eases the normative problems it might encounter in curtailing parties whose goal is to destroy such rights. Constitutionalism openly posits that a truly civil society must foster certain substantive values—the most basic of which is the dignity of each person—and asserts a governmental duty to protect such values against its own officials, private factions, and even the mass of its own citizens acting peacefully through regular political channels. For constitutionalism, democracy's procedural criteria are at most necessary, not sufficient, conditions for the legitimacy of political structures or particular policies. Constitutionalism imposes an additional criterion: political arrangements and policies must also accord with certain substantive values, not merely with those listed in a constitutional text but also with principles relating to the dignity of all human beings.[10] Because establishment of a tyrannical regime is squarely at odds with constitutionalism's principles, that normative theory would brand as illegitimate all efforts, peaceful as well as violent, so to replace a constitutional democracy.

Difficulties

However convincing the logic of my basic argument, it spawns several problems. Some of these relate to the probability of mistakes, destructively selfish even if honest, committed by ambitious and egotistical public officials. Others relate to normative issues of radical change in a constitutional democracy.

Emotional Difficulties

First of all, the argument presented here is likely to raise the hackles of many Americans who fear abuses of power. Memories of Cold War hysteria and Red scares are recent enough to smart. State and federal officials were obsessed with discovering communists and communist influence behind every American failure. Only a few leaders like William O. Douglas both understood and had the courage to say publicly that American communist leaders were no more than "miserable merchants of unwanted ideas" (Douglas, dissenting in *Dennis* [1951]). Marxists could not even make many converts among African Americans, surely at the time a downtrodden minority (Record 1951; Draper 1957; Howe and Coser 1957). There was more truth than humor in the joke, circulated while the prosecutions in *Dennis* were under way, that most of the dues paid to the American Communist Party came indirectly from the FBI, whose undercover agents and informants outnumbered committed members of the party. American efforts against domestic communism were epitomized by the fact that Junius Irving Scales, the only person to go to jail in the United States for "knowing" membership in the Communist Party, had rejected that affiliation years before his conviction.

I share this emotional reaction, which is why I have insisted on the distinction between constitutionality and wisdom. As Felix Frankfurter said in his concurring opinion in *Dennis*: "Focusing attention on constitutionality tends to make constitutionality synonymous with wisdom. When legislation touches freedom of thought and freedom of speech, such a tendency is a formidable enemy of the free spirit." Christopher Eisgruber's principle of "no pain, no claim" is especially relevant here: "Only those constitutional theorists who ascribe painful consequences to constitutional fidelity can claim to offer genuine theories of constitutional meaning" (1993, 7).

A conclusion that excluding tyrannical parties is legitimate carries significant consequences, for, in a constitutional democracy, any public policy that violates the polity's basic norms is, by definition, forbidden. Were it "unconstitutional" for a polity to protect itself against tyrannical parties, constitutional democracy would face a dilemma: either to permit its own destruction or, by violating its fundamental principles, deny the validity of those tenets. If, however, those principles permit defense against parties who would use the processes of constitutional democracy to destroy constitutional democracy, the issue switches from one of legitimacy to one of prudence and should move us to focus on that aspect of the problem.

Practical Difficulties

The costs of exclusion are apt to be high, and weighing putative harms against expected benefits is more a matter of what Aristotle aptly called practical judgment than of constitutional interpretation. Some of these costs, however, have serious implications for constitutional democracy and its basic normative principles and need to be addressed.

Lost Opportunities for Co-option

Deciding whether the odds of socializing would-be tyrants into the norms of constitutional democracy warrant the risks requires political wisdom.[11] One can cite examples of success and failure in making these estimates. Among the more dramatic successes was Bismarck's decision (though Imperial Germany was only reluctantly crawling toward constitutional democracy) to tempt radicals to work for social reform through rather than against the system. Eduard Bernstein's decision to utilize this opening made him anathema to militant Marxists, but a great deal of social and some political reform did come; and Germany's modern (and powerful) Social Democratic Party had its first reincarnation (Gay 1952). So, too, after World War II, a legally tolerated Italian Communist Party moved from a revolutionary Marxist movement to a prickly reform organization and, before shattering, helped create the concept of "Euro-Communism." The neo-Fascist MSI (Movimento Sociale Italiano) made somewhat the same transition, actively competing for seats in parliament and even, during much of 1994, participating as a partner in Silvio Berlusconi's governing coalition. Mussolini's heirs carried on this work despite Article 12 of the constitutional text, "The reorganization in any form whatever of the now dissolved Fascist party is prohibited," and the so-called Scelba Law that criminalized efforts to renew the party.

On the other hand, Weimar's inaction against Nazi threats brought tragic results.[12] Despite the hopes of democratic politicians and the prayers of Vatican diplomats, many of whom assumed that Hitler and his crew did not mean what they were saying (Friedländer 1966; Lewy 1964; Rhodes 1973), participation in free political processes did nothing to civilize the Nazis; on the contrary, it gave them an opportunity to murder in the name of the state. So, too, the chance to compete for votes in Italy had done nothing to tame Mussolini and his Black Shirts.

Given German history, banning the neo-Nazi Socialist Reich Party (SRP) seemed wise to the government in 1951 and constitutional to the *Bundesverfassungsgericht* in 1952. The party's message, including anti-Semitic vitriol, had not changed. The leaders of the SRP were not only ridiculing the Federal Republic and its allegedly demeaning relationship with the Western occupiers—an ominous reprise of the Nazi chorus about German humiliation at Versailles—but were also organizing a version of the old Hitler Youth. And, seven years after the end of the war, before the economic miracle had delivered Germans from the hunger of desperate poverty, it was impossible to know how many people yearned for the fleshpots of the Third Reich. After all, Weimar had died in 1933 without much of a record of good government; most West German citizens were strangers to constitutional democracy; and, until the final stages of the war, support for the Nazi regime had been strong and solid (Grunberger 1971), though small pockets of resistance endured (Gill 1994; Powers 1997).

In that same era, the threat of the revamped German Communist Party was real. Immediately after the war, Communist parties in East Germany, Poland, Hungary, and the rest of Eastern Europe showed how an organized group opposed to constitutional democracy could abort that system. Most of these countries began the postwar era with what looked like open political competition; but soon Marxist parties, backed by the power of the Red Army, destroyed both constitutionalism and democracy.

In the context of the 1950s, it is difficult to say West German officials were acting imprudently when they invoked Article 21 of the Basic Law and persuaded the *Bundesverfassungsgericht* to outlaw the Communist Party (Communist Party Case [1956]). Kenneth H. F. Dyson has questioned whether the purpose of that ban was "to protect the constitution's free democratic basic order or . . . by restrictive constitutional interpretation to protect a particular economic and social system against criticism and reform" (1974, 65). If exclusion had been directed against "criticism and reform," it violated the tenets of constitutional democracy. But, in light of what had just happened to the east, it would have taken a very naive person to believe that the objectives of the KPD (Kommunistische Partei Deutschlands) were "criticism and reform." It is tempting to retrofit our perceptions of a failed empire back four decades; but then the Cold War was close to being a hot war (indeed, was very hot on the Korean peninsula), and it was quite unclear who would be the buriers and who would be the buried. Would it have been wise for German officials to shrug off with "it can't happen here as it did to our next-door neighbors" the threat that a strong and lawful Communist Party posed to free government?

One can ask much the same question about the wisdom of the Russians' outlawing the old Communist Party of the Soviet Union and seizing its assets in 1991.[13] Party leaders had been adamantly opposed to the new regime's struggle to educate itself and its citizens for constitutional democracy, and the old guard's attempted coup against Mikhail Gorbachëv hardly indicated devotion to civil society. That later, during the presidential campaign of 1996, some Communists would claim to be reformers who merely wanted to go slowly in building the new political and economic order and would express willingness to compete within the rules of constitutional democracy tells very little about either their immediate aims in 1991 or their long-range plans. Whatever message they tried to transmit through peaceful competition has been obscured by their efforts in 1993 to establish a "national salvation front" allied with Vladimir Zhirinovsky's right-wing, anti-Semitic, Liberal Democratic Party to crush the developing political system. Moreover, during the campaign of 1996, Gennadi A. Zyuganov, the Communist Party's candidate, spoke ominously of a secret agenda, while praising Stalin. In sum, little in Russian history,[14] the course of Soviet communism, or Russia's hesitant moves toward constitutional democracy justifies the conclusion that, in 1991, the party's threat to civil society was merely a phantom reflected in Yeltsin's vodka or that participation in electoral processes would cause its members to be reborn as good constitutional democrats.

Who Guards the Excluders?

Ambition, power, and distrust snuggle warmly together. Even democratically chosen officials are apt to mistake opposition to their own policies as opposition to the political system. It was easy, for example, for Federalists like Luther Martin to believe Thomas Jefferson was a Jacobin radical who would transplant the French Revolution in American soil. This sort of flaw is compounded by a human tendency to conflate one's own career with the advancement of much-needed public policies. In short, we should be suspicious of any official's labeling his or her opponents as subversives.

Can a constitutional democracy establish procedures to minimize the chances of a corrupt or mistaken exclusion? There are two obvious, interrelated, problems here: What evidence should be conclusive, and who should have authority to decide? We can address the first only in the abstract. There should be a presumption against exclusion but not an irrebuttable one. Speeches of a party's leaders, party platforms, and internal memoranda—in sum, its avowed aims—may, as they did with the Nazi and Communist Parties in Germany and the Fascists in Italy, provide probative evidence. So, too, may the party's scheme of internal organization, its history and heroes, its links to similar organizations in other countries, and the behavior of its rank and file as well as its leaders.

Even if we agreed on these and similar criteria, the second question would remain crucial: Who will gather and judge the evidence? The worst solution would be to write into the constitutional text the principle of banning parties that warred on constitutional democracy and then neglect to designate responsible decision makers. Both the Hungarian and Russian documents commit this sin. At the very least—and there is likely to be more—such an omission casts a shadow on the legitimacy of any particular exclusion. As one of the dissenting judges on the Russian Constitutional Court said in explaining his vote against the validity of 1991 Yeltsin's decrees banning the old Communist Party: "They were issued by an inappropriate person. The President did not have authority to issue those decrees" (*Current Digest of the Post-Soviet Press* 44, no. 48 [1992], 12).[15] The new text, adopted in 1993, did nothing to clarify the issue.

At least in common-law countries, the executive branch may be in the best position to gather the data needed to decide on exclusion. But reliance on the executive branch to exclude runs grave risks of abuse of authority. Even Abraham Lincoln does not provide a happy model. His military action against armed guerrilla bands of Southern sympathizers in Indiana and the border states, though ultimately held unconstitutional by the Supreme Court in *Milligan* (1866), was not unreasonable: These people had taken up arms against the United States; they were not using political forums to try to peacefully persuade others. The president's efforts to imprison such men may have trespassed on congressional authority; but, in this regard, he did not interfere with free electoral processes. One could even defend his "detaining" Maryland legislators who might have voted for secession in 1861. On the other hand, imprisoning editors and other private citizens who criticized his constitutional interpretation, locking up a lawyer who tried to defend a captured captain of a Southern raider against charges of piracy, and exiling a dissenting congressman did not display a leader who revered government of, by, and for the people.

Yeltsin, as would be expected, performed no better. However one judges his decrees in 1991 banning the Communist Party, his efforts in 1993 to deny places on the ballot to two parties that were urging voters to reject his proposed constitutional text and in 1995 to bar several minor parties as well as the larger Yabloko party smack of partisan efforts to win particular elections, not to protect constitutional democracy. The Russian Supreme Court agreed and reversed the Central Election Commission's decision to strike these parties and their candidates from the ballot (*New York Times*, Nov. 4, 1995).

Delegating to the legislature authority to exclude may inhibit gathering data in most countries, though the American Congress has shown that legislative investigations can be excellent mechanisms for collecting reliable information. Furthermore, the large and usually diverse membership of legislatures may make them less apt than executive branches to act arbitrarily. The Parliament of the United Kingdom has historically had authority to outlaw parties and, in modern times, has not abused that prerogative, at least outside of Ireland. On the other hand, resting such authority in legislatures, whose members do not feel so tightly bound by, or even aware of, an ancient parliamentary culture, may court disaster. In most constitutional democracies, legislative action is subject to judicial review,[16] and that check provides an additional, though hardly insuperable, barrier to legislative abuse.

There is, of course, the possibility of relegating to judges responsibility for deciding whether to exclude a party. In common-law systems, the judicial process would most likely provide a poor investigative institution. In those systems, courts are largely passive. They lack, as Justice Robert H. Jackson once said, "a self-starting capacity" (1955, 24). Judges must wait for someone to bring a legal action before them for decision; they cannot act on their own initiative. Their investigative instruments, like a special master, would probably not be effective. On the other hand, in civil-law systems, procurators, although members of an independent judiciary, have wide investigatory powers, as several former Italian prime ministers, hundreds of lesser officials, and even some Mafiosi godfathers have painfully learned.

Germany's Basic Law puts judges at center stage. As augmented by statute, Article 21 authorizes the government to present evidence to the Constitutional Court and ask the judges to ban a party. The party may respond with its counterevidence. The judges then hold hearings, listen to arguments, review the evidence, and decide. These judges, operating within a civil-law context, are free from a limitation their common-law colleagues would face: German judges may gather their own evidence if they are not satisfied with what the government and the party have offered.

The Basic Law also avoids some psychological problems that the American form of judicial review creates. When reviewing congressional legislation dealing with almost any subject, especially when it has the president's approval, the justices frequently beat their breasts, professing anguish at playing an undemocratic role. Although a cynic might draw a different conclusion, they are probably under considerable internal pressure to find that the constitution permits the challenged action. Judges of the German Constitutional Court do not review the legislature's constitutional interpretation but make their own. Furthermore, the Germans have been more sophisticated (or perhaps merely more candid) than their American cousins in describing their political system as a constitutional democracy rather than a representative democracy and thus accepting, without apology, that restraining the choices of democratically elected officials is one of their most important functions.

Delegating responsibility to judges by no means ensures impartiality on such emotionally charged issues. As Benjamin N. Cardozo once noted, "The great tides and currents which engulf the rest of men do not turn aside in their course and pass the judges by" (1921, 168). The Russian Constitutional Court's affirmation of part of Yeltsin's decrees outlawing the old Communist Party of the Soviet Union may provide a case directly in point. At a press conference the day after the decision, Viktor Luchin, one of the dissenting judges, said: "To a significant degree, the Constitutional Court's decision was dictated by the situation. What it reflects is the political realities of the day, not the spirit of the Constitution. We acted not as legal experts but as politicians and political scientists guided by expediency rather than by the law—although I am not condemning anyone" (*Current Digest of the Post-Soviet Press* 44, no. 48 [1992], 12).

Moreover, acting as investigating officials or as judges, magistrates may pursue their own agendas. Despite the numerous victories of the Italian campaign, dubbed *mani puliti* (clean hands), against widespread bribery at the highest levels, suspicions have been rife that magistrates concentrated on leaders with whom they had disagreed and even fired occasional salvos at their critics in academia.[17]

Although judges are apt to want to make wise, as well as constitutional, policy—and thus to consider factors that do not fit a purist's conception of "legal" concerns[18]—and, as the Italian experience shows, are occasionally not above pursuing personal vendettas, they are, on the whole, less likely than elected officials to perceive much self-interest (beyond preservation of the political system itself) in banning a particular party. German procedures dramatically reduce the possibility that a party will be excluded merely because it threatens the political power of a ruling coalition or the careers of elected officials. But even this method is not infallible. No decision-making process is. Certainly, adopting Oliver Wendell Holmes's policy of allowing all parties to compete for votes has produced disaster. At most, we can only reduce the risks of error by estimating the likely costs and probabilities of the errors each procedure might produce.

INFORMATIONAL COSTS

Exclusion may prevent citizens from gaining information that they wish to obtain about the political options open to them. This problem is much more serious for democratic than for constitutionalist theory, even if one accepts that the choice of a tyrannical system is simply not open under the norms of democratic theory. Exclusion, even the possibility of exclusion, reflects wariness about the political maturity and good sense of the electorate. But then so does a democratic precommitment to bind a majority and its representatives to follow certain procedures (Holmes 1988). Even John Hart Ely (1980), an eloquent advocate of democracy over constitutionalism, devotes much of his major work to showing how the American form of democracy restricts the range of democratic choice. For its part, constitutionalism has as one of its primary purposes limiting the power of ruling groups, including democratic majorities. Although some recent justices of the Supreme Court do not seem to realize it, the Federalists won the great debate of 1787–88, and their purpose in pitting power against power and ambition against ambition was to limit democratic government. As James Madison quoted himself as saying at the Constitutional Convention, "In all cases where a majority are united by a common interest or passion, the rights of the minority are in danger" (quoted in Farrand 1966, 1:136). A year later, he wrote to Jefferson, explaining his conversion to the necessity of a bill of rights:

> Wherever the real power in a Government lies, there is the danger of oppression. In our Governments the real power lies in the majority of the community, and the invasion of private rights is *chiefly* to be apprehended, not from acts of Government contrary to the sense of its constituents, but from acts in which the Government is the mere instrument of the major number of the Constituents.... Wherever there is an interest and a power to do wrong, wrong will generally be done. (Smith 1995, 1:564–65)

Wariness about the electorate's judgment reflects not disdain for citizens but the same hard-headed understanding of the flawed nature of humanity as does the prayer, "Lead us not into temptation." Democratic and constitutionalist precommitments reflect more of Rousseau's notion of forcing people to be free than we might like to think.

Theoretical Difficulties

Better Dead than Red?

Perhaps the strand of argument about binding the future proves too much, even for the limited purpose of preserving freedom of political choice. After all, a constitutional democracy may face conditions under which its people have only the options of accepting a quasi-totalitarian system or of being exterminated. Under such circumstances, citizens may reasonably prefer to be Red (or black, brown, or some other color) than dead. Does the temporal dimension of democratic theory require martyrdom?

The first response is itself a question: To what extent would citizens face a free choice? Coerced agreement is not what we mean when we speak of the expression of democratic preferences.[19] But, leaving that important issue aside, a people could agree to submit for now in the hope that they or their children could later regain a system of free government. They would, in effect, be trying to maintain the possibility of a civil society. Such a choice is hardly happy, but we have no data that indicate the dead can maintain constitutional democracy for themselves or their posterity.[20]

A related question arises: May a nation legitimately abandon constitutional democracy when it faces a domestic crisis that overwhelms established political processes? The constitutional texts of many polities anticipate such contingencies by prescribing procedures for the temporary suspension of democratic and constitutional guarantees. The American document provides the least guidance, the German Basic Law perhaps the most.[21] The point is that temporary suspension of constitutional democracy, providing it is accomplished according to rules laid down in advance that clarify what opens and closes such "a state of siege," differs greatly from abandoning constitutional democracy and its scheme of values (Finn 1990).

"Perpetual Constitutions" and Future Choice

Does establishment of any permanent constitutional order violate the future's right to self-government? The question is fair, though any answer must be complex. In 1790, Noah Webster claimed that "the very attempt to make *perpetual* constitutions, is the assumption of a right to controul the opinions of future generations; and to legislate for those over whom we have as little authority as we have over a nation in Asia" (47). Without doubt, any constitutional arrangement, especially if written into a covenant that citizens and public officials take seriously, restricts not only current but also future choices. Indeed, the basic purpose of constitutional agreements, often likened to Ulysses's binding himself to the mast and putting wax in his crewmen's ears so he could safely hear the legendary call of the Sirens, is precisely to constrain political choices.

The critical difference between an agreement to form a tyrannical system and a constitutional democracy is that in the former the people submit to masters, and in the latter they unite to protect their right to self-government under conditions that they believe will also best protect other rights. In sum, the purpose of constitutional democracy is to preserve as much individual dignity, independence, and autonomy as group living allows. Perhaps paradoxically, achieving that purpose often requires what some of the American founders termed "energetic government." To substitute a tyrannical system for constitutional democracy would require a revolution.

Because constitutional democracy is compatible with a broad range of structures and policies, citizens have wide room to change governmental structures and public policies. The sole requirement is that these must not be inconsistent with self-government and the protection of individual liberty. Even Jefferson, who was as implacable a foe of "perpetual constitutions" as was Noah Webster, would have put an enormous limitation on political transformations: "Nothing is unchangeable," he wrote, "but the inherent and unalienable rights of man" (letter to John Cartwright, June 5, 1824, in Lipscomb 1903, 16:48).

In a real sense, then, both democratic and constitutionalist theory restrict legitimate political change. They also allow government to curb those people and organizations who would use free and open processes to destroy the polity's fundamental values. In sum, both normative theories guard against political self-destruction. But what is self-destruction and what is self-improvement is not always self-evident. Reasonable men and women may reasonably—and passionately—disagree. The norms underlying constitutional democracy speak clearly about the legitimate goals of politics; but both theories become more vague about valid means. Both, therefore, carry a severe risk that overly ambitious or misguided officials will squelch the very values they claim to be protecting. The earlier point about normative theories not substituting for prudence still holds.

Is Constitutional Democracy "Perpetual"?

It seems that the logic of this chapter requires the conclusion that, once a people have adopted constitutional democracy, they, as well as future generations, are forever trapped in that sort of political system unless "freed" by foreign or domestic crises of a massive sort or a (temporarily) populist revolution. Does it follow, then, that constitutional democracy may ban any party that is radical in the true sense of that term, that is, any party that wants changes that go to the root of the system?

The answer is largely, but not completely, no. That qualified response provides additional cause for worry.[22] Let me back up a bit. The gist of the argument for constitutional democracy runs along these lines: We are intelligent men and women who think we can choose our form of government by "reflection and choice." Reason and experience convince us that constitutional democracy is the best form of government for achieving a mix of protections from our fellow citizens and from public officials, on the one hand, and, on the other, a capacity to aggregate power to accomplish goals beyond the reach of individuals acting alone or in small groups.

This form of government, we believe, best protects those values Benjamin N. Cardozo summed up in *Palko v. Connecticut* (1937) under the rubric of "ordered liberty." Not only do reason and experience lead us to try to create a constitutional democracy, but the legitimacy of that sort of system depends heavily on reasoned argument buttressed by experience, rather than on threats of violence. Thus, constitutional democracy has a double appeal to people who value reason.

Indeed, despite objecting to "perpetual constitutions," Noah Webster claimed that successful constitutional government would create an "empire of reason."

But does not the primacy of reason, tested by experience, raise additional problems for my argument? Barber, for example, maintains that a full commitment to reason allows only a provisional commitment to constitutional democracy because we must be open to rational persuasion about the moral necessity, or at least desirability, of systemic transformation of the polity (1993, 60–61, 186–87, 232–34, 265n; 1984, 49–51, 59–61).[23] And that openness must also entail openness to radical political parties. I agree. Still, a plenary commitment to reason does not permit *every* sort of systemic transformation, only those that will, at least equally as well as constitutional democracy, protect the capacity of humans to reason together about basic values and political change and to carry out changes that reason indicates. Thus, constitutional democracy would allow a transformation to another system that would enlarge reason's empire or strengthen its reign. But a move from constitutional democracy to a quasi-totalitarian system, except when forced by a stronger foreign power or temporarily during otherwise unmanageable domestic emergencies, would restrict reason's ambit for all citizens except the ruler and his or her coterie. Moreover, it is far from obvious that such a system would push even that elite to rule by reason.[24]

Tyrannical systems aside, the question would remain about what other kinds of transformations might be validly open to a constitutional democracy. I have not yet seen any options I would willingly accept. I do not, however, mean this response as anything more than a rejection of the other models, theocratic and secular, the world has witnessed in this century and also a less firm rejection of representative democracy unrestricted by constitutionalism.[25]

Someday we may be able to imagine and create a kind of political system that protects, better than does constitutional democracy, our capacity to reason together and more efficiently advances the values of individual human dignity. Finality, as Disraeli said, is not in the language of politics. When—if—the day comes when we can envision a practically attainable political order that will better protect those values, constitutional democracy's commitment to reason will demand that the change be made and that the polity encourage, not simply permit, political parties to advocate adoption of the new system. (Experience, of course, may dictate that we proceed slowly in trying to turn such a vision into reality.)

The thorniest problem of all involves our ability to discern the difference between a new system that would enhance our lives and one that would enslave us. Once more, we return to issues of practical wisdom.

Notes

1. *The Current Digest of the Post-Soviet Press* 45, no. 45 (1993), 4 ff., translates and reprints the entire text. See also Article 29:

1. Everyone is guaranteed freedom of thought and of speech.

2. Propaganda or agitation that instigates social, racial, national, or religious hatred and enmity is not permitted. The propaganda of social, racial, national, religious, or linguistic superiority is prohibited. . . .

5. Freedom of the press is guaranteed. Censorship is prohibited.

2. One can question the appropriateness of this term, but, with the possible exception of North Korea, no regime has yet been able to do more than aspire to being totalitarian, that is, to break down the distinction between private and public aspects of life and totally to control all of its denizens' choices.

3. This differentiation is more complex than it might seem. Some American constitutional theorists reject the notion that their "constitution" opposes justice and lawfulness. Eisgruber both analyzes American theorists who try to distinguish or merge justice and constitutionality and constructs an appealing theory of his own to justify his belief that one of the purposes of the "American Constitution" (a term he does not explicitly define) is "to foster the prudent pursuit of justice" (1993, 14). I agree with much of what Eisgruber says about the "American Constitution," either as merely the text or as a larger conception. Indeed, any reader who takes the document seriously must agree. (I do not, however, imply that all interpreters, on and off the bench, take that charter seriously.) After all, the Preamble lists as one of its basic purposes "to establish Justice." My assumption in this chapter, which I think is about as close to self-evident truth as we are likely to come in this flawed world, is merely that fallible humans cannot construct a constitution, whether text or system, that can ensure that every public policy it permits will be wise or just. I do not think that Eisgruber would dispute this limited claim.

4. Some commentators and judges, mostly in the United States, also claim that the "constitution" includes the "intent" or understanding of the founding generation(s). Justice Antonin Scalia (1989) has offered the most eloquent presentation of this claim; the problems with such claims are enormous. Often, perhaps typically, the explication of such "intent" or "understanding" boils down to this: "I am an intelligent person of good will and judgment. The framers were also intelligent people of good will and judgment. Therefore, they must have intended or understood the document's words to mean what I would have intended or understood had I been a framer." For discussions and bibliographies, including a slightly abridged reprinting of Scalia's article, see Murphy, Fleming, and Barber (1995, 112–14, 231–43, 389–93).

5. For differentiations of *constitution* with a small *c* and a capital *C*, see Harris 1993.

6. My contention, of course, is that such a decision would fall under John Stuart Mill's famous exception to his general principle of individual liberty.

7. Even Central and Eastern Europe, where tyrannical rule was overthrown in 1989–90 more peacefully than anyone had imagined possible, experienced considerable violence during the early days of the Velvet Revolution. The Communist leaders acceded not to

the outcome of free elections but to the very real threat of widespread, violent revolt, which, when Gorbachëv refused to intervene, would have probably meant their own deaths, as indeed happened with Nicolae Ceauşescu. Augusto Pinochet's relinquishment of the presidency of Chile in 1988–89 may seem to be another exception, but it is a complicated one. He had no intention of allowing fair competition until his supposed lackeys on the Constitutional Court ordered the government to allow his opponents equal time on state-owned television. Even after his defeat at the polls was apparent, Pinochet ordered troops into the streets and convened his junta. The air force's chief of staff, however, had been miffed at Pinochet's favoritism toward the army and held an impromptu news conference on the steps of the presidential palace and, by publicly conceding electoral defeat, forced Pinochet to concede.

8. There are, of course, further complications. For instance, the refractions caused by every known means of representation make it difficult to be certain about a people's current preferences. How can one then speak of the preferences of the future other than by, as Judge Learned Hand would have put it, "shoveling smoke"? Perhaps the preference we can identify with most assurance that rational men and women would prefer is the right to have some significant choices about the kind of society in which they would exist and the sorts of lives they could lead. In the political realm, so a democratic theorist would argue, such a preference would require a form of democratic governance. That sort of conclusion rests, however, on several typical—and typically unspoken—assumptions of modern Western societies that have achieved both large measures of economic development and constitutional democracy, the most obvious of which is that there will be enough basic necessities like food available to sustain life so that human beings may make meaningful choices. This conclusion might not hold in many areas of the world, such as the Horn of Africa. In places like that, preference for survival would probably come first. "Being," as Franklin Roosevelt once remarked, "comes before well being." There are also deeper cultural assumptions at work here about the desirability of individual autonomy. Compare Nandy 1989 and Vaidyanathan 1989.

The problem becomes even more complex when one adds the dimension of the past. One might, as Thomas Jefferson did, simply say that "life belongs in usufruct to the living." But then one runs afoul of the legitimacy of all sorts of traditional bonds that tie a people together and validate processes of decision making as well as more overtly substantive values.

9. My argument, of course, parallels that of "militant" or "fighting democracy," which Karl Loewenstein developed six decades ago (1937a, 1937b, 1938a, 1938b). The opinion of the *Bundesverfassungsgericht* in the Socialist Reich Party Case (1952) offers a more recent exposition but from within the framework of "fighting democracy" itself.

10. See the German Constitutional Court's discussion of this issue in the Southwest Case (1951); see also the Privacy of Communications Case (1970), which Kommers (1997) calls the Klass Case:

> Constitutional provisions must not be interpreted in isolation, but rather so they are consistent with the Basic Law's fundamental principles and system of values. . . . It is especially significant that the Constitution . . . has decided in favor of a "militant democracy" that does not submit to abuse of basic rights for an attack on the liberal

order of the state. Enemies of the Constitution must not be allowed to endanger, impair, or destroy the existence of the state while claiming protection of rights granted [*sic*] by the Basic Law. (Translated in Murphy and Tanenhaus 1977, 660)

11. In a sense, this problem is the mirror image of that which Giuseppe DiPalma (1990) examines, for the task is not to persuade those in office to loosen their grip on power and accommodate themselves to constitutional democracy but to persuade those who have not had power and want it badly to temper their ambitions and accept the restraints constitutional democracy imposes on rulers and aspiring rulers.

12. One of the charges against Weimar was that it took a politically neutral stance toward extremist parties. In fact, however, Weimar enacted ample legislation to cope with the Nazis and Communists, including sedition laws, a ban against paramilitary organizations, and special statutes allowing the government to implement its authority under Article 48—which permitted the president to declare a state of emergency. The Republic also kept intact §128 of the *Criminal Code* of 1871, which forbade secret political societies. The government often did react swiftly and harshly against Communists; but, for a variety of reasons, enforcement against groups from the Right was typically feeble. Finn 1990, ch. 4, and Office of the U.S. Chief of Counsel 1946, 2:10 ff.

13. In 1992, the Russian Constitutional Court, by a vote of 13–2, handed down a ruling that was widely called "ambiguous," a characterization caused in part by the fact that the court announced its decision without issuing, at the time, any opinion to explain or justify its decision. The judges upheld those parts of the decrees prohibiting further activities by the party and disbanding the organization at the level of the republic, province, and city. On the other hand, the court said that lower level organizations could be relieved of responsibility for the actions of higher officials. In addition, the judges held that seizing the party's assets was unconstitutional. Two judges dissented. *New York Times*, Dec. 1, 1992; and *Current Digest of the Post-Soviet Press* 44, no. 48 (1992), 11–13. It should be noted that Yeltsin's decrees and the Constitutional Court's rulings came before adoption of the current constitutional text in December 1993. In October 1993, Yeltsin's Ministry of Justice suspended the activities of the party's successor, but the ban was lifted in time to compete in the elections of December 1993.

14. Victor Sergeyev and Nikolai Biryukov (1993) see almost no democratic roots in Russian history; Nicolai Petro (1996) finds much more hope in the past.

15. Because Yeltsin and the court both acted before adoption of the current constitutional text and well before any constitutional "tradition" or even long usage had developed, it is unclear how one judges who then had authority to exclude a political party— or to perform many other governmental functions.

16. Even many actions of the British Parliament are subject to review by the European Court of Justice, which can declare legislation and executive orders void as violations of the European Community's agreements. The European Court of Human Rights, located in Strasbourg, performs a somewhat analogous function in that it can declare that national actions contravene the European Convention on Human Rights.

17. The efforts of some magistrates to imprison enemies became especially noticeable when they indicted their principal academic critic, Professor Giuseppe Di Federico. Over the decades, he and members of his Center for the Study of the Ordinary Judiciary

at Bologna had published a series of articles and monographs detailing how many magistrates had failed the entry examination and how, once they had passed that examination, they manipulated the system for personal financial gain. Several times magistrates had warned Di Federico to stop his attacks, threatening to "get" him if he continued. He did continue; and, in 1995, magistrates brought formal, though frivolous, criminal charges, which in true Italian fashion were still in trial more than two years later.

18. At least since the time of Jefferson, some Americans have bemoaned, while other have celebrated, the inevitable mixture of concerns about practical policy and abstract legal principles that typify judicial decision making. Indeed, much of the scholarship in the subfield of public law in political science addresses (and documents) this dual involvement, not only in the United States but also in most other constitutional democracies. For a recent study of those phenomena in the Russian Federation, see Sharlet 1993.

19. The problem of deciding what conditions determine whether consent is freely given and thus binds the giver is at least as old as Aristotle and as recent as pending cases regarding the law of contracts and annulments of marriage. For general discussions, see Herzog 1989, Raz 1987, and Murphy 1992a. Economists, especially those concerned with "rational choice," have developed a huge literature that is relevant to consent. See in particular Buchanan 1991, Buchanan and Brennan 1985, and Buchanan and Tullock 1962.

20. Of course, no student of American parties would claim that deceased persons are always unable to help maintain a regime in office. Boss Hague was not alone in possessing the power to raise the dead on election day.

21. See especially Articles 115a–115l. The Spanish constitutional charter of 1978 also makes elaborate provisions for a state of siege in Articles 55 and 116. Article 56 of the new Russian constitutional text has more general provisions, but it specifically exempts from emergency restriction a long list of rights including those to life, dignity (which encompasses protection against torture), personal honor and familial privacy, freedom of conscience and religion, private property, housing, access to the courts, counsel, presumption of innocence, reimbursement for illegal governmental action, and protection against double jeopardy, ex post facto laws, and testifying against oneself, one's spouse, or close relatives.

22. I mention in passing two other such causes for concern. First is the problem of gradual systemic transformation from constitutional democracy. The reasoning I have used here would apply to that situation, but the practical difficulties, including but not limited to those of recognition of the change, would be far more serious. Second is the problem, however open or rapid the attempt at transformation, of whose duty it is to stand up and shout foul. The short reply is "All citizens, in and out of public office." A long answer would have to take into account the institutional structures and procedures of specific constitutional democracies.

23. I am indebted to Barber for helping to clarify my thinking by arguing with me, a task he performs with great gusto and skill.

24. One could make a strong case that brutal dictators like Adolf Hitler, Benito Mussolini, Francisco Franco, Josef Stalin, Gamal Abdel Nasser, Hafez al-Assad, Mu'ammar Qadafi, Saddam Hussein, "Papa Doc" Duvalier, Mao Zedong, Augusto Pinochet, and Joseph Mobutu have been cunning, shrewd, and even quite adept at deploying some versions of rational choice. It would be fair, however, to classify only Pinochet and Franco

among these as having depended much on reason to rule or valuing that capacity in subjects; and both these men heavily spiced their reason with terror and torture. See Arriagada 1988, Constable and Valenzuela 1991, Politzer 1989, Anderson 1970, and Preston 1995.

25. The careful reader will note the lack of literary parallelism in this sentence. I deliberately did not say "models of representative democracy" because I am not sure any exist in the real world, other than perhaps in New Zealand. Constitutionalists feel more secure with such institutional arrangements as judicial review, but I am not—at least not yet—willing to argue that a political culture cannot adequately protect constitutionalism's values.

References

Books and Articles

Anderson, Charles W. 1970. *The Political Economy of Modern Spain: Policy Making in an Authoritarian System*. Madison: University of Wisconsin Press.

Arriagada, Genaro. 1988. *Pinochet: The Politics of Power*. London: Unwin Hyman.

Barber, Sotirios A. 1984. *On What the Constitution Means*. Baltimore: Johns Hopkins University Press.

————. 1993. *The Constitution of Judicial Power*. Baltimore: Johns Hopkins University Press.

Buchanan, James M. 1991. *The Economics and the Ethics of Constitutional Order*. Ann Arbor: University of Michigan Press.

Buchanan, James M., and Geoffrey Brennan. 1985. *The Reason of Rules*. New York: Cambridge University Press.

Buchanan, James M., and Gordon Tullock. 1962. *The Calculus of Consent*. Ann Arbor: University of Michigan Press.

Cardozo, Benjamin N. 1921. *The Nature of the Judicial Process*. New Haven: Yale University Press.

Constable, Pamela, and Arturo Valenzuela. 1991. *A Nation of Enemies: Chile under Pinochet*. New York: Norton.

DiPalma, Giuseppe. 1990. *To Craft Democracies: An Essay on Democratic Transitions*. Berkeley: University of California Press.

Draper, Theodore. 1957. *The Roots of American Communism*. New York: Viking.

Dyson, Kenneth H. F. 1974. "Anti-Communism in the Federal Republic of Germany: The Case of the 'Berufsverbot.'" *Parliamentary Affairs* 28:51.

Eisgruber, Christopher L. 1993. "Justice and the Text: Rethinking the Constitutional Relation between Principle and Prudence." *Duke Law Journal* 43:1.

Ely, John Hart. 1980. *Democracy and Distrust*. Cambridge: Harvard University Press.

Farrand, Max, ed. 1966. *The Records of the Federal Convention of 1787*. Rev. ed. New Haven: Yale University Press.

Finn, John E. 1990. *Constitutions in Crisis: Political Violence and the Rule of Law*. New York: Oxford University Press.

Friedländer, Saul. 1966. *Pius XII and the Third Reich: A Documentation.* New York: Knopf.

Gay, Peter. 1952. *The Dilemma of Democratic Socialism: Eduard Bernstein's Challenge to Marx.* New York: Columbia University Press.

Gill, Anton. 1994. *An Honourable Defeat: A History of German Resistance to Hitler, 1933–1945.* New York: Holt, Rinehart and Winston.

Grunberger, Richard. 1971. *The Twelve-Year Reich: A Social History of Nazi Germany, 1933–1945.* New York: Holt, Rinehart and Winston.

Harris, William F., II. 1993. *The Interpretable Constitution.* Baltimore: Johns Hopkins University Press.

Herzog, Don. 1989. *Happy Slaves.* Chicago: University of Chicago Press.

Holmes, Stephen. 1988. "Precommitment and the Paradox of Democracy." In *Constitutionalism and Democracy,* ed. Jon Elster and Rune Slagstad. New York: Cambridge University Press.

Howe, Irving, and Lewis Coser. 1957. *The American Communist Party: A Critical History.* New York: Praeger.

Jackson, Robert H. 1955. *The Supreme Court in the American System of Government.* Cambridge: Harvard University Press.

Kommers, Donald P. 1997. *The Constitutional Jurisprudence of the Federal Republic of Germany.* 2d ed. Durham: Duke University Press.

Lewy, Guenter. 1964. *The Catholic Church and Nazi Germany.* New York: McGraw-Hill.

Lipscomb, Andrew A., ed. 1903. *The Writings of Thomas Jefferson.* Washington, D.C.: Jefferson Memorial Association.

Loewenstein, Karl. 1937a. "Militant Democracy and Fundamental Rights." *American Political Science Review* 31:417.

———. 1937b. "Militant Democracy and Fundamental Rights." *American Political Science Review* 31:638.

———. 1938a. "Legislative Control of Political Extremism in European Democracies." *Columbia Law Review* 38:591.

———. 1938b. "Legislative Control of Political Extremism in European Democracies." *Columbia Law Review* 38:725.

March, James G., and Johan P. Olsen. 1989. *Rediscovering Institutions: The Organizational Basis of Politics.* New York: Free Press.

Meiklejohn, Alexander. 1948. *Free Speech and Its Relation to Self-Government.* New York: Harpers.

Mennel, Robert M., and Christine L. Compston, eds. 1996. *Holmes and Frankfurter: Their Correspondence, 1912–1924.* Durham: University of New Hampshire/University Press of New England.

Murphy, Walter F. 1980. "An Ordering of Constitutional Values." *Southern California Law Review* 53:703.

———. 1986a. "*Slaughter-House, Civil Rights,* and Constitutional Change." *American Journal of Jurisprudence* 21:1.

———. 1986b. "Who Shall Interpret the Constitution?" *Review of Politics* 48:401.

———. 1990. "The Right to Privacy and Legitimate Constitutional Change." In *The Constitutional Bases of Political and Social Change in the United States,* ed. Shlomo Slonim. New York: Praeger.

————. 1992a. "Consent and Constitutional Change." In *Human Rights and Constitutional Law,* ed. James O'Reilly. Dublin: Round Hall Press.

————. 1992b. "Staggering toward the New Jerusalem of Constitutional Theory." *American Journal of Jurisprudence* 37:337.

————. 1993a. "Constitutions, Constitutionalism, and Democracy." In *Constitutionalism and Democracy,* ed. Douglas Greenberg, Stanley N. Katz, Melanie Beth Oliviero, and Steven C. Wheatley. New York: Oxford University Press.

————. 1993b. "Excluding Political Parties." In *Germany and Its Basic Law,* ed. Paul Kirchhof and Donald P. Kommers. Baden-Baden: Nomos Verlagsgesellschaft.

————. 1995. "Merlin's Memory." In *Responding to Imperfection: The Theory and Practice of Constitutional Amendment,* ed. Sanford V. Levinson. Princeton: Princeton University Press.

Murphy, Walter F., James E. Fleming, and Sotirios A. Barber. 1995. *American Constitutional Interpretation.* 2d ed. Westbury, N.Y.: Foundation Press.

Murphy, Walter F., and Joseph Tanenhaus. 1977. *Comparative Constitutional Law.* New York: St. Martin's.

Nandy, Ashis. 1989. "The Political Culture of the Indian State." *Daedalus* 118:1.

Office of the U.S. Chief of Counsel for the Prosecution of Axis Criminality. 1946. *Nazi Conspiracy and Aggression.* Washington, D.C.: Government Printing Office.

Petro, Nicolai N. 1996. *The Rebirth of Russian Democracy.* Cambridge: Harvard University Press.

Politzer, Patricia. 1989. *Fear in Chile: Lives under Pinochet.* New York: Pantheon.

Powers, Thomas. 1997. "The Conspiracy That Failed." *New York Review of Books,* Jan. 9, 49 ff.

Preston, Paul. 1995. *Franco: A Biography.* New York: Basic Books.

Rawls, John. 1971. *A Theory of Justice.* Cambridge: Harvard University Press.

————. 1993. *Political Liberalism.* New York: Columbia University Press.

Raz, Joseph. 1987. "Government by Consent." In *Authority Revisited,* ed. J. Roland Pennock and John W. Chapman. New York: New York University Press.

Record, Wilson. 1951. *The Negro and the Communist Party.* Chapel Hill: University of North Carolina Press.

Rhodes, Anthony. 1973. *The Vatican in the Age of the Dictators (1922–1945).* New York: Holt, Rinehart and Winston.

Sartori, Giovanni. 1987. *The Theory of Democracy Revisited.* Chatham, N.J.: Chatham House.

Scalia, Antonin. 1989. "Originalism: The Lesser Evil." *University of Cincinnati Law Review* 57:849.

Sergeyev, Victor, and Nikolai Biryukov. 1993. *Russia's Road to Democracy: Parliament, Communism, and Traditional Culture.* Brookfield, Vt.: Edward Elgar.

Sharlet, Robert. 1993. "Chief Justice as Judicial Politician." *East European Congressional Review* 2:32.

Smith, James Morton, ed. 1995. *A Republic of Letters: The Correspondence between Jefferson and Madison, 1776–1826.* New York: Norton.

Vaidyanathan, T. G. 1989. "Authority and Identity in India." *Daedalus* 118:147.

Walzer, Michael. 1981. "Philosophy and Democracy." *Political Theory* 9:379.

Webster, Noah. 1790. "Bills of Rights." In *Collection of Essays and Fugitive Writings on Moral, Historical, Political, and Literary Subjects*, ed. N. Webster. Boston: Thomas and Andrews.

Legal Cases

Communist Party Case, 5 BVerfGE 85 (1956); translated in Murphy and Tanenhaus 1977.
Dennis v. United States, 341 U.S. 494 (1951).
Gitlow v. New York, 268 U.S. 652 (1925).
Milligan, Ex parte, 71 U.S. 2 (1866).
Palko v. Connecticut, 302 U.S. 319 (1937).
Privacy of Communications Case, 30 BVerfGE 1 (1970); translated and reprinted in shortened form in Murphy and Tanenhaus 1977.
Schleswig-Holstein Voters' Association Case, 1 BVerfGE 208 (1952); quoted in Kommers 1997.
Socialist Reich Party Case, 2 BVerfGE 1 (1952); translated in Kommers 1997 and Murphy and Tanenhaus 1977.
Southwest Case, 1 BVerfGE 14 (1951); translated in Kommers 1997 and Murphy and Tanenhaus 1977.
United States v. Schwimmer, 279 U.S. 644 (1929).

Conclusion

CHAPTER 13

Politics as Vocation: Variations on Weber

Stanley Kelley Jr.

At the end of the first World War and about two years before his death, Max Weber delivered a now-famous lecture, "Politics as a Vocation," under the sponsorship of a group of students at the University of Munich.[1] The lecture was one in a series on vocations, and at the heart of it was a discussion of the difficulties, rewards, and opportunities of a political career, the qualities and talents required of politicians, and the ethical issues that confront them—all matters of immediate interest to young people actively considering politics as a career. Most probably, some of Weber's student-listeners did not get all that they had hoped for, for he had little explicitly to say about the political problems, issues, and movements of their own time and place; to our benefit, and perhaps to theirs, Weber addressed more enduring concerns about politics as a vocation. Moreover, to some of the political activists in his audience, the sweeping historical review of politics (and of party politics in particular) that went with what he had to say about politics as a vocation may have been more than they wanted to hear; but, if so, their cause for complaint is ours for gratitude.

The decision to enter, or not to enter, political life is a socially as well as personally important one, and Weber's joining of the perspective of the social theorist and historian with that of the politician and potential politician helps us to see the latter viewpoint as a valuable alternate point of entry into a better understanding of what party politics involves, an entry point that is all the more interesting because it is all too rarely taken. Contemporary scholarship on party politics devotes a great deal of attention to the institutions and activities associated with it but relatively little to what it means to lead the life of a full-time party politician. This emphasis makes it easy to miss the fact that the two perspectives complement each other in the same way that alternately looking at medicine and doctors, writing and writers, or music and musicians can tell us more about both than we could learn from looking at either alone. Sensible constitution makers, among whom our own must certainly be included, do not design governmental institutions without thinking about the kinds of people likely to occupy important positions in them and about the likely fate of those institutions in their hands.

Because I subscribe to the things that I have just said, I want here to recall and to elaborate on some of the principal themes of "Politics as a Vocation"—specifically, those that I have already described as central to it—thus offering a perspective on party politics that, if not new, is at least uncommon in our times. Much of what Weber said in developing those themes was speculative, and I must be speculative, too, because information on many of the points he raised is either lacking or fragmentary. Such speculation is justified by what motivates most justifiable speculation—the service it can render in clearing the way for learning more about an important subject. The present, moreover, is a particularly good time to think about politics as a vocation: we are in an era in which a large part of the American electorate seemingly would like to drive career politicians from office en masse by limiting the time they can serve there, putting in their place citizen-politicians for whom public office and public duties are a brief time-out in their usual occupations. What Weber had to say about politics as a vocation can help us to think about whether we either can or should want to make careers in politics less accessible in this way, and so I address that issue in closing.

The Material Bases of a Political Vocation

What sort of politics did Weber have in mind as a possible vocation, and how did he think it could be made one? To the first of these questions, a temporarily sufficient answer is that he was thinking of a politics that involves the seeking of governmental leadership, or a share in it, through efforts to win and maintain popular support. In the United States today, Weberian career politicians are thus to be found mainly among those whose eyes are on elective policy-making positions, whether as candidates and officeholders, leaders in political parties, or heads of other groups devoted to influencing choices of either officeholders or governmental policy makers or both. Weber did not have in mind the careers of bureaucrats, military men, or mere yea-sayers in a party or a legislative body. A brief (and adequate, for present purposes) answer to the second question—how can politics be made a vocation—is that (in Weber's view) one must devote one's life to it; occasional participation is not enough.

Thus, politicians' arrangements for getting the necessities of life while they work at politics become important both for themselves and for their societies, and early in his lecture Weber made a distinction that is helpful in thinking about the material bases for politics as a vocation, a distinction between living *for* politics and living *off* politics (Weber 1958, 84). To live *for* politics means to make politics the focal point of one's life, either because one "enjoys the naked possession of the power he exerts, or he nourishes his inner balance and self-feeling by the consciousness that his life has *meaning* in the service of a 'cause'" (ibid., emphasis in original). To live *off* politics means to make it one's source of income. What this simple distinction makes immediately obvious is that those who lack private means cannot live for politics unless they can also live off it; in Weber's words, "The leadership of a state or of a party by men who (in the economic sense of the word) live exclusively for politics and not off politics means necessarily a 'plutocratic' recruitment of the leading political strata" (85–86). Unless one favors such a result—that is, unless one wants vocations in politics to be the exclusive preserve of those who can afford to work for no pay—then both society and those who incline toward political careers have problems to solve.

Indeed, the problem for democratic societies goes beyond avoiding a corps of career politicians recruited only from among the rich: Such societies should care also about the supply of career politicians, the amount of competition among them, and the kind of people who become such—whether plutocrats or nonplutocrats. The measures taken by democratic governments that bear most directly on material support for political careers— paying for public service and regulating the financing of campaigns—have an uncertain relation to any of these concerns, in part because we are ignorant of many of the facts about public service and in part because we are unsure about what we should regard as desirable states of affairs. How many career politicians do we have? Is that number too many—as some heatedly argue—or too few? If some number of people making a career of politics is either desirable or permissible or inevitable, what sort of people should they be? How nearly does our body of career politicians come to meeting some reasonable set of ideal standards in its size and composition? in its contribution to diversity in the viewpoints brought to bear on social and political problems?

If the material basis for making politics a vocation presents society with difficult questions of this sort, it turns another face, and poses equally difficult questions, to those attracted to that vocation. Think of the prospect it presents to a poor but ambitious boy or girl also considering how to rise from rags to riches, considering how to become not just comfortably well off but, say, as rich as Ross Perot or William Gates. Fabulously wealthy politicians are not unknown —Ferdinand Marcos and "Papa Doc" Duvalier are examples—but in the United States the plums of a political career—the presidency, governorships, Senate seats—come with salaries attached to them that are unrelated to performance and much lower than those paid the most successful people in many other lines of work, even taking perquisites into account. Terms are short in these and other public offices, and those who aspire to them run a significant risk of being jobless at one or more points in their careers. Winning and keeping elective offices usually means campaigning for them, repeatedly or continually, and the amount of money that must be spent on a single campaign is often much more than the salaries attached to the jobs. Can one start out poor and yet amass a great fortune in a political career? How? Probably no one can, our poor boy or girl should be told, without either breaking the law, doing things that, if discovered, would end the career, or destroying the ability of others to remove one from power. The poor but honest boy or girl should ask not "How can a political career maximize my wealth?" but "How can I support myself and my family while devoting myself to politics?"

This question has at least four answers, the realism and appeal of which will vary with one's precise circumstances:

1. *Have an income sufficient for a living for which you do not have to work,* or, to use Weber's terminology, be "economically dispensable" (1958, 85). He cited rentiers as the prime example of an economically dispensable class; were he lecturing today, he might point to some members of the Rockefeller and Kennedy families as examples of rentier-politicians.

2. *Be ready to serve in varying kinds of political positions and to move from one to another with considerable frequency.* To many, a political career may seem a particularly risky one, but it is less risky than it appears at first glance. While waiting for the best occasion or occasions to make a run for (for instance) Congress, an aspirant to eventual membership in that body can serve in other elective offices, in politically appointive positions in government, or in staff positions in party organizations, advocacy organizations, and interest groups. With three levels of government in the United States, three branches for each level, and a vast array of groups that exist to influence government, our would-be member of Congress is not without places to wait, provided only that he or she is willing to make lateral as well as upward moves and to do so more frequently than some would find comfortable.

3. *Acquire expert knowledge of one or more of the techniques of politics.* In his lecture Weber noted in passing that some "men to whom leadership qualities were ascribed were approached by people willing to take over propaganda, at fixed rates for every vote" (1958, 113). These entrepreneurial propagandists were evidently the forerunners of tillers of the now thriving field of political consulting who (among other things) create advertisements, write and coach speeches, poll the electorate, organize get-out-the-vote drives, and offer advice

about the best ways to win elections—not usually "at fixed rates for every vote," it is true, but for often quite handsome fees. Someone knowledgeable about survey research and adept in quantitative analysis can now often be found at an early age discussing campaign strategy with a member of Congress. As yet not many consultants have gone on to high elective office—that step could be a hard one for a consultant of any prominence—but one leading consultant, Lee Atwater, has served as chair of his party's national committee, surely a position in which one can share in the nation's leadership.

4. *Have the ability to pursue a complementary career.* Ideally, such career would be lucrative; involve skills and knowledge that are also useful in politics; yield politically useful personal connections; allow one to practice it part-time, or to reenter it, without severe losses in earning power; have, or make possible, easily adjusted day-to-day schedules; and permit one to acquire a politically valuable reputation. As everyone knows, law fits this bill about as well as it can be fit; moreover, some public offices are reserved for lawyers, a fact that gives them more options in politics than are available to nonlawyers and thus a competitive advantage in pursuing a political career.[2] Journalism is another occupation that may serve as a backup for political careerists. Knowledge of politics and skill in using words are of great value to both journalist and politician, and the recent career of Patrick Buchanan shows how vague the boundaries between politics and journalism can be. Weber duly noted both law and journalism as avenues into politics, and he might also have mentioned academic life, which has some of the attributes of a good complementary career. As occupations hard to combine with a political vocation, he pointed to medicine and industrial entrepreneurship.

These observations about ways to make politics a vocation create several reasonable expectations about careerism in politics. Since there are practicable ways for a considerable number of people to make a career in politics, we should not be unduly surprised that careerists exist in fact. In the United States, a sizable proportion of those who have become presidents, senators, governors, cabinet members, and members of the U.S. House of Representatives can be described as political careerists without stretching that notion unduly, though no one keeps a running count. As we would expect also, where there are many career politicians, there are representatives of the professions just discussed. In the five Congresses before the present one, for instance, 42 percent of the members, on average, have been lawyers; 13 percent, educators; and 5 percent, journalists.[3] Finally (on the theory that the more one starts out with, the more one has to fall back on), we would expect a disproportionate number of those in political careers to come from economically well-off families. On this point few good data exist, but information collected by Donald Matthews from U.S. senators in the Eightieth to Eighty-fourth Congresses is at least suggestive. Matthews found that the "children of low-salaried workers, wage earners, servants, and farm laborers, which together comprised 66 percent of the gainfully employed in 1900, contributed only 7 percent of the postwar senators" (1960, 19).[4] We should, of course, want senators themselves to be unrepresentative of the population at large in educational attainment and in other ways as well, but this kind of unrepresentativeness of senators' *parents* sits much less well with the aspirations of egalitarian democracy.

How should those interested in (in Weber's phrase) living for politics view the arrangements that society has made for them to live off it? Clearly, those arrangements make a life in politics a feasible one for many people, and occasionally a political career may yield opportunities, honestly arrived at, for making substantial amounts of money—by writing a best selling book, for instance. Nonetheless, it is probably true that many who have made careers in politics— when they were unwilling to abuse the powers they acquired there—have lived less securely and less well than they would have in another line of work undertaken with equal talent and diligence.

Some Rewards of Politics as a Vocation

Why, then, do such people pursue a political career? Why do they accept its financial risks and sacrifices?

We could reply flippantly that money is not everything—that status and power count, too—but if we do so, we must immediately concede that the status achieved by politicians comes at a price, and one that is normally higher, the higher the status. That price is infringement of privacy. We must also concede that the status of politicians is by no means unambiguously high. Public officeholders are deferred to by most of those with whom they are in frequent contact, and individual politicians, certainly, may be respected and admired: consider, for instance, the praise that William Jennings Bryan received in 1896 from a fifteen-year-old who wanted to be like Bryan, he said, because the Great Commoner was "a good looking gentleman, and one of the smartest men in the United States . . . and . . . without exception, the greatest orator on the face of the globe" (quoted in Greenstein 1965, 145). Who, looked up to in that way, could fail to be gratified? But consider also Walt Whitman's description of the elite corps of the Democratic Party, the delegates to its national convention:

> The meanest kind of . . . blowing office-holders, office seekers . . . malignants, conspirators, murderers, fancy-men, custom-house clerks, contractors, kept-editors, spaniels well trained to carry and fetch, jobbers, infidels, disunion-

ists, terrorists, mail-riflers, slave-catchers, pushers of slavery, creatures of the
President, creatures of would-be Presidents, spies, bribers, compromisers, lob-
byers, spongers, ruined sports, expelled gamblers, policy backers, monte-deal-
ers, duellists, carriers of concealed weapons, deaf men, pimpled men, scarred
inside with vile disease, gaudy outside with gold chains made from the people's money; crawling, serpentine men; the lousy combings and born freedom-
sellers of the earth. (Whitman 1892, 259)

Elsewhere, Whitman wrote in a less partisan vein of "the antics of the parties and their leaders, these half-brained nominees . . . and many elected failures
and blatherers" (ibid., 234). Obviously dated concerns being edited out, one
would not be surprised to hear similar references to politicians on today's political call-in programs, supposing only that the disgruntled callers were endowed with a poetic imagination anything like Whitman's.

A study in the late 1950s of public attitudes toward American politicians
reached a conclusion that probably holds true for a long span of time, namely,
that "Americans appear to be cynical about politics and quite idealistic about
certain politicians, especially dead ones, and about certain offices" (Mitchell
1959, 695). Thus, political positions (governor, cabinet member) ranked among
the occupations rated most highly by respondents in a national sample (ibid.,
688–89), political figures have often topped the Gallup Poll's list of most-
admired men, and George Washington and Abraham Lincoln are enduring
American heroes, even though large numbers of Americans at the same time reject politics as a lifework for their sons. Some do so, it is true, because they think
political careers are too insecure and pay too poorly, but (in one study) almost
half rejected the idea of a politician-son because they believed politics to be fundamentally dishonest. A typical observation went thus: "If he [the son] is a good
Christian man, politics will ruin him. I believe no man in politics remains honest" (quoted in Mitchell 1959, 690). If some politicians win widespread approval,
they seem to do so only when they are not seen as members of the class of
"politicians," a word that seems unredeemably associated with scheming and
opportunism.

Is power an unambiguously attractive feature of political life? Although for
Weber those who live for politics were by definition power seekers, there is
ample reason to expect the desire for power to be one of the chief appeals of a
political career, even if we do not make that proposition true by definition.
Power is the ability to do things, the ability to do things is universally valued,
and the politician is often in a position to do things that others cannot. Still,
many of us view power seeking with great suspicion. In nations that enjoy full
civil liberties, Lord Acton's "Power tends to corrupt and absolute power corrupts
absolutely" is surely one of the most frequently quoted observations in politi-

cal commentary, and Acton is by no means alone in having depicted power as more nearly an evil than a value. "The effect of power and publicity on all men," wrote Henry Adams, "is the aggravation of self, a sort of tumor that ends by killing the victim's sympathies. . . . One can scarcely use expressions too strong to describe the violence of egotism it stimulates" (Adams 1918, 147). And Weber saw the power-seeking politician as prone to fall victim to "a quite trivial and all-too-human enemy: a quite vulgar vanity, the deadly enemy of all matter-of-fact devotion to a cause" (Weber 1958, 116).

In fact, our attitudes toward power and power seeking are severely conflicted. We distrust power seekers but like people who know how to take charge; we cherish independence but forget that it is the power to do as we like. Such contradictory attitudes pull us up short before what otherwise might seem uncomplicated choices. Consider these observations of John F. Kennedy in an interview of December 17, 1962:

> I think that there are a lot of satisfactions to the Presidency, particularly, as I say, we are all concerned as citizens and as parents and all the rest, with all the problems we have been talking about tonight. They are all the problems which if I was not the President, I would be concerned about as a father or as a citizen. So at least you have an opportunity to do something about them. And if what you do is useful and successful, then of course that is great satisfaction. When as a result of a decision of yours, failure comes or you are unsuccessful, then of course that is a great setback. (Kennedy 1963, 903)

This matter-of-fact statement is notable for its suggestion that a career in politics needs no elaborate justification: full-time work in politics is a way for some to go beyond what ordinary citizens can do in working toward solutions of a community's problems. To put it another way, a position of political power is a point of leverage that can enable one to make a substantial contribution to his or her community and, once in a while, to move the world. It is true that people can be too eager for power or have too much of it, but the same can be said of other values as well—we can, for instance, be too eager for love and pampered beyond what is good for us.

If a career in politics promises the chance for power, it, like athletics or the performing arts, also offers repeated opportunities for some to exercise talents and capacities pleasurably, sometimes to cheering and applause. These words of Winston Churchill, spoken at an affair honoring him on the occasion of his eightieth birthday, can help to make the point:

> I have never accepted what many people have kindly said, namely, that I inspired the nation. Their will was resolute and remorseless, and, as it proved, unconquerable. It fell to me to express it, and, if I found the right words, you must remember that I have always earned my living by my pen and by my

tongue. It was the nation and the race dwelling all round the globe that had the lion heart. I had the luck to be called upon to give the roar. (Churchill 1974, 8608)

Churchill's masterly use of words is evident even in the few I have just quoted, and even without hearing his engaging delivery of them. Note his use of the word, "luck." What Michelangelo's frescoes in the Sistine Chapel are to painting, Churchill's wartime speeches are to rhetoric. Is it any wonder that someone with his rhetorical skills should feel lucky to have had the kind of opportunity to use them that came with his position as prime minister in time of war? Pleasure in the exercise of politically important talents is not just an on-stage pleasure; it can become generalized into fascination with "the game." Henry Adams wrote that Thurlow Weed, a seemingly selfless and personally undemanding master of political management, was drawn to politics in this way: "Management was an instinct with Mr. Weed; an object to be pursued for its own sake, as one plays cards" (Adams 1918, 147). It is true that Adams did not find Weed's preoccupation with the game entirely admirable ("he appeared to play with men as though they were only cards"), but we should not be surprised that politicians do what they do in part because they like doing it very much, even if in particular cases we might wish that they were doing something else.

Why would anyone accept financial risks and sacrifices to follow a political career? One good answer to this question should now be evident, if it was not always so: For the same reason that not everyone marries for money. Politics offers satisfactions that some more lucrative pursuits do not.

This answer may be a sufficient one for individuals, but those with an interest in our well-being as a community should note further that our general culture does little to bring the possible satisfactions of a political career to the attention of young people. Indeed, the representatives of that culture—parents, teachers, neighbors, peers—are more likely to make young people embarrassed to admit to a desire to go into politics. Of course, things are quite different in some subcultures; it seems doubtful, for instance, that presentable scions of political families face skeptical looks when they declare an interest in political careers. If political careerists are unrepresentative of Americans generally, our culture, as well as financial barriers, help to make them so.

Personal Qualities

What skills, talents, and dispositions aid one in a political career? For democratic societies this question is important because the personal qualities and resources that yield a competitive advantage in struggles for their leadership are likely to matter for their long-run health. The same question is even more obviously important for those considering a political career. To choose sensibly among occupations, one needs to assess one's strengths and weaknesses relative to the things that they seem to require for success and happiness in them. As the politically correct would have it, we are all "differently abled," and so the tone deaf do not become musicians and hundred-pound weaklings do not become heavyweight boxers. Of course, no particular dispositions, skills, or talents, nor any sets of them, will guarantee success in politics, because their value will vary from situation to situation, and in some situations they may not matter at all. Over the course of a career, however, personal qualities are likely to count for a good deal *just because* circumstances will change. In specifying occasions in which the personal characteristics of leaders are likely to make a difference, Fred Greenstein makes this point well: "Skill is of the utmost importance, since the greater the actor's skill, the less his initial need for a favorable position or a manipulable environment, and the greater the likelihood that he himself will contribute to making his subsequent position favorable and his environment manipulable"(Greenstein 1987, 45).

Weber called attention to several qualities he believed to be of crucial importance to anyone who would make a vocation of politics. One of these was passion—"passion in the sense of matter-of-factness, of passionate devotion to a 'cause,' to the god or demon who is its over-lord" (Weber 1958, 115). *Will* or *zeal* most probably conveys his meaning for "passion" better than *ardor* or *enthusiasm*. If so, we could include among passionate politicians not only an obvious case, like Martin Luther King, but a less obvious one, like Lyndon Johnson. As depicted by some biographers, Johnson was a man wholly wrapped up in politics and continually striving for perfection of technique.[5] Just as the successful real estate developer sees condominiums where most of us see only a lovely wood, Johnson, it seems, saw virtually everything in its relevance or irrelevance to his political projects.

A second disposition that Weber held to be important is detachment, or a sense of proportion: "The decisive psychological quality of the politician," he said, ". . . is his ability to let realities work upon him with inner concentration and calmness" (Weber 1958, 115). The highly successful in most fields seem likely to have passion in Weber's sense, but Weberian detachment may be both more necessary in politics than in some other callings and harder to achieve there than in many. Working to undermine detachment are both the wishful thinking that may accompany passionate devotion to a cause and politicians' necessary concern with what people will think of them, which may lead to confusing what is good for the self with what is good for the cause, or, in Weber's words, to "purely personal intoxication" (115). Most of us would also find it difficult to maintain analytical objectivity in the face of some of the decisions that politicians have to make. Friendship, Rexford Tugwell observes, "is a difficult—almost impossible—luxury for the leader. Sooner or later he sacrifices loyalty to a friend for some other value—usually his own ambition in combination with a conviction that it also involves a people's interest" (1958, 222).

The "force of demagogic speech" is a third thing that Weber saw as of decisive importance to a successful politician (107). In using that phrase he clearly had in mind speech to large groups of people and speech that appealed to the emotions as well as to the intellect, but he failed to elaborate much further on what he meant. Thus left mostly to ourselves, we may note that speaking ability seems to involve a blending of two sets of skills and that one of these involves special sensitivity to the ways in which language can be deployed to achieve various effects. Let us pay particular attention, with Cicero (1970, 235ff.), to metaphor, and for a better appreciation of the power of metaphor, let us consider speeches by two leaders in similar circumstances—Jimmy Carter, when the Soviet Union invaded Afghanistan in 1979, and Franklin Roosevelt, when Italy invaded France in 1940. Arousing listeners' indignation was an important objective of each of these speeches, and in each case the event about which listeners were to be asked to be indignant was one remote from their everyday concerns.

How did FDR go about his task? After briefly tracing his efforts to limit the war in Europe and to mediate differences between Italy and France and Britain, he said, "On this tenth day of June, nineteen hundred and forty, the hand that held the dagger has struck it into the back of its neighbor" (Roosevelt 1941, 263). This metaphorical rendering of the Italian invasion invokes a vivid visual image of a treacherous and cowardly act. Indignation is its virtually automatic accompaniment. The remote event is brought home by portraying relations between nation-states as relations between neighbors and by equating national aggression with personal villainy.

Carter, after lengthy introductory remarks (some of which had nothing to do with Afghanistan), eventually told his prime-time audience, "Recently there has been another very serious development which threatens the maintenance of the peace in Southeast Asia. Massive Soviet military forces have invaded the small, non-aligned sovereign nation of Afghanistan, which hitherto has not been an occupied satellite of the Soviet Union. . . . This is a callous violation of international law and of the United Nations Charter" (Carter 1980, 22). This account of events is literal; the only metaphor ("satellite") is a dead one. There is, it is true, a bare suggestion that a big guy has picked on a little guy ("massive" forces have invaded a small nation), but the victim is a virtual abstraction ("the small, non-aligned sovereign nation of Afghanistan"), the threat of the action is to peace on a faraway continent, and the offense described—violation of international law and of the United Nations Charter—is not of a sort calculated to induce any shudders. Carter's literal account is less successful in stimulating a strong feeling of indignation than FDR's metaphorical one, because it fails to reduce the great psychological distance between his listeners and the plight of Afghanistan. Remote things, literally described, remain remote things.

Effective deployment of the "force of demagogic speech," however, comes to more than skill in using words; it is also grounded in social skills, particularly in sensitivity to ways in which one can increase or decrease people's resistance to ideas. Suppose for a moment that you are a junior partner in a law firm, charged with matching offices and new associates. You might send a memorandum to one of these new associates which says, either, "I am assigning you to office 15" or "I am assigning office 15 to you." From one point of view you are saying the same thing, but from another you are not. The first wording reads as an assertion of your authority over the recipient, the second presents your action as a service to him or her.

There are thousands of examples of politicians' alertness to the differences in the tone and feeling of communications that come with different ways of expressing ideas. A crude example is the attempt to make taxes more palatable by calling them "revenue enhancements." One that is not at all crude is the way in which Franklin Roosevelt and Winston Churchill eased the passage of the Lend-Lease Act of 1941.[6] That act found formidable obstacles to its acceptance in sour memories of defaults on U.S. loans in World War I, fears of being drawn into outright war with the Axis powers, and the extraordinary power that it lodged in the president. Roosevelt met the first of these challenges by deftly brushing issues of money aside:

> Suppose my neighbor's home catches on fire, and I have a length of garden hose. . . . If he can take my garden hose and connect it up with his hydrant, I may help to put out his fire. Now what do I do? I don't say to him before that operation, "Neighbor, my garden hose cost me $15; you have to pay me $15 for it." . . . I don't want $15—I want my garden hose back after the fire is over. . . . If it goes through the fire all right, intact, without any damage to it, he gives it back to me and thanks me very much for the use of it. (Quoted in Goodwin 1994, 194)

Would aid to Britain draw the United States into war? To the contrary, Roosevelt said, making the United States "the great arsenal for democracy" was our best chance for keeping out of it. Churchill helped him to advance this argument by addressing the words of a major speech directly to FDR (and indirectly to the Congress): "Put your confidence in us. . . . We shall not fail or falter. . . . Give us the tools and we will finish the job" (quoted in Goodwin 1994, 213). The wide discretion that the act gave the president was neither easily masked nor easily forgone, since Roosevelt believed that aid might at some point be required for the Soviet Union, a possibility abhorrent to his isolationist opponents. This line of attack on lend-lease, however, was dulled by pointing to a precedent—a law of 1892 that had given the secretary of war the right to lease Army property when he found doing so to be in the public interest (Sherwood 1948, 228).

The contribution that social skills can make to the careers of politicians goes much beyond helping them to persuade mass audiences. What politicians (often) need to do relative to other people is fairly evident. They have to strike up alliances, work to maintain such alliances, and coordinate members' actions in them. They must negotiate with opponents and mediate among friends. They need to know when to trust others and how to win trust for themselves. They must estimate, often instantly, how others will react to words and deeds. They are benefited by a quick and accurate grasp of what convention says may be done, or not done, in a wide range of situations. Although no one is in a position to be dogmatic on the subject, to do these things skillfully seems to depend on two basic abilities: (1) facility in seeing situations from many perspectives, the capacity that enables us to act more or less effectively as members of teams; and (2) empathy, or what Howard Gardner has called "interpersonal intelligence." Of this latter ability Gardner says:

> Examined in its most elementary form, the interpersonal intelligence entails the capacity of the young child to discriminate among the individuals around him and to detect their various moods. In an advanced form, interpersonal knowledge permits a skilled adult to read the intentions and desires—even when these have been hidden—of many other individuals and, potentially, to act upon this knowledge—for example, by influencing a group of disparate individuals to behave along desired lines. We see highly developed forms of interpersonal intelligence in political and religious leaders (a Mahatma Gandhi or a Lyndon Johnson), in skilled parents and teachers, and in individuals in the helping professions, be they therapists, counselors, or shamans. (Gardner 1983, 239)

For the student of politics, whether "interpersonal intelligence" is the proper name for the abilities Gardner describes under that rubric—a matter of controversy among psychologists—is of much less moment than whether those abilities exist and whether people vary in the extent to which they possess them. Experience and observation, of politics and of everyday life, suggest affirmative answers to both questions. In a study of Connecticut legislators, for instance, James Barber found that "lawmakers" (his term for one of the two groups of legislators most devoted to a career in politics) had "unusual empathic abilities" that made it easy for them "to like others because they understand how others feel" (1965, 182). A member of the U.S. House of Representatives, says Richard Fenno, tries to convey "a sense of empathy with his constituents. Contextually and verbally, he gives them the impression that 'I understand your situation and I care about it'; 'I can put myself in your shoes'; and 'I can see the world the way you do'" (1978, 59). Some or much of this empathy may be feigned, but, if so, it stands, like all hypocrisy, as a tribute to the real thing.

Weber and others have noted still other dispositions, talents, and skills useful to the politician that also deserve mention here, even if they cannot be discussed at any great length. Politicians, Weber said, must "always and necessarily" be ready to fight (1958, 95), and so, presumably, they are better off with a good stomach for fighting. In a profession in which crises are frequent and in which requirements for success are often both uncertain and open ended, energy and stamina should be valuable traits, and biographical studies of political leaders are indeed full of references to long hours and hard work. Self-confidence and adaptability seem clearly useful endowments for politicians, and so, finally, does inventiveness. Great politicians, Charles Merriam argues, are adept at creating new political situations out of apparently intractable old ones (Merriam 1926).

As a case in point, consider the formula for settling the Irish-British conflict that Eamon de Valera advanced in negotiations with the British government in 1921. As conditions for granting autonomy to Ireland, the British at that time were insisting that it accept membership in the British Commonwealth of Nations and that its leaders swear allegiance to the king. Some of the Irish were ready to accept these conditions grudgingly, but many found them wholly unacceptable. De Valera proposed a formula for breaking the deadlock, the seeds of which had popped into his head, we are told, while he was tying his shoelaces one morning (Longford and O'Neill 1971, 128 ff.). Ireland would not become a member of the Commonwealth but would attach itself to it as an "external associate," as Switzerland had become associated with the League of Nations. Furthermore, as officials of a nation in association with the Commonwealth, members of the Irish Dail, though not swearing allegiance to the king, would recognize him as the Commonwealth's leader. De Valera, faced with a knotty symbolic problem, had attempted to solve it by this deft manipulation of symbols. His formula won unanimous approval from the Irish cabinet, but unfortunately for him and for the Irish, it was rejected by the British, and the Irish were condemned to a bitter and bloody civil war. Virtually the same formula, however, was later put to good use in resolving the symbolic conundrums involved in granting India its independence from Britain.

Reviewing the list of traits I have presented, a young person considering a career in politics should notice two things: such traits are not found in everyone in high degree, and they are a rather odd set of qualities to find in combination. Weber asked, "How can warm passion and a cool sense of proportion be forged together in one and the same soul?" (1958, 115). We may ask the same question about empathy and a taste for fighting, adaptability and passionate determination, creativity and sensitivity to convention. If our list indeed includes the qualities most useful to politicians, evidently nature and nurture do not equip all of us equally well for a life as such.

Ethics and Politics

A student of ethics might notice something else about the traits on our list: They are essentially neutral in their relation to the content and objectives of political action, that is, they are traits useful to unscrupulous as well as scrupulous politicians, to misleaders as well as leaders. For that reason (though not only for it), those who care about democratic government should be concerned with the ethical standards of the nation's politicians, the forces that influence those standards, and what, if anything, can be done to make the norms of political practice maximally consistent with the chief objectives of democratic societies. Those who think of politics as a possible career should have the same concerns, but they will have two others that are distinctly personal. They will want to know whether what politics requires of them will square with their sense of right and wrong: few of us want to play an ignoble role in our own life story. And, knowing that equally honest parsons and used-car dealers hardly ever enjoy equal reputations for honesty, they will also care about the kind of reputational baggage that a career in politics may force them to carry.

Knowing how to act rightly and how to explain the rightness of actions to others would be a good deal easier for politicians if there existed for their guidance a reasonably detailed body of doctrine on which both they and citizens were agreed. In the average citizen's manual of democracy they are faced instead with a skimpy text and with Abelardian *sic-et-non* on many matters of importance. Our imaginary manual's commentary on leadership is confusing at best. It praises independence in representatives but says that they hold office to serve their constituents' interests (always) and to do their bidding (most of the time). The manual is confusing about nation and constituency, saying that first one, then the other, should be paramount for the legislator. It praises compromise on some pages, condemns it as unprincipled on others, decries political violence, and celebrates our violent Revolution. It says that representatives should decide the issues that come before them on their merits, though citizens in their everyday lives often sacrifice views on one point to win support on another.

Of course, there are sophisticated responses to these apparent contradictions. For instance, Dennis Thompson interprets the principle of autonomy—the principle that issues must be decided on their merits—in a way that legitimizes the trading of votes. Legislators act autonomously (or autonomously enough), he argues, if their reasons for acting as they do are relevant to "either the merits of legislation or the means necessary for adopting the legislation, where the means are consistent with a legislative process that generally considers legislation on the merits" (Thompson 1987, 113). Politicians who accept this argument, or who arrive at a similar one for themselves, are doing what citizens presumably want them to do—taking ethics seriously. That fact may fail to increase their moral standing with citizens, however, unless citizens, too, acquire greater sophistication about what is politically right and wrong, something that the long run may bring but in the short run can hardly be counted on.

Although Weber argued that no body of ethics could establish "commandments of identical content for erotic, business, familial, and official relations; for the relations to one's wife, to the green grocer, the son, the competitor, the friend, the defendant" (1958, 118–19), he nonetheless saw politicians as like everyone else in having to face up to the fact that "all ethically oriented conduct may be guided by one of two fundamentally differing and irreconcilably opposed maxims" (120). These are an "ethic of ultimate ends" and an "ethic of responsibility." To act in accordance with the first of these, "the Christian does rightly and leaves the results with the Lord"; to follow the second, "one has to give an account of the foreseeable results of one's action." Those who subscribe to the ethic of ultimate ends follow a set of absolute rules (rules like the Ten Commandments, but without the benefit of Jewish and Christian commentary on them), and if doing so brings grief, it is God's will, or the fault of the wicked. Those who accept an ethic of responsibility must take the likely responses of the wicked and ignorant into account in deciding which is the better among the alternative courses of action open to them.

Weber clearly thought that politicians, most of the time, should adopt an ethic of responsibility. They are agents engaged in the public's business who are held accountable by their fellow citizens for their actions and the results of their actions; since following absolute rules sometimes risks bad results (one of which may be the success of unworthy opponents), politicians may sometimes have to do bad in order to do good. Can they, like farmers, regard their dirtied hands simply as a mark of honest labor? Not in Weber's view. His "fundamentally differing and irreconcilably opposed maxims"—the ethic of ultimate ends and the ethic of responsibility—are not "absolute contrasts but rather supplements, which only in unison constitute a genuine man—a man who can have the 'calling of politics'" (1958, 127). Thus, he said, "it is immensely moving when a mature man—no matter whether old or young in years—is aware of a responsibility for the consequences of his conduct and really feels such responsibility with heart and soul. He then acts by following an ethic of responsibility and somewhere he reaches the point where he says: 'Here I stand; I can do no other'" (127).

Politicians, he is saying in this passage, mostly committed to the ethic of responsibility, may reach a point at which they will feel compelled to act as if guided by an ethic of ultimate ends, and we will admire them for doing so. At other times, however, when not ignoring moral rules, they are busily making amendments to them, and so, "he who seeks the salvation of the soul, of his own and of others, should not seek it along the avenue of politics" (126). He should not, because—as Weber puts the matter—he will sometimes be quite literally damned if he does and damned if he does not.

This is a gloomy message from a man who cared about politics, whose father was a professional politician, and who was an occasional politician himself. What sort of credit should it be given by a young person who wants a career in politics but is unwilling to check his or her ethical concerns at the point of entry? At the very least, it seems proper to answer, Weber was correct that politicians may sometimes face painful moral choices, ones made no less so because in particular cases it can be plausibly argued that the politician *should* take actions normally regarded as immoral or should even commit what we usually regard as crimes. Who would not think it permissible to lie or worse, if a lie or worse might reasonably be supposed to defeat a Hitler? The rightness of lying seems as evident in this case as it ever could be, but what if the "or worse" should include, say, torture or murder; work to the detriment not of a Hitler but of some less threatening tyrant; and be less than certain of achieving its objective? Would politicians in such a case come away with clean hands and easy consciences, if they had been scrupulous in canvassing the alternatives, gathering information about them, weighing the consequences, and so doing the best they could, "standing alone in a moment of time, forced to choose" (Walzer 1973, 169)?

Like Weber, Michael Walzer is unwilling to let politicians off so easily. He rejects an affirmative answer to this question, even if the position it represents is qualified to stipulate the normal claims of moral rules to obedience:

> Moral life is a social phenomenon, and it is constituted at least in part by rules, the knowledge of which (and perhaps the making of which) we share with our fellows. The experience of coming up against these rules, challenging their prohibitions, and explaining ourselves to other men and women is so common and so obviously important that no account of moral decision-making can possibly fail to come to grips with it. . . . It might be well to say that moral rules ought to have the character of guidelines, but it seems in fact that they do not. Or at least, we defend ourselves when we break the rules as if they had some status entirely independent of their previous utility (and we rarely feel proud of ourselves). (1973, 169–70)

One does not have to accept fully the moral position that Walzer develops in "Dirty Hands" to believe that he sees the sociology and psychology of morality correctly for some—perhaps many—people. Depending on the situation and the rules involved, transgressions of them by the ethically serious politician are likely to come with a twinge, qualm, feeling of shame, or sense of guilt, for the rules have been incorporated into his or her sense of self long before any thoughts of public office or public service. It is certainly possible, then, that politics may force choices on nonsociopathic politicians that may sometimes make them feel bad about themselves, even very bad.

Not everyone, however, sees political life as confronting politicians with ethical alternatives quite so bleak as Weber depicts them, bleak because doing the responsible thing may risk salvation. Against the position he takes, one can reasonably argue that an action conscientiously and intelligently taken to achieve the best overall consequences that a situation permits involves no moral wrongdoing, even if it violates a normally binding moral rule. Politicians may understandably regret being forced to take such actions, this argument goes, but they need not feel bad about themselves for having done so. Even if we reject this view of ethics, one may still believe that Weber's is one-sided and incomplete. If politics sometimes forces actions with high moral costs, it also offers unusual opportunities to advance moral objectives, among them, ending wars, righting injustices, and helping those deserving of help.

Moreover, politicians who have acted wrongly have chances to make amends; indeed, more than most sinners, they may be able to change the circumstances that tempt them to sin. Weber may exaggerate the seriousness of the moral transgressions into which politicians are likely to fall. We may suppose that murder, torture, and violence against opponents are not often realistic courses of action for politicians in democratic societies, quite apart from the immorality of such acts. More likely, the bad acts sometimes required for the overall good may, as Bernard Williams puts it, be simply squalid, involving "lying, or at least concealment and the making of misleading statements; breaking promises; special pleading; temporary coalition with the distasteful; sacrifice of the interests of worthy persons to those of unworthy persons; and (at least if in a sufficiently important position) coercion up to blackmail" (1978, 59). We (and politicians themselves) might reasonably hope that transgressions of this sort, however justified in particular cases, will never be taken without qualms, because "only those who are reluctant or disinclined to do the morally disagreeable when it is really necessary have much chance of not doing it when it is not necessary" (64).

Finally, we should keep in mind that politicians, even if they cannot always avoid ethical paradoxes, are under no obligation to seek them out. Any particular fall from right-doing is justifiable only if it is also necessary to the realization of an important public objective. Forethought about the choices one will face in the game of politics, skill in playing it, and what Williams calls "moral cunning" (1978, 62) will sometimes make the dirtying of hands needless. Politicians can shame themselves unnecessarily, and those most likely to do so are second-rate politicians, caught off guard, their minds focused only on the immediate situation, too timid to risk anything for what their conscience tells them is right, and so acting in what may be to their disadvantage both politically and morally. Francesco Guicciardini, no sentimentalist, argued that "it is a great error not to know where true interest lies" and noted that it sometimes lies "in honor, in knowing how to keep a reputation, and in a good name" (1965, 97). In the uncertain world of politics, to err on the side of ethics can be both the ethical and the prudent thing to do.

Even taking prudence, foresight, and skill into account, however, it seems clear that politics will routinely lead politicians to do things that in the best of lights will be seen as morally ambiguous, in the eyes of others and sometimes in their own. The problem of dirty hands will not be the only source of such ambiguity. An ethic of responsibility requires a calculation of the probable consequences of actions. Estimates of probable consequences depend on the information available to one, so that politicians, seeing one reality, may find an action justifiable that some citizens, seeing another, regard as wrong. The ethic of responsibility calls for unbiased estimates of consequences: no one is entitled to do wrong for the sake of one's own ease and comfort. In politics it is frequently the case, however, that politicians, to advance a public purpose, must also advance themselves. In any given case, which of these goals provides the real motive? For outsiders this question is unanswerable most of the time, and it is sometimes a difficult question even for politicians themselves, for, as we all know, we tend to be poor judges in our own cases.

Consider Lyndon Johnson's role in, and contribution, to the movement to secure full civil rights for African Americans. Rowland Evans and Robert Novak, writing about his career in Congress, observe that "ever since 1937, when he first entered the House, Johnson had voted *no* on civil rights 100 percent of the time" (1966, 121). He had voted against an antilynching bill, against abolition of segregation in the armed forces, against anti-poll-tax bills, and against a move to forbid discrimination in the use of federal moneys for school lunches. He had ridiculed the Truman civil rights program and had complained that all he ever heard from liberals was "Nigra, Nigra, Nigra" (Evans and Novak 1966, 119). He had taken the lead in the passage of the Civil Rights Act of 1957, it is true, but this measure had little substance and was seen by many as testimony more to Johnson's national political ambitions than to his belief in civil rights for all.

Then, as vice president, Johnson became an outspoken advocate of civil rights, and in his first year as president secured the passage of the Civil Rights Act of 1964. The next year, in the midst of an ugly series of repressive actions in George Wallace's Alabama, he called a joint session of the Congress and asked it to eliminate the barriers to voting by blacks.[7] He put the issue this way: "There is no constitutional issue here. The command of the Constitution is plain. There is no moral issue. It is wrong—deadly wrong—to deny any of your fellow Americans the right to vote in this country" (Johnson 1966, 283). Though Johnson had never been conspicuous for strong and principled stands during most of his legislative career, in what he had to say about action to secure voting rights, he showed no interest in compromise:

> The last time a President sent a civil rights bill to the Congress it contained a provision to protect voting rights in Federal elections. That civil rights bill was passed after eight long months of debate. And when that bill came to my desk from the Congress for my signature, the heart of the voting provision had been eliminated.
>
> This time, on this issue, there must be no delay, no hesitation and no compromise with our purpose. (Ibid.)

Toward the end of the speech, Johnson struck a personal note:

> My first job after college was as a teacher in Cotulla, Texas, in a small Mexican-American school. Few of them could speak English, and I couldn't speak much Spanish. My students were poor and they often came to class without breakfast, hungry. They knew even in their youth the pain of prejudice. They never seemed to know why people disliked them. But they knew it was so, because I saw it in their eyes. I often walked home late in the afternoon, after the classes were finished, wishing there was more that I could do. But all I knew was to teach them the little that I knew, hoping that it might help them against the hardship that lay ahead.
>
> Somehow you never forget what poverty and hatred can do when you see its scars on the hopeful face of a young child.
>
> I never thought then, in 1928, that I would be standing here in 1965. It never even occurred to me in my fondest dreams that I might have the chance to help the sons and daughters of those students and to help people like them all over this country.
>
> But now I do have that chance—and I'll let you in on a secret—I mean to use it. (Ibid., 286)

And, as we know, use it he did, with far-reaching consequences for American society and politics.

But what credence should be given his account of his reasons for welcoming the opportunity that history gave him? Had he opposed civil rights for blacks for so long only because he believed that he had to do so, to be a senator from Texas? Could his fervor for civil rights as vice president have been grounded mainly in presidential ambitions? If he believed that opposition to civil rights for blacks was a necessity for a senator from Texas, might he not have been wrong? In 1957, after all, Texas had elected a senator who favored civil rights, Ralph Yarborough, albeit in a special election and with less than a majority of the votes. If Johnson was right about the political necessities for a senator from Texas, might he nonetheless have had more influence for the good as a nonofficeholder, speaking out for the rights of blacks in all those years when he had upheld the racial status quo and scorned those who found it shameful? Or was the task of persuasion better left to a great orator like Martin Luther King, while Johnson, the magnificently skilled political insider, waited for a chance to right wrongs? I have no answers to these questions, and Johnson may himself have been unclear about the answers to some of them. What is clear, however, is that Americans are indebted to Johnson for a great political achievement, one extremely difficult of attainment and one that brought American democratic ideals and American democratic practices measurably closer to each other.

If the ethical ambiguities of politics as a vocation matter to individual politicians, they also matter to us collectively. Such ambiguities, both in themselves and as they are reflected in public attitudes toward politicians, almost certainly discourage some people of high ethical standards from careers in politics. Collectively, we cannot remove all the hard choices politicians face, but in the right circumstances some could be removed, thus helping to improve the reputation of politicians, as we decrease their burdens. We could change our present system of financing of political campaigns, which, by making most elected public servants dependent on private donations for campaigns, creates an obvious conflict of interest for the great majority of holders of elective office. If payments are at all substantial, what average citizen is ever likely to believe that those who pay the piper have nothing to do with the choice of the tunes? We could pass stricter codes of ethics for public servants of all kinds, taking care that such codes address what has been called "institutional corruption" as well as personal corruption and arranging credible enforcement procedures for them.[8] We could encourage debate-like forms of campaign discussion, thus decreasing incentives to distort facts in campaigns.[9] We could think much more than we have about educating politicians, educating them both about political techniques and about the ethical issues that arise in the pursuit, maintenance, and use of power. "We Americans," Robert Dahl has written, "have been so bemused by our belief in the supposed superiority of the amateur (a belief we hold to only in politics and in the athletic activities of a small number of private colleges and universities whose alumni permit them the luxury of bad football teams) that we have never systematically used either our intelligence or our resources to improve the training of politicians" (Dahl 1957, 4).

Politics as a Vocation and the Citizen-Legislator

As Weber's lecture proceeded, it would have become increasingly evident that he did not regard everyone in politics, or living for politics, as having a calling to it. Politicians who were in politics for the money he did not think of as politicians at all, and the "mere 'power politician,'" he said near the end of the lecture, "may get strong effects, but actually his work leads nowhere and is senseless" (1958, 116). Politicians with a Weberian vocation for politics are men and women who serve their communities by working in, through, and around party politics. Though not heedless of their ability to fight another day, they are sensitive to the ethical issues that politics involves and proceed with fervor, balance, and skill in pursuit of the common good as they see it. They are persistent and tough: "Politics is a strong and slow boring of hard boards. . . . Only he has the calling for politics who is sure that he shall not crumble when the world from his point of view is too stupid or base for what he wants to offer" (128). For Weber, politics is a high calling. We might be tempted to think that he has limned a class of heroes to which no one in the real world has ever borne any resemblance, but then we recall Lincoln or Churchill, Gandhi or King, Roosevelt or DeGaulle, or many other career politicians who have performed magnificently on stages large and small.

Today, any kind of advocacy of politics as a vocation places the advocate directly at odds with much of the rhetoric of the contemporary movement to limit the terms of legislators. That movement is about many things, but a revolt against career politicians is one important element of it. George Will, one of the most thoughtful advocates of limits on legislative terms, finds that political careerism is associated with mischief and that "the skills, expertise, and attitudes characteristic of professional politicians are irrelevant to, or inimical to, the good functioning of government" (1992, 141).[10] "A Congress purged of careerism," he argues, "would beget an electorate purged of its virulent cynicism about politicians, a cynicism born of suspicion about politicians' motives" (183). In Mark Petracca's view, "Although it may be useful for society to encourage the development of professional lawyers, nurses, social scientists, journalists, or physicians, the qualities and characteristics associated with being a 'professional' politician run counter to the essential requirements of representative democracy" (1994, 73). For those in the movement for term limits, the nation's politics would ideally be in the hands not of men and women who make a life vocation of it but of citizen-legislators (or citizen-politicians), serving "only briefly, going to . . . [legislatures] . . . from other careers, to which they would return in a few years" (Will 1992, 36).

As concepts, "career politician" and "citizen-politician" suggest very different kinds of representation by public officials. Ideally, Weberian career politicians are skilled and knowledgeable agents who act to further the best interests of the communities that put them into positions of leadership. To entrust them with the conduct of governmental affairs is akin to turning to a lawyer to protect one's legal interests or to a carpenter to build one's garage; in each case one sees the agent—politician, lawyer, carpenter—as better equipped to handle certain tasks than one is oneself. The citizen-politician, in contrast, is in the tradition of the New England town meeting, that is, in the tradition of ordinary citizens acting together to govern themselves. If "legislators were not too separated, for too long, from normal citizens and normal life in normal communities," Will argues, "they might retain the ability to discriminate between appropriate and inappropriate functions for the federal government" (1992, 36). Citizen-legislators would represent our interests well because they are people like ourselves (or, more accurately, people taking a brief time-out from being like ourselves), who will soon be punished or rewarded for what they do, to the same extent, and in the same way, as are all the rest of us.

As compelling as each of these conceptions of representation is in its own way, exalting either in opposition to the other can easily lead us astray. No follower of James Madison would expect skilled agents, political or nonpolitical, to be angels, and if they are not, they may put their own interests ahead of those of their principal, often flattering the prejudices of the principal as they do so. Many advocates of limiting legislative terms seem to believe that most of the professional politicians in our legislative bodies have done just that. The movement to limit terms is almost certainly not a reaction against the professionalism of those who come close to embodying the skills and virtues of the Weberian politicians—a Lincoln or a Churchill—but one against the (perceived) absence of Lincolns and Churchills among our career politicians.

Representation by people like ourselves also has obvious pitfalls. Sometimes we lack the skill or knowledge to further our own interests. If the lawyer who handles his or her own case has a fool for a client, what can be said for the non-lawyer who does the same? A legislative body filled with citizens like ourselves could almost certainly represent our preferences well, and possibly our interests also, but is the citizen-politician the equal of the professional in fashioning reasonable policies out of our often disparate preferences and conflicting interests? This latter question is not one that can confidently be given an affirmative answer. Note also that the ideal of representation by citizen-legislators assumes not just that they are ordinary people but that they are close to a representative sample of those whom they will represent. The claim of citizen-legislators to authority derives from the likeness of their interests to ours, not from any special talents or knowledge. But imagine a society populated only by greens and blues. If the interests and outlooks of these two groups differ, an all-blue legislature is unlikely to serve that society well, however ordinary these blues may be and however temporarily each may serve. The blue-green society simply has a badly malapportioned legislative body that is likely, if citizen-legislators are indeed ordinary, to put the interests and values of blues ahead of those of greens—and ahead of social cohesion.

As an ideal, representative institutions in which only citizen-politicians serve has an attractive face, but it is a face that the harsh light of reality would be sure to show to much less advantage. Exponents of the ideal appear to have given little thought to what sort of people might voluntarily choose to take leaves-of-absence of several years duration from their normal careers, what motives might lead them to do so, or who would pay for advertising the availability, qualifications, and views of those willing to serve. Service as a citizen-official, however, would often involve large sacrifices, like—but much larger than—those involved in jury duty, and these sacrifices would be unequal, as between those in different income groups, age groups, and lines of work. Such being true, a body of citizen-politicians would be virtually certain to be a badly skewed sample of citizens generally, quite unlike the society they would seek to govern. One can make a good case for greater influence for the informed opinion of ordinary citizens in governmental affairs,[11] but government by volunteer citizen-politicians in practice is highly likely to give short shrift to the interests and values of some groups in society, even if it is not fully predictable in advance which groups those would be.

If, up close, government by citizen-politicians looks less good than it does from farther away, driving career politicians from influence in government looks, after serious reflection, both less good and less possible. Are the skills and outlooks that serve to advance a political career truly irrelevant to good government? Are such skills widely and evenly distributed in the population? Though we should not rest content with mere speculation about these propositions, we may doubt that either is true. Can we banish career politicians from public life? Certainly not by limiting terms of legislators. Even a truly sweeping limit on service in public office—one permitting only a brief period of service in local, state, and federal office over a lifetime—would do no more than force those interested in political careers to spend less time as public servants than they now do and more time as servants of interest groups and party organizations. Limits on terms of office doubtless could affect the kinds of people who make careers in politics and perhaps their number (though not in easily foreseeable ways), but surely no free society can deny such careers to those with the desire, talents, and means to pursue them.

To conclude that free societies cannot purge career politicians from political life is to conclude that efforts to do so ought to give way to better-considered objectives. One of these, surely, should be preventing abuses of power by those possessed of it, and another, keeping politicians faithful to the collective interests of citizens. To these one can add a third, an objective that has been largely neglected, both in thought and in action: encouraging those with a conception of the political vocation akin to Weber's to enter—and to stay in—public life. Exasperated with particular doctors or doctors as a class, we are yet likely to realize that it is mediocrity or malfeasance in medicine we want to be rid of, not doctors, because we know that excellent doctors exist and have existed—doctors guided by high aspirations to service, whose work has benefited from long study and experience. Have there been no politicians who have served us well? Of course there have been, unless one plays games with words. Are the skills they have displayed common ones? skills of a sort to which experience has nothing to contribute? Surely not. Has politics no high ideals of service akin to those of medicine? Here, let us give Weber the last words, those with which he summed up his complex view of the requirements of the political vocation:

> It takes both passion and perspective. Certainly all historical experience con-
> firms the truth—that man would not have attained the possible unless time
> and again he had reached out for the impossible. But to do that a man must be
> a leader, and not only a leader but a hero as well, in the very sober sense of the
> word. And even those who are neither leaders nor heroes must arm themselves
> with that steadfastness of heart which can brave even the crumbling of all
> hopes. This is necessary right now, or else men will not be able to attain even
> that which is possible today. Only he has the calling for politics who is sure that
> he shall not crumble when the world from his point of view is too stupid or
> too base for what he wants to offer. Only he who in the face of all this can say
> 'In spite of all!' has the calling for politics. (1958, 128)

Notes

John Geer and Fred Greenstein encouraged me to write this essay, which enlarges upon a lecture I developed for my undergraduate course on party politics. In that course, year after year, I found many of my students interested, some keenly, in careers in elective politics; I wanted to speak to that interest, and Max Weber helped me to do so. I am extremely grateful for suggestions for, and comments on, earlier versions of the essay from Ira Cohen, Fred Greenstein, Amy Gutmann, Suzanne Keller, Marion J. Levy Jr., Tali Mendleberg, Thomas Rochon, and Dennis Thompson. My debt to all is substantial, but that to Greenstein and Thompson is particularly heavy. The former put at my service both his keen insight into leadership and his encyclopedic knowledge of its literature, while the latter's carefully constructed critique of what I had to say about ethics and politics emboldened me to stray some distance from Weber's view of that subject.

1. Sources disagree in dating the lecture, but little doubt exists that it was delivered in late 1918 or early 1919. On this issue, see Roth and Schluchter 1979, 113–16. For an English translation of "Politics as a Vocation," see *From Max Weber: Essays in Sociology*, ed-

ited and translated by H. H. Gerth and C. Wright Mills (Oxford University: New York, 1958), 77–128.

2. See Schlesinger 1957, 26–39, Matthews 1960, 33–35, and Hain and Piereson 1975, 41–51, for excellent discussions of lawyers in politics.

3. Calculated from data presented in table 7.3 in Stanley and Niemi 1995, 23. The proportions are not additive, because some members listed themselves as having more than one occupation. In these same Congresses about one-third of the members of the House listed themselves as business people. Some of these came to politics relatively late in life, but their numbers also reflect the fact that some kinds of business careers—real estate, for example, insurance, or advertising—can complement a political career rather well. It is an interesting fact that the proportion of lawyers in the decade 1789–1800 (44.8 percent) was nearly the same as it has been recently (Bogue et. al. 1976, 284).

4. Among Matthews' senators, "almost half held their first public offices before their thirtieth birthdays" (1960, 50).

5. See especially Evans and Novak 1966 and Kearns 1976.

6. I am indebted to Fred Greenstein for calling this example to my attention.

7. For a brief but excellent account of the crisis, see Woodward 1974, 184–85.

8. For an excellent discussion of reforms of this sort, see Thompson 1995.

9. I pursue this line of thought in my *Political Campaigning: Problems of Creating an Informed Electorate* (Washington, D.C.: Brookings Institution Press, 1960), 50–84 and passim.

10. Will does not mean, however, to include among such skills, expertise, and attitudes "the traditional arts and crafts and skills of negotiating, conciliating, logrolling and the rest," which, he says, "no one wants to purge from politics" (1992, 145).

11. Robert Dahl does so very persuasively in *Democracy and Its Critics* (1989). As one way to give a larger place in government to the views of ordinary citizens, he suggests lengthy deliberation on issues of public policy by randomly selected bodies of citizens, whose judgments would carry the authority of *demos* because they would in fact reflect accurately the composition of, and currents of opinion in, society (Dahl 1989, 338–41). See also Fishkin 1991, especially 1–13 and 81–104. The objectives that Fishkin seeks to advance through his "deliberative opinion polls" are essentially the same as those that Will hopes would be furthered by citizen-legislators, that is, less attention in government to ill-informed popular opinion, more attention there for the thoughtfully considered opinions of ordinary people.

References

Adams, Henry. 1918. *The Education of Henry Adams: An Autobiography.* Boston: Houghton Mifflin (Sentry Edition).

Barber, James David. 1965. *The Lawmakers: Recruitment and Adaptation to Legislative Life.* New Haven: Yale University Press.

Bogue, Allan G., Jerome M. Clubb, Carroll R. McKibbin, and Santa A. Traugott. 1976. "Members of the House of Representatives and the Processes of Modernization, 1789–1960." *Journal of American History* 63 (Sept.): 275–302.

Carter, Jimmy. 1980. "American Hostages in Iran and Soviet Intervention in Afghanistan: Remarks to Reporters." In *Public Papers of the Presidents of the United States: Jimmy Carter, 1979*, vol. 2. Washington, D.C.: Government Printing Office.

Churchill, Winston S. 1974. "Remarks on His Eightieth Birthday." In *Winston S. Churchill: His Complete Speeches 1897–1963*, vol. 8., ed. Robert Rhodes James. London: Chelsea House.

Cicero. 1970. *Cicero on Oratory and Orators*. Edited and translated by J. S. Watson. Carbondale: Southern Illinois University Press.

Dahl, Robert. 1957. Preface to *How They Became Governor*, by Joseph A. Schlesinger. East Lansing: Michigan State University.

———. 1989. *Democracy and Its Critics*. New Haven: Yale University Press.

Evans, Rowland, and Robert Novak. 1966. *Lyndon B. Johnson: The Exercise of Power*. New York: New American Library.

Fenno, Richard. 1978. *Home Style: House Members in Their Districts*. Boston: Little, Brown.

Fishkin, James. 1991. *Democracy and Deliberation*. New Haven: Yale University Press.

Gardner, Howard. 1983. *Frames of Mind: The Theory of Multiple Intelligences*. New York: Basic Books.

Goodwin, Doris Kearns. 1994. *No Ordinary Time*. New York: Simon and Schuster.

Greenstein, Fred. 1965. *Children and Politics*. New Haven: Yale University Press.

———. 1987. *Personality and Politics: Problems of Evidence, Inference, and Conceptualization*. Princeton: Princeton University Press.

Guicciardini, Francesco. 1965. *Maxims and Reflections*. Philadelphia: University of Pennsylvania Press.

Hain, Paul L., and James E. Piereson. 1975. "Lawyers and Politics Revisited: Structural Advantages of Lawyer-Politicians." *American Journal of Political Science* 19 (Feb.): 41–51.

Johnson, Lyndon B. 1966. "Special Message to the Congress: The American Promise." In *Public Papers of the Presidents of the United States: Lyndon B. Johnson, 1965*, vol. 2. Washington, D.C.: Government Printing Office.

Kearns, Doris. 1976. *Lyndon Johnson and the American Dream*. New York: Harper and Row.

Kennedy, John F. 1963. "Television and Radio Interview: 'After Two Years—A Conversation with the President.'" In *Public Papers of the Presidents of the United States: John F. Kennedy, 1962*. Washington, D.C.: Government Printing Office.

Longford, the Earl of, and Thomas P. O'Neill. 1971. *Eamon de Valera*. Boston: Houghton Mifflin.

Matthews, Donald R. 1960. *U.S. Senators and Their World*. Chapel Hill: University of North Carolina Press.

Merriam, Charles. 1926. *Four American Party Leaders*. New York: Macmillan.

Mitchell, William C. 1959. "The Ambivalent Social Status of the American Politician." *Western Political Quarterly* 12 (Sept.): 683–98.

Petracca, Mark P. 1994. "Restoring 'The University in Rotation': An Essay in Defense of Term Limitations." In *The Politics and Law of Term Limits*, ed. Edward H. Crane and Roger Pilon. Washington, D.C.: Cato Institute.

Roosevelt, Franklin D. 1941. "Address at the University of Virginia." In *Public Papers and Addresses of Franklin D. Roosevelt*, vol. 9. New York: Macmillan.

Roth, Gunther, and Wolfgang Schluchter. 1979. *Max Weber's Vision of History*. Berkeley: University of California Press.

Schlesinger, Joseph A. 1957. "Lawyers and American Politics: A Clarified View." *Midwestern Journal of Political Science* 1 (May): 26–39.

Sherwood, Robert E. 1948. *Roosevelt and Hopkins: An Intimate History*. New York: Harper and Brothers.

Stanley, Harold W., and Richard G. Niemi. 1995. *Vital Statistics on American Politics*. Washington, D.C.: Congressional Quarterly Press.

Thompson, Dennis F. 1987. *Political Ethics and Public Office*. Cambridge: Harvard University Press.

———. 1995. *Ethics in Congress: From Individual to Institutional Corruption*. Washington, D.C.: Brookings Institution Press.

Tugwell, Rexford. 1958. *The Art of Politics*. Garden City, N.Y.: Doubleday.

Walzer, Michael. 1973. "Political Action: The Problem of Dirty Hands." *Philosophy and Public Affairs* 2 (winter): 60–80.

Weber, Max. 1958. "Politics as a Vocation." In *From Max Weber: Essays in Sociology*, ed. and trans. H. H. Gerth and C. Wright Mills. New York: Oxford University Press.

Whitman, Walt. 1892. *Complete Prose Works*. Philadelphia: David McKay.

Will, George. 1992. *Restoration: Congress, Term Limits, and the Recovery of Deliberative Democracy*. New York: Free Press.

Williams, Bernard. 1978. "Politics and Moral Character." In *Public and Private Morality*, ed. Stuart Hampshire. Cambridge: Cambridge University Press.

Woodward, C. Vann. 1974. *The Strange Career of Jim Crow*. New York: Oxford University Press.

CHAPTER 14

The Expanding Universe of Party Politics

Fred I. Greenstein

By liberating the analysis of party politics from its conventional boundaries, the authors whose work appears in this volume honor a rich scholarly tradition. Many of the seminal contributors to the political parties literature range widely in their writings, exploring topics that appear to be unrelated to the party system, showing that they are integral to it.

Two scholars in whose writings this breadth is particularly evident are E. E. Schattschneider and Stanley Kelley Jr., author of the preceding chapter. At the time of his retirement, Schattschneider had made his mark as the author of *Toward a More Responsible Two-Party System* (American Political Science Association 1950), a much discussed report on the condition of the nation's political parties, and three influential books, *Politics, Pressures, and the Tariff* (1935), *Party Government* (1942), and *The Semi-Sovereign People* (1960).

Schattschneider's first and third books might seem to be unrelated to the study of political parties, dealing as they do with the effects of interest groups on tariff legislation and the imperfect capacity of citizens to control government. But in fact all of his writings are preoccupied with a particular theme that bears on the party system. In each work his emphasis is on the shortcomings of interest group mobilization as a means of advancing the public interest and the desirability of moving toward a system of cohesive, issue-oriented political parties that would afford voters clearly defined policy choices and make it possible for like-minded coalitions to control the government, transforming public preferences into public policy.

When Stanley Kelley assumed emeritus status from Princeton University, he had published three books and a number of articles and book chapters. There is less awareness of the scope of Kelley's contributions than of Schattschneider's, and at first glance those contributions seem even more varied. But on closer examination Kelley and Schattschneider prove to be united by issues that bear on the party system. A brief review of Kelley's books and two of his most influential articles supports that point and prompts a larger observation about the study of political parties.

Professional Public Relations and Political Power (Kelley 1956) was the first scholarly account of the role of political consultants in American politics. It identified the importance of such professionals at a time when the application of public relations techniques to politics was in its infancy, reporting a series of richly textured case studies of the actions of public relations specialists in post–World War II politics. The emergence of public relations practitioners as key players in electoral politics, Kelley argues, was a predictable consequence of changes in the American party system. As the antipartisan reforms of the Progressive Era took hold, party machines gave way to public relations. Instead of employing material incentives to buy the support of voters, politicians began to appeal to them in the aggregate on the basis of issues and candidates. Specialists in mass communication became latter-day equivalents of machine politicians.

For all its shortcomings, the politics of public relations has an insufficiently recognized merit, according to Kelley. It makes for a "closer approach of democracy to its own ideal" by encouraging citizens to cast their votes on the basis of more than narrow personal benefits (Kelley 1956, 219). The rub, of course, is that since the demise of machine politics, well-heeled candidates have a distinct advantage: they can afford more-expensive campaigns and more-skilled public relations specialists than the less affluent.

This depressing conclusion provides the stimulus for Kelley's insufficiently recognized exploration of the problem of creating an informed electorate. *Political Campaigning* (Kelley 1960) is a deductive normative analysis of what would be called for if the campaign process in the United States maximized the potentialities for informed electoral choice. Kelley identifies a series of broad requirements: The contending candidates should have equal access to audiences. The issues should be clearly stated, with alternatives spelled out. The caliber of debate should not be debased by unfair personal attacks on candidates, such as the McCarthy-era assaults on the patriotism of candidates that were prevalent when Kelley was writing. And voters should be protected from self-interested propaganda that is promulgated without divulging its source.

These ends cannot be attained in any absolute sense, Kelley acknowledges, but he proposes a variety of practical means for moving toward their accomplishment, a number of which have gradually been incorporated in political practice—for example, careful comparison in the media of the claims of competing candidates and the factual basis of political advertising. One reform that Kelley did not mention in *Political Campaigning*—but that he later helped to institute—involves making the skills of political management broadly available by creating a training program in this seemingly arcane art. As the "founding provost" of the Graduate School of Political Management (now at George Washington University), Kelley placed a powerful stamp on an institution that helps to demystify the politics of mass communications.

In "Putting First Things First" (Kelley, Ayres, and Bowen 1967), Kelley and his collaborators examine a distinctly American impediment to the achievement of high levels of participation in elections—the inability of many citizens to cast a vote on election day because they had failed at some earlier period to go through the burdensome process of registering to vote. With laudable thoroughness, they identify the correlates of voter turnout in 104 of the nation's largest cities, establishing that by far its strongest determinant is the provisions governing registration. The simpler the process of voter registration, the higher the turnout.

Much follows from this finding. Once one accounts for the requirement that voters must not only go to the polls in the heat of a campaign but also register to vote at some early time when there may be little to motivate them, it becomes understandable that the United States has lower electoral turnout than other democracies. It also becomes evident why there was a mysterious decline in voting in the early decades of the twentieth century, precisely when voter registration was instituted as one of the Progressive Era reforms.

"Putting First Things First" has spawned a significant literature on the determinants of turnout, including the important national study by Raymond Wolfinger and Steven Rosenstone (1980), and it figures in the literature on historic patterns of electoral participation (see, for example, Converse 1972). Just as *Professional Public Relations and Political Power* and *Political Campaigning* had a practical consequence in the creation of an educational institution to prepare campaign managers, "Putting First Things First" also has had a nonacademic consequence. Wolfinger not only set about, with Rosenstone, to replicate and expand upon Kelley's work, but he also was responsible for a more extensive body of scholarship that laid the foundation for the 1993 "motor-voter act," which makes it possible for citizens to register when they are engaging in such routine actions as renewing a driver's license or reporting a change of address.

"The Simple Act of Voting" (1974) and *Interpreting Elections* (1983) are parts of a common endeavor. In the former, Kelley and Mirer document the validity of an uncomplicated, but highly predictive, method of identifying the considerations voters take into account in making their electoral choices. In effect, members of the electorate add up pros and cons, much as any decision maker might tote up the positives and negatives in making any choice. Specifically, Kelley's method calls for aggregating the positive and negative statements survey respondents make in response to a series of open-ended questions posed by the University of Michigan Survey Research Center to national samples of the electorate since 1952—questions about what the voters like and dislike about each of the two major parties and their candidates. In addition to providing a better predictor of voters' choices than other existing metrics, Kelley's procedure provides a singularly informative account of the specific attitudes that go into electoral outcomes.

Interpreting Elections (Kelley 1983) reports an extensive application of the procedure. Kelley shows that, except for possible rare instances such as the 1932 landslide that elected Franklin D. Roosevelt, the substantive mandates that electoral winners claim they have been accorded by the public are (as Robert A. Dahl notes in chapter 9 of this volume) largely mythical. Indeed, it is sometimes possible for a candidate to be swept into office in what Kelley calls a weak landslide, as in 1972 when voters were more anti-McGovern than pro-Nixon, and much of Nixon's majority came from voters on the razor's edge between the two candidates.

Interpreting Elections affords an unprecedented transparency to the considerations that shape election outcomes. Many of its insights remain to be adequately mined—for example, a profoundly subversive, six-page critique of the validity of the fixed-choice survey items that are the basis of the great bulk of existing survey-based studies of voting (Kelley 1983, 64–70).

But the book reflects more than Kelley's interest in the academic study of elections. As he points out, it also is informed by two other preoccupations:

> The efforts of campaigners to understand how the many particular concerns of voters translate into victory and defeat at the polls have interested me for a long time and have shaped my own conception of that process in many ways. Political philosophy, my first love in the study of politics, has ... urged me continually toward attempts to puzzle out how elections contribute to, or impair, the health and stability of democratic government. (Kelley 1983, xiii)

In the last of these remarks lies not only the connecting logic of Kelley's scholarship but also a larger perspective on the study of political parties. Properly understood, it is a normative as well as an empirical concern, and its scope reaches far beyond party organizations, parties in government, and parties in the electorate. It extends to all processes and institutions that foster democracy in the modern nation-state.

References

American Political Science Association, Committee on the Political Parties. 1950. *Toward a More Responsible Two-Party System*. New York: Rinehart.

Converse, Philip E. 1972. "Change in the Electorate." In *The Human Meaning of Social Change*, ed. Angus Campbell and Philip E. Converse. New York: Russell Sage Foundation.

Kelley, Stanley, Jr. 1956. *Professional Public Relations and Political Power*. Baltimore: Johns Hopkins University Press.

————. 1960. *Political Campaigning: Problems of Creating an Informed Electorate*. Washington, D.C.: Brookings Institution Press.

————. 1983. *Interpreting Elections*. Princeton: Princeton University Press.

Kelley, Stanley, Jr., Richard E. Ayres, and William G. Bowen. 1967. "Registration and Voting: Putting First Things First." *American Political Science Review* (June): 359–79.

Kelley, Stanley, Jr., and Thad W. Mirer. 1974. "The Simple Act of Voting." *American Political Science Review* (June): 572–91.

Schattschneider, E. E. 1935. *Politics, Pressures, and the Tariff*. Englewood Cliffs, N.J.: Prentice-Hall.

————. 1942. *Party Government*. New York: Holt, Rinehart and Winston.

————. 1960. *The Semi-Sovereign People: A Realist's View of Democracy in America*. New York: Holt, Rinehart and Winston.

Wolfinger, Raymond E., and Steven J. Rosenstone. 1980. *Who Votes?* New Haven: Yale University Press.

Contributors

Larry M. Bartels is professor of politics and public affairs and Stuart Professor of Communications and Public Affairs in the Woodrow Wilson School at Princeton University. He is author of *Presidential Primaries and the Dynamic of Public Choice* and of scholarly articles on electoral politics, public opinion, the mass media, and political methodology.

Robert A. Dahl is Sterling Professor of Political Science emeritus at Yale University. He is the author of numerous books, including *Preface to Democratic Theory, Who Governs?,* and *Democracy and Its Critics.*

James DeNardo is professor of political science at UCLA. He is the author of *Power in Numbers,* and *The Amateur Strategist.* His research addresses the ideological and factional roots of party strategy.

John G. Geer is professor of political science at Vanderbilt University. He is author of *From Tea Leaves to Opinion Polls* and of scholarly articles on party politics, public opinion, elections, and the mass media that have appeared in the *American Journal of Political Science* and the *Journal of Politics.*

Fred I. Greenstein is professor of politics and director of the Research Program in Leadership Studies at Princeton University. His writings include *The American Party System and the American People, Children and Politics, Personality and Politics,* and *The Hidden-Hand Presidency.*

Ikuo Kabashima is professor of political science in the Faculty of Law at Tokyo University. He is author of many articles on elections and voting in Japan.

Stanley Kelley Jr. is professor of politics emeritus at Princeton University. He is author of *Professional Public Relations and Political Power, Political Campaigning,* and *Interpreting Elections.* He has also published articles in the *American Political Science Review* and is currently working on a book about party politics.

Jonathan S. Krasno is senior policy analyst at the Brennan Center for Justice at the New York University School of Law. He is author of *Challengers, Competition, and Reelection* and of scholarly articles on electoral behavior and is currently writing a book about campaign finance.

David R. Mayhew is Alfred Cowles Professor of Government at Yale University. He is the author of *Congress: The Electoral Connection* and *Divided We Govern*. His interests include Congress, party politics, and policy making.

Walter F. Murphy is the McCormick Professor of Jurisprudence emeritus of Princeton University. He has written extensively in public law and comparative politics and is currently working on a book on constitutional democracy, to be published by the Johns Hopkins University Press.

Gerald M. Pomper is Board of Governors Professor of Political Science at Rutgers University. His interests included party politics, campaigns, and elections. His most recent book is *The Election of 1996*, the latest in a quadrennial series that dates back to 1976.

Thomas R. Rochon is professor and director of the School for Politics and Economics at Claremont Graduate University. His most recent book is *Culture Moves: Ideas, Activism, and Changing Values.*

Carol M. Swain is associate professor of politics and public affairs, Woodrow Wilson School, Princeton University. She is author of *Black Faces and Black Interests*, which won the Woodrow Wilson Foundation Award for the best book in American politics, the V. O. Key Award for the best book on southern politics, and the D. B. Hardeman Prize for the best scholarly work on Congress. She is currently writing a book about the politics of race relations.

John Zaller is professor of political science at UCLA. He is the author of *Nature and Origins of Mass Opinion*. His interests are mass communication, public opinion, and elections.

Index of Names

Subject Index

Library of Congress Cataloging-in-Publication Data

Politicians and party politics / edited by John G. Geer.
    p.   cm.
Based on a conference held in Baltimore, Md., in 1995.
Includes index.
ISBN 0-8018-5845-3 (alk. paper).—ISBN 0-8018-5846-1 (pbk.: alk. paper)
    1. Political parties—United States—Congresses. 2. Politicians—United States—
Congresses. I. Geer, John Gray.
JK2261.P645   1998
324.273—dc21   98-10047
                                  CIP